NORTHERN IRELAND AND THE DIVIDED WORLD

Northern Ireland and the Divided World

The Northern Ireland Conflict and the Good Friday Agreement in Comparative Perspective

Edited by
JOHN McGARRY

OXFORD
UNIVERSITY PRESS

OXFORD

UNIVERSITY PRESS

Great Clarendon Street, Oxford OX2 6DP

Oxford University Press is a department of the University of Oxford.
It furthers the University's objective of excellence in research, scholarship,
and education by publishing worldwide in

Oxford New York

Athens Auckland Bangkok Bogotá Buenos Aires Cape Town
Chennai Dar es Salaam Delhi Florence Hong Kong Istanbul Karachi
Kolkata Kuala Lumpur Madrid Melbourne Mexico City Mumbai Nairobi
Paris São Paulo Shanghai Singapore Taipei Tokyo Toronto Warsaw

and associated companies in Berlin Ibadan

Oxford is a registered trade mark of Oxford University Press
in the UK and in certain other countries

Published in the United States
by Oxford University Press Inc., New York

British Library Cataloguing in Publication Data

Data available

Library of Congress Cataloging in Publication Data
Northern Ireland and the divided world: the Northern Ireland
conflict and the Good Friday Agreement in comparative
perspective / edited by John McGarry.
p. cm.
Includes bibliographical references and index.
1. Northern Ireland—Politics and government—1994– .
2. Divided government—Case studies. I. McGarry, John.
DA990.U46 M437 2001 941.60824—dc21 2001024668
ISBN 0–19–829633–9
ISBN 0–19–924434–0 (pbk.)

1 3 5 7 9 10 8 6 4 2

Typeset by Hope Services (Abingdon) Ltd.
Printed in Great Britain
on acid-free paper by
Biddles Ltd.,
Guildford & King's Lynn

For
Margaret, Séan, and Paul

ACKNOWLEDGEMENTS

I would like to thank the Social Sciences and Humanities Research Council of Canada and the United States Institute of Peace for providing funding that facilitated this project. Patti Lenard, a graduate student and research assistant, provided invaluable help throughout. Michael Keating, Margaret Moore, and Brendan O'Leary were sources of inspiration, as usual. Dominic Byatt, at Oxford University Press, was very professional and encouraging. Finally, my thanks go to my contributors, several of whom took time away from other important projects to indulge me.

J.M.G.

CONTENTS

LIST OF FIGURES

LIST OF TABLES

LIST OF ABBREVIATIONS

AERT	Autonomous European Region of Tyrol
ANC	African National Congress
ARC	Azzione per a Rinascita Corsa (Action for a Reborn Corsica)
AV	alternative vote
DUP	Democratic Unionist Party
EC	European Community
EOKA	Ethniki Organosis Kyprion Agoniston (National Organization of Freedom Fighters (Cyprus)
ETA	Euzkadi ta Azkatasuna ('Basque homeland and liberty')
EU	European Union
FAIT	Families Against Intimidation and Terror
FLNC	Front Libération National de la Corse (National Liberation Front of Corsica)
FRANCIA	Front d'Action nouvelle Contre l'indépendance et l'Autonomie (New Action Front against Independence and Autonomy) (Corsica)
FRETILIN	Frente Revolucionaria do Timor Leste Independent (Revolutionary Front of Independent East Timor)
GAL	Grupos Antiterroristas de Liberación (Spain)
IFP	Inkatha Freedom Party (South Africa)
IPKF	Indian Peace-Keeping Force (Sri Lanka)
IRA	Irish Republican Army
ISPO	International Study of Peace/Conflict Resolution Organizations
KKK	Ku Klux Klan
LTTE	Liberation Tigers of Tamil Eelam (Sri Lanka)
LVF	Loyalist Volunteer Force
MNLV	Movimiento de Liberación Nacional Vasco (Basque Country)
NATO	North Atlantic Treaty Organization
NGO	non-governmental organization
NICVA	Northern Ireland Council for Voluntary Action
NSMC	North–South Ministerial Council
P–CRO	peace–conflict resolution organization
PLO	Palestine Liberation Organization

PNP	Partido Nuevo Progresista (New Progressive Party) (Puerto Rico)
PNV	Partido Nacionalista Vasco (Basque Nationalist Party)
PP	Partido Popular (Popular Party, Spain)
PPD	Partido Popular Democratico (Popular Democratic Party) (Puerto Rico)
PR	proportional representation
PSOE	Partido Socialista Obrero Español (Socialist Party of Spain)
PSP	Progressive Socialist Party (Lebanon)
PUP	Progressive Unionist Party
RUC	Royal Ulster Constabulary
SACP	South African Communist Party
SDLP	Social Democratic and Labour Party
SMP	single-member plurality
SOV–ELA	Solidartidad de los Obreros Vascos–Euskal Langileen Alkartasua (Union of Basque Workers)
STV	single transferable vote
TMT	Turk Mukavenet Testikali (Turkish Defence Organization) (Cyprus)
UCAN	Ulster Community Action Network
UDA	Ulster Defence Association
UDP	Ulster Democratic Party
UFF	Ulster Freedom Fighters
UKUP	United Kingdom Unionist Party
UNFICYP	Uniter Nations Force in Cyprus
UUP	Ulster Unionist Party
UVF	Ulster Volunteer Force

LIST OF CONTRIBUTORS

Antony Alcock is Professor of European Studies at the University of Ulster, Coleraine, Northern Ireland. His most recent publicatioins include *A Short History of Europe: from the Greeks and Romans to the Present Day* (1998) and *A History of the Protection of Regional Cultural Minorities in Europe: From the Edict of Nantes to the Present Day* (2000). He served on the Ulster Unionist Party team in the negotiations leading to the 1998 Belfast (Good Friday) Agreement.

Feargal Cochrane is Lecturer in Politics within the Richardson Institute for Peace and Conflict Research in the Department of Politics and International Relations at Lancaster University. He is the author of *Unionist Politics and the Politics of Unionism since the Anglo-Irish Agreement* (1997 and 2000). He is co-author (with Professor Seamus Dunn) of *People Power? The Role of the Voluntary and Community Sector in the Northern Ireland Conflict* (2001).

Adrian Guelke is Professor of Comparative Politics and Director of the Centre for the Study of Ethnic Conflict in the School of Politics at Queen's University, Belfast. His books include *South Africa in Transition: The Misunderstood Miracle* (1999); *The Age of Terrorism and the International Political System* (1995); and *Northern Ireland: The International Perspective* (1988).

Donald L. Horowitz is James B. Duke Professor of Law and Political Science at Duke University. In 2001 he will serve as Centennial Professor at the London School of Economics. He is the author of *Ethnic Groups in Conflict* (1985; 2000); *A Democratic South Africa? Constitutional Engineering in a Divided Society* (1991); and *The Deadly Ethnic Riot* (2000).

Michael Keating is Professor of Regional Studies at the European University Institute, Florence, and Professor of Scottish Politics at the University of Aberdeen. He is the author of *State and Regional Nationalism: Territorial Politics and the European State* (1988); *Comparative Urban Politics: Power and the City in the United States, Canada, Britain and France* (1991); and *Nations against the State: The New Politics of Nationalism in Quebec, Catalonia and Scotland* (1996, 2001). He is the co-editor, with John McGarry, of *Minority Nationalism and the Changing International Order* (2001).

John McGarry is Professor of Political Science at the University of Waterloo, Canada. He is the author with Brendan O'Leary of *Explaining Northern Ireland: Broken Images* (1995); *The Politics of Antagonism: Understanding Northern Ireland* (1993, 1996); and *Policing Northern Ireland: Proposals for a New Start* (1999). He is the co-editor, with Michael Keating, of *Minority Nationalism and the Changing International Order* (2001).

S. J. R. Noel is Professor of Political Science at the University of Western Ontario, Canada. He is the author of *Politics in Newfoundland* (1971) and *Patrons, Clients, Brokers: Ontario Society and Politics, 1791–1896* (1990). He has also written several articles on consociationalism and federalism, and on the politics of divided societies, including Canada and South Africa.

Brendan O'Leary is Professor of Political Science and head of the Department of Government at the London School of Economics. He is the author with John McGarry of *Explaining Northern Ireland: Broken Images* (1995); *The Politics of Antagonism: Understanding Northern Ireland* (1993, 1996); and *Policing Northern Ireland: Proposals for a New Start* (1999). He has acted as a constitutional advisor to the European Union, the United Nations, and the UK's International Department for Development. He is a former adviser to the British Labour Party on Northern Ireland.

Padraig O'Malley is Senior Fellow at the John McCormack Institute, University of Massachusetts (Boston). He is the author of *The Uncivil Wars: Ireland Today* (1983); *Northern Ireland: Questions of Nuance* (1990); and *Biting at the Grave: The Irish Hunger Strikes and the Politics of Despair* (1990).

Kirsten E. Schulze is Lecturer in International History at the London School of Economics. She is the author of *Israel's Covert Diplomacy in Lebanon* (1998); *The Arab–Israeli Conflict* (1999); and *The Jews of Lebanon: Between Conflict and Coexistence* (2001). She has also written numerous articles on conflict and conflict management in the Middle East, Northern Ireland, and Indonesia.

Sammy Smooha is Professor of Sociology at the University of Haifa, Israel. He is the author of *Israel: Pluralism and Conflict* (1978) and *Arabs and Jews in Israel* (1992).

Rupert Taylor is Senior Lecturer in Political Studies at the University of the Witwatersrand, Johannesburg. His publications include articles in *Telos, Race and Class, Transformation, Ethnic and Racial Studies, Peace and Change,* and *Voluntus*.

1

Introduction: The Comparable Northern Ireland

JOHN MCGARRY

> Northern Ireland is truly a place apart
>> (editorial, *Belfast Telegraph*, 5 April 2000)

> For 30 years the politicians . . . of Northern Ireland have insisted their conflict cannot be compared to others
>> (Kevin Cullen, journalist, *Irish Times*, 13 May 2000)

> 'Ulster', the world's best laager!
>> (sign in David Trimble's Westminster office)

> We tried to answer, spoke of Arab, Jew,
> of Turk and Greek in Cyprus, Pakistan
> and India, but no sense flickered through
> that offered reason to a modern man
> why Europeans, Christians, working-class
> should thresh and struggle in that old morass
>> (John Hewitt, Ulster poet)[1]

> Say it once, Say it loud, I'm Black an' I'm proud . . . The Irish are the niggers of Europe, lads.
>> (Roddy Doyle, *The Commitments*)[2]

For many people, like the editorialists of the *Belfast Telegraph* or the audience of John Hewitt's poem, Northern Ireland is a place apart, its conflict the result of some unique pathology. This view was particularly dominant from the outbreak of the troubles until the early 1990s, although it is still subscribed to. Northern Ireland has been seen, variously, as a 'sui generis, untypical and even anachronistic phenomenon',[3] a 'peculiarly local conflict',[4] an 'outlandish exception to all the rules',[5] or as possessing a 'peculiar intractability'.[6]

However, many people, not just John Hewitt and Roddy Doyle, reject the idea that Northern Ireland is incomparable. Political partisans, contrary to

Kevin Cullen's insight, have been drawing parallels between Northern Ireland and other divided societies since at least the nineteenth century. Some of the best academic work on the Northern Ireland conflict, written by leading scholars from both outside and inside Northern Ireland, is comparative in focus.[7]

The scope for comparative analysis has increased in recent years. As a result of better international communications, it has become easier for those inside and outside Northern Ireland to compare its conflict with others. With outside governments, particularly the United States, and nongovernmental organizations playing an increasingly prominent role in Northern Ireland, there are more incentives for the region's partisans to seek to influence external opinion through the drawing of appropriate parallels. There also appear to be more conflicts with which Northern Ireland can be compared: the end of the cold war has been followed by a series of confrontations in south-eastern Europe and the Caucasus, and has made it possible to focus more on other ongoing violent intra-state conflicts, in Spain, Indonesia, Sri Lanka, and Cyprus, as well as the non-violent dispute between Quebec and the rest of Canada. It has also ushered in peace processes in South Africa and Israel–Palestine that have been the focus of global attention. Finally, the process of European integration led some scholars to examine the possibilities it offers for different national minorities, including those in Northern Ireland, the Basque Country, and South Tyrol.

This collection was assembled in part to allow leading comparativists to discuss Northern Ireland in light of these broad developments. Northern Ireland is compared with a significant number of the cases mentioned, including the Åland Island, Cyprus, and South Tyrol (Alcock); the Basque Country (Keating); Canada (Noel); Cyprus, Corsica, East Timor, Puerto Rico, and Sri Lanka (Guelke); Lebanon (Schulze); South Africa (O'Malley); and Israel–Palestine (Smooha).

The collection is also a response to the Good Friday Agreement, the landmark settlement reached in April 1998. Contributors were asked to use comparative analysis to evaluate the Agreement and to assess whether it represents the optimal way forward. The judgements are rich and varied. Several of the contributions are written from a pro-Agreement perspective. These include chapters written from a unionist perspective (Alcock), a loyalist perspective (Schulze), and a position that has been associated with that of moderate nationalists (McGarry, O'Leary). Other chapters are critical of the Agreement, including one that appears close to the position of republican rejectionists (Taylor) and another that reflects concerns held by the Alliance Party (Horowitz). The various contributions offer a wealth of prescriptive suggestions, including advice on how to design institutions for a bi-national society (McGarry, O'Leary); strengthen the Agreement to prevent breakdown (O'Leary); address the vexed question of the decommissioning of paramilitary weapons (Schulze); ensure that negotiations between rival groups succeed (O'Malley); build a multi-ethnic executive coalition that will last (Horowitz, Noel); and construct an integrated society from the grass roots up (Taylor). While a number of academics have examined Northern Ireland comparatively in monographs and journal articles, this is the first collection of essays on the subject.

This introductory chapter provides an overview of the use of comparative analysis in Northern Ireland. The first section discusses the ways in which nationalist and unionist partisans have drawn links between Northern Ireland and other divided societies since before the conflict began in the late 1960s. The second section examines comparative analysis by academics over this same period. The chapter ends with a brief summary of the various contributions to the collection, and situates these in relation to the existing literature.

Partisans and Parallels[8]

Partisans everywhere draw parallels with other conflicts. Particular parallels are selected because they are considered appropriate: the partisans see the two cases as essentially similar. However, comparisons may also be used for their instrumental value. As the parallels invariably portray the group making them in a positive light and depict rivals negatively, they can help to rally one's domestic constituency and attract sympathy from outsiders.[9] Preferred parallels change, depending on circumstances: a comparison with a particular conflict may be dropped if the conflict ends or loses its international salience. There is also some evidence that an ethnic group's choice of comparison may have real political consequences. If outsiders, including external governments and non-governmental organizations, accept the validity of a parallel between two conflicts, it may lead them to adopt the same approach towards one that they have taken towards the other. If actors in one conflict come to identify sufficiently with the actors in another, the latter's behaviour may influence the former's. There is evidence of both effects in Northern Ireland.

During the 1960s Northern Ireland's nationalists, particularly moderates, identified their plight with that of American blacks struggling for civil rights.[10] This had the advantage of identifying Northern Ireland's unionist regime with the white racist regimes of Alabama, Mississippi, and other parts of the Deep South. The parallel embarrassed Britain on the world stage and encouraged pressure from the United States for the reform of Northern Ireland. Like the US campaign, the appeal for civil rights in Northern Ireland was aimed at metropolitan citizens. The Northern Ireland Civil Rights Association, which began to challenge the unionist regime in 1964, was based on its American counterpart, although it was also inspired by the UK-based National Council for Civil Liberties. Catholics used the same slogans, 'One man, one vote' and 'The world is watching', and the same song, 'We shall overcome', as their American counterparts. More importantly, they employed the same tactics: civil disobedience and peaceful protest marches. It was thought that these tactics would have the same effect in Northern Ireland as they had in the United States, that is, that they would appeal to moderates in the dominant group and expose the intransigence of local chauvinists to liberal metropolitans. This was what happened.

Nationalists have been less inclined to portray their situation as similar to that of American blacks in recent years. This is because the American case, which featured a minority peacefully demanding civil rights, became less appropriate as the struggle of Northern Ireland's Catholics developed into a violent campaign for national rights. It is also because the American civil rights campaign lost its salience, partly because its core demands were met. However, nationalists continue to compare themselves to American blacks when it suits them. Nationalists who want to stop Orange parades through their neighbourhoods frequently refer to the Orange Order as akin to the Ku Klux Klan (KKK), and to the idea of it marching through a nationalist community as equivalent to the Klan parading through a black area in the United States.[11] During congressional hearings into police reform in Northern Ireland in April 1999, at which I was a witness, a nationalist woman giving evidence claimed that Northern Ireland reminded her of Alabama in the 1950s.[12] The parallel resonated with several of the black congressmen in attendance, and they accordingly condemned the Royal Ulster Constabulary (RUC). If a report in the *Guardian* is to be believed, President Clinton also accepts that the two cases are similar. He apparently rebuffed a request from Tony Blair to put pressure on Irish republicans to make concessions on police reform because he believed that bowing to unionist demands on the RUC 'would be like leaving Alabama and Georgia under all-white cops'.[13]

By the 1980s the favourite comparison of nationalists and republicans was between their struggle and that of the anti-apartheid movement in South Africa.[14] Ironically, at the beginning of the century Irish republicans identified with Boers, who, like them, were engaged in a militant campaign against British imperialism.[15] This comparison lost its appropriateness after the apartheid regime came to power in 1948, and after the salient conflict in South Africa became between whites and blacks rather than between Afrikaners and Britain. The comparison with the anti-apartheid movement was pressed into service as early as the 1970s. Michael Farrell, a leader of the civil rights movement, pointed out in an important book published in 1976 that the South African prime minister had offered, when introducing a new Coercion Bill in the South African Parliament in 1963, to 'exchange all the legislation of that sort for one clause of the Northern Ireland Special Powers Act'.[16] However, it was not until the 1980s that the comparison became widespread. The emerging violent anti-state protests in South Africa; the even more violent response from Pretoria; the armed, even if relatively low-key, campaign of the African National Congress (ANC)'s paramilitary wing Umkhonto we Sizwe; and the greater international profile of the conflict against apartheid, all helped to make South Africa a more compelling parallel for nationalists than the American civil rights movement.

Republicans constantly refer to the similarity between their struggle and that of the ANC, as can be seen from Belfast wall murals celebrating ANC–IRA solidarity, and from their speeches and books.[17] The analogy has been given the blessing, to the consternation of the British government, of Nelson Mandela and other ANC leaders.[18] It is also accepted by constitutional nationalists. In a book published two years before the Good Friday Agreement was reached, the Social Democratic and Labour Party leader, John Hume, claimed that what Northern Ireland needed was a unionist version of F. W. de Klerk, the white South African leader who negotiated an end to apartheid with Nelson Mandela.[19] Two years after the Agreement was signed, Hume allegedly continued to see unionists as possessing an 'Afrikaner mindset'.[20]

Equating unionists with the defenders of apartheid is intended to suggest that it is for unionists, as defenders of the status quo, to make concessions. However, it is also meant to convey a *nationalist* interpretation of the conflict, and of the prescription that is necessary to end it. It infers that unionists, like whites, not only defend the status quo, but are also a *minority*, who should seek agreement with the nationalist *majority* in the island of Ireland. Just as South Africa's majority was denied its right to self-determination by the apartheid regime, Ireland's majority has been similarly deprived by the British state. The attempt to carve Northern Ireland out of Ireland is seen as analogous to attempts by whites to carve out a white-dominated South Africa through the creation of black 'homelands'.[21] Just as the context for the solution to South Africa's conflict was the reintegration of these territories into South Africa, so the context for a solution to the conflict in Northern Ireland is an end to the partition of Ireland (the hardline nationalist version) or a process which leads to this (the moderate and currently dominant version).

Towards the end of the 1960s and early 1970s some radical republican groups drew parallels between Northern Ireland and Vietnam, and this had echoes on the British Left. It was never a dominant comparison, however, perhaps because there was concern that repetition of it would alienate Irish American support. Republicans have also compared Ireland and Israel–Palestine. In the first half of the century republicans sympathized with Zionists, who, like them, were being blocked from self-determination by British authorities. However, after Israel conquered the West Bank and Gaza Strip in 1967, and particularly after the outbreak in 1987 of the *infada*, the Palestinian uprising against Israeli control, nationalists began to draw parallels between themselves and Palestinians. The parallel, however, has not been as popular as that with black South Africans.[22] There are two obvious reasons: the Palestine Liberation Organization (PLO)'s greater proclivity for using indiscriminate terror made them a less attractive parallel; and Israeli Jews have been considered less of a pariah people than South African whites, at least in a West that continues to harbour guilt about the Holocaust. Israeli Jews may indeed be a pariah people in certain Arab societies, but Irish republicans are not primarily interested in influencing them.

More generally, Northern Ireland has been seen by its nationalist population, and in particular by republicans, as a colony, like those in pre-1960s Africa and Asia. This has helped to underline the republican position that Ireland, unlike Scotland and Wales, had never been a candidate for integration into the British nation. It has further suggested that the conflict is unfinished business left over from the imperial era, and that the appropriate prescription is a British withdrawal. Labelling Ireland (later Northern Ireland) as a colony entitled to national self-determination has the additional advantage of calling international law in aid. Colonies are entitled in international law to the right of self-determination, but integral parts of states are not. Designating Northern Ireland as Britain's colony is also consistent with the nationalist argument that the conflict is externally imposed, and masks over internal divisions between unionists and nationalists.

The international community largely accepts the colonial analogy, which helps to explain why nationalists and republicans have received more external support than unionists.[23] Many Americans, Europeans, and people from developing countries have a rather simplistic view of the conflict as taking place between Irish people and imperialist Britain. Even more damaging for the unionist cause, there is considerable evidence that people in Britain accept the colonial analogy. The public in Britain do not consider Northern Ireland an integral part of the United Kingdom. London has exclusion clauses in the Prevention of Terrorism Act that allow people from Northern Ireland to be denied entry to Britain. The main British political parties do not contest elections in Northern Ireland. Regular comments by British political elites suggest that many of them think of Northern Ireland in a colonial context. Reginald Maudling, when commenting on the failure of Stormont, said that it showed the Westminster constitution was not 'easily exportable'. In 1969 Jim Callaghan, the British home secretary who introduced troops into Northern Ireland, compared it with Cyprus, suggesting that it was much easier to get involved in these conflicts than to get out of them. In the mid-1990s Home Secretary Douglas Hurd sounded a similar note to European Union foreign ministers: they should avoid military intervention in Bosnia lest they end up with a protracted commitment like the British government's in Northern Ireland.[24] London's decision, in the Joint Declaration for Peace in 1993, and in the Good Friday Agreement of 1998, to grant the right of self-determination to the people of Ireland (north and south) and to allow a united Ireland as soon as a majority in Northern Ireland assents, is further evidence that the British government sees Northern Ireland as a colony. States have granted such rights to colonies, but seldom, if ever, to integral parts of their territory.[25]

Nationalists have also argued that they are 'republicans', that is, 'civic' nationalists committed to an inclusive vision of the nation in which Protestants and Catholics are treated equally.[26] This argument treats Irish nationalism, at least implicitly, as similar to French or American nationalism, both of which are predominantly civic in character. Unionists, by contrast, are identified as ethnic chauvinists, or, as locals might put it, 'sectarian' bigots.[27] The message is that they are more like militant Serbs than Americans. This civic–ethnic distinction pervades the other analogies favoured by nationalists. It may be another reason why republicans prefer identification with the ANC, a civic nationalist movement, over the PLO, which is more clearly ethnic nationalist. It is consistent with the colonial analogy, as colonial movements were generally multi-ethnic and inclusive national liberation movements. It is implicit in the common description of unionists as analogous to South African whites, the KKK, or European fascist organizations. In each of these cases the consistent nationalist message is that they are on the right side of enlightenment values while unionists cling to old prejudices.

Unionist Analogies

A key theme running through nationalist comparisons is the depiction of Northern Ireland as a colony and of British rule as illegitimate. Unionists reject such arguments. Before political correctness became fashionable, Brian Faulkner famously explained that Northern Ireland was not a 'coconut colony'.[28] Unionists have consistently rejected the idea that Ireland was a colony before 1921. It was, rather, an integral part of the United Kingdom governed by the same legislative procedures as the rest of the state. What happened in 1921 was not decolonization but secession from the United Kingdom by ethnocentric nationalists. One academic who is sympathetic to unionism, Hugh Roberts, has devoted an entire book to rejecting the argument that Northern Ireland is similar to the French colony of Algeria and that the appropriate prescription is an end to metropolitan rule.[29]

However, since 1972, and especially after 1985, many unionists have come to see Northern Ireland as an 'internal colony' whose inhabitants are treated as second-class citizens.[30] They are referring here to the British government's use of special 'Order in Council' procedures to limit debate on legislation pertaining to Northern Ireland and to its decision in 1985 to allow a 'foreign' government, the Irish Republic, a say over the affairs of Northern Ireland. Unionists have also criticized the major British parties, those with the only chance of winning office, for refusing to organize in Northern Ireland.[31] The use of the term 'internal colony' is deliberate, because the solution for this condition is integration, whereas 'decolonization' is the remedy for a colony.

While nationalists identify with the internationally recognized right of colonies to self-determination, unionists rest their case on an even older international principle: the right of states to sovereignty and territorial integrity. The conflict, from this perspective, is a result of irredentism and external aggression from the Irish Republic, and parallels are chosen to make this point. During the Gulf crisis in the early 1990s former Ulster Unionist Party (UUP) leader James Molyneaux compared Northern Ireland with Kuwait, casting the former Irish prime minister Charles

Haughey in the role of Saddam Hussein. His colleague Chris McGimpsey likened Northern Ireland with the Sudetenland, with Irish nationalists as Nazi aggressors and the unionists as doughty liberal Czechs. McGimpsey claimed that 'the South's demand for the destruction of Northern Ireland—Eire's claim to *Lebensraum*—is equivalent to Hitler's claim over Czechoslovakia'.[32]

In his contribution to this volume (Chapter 7) Antony Alcock, a member of the UUP, provides another version of this argument. He explains that unionists traditionally refused to accommodate nationalists only because the latter rejected the territorial integrity of the United Kingdom and because the Irish Republic, in Articles 2 and 3 of its Constitution, expressed an irredentist claim to Northern Ireland. He draws on a number of cases from continental Europe to show that unionist behaviour was not deviant. Alcock claims that the accommodation of the Swedish minority in the Åland Islands and the Austrian minority in South Tyrol was greatly facilitated when Sweden and Austria dropped their claims to these respective areas. In Cyprus, Slovakia, and other parts of eastern Europe, on the other hand, continuing uncertainty over territorial integrity has prevented majority-minority settlements.

This account helps to explain, from a pro-Agreement unionist perspective, why unionists signed the Good Friday Agreement. It was because the Republic agreed to remove its constitutional claim to sovereignty over Northern Ireland; because nationalists accepted that a united Ireland required the consent of a majority within Northern Ireland; and because the 1998 Agreement replaced the Anglo-Irish Agreement of 1985, which gave the Irish Republic a role in policy-making in Northern Ireland. Alcock also offers an explanation of why many unionists are ambivalent about the Agreement or opposed to it. This is because Irish irredentism remains a potent political force. It is also because the Irish government, while it no longer has the right to be consulted in areas of jurisdiction that have been devolved to the Northern Ireland Assembly, continues, under the Agreement, to be able to 'put forward views and proposals' on 'non-devolved Northern Ireland matters'.[33]

Their concern with the territorial integrity of states has led unionists to be sceptical of 'internationalizing' conflicts. Their opposition to international intervention led some of them to denounce the North Atlantic Treaty Organization (NATO)'s intervention in Kosovo (or, as they would have it, Yugoslavia) in 1999. During the parliamentary debate on NATO's bombing campaign, the UUP's deputy leader, John Taylor, stated that he condemned it 'without hesitation'. In a defence of Yugoslavia's territorial integrity, he argued that it was as wrong to recognize Kosovo as it had been to recognize Croatia, Bosnia, and the other states of the former Yugoslavia.[34] A member of the Democratic Unionist Party, Ian Paisley Jr., complained that the Kosovo Liberation Army, like the IRA, had got its way 'by internationalising the crisis in the Balkans, and just like their Irish counterpart in the IRA, they are looking for a way of seizing power in this region of the Balkans' in the name of a 'mystical-romantic nationalism'.[35] While the younger Paisley relied on secular arguments, other Protestants did not. According to a 'Professor' Arthur Noble, writing on the elder Paisley's web site, internationalization should be resisted because it is orchestrated by the Vatican. What links the bombing of Serbia and the Good Friday Agreement, in this view, is that both were directed by Rome. The Vatican, apparently, is planning a papal 'super-state' in Europe, and has ordered its vassals in Washington and London to subdue the Serbs and Ulster's Protestants, the two groups who 'refused to bow the knee' to Rome.[36]

Given the support among unionists for an integrated United Kingdom, it is hardly surprising that their favourite parallel is with Scotland and Wales. Integrationist unionists have long argued that Northern Ireland should be treated in the same way as these other parts of the United Kingdom. They have criticized the British government's practice of passing legislation for Northern Ireland in ways that are different from Scottish and Welsh legislation, and the tendency of the major British parties to organize in Scotland and Wales but not in Northern Ireland. Northern Ireland's distinctiveness, including the fact that it has a large Irish nationalist population, can be managed, it is claimed, within the United Kingdom, which also has sizeable Scottish and Welsh national communities. As Britain would not allow a foreign government a say in Scottish or Welsh policy, unionists argue that it should not allow a 'foreign' government a say over Northern Ireland policy. Prior to the Labour government's decision in 1997 to devolve power to a Scottish parliament and a Welsh assembly, unionist integrationists used the fact that Scotland and Wales had no such institutions to argue against devolution for Northern Ireland. Since devolution anti-Agreement unionists have expressed a preference for the Welsh over the Scottish model, as the powers Wales received are relatively insubstantial and, therefore, more compatible with integrationism.

Some unionists go beyond the Scotland and Wales analogy to compare Northern Ireland with parts of England. Margaret Thatcher once famously asserted that Northern Ireland is 'as British as Finchley', her suburban London constituency, although her autobiography suggest her views on Northern Ireland were more traditionally British than this statement suggests. A Marxist integrationist clique, the British and Irish Communist Organization, once supported its case for integration by arguing that 'parts of Ulster' are physically similar to parts of England and could 'be placed in Worcestershire without arousing comment'.[37]

Just as nationalists occasionally deviate from the rule of comparing their conflict with national liberation struggles, as when they identify with American blacks, unionists also stray from a consistent defence of the territorial integrity of states. Rather than defending the territorial unity of Cyprus and opposing outside interference in Cypriot affairs, two leading unionist politicians, John Taylor and Ken Maginnis, support the partition of Cyprus by Turkish forces and are sympathetic to the claims of Turkish Cypriots in the northern part of the island.[38] Steven King, an adviser to the UUP leader, David Trimble, has argued the merits of partition not only in Ireland and Cyprus, but also in India and the former Yugoslavia. King claims that partition can maintain peace between warring enemies and that 'people who cannot hang together are better hanging apart'. His solution to the recent Kosovo conflict is the creation of a Greater Serbia and a Greater Albania, and an end to the illusion that one can have multi-ethnic states in this region.[39] This support for partition represents a divergence from the traditional unionist position that it was Irish nationalists who were partitionists, not unionists. The support for homogeneous states is also inconsistent with civic unionist support for the United Kingdom as a multicultural and multinational state.

Unionists have been less adroit, or less concerned, than republicans about selecting politically correct analogies. In the 1960s they expressed sympathy with the white regime in Rhodesia, which they saw as, like them, under siege by a larger group and without friends. Ulster loyalists made contact with the South African apartheid regime during the 1980s, and currently enjoy links with fascist groups in Great Britain.[40] As we have just seen, some unionists are happy to associate themselves with the Serbs. However, mainstream unionists have become increasingly disenchanted with such comparisons, probably because of the propaganda pitfalls associated with them. Since the Anglo-Irish Agreement of 1985 unionist politicians and intellectuals have increasingly presented their position in modern inclusive language.[41] They claim that unionists want a modern and tolerant multi-ethnic state capable of accommodating all its citizens, including Irish Catholics and nationalists. It is Irish nationalists who are said to seek a homogeneous nation-state on the Eastern European model. To the nationalist accusation that they are like the KKK, the Loyal Orders respond by framing their demand to march through nationalist areas in the liberal language of rights of assembly. One of these Orders, the Apprentice Boys, claims it wants the 'right' to march while nationalists want to impose 'apartheid' on Northern Ireland by keeping Orangemen and nationalists separate.[42] Launching his bid for the UUP leadership in March 2000, unionist right-winger Martin Smyth suggested that it was Sinn Féin which was fascist, and claimed that the European Union was being hypocritical in opposing the inclusion of Jörg Haider's Freedom Party in the Austrian government while permitting Sinn Féin's participation in Northern Ireland's government.[43] When told by a reporter that John Hume had called for a unionist de Klerk, David Trimble responded that the analogy was incorrect: it was a *nationalist* de Klerk that was necessary. Trimble was making the point that if one took Northern Ireland, or the United Kingdom, as one's point of reference, it was nationalists who were in a minority, but his response also had the advantage of associating nationalists with an erstwhile pariah people.

Do Parallels Matter?

One should be careful about exaggerating the effect of parallels. Developments in divided societies, whether of a violent or peaceful kind, are usually influenced by a myriad of exogenous and endogenous factors. However, there is evidence that a parrallel, once accepted, can influence subsequent developments. In the 1960s the norm spread by the US civil rights movement that second-class citizenship was unacceptable helped to motivate Catholics, after decades of passivity, to challenge the Stormont regime. The event that is thought by many to have started the troubles, the Belfast to Derry march of January 1969, was modelled consciously on the Selma–Montgomery march undertaken by the American civil rights movement in 1965. The use of tactics of civil disobedience had roughly the same effect in Northern Ireland as in the American South: it exposed the illiberalism of the local governors, split the dominant group, and provoked metropolitan intervention. If the *Guardian* report referred to on page four is accurate, the analogy between Northern Ireland's Catholics and America's blacks continues to influence US policy on Northern Ireland.

The Northern Ireland-South Africa Parallel was used explicitly by Irish Americans to shape US policy towards Northern Ireland. The MacBride principles, adopted in the 1980s to promote regulation of US investment in Northern Ireland, were modelled on the Sullivan principles established to govern trade between the United States and apartheid South Africa. This American pressure helped to secure anti-discrimination reforms in

Northern Ireland, including the Fair Employment Act of 1989. By the 1990s the ANC's decision to suspend its armed struggle, and, to a lesser extent, the PLO's decision to embrace the Oslo process, made it easier for the IRA to explore peace. According to Guelke, the ANC's decision to abandon its armed struggle was one of the factors that led the IRA to declare a ceasefire in 1994.[44] Others, including O'Malley in this collection, argue that the ability of South Africans to settle their conflict exercised a positive influence on Northern Ireland nationalists (and unionists) as they negotiated the Good Friday Agreement. A number of journalists attributed the IRA's decisions in May 2000 to allow two international inspectors to examine some of its arms dumps to pressure from the ANC, particularly from one of Mandela's leading lieutenants, Mac Maharaj. It was noted by anti-Agreement unionists and others that an important aspect of the IRA's offer was that one of the two inspectors be the former ANC secretary-general, Cyril Ramaphosa.[45] A reporter from the *Boston Globe* claimed, albeit without offering a shred of evidence, that 'there is little doubt that [the IRA offer] would not have been issued if not for the influence of Maharaj and Ramaphosa, and if Ramaphosa had not been chosen by the British and Irish governments as one of their arms inspectors'.[46]

Unionists also appear to have been affected by their choice of parallels. After years in which they argued that Northern Ireland should be treated the same as Scotland and Wales, their case for integration was dealt a serious blow when the Blair government devolved power to Edinburgh and Cardiff in 1997.[47] This created space for UUP moderates to support proposals for devolution in the Good Friday Agreement. The fact that the arrangements for Scotland and Wales were asymmetrical, reflecting the particular circumstances of each case, made it easier to accept, or at least more difficult to argue against, peculiar institutions for Northern Ireland, including a power-sharing executive and a North–South Ministerial Council and all-island 'implementation bodies'.[48] Supporters of reform sought to take advantage of these parallels, pointing out that a new oath to be sworn by police constables from 1998, and proposed changes to the prosecution system, were based on Scottish precedents.

It is not only Northern Ireland partisans who are influenced by the analogies they use. Keating points out in this volume that Basque nationalists have looked to Northern Ireland rather than vice versa.[49] According to him, the Basques followed the Northern Ireland peace process closely, and it was not a coincidence that ETA called a ceasefire shortly after the signing of the Good Friday Agreement.

Academics and Comparative Analysis

Comparisons are not a preserve of partisans, of course. Northern Ireland has also been a focus of study for several intellectuals who have used comparative analysis. The most prominent of these approaches are based on classical pluralist theory, consociational theory, integrationist theory, linkage theory, and settler colonial theory. My intention here is to offer a brief summary of these approaches rather than a lengthy analysis and critique. Those interested in the latter should see the discussion by Brendan O'Leary and me in *Explaining Northern Ireland,* particularly chapter 8.[50]

Classical Pluralist Theory

Classical pluralist theory dominated political science during the 1950s and 1960s.[51] Sometimes referred to as 'cross-pressures' theory, it explained instability as resulting from the absence of a balanced distribution of conflicting interests. Conflict flowed, in this view, when social divisions, whether linguistic, racial, religious, or otherwise, reinforced rather than cross-cut each other, when, for instance, memberships in different voluntary associations were cumulative rather than overlapping.[52] Given its dominance in the 1960s, it is not surprising that it shaped some of the early prominent attempts to explain the conflict in Northern Ireland. In one of the first major works on Northern Ireland, Richard Rose argued that Northern Ireland's reinforcing pressures accounted for its surplus of republican 'rebels' and loyalist 'ultras'. It had, according to Rose, insufficient cross-pressures to generate enough allegiant or passive citizens, and it consequently lacked the consensus required for legitimate democratic government.[53]

Edmund Aunger, a French Canadian political scientist, also employed cross-pressures theory in a comparative study of Northern Ireland and the Canadian province of New Brunswick. According to Aunger, New Brunswick was stable, despite its English–French ethnic cleavage, because the language division was cross-cut by others based on religion and class. Northern Ireland was unstable, by contrast, because its various social divisions were reinforcing.[54] In a comparative study of Belfast and Glasgow which used survey evidence, Ian Budge and Cornelius O'Leary made the 'discovery' that there was much lower cross-cutting between party and religion in Belfast than between party and any social characteristic in Glasgow.[55] In their view, the fact that political parties in Belfast were subject to fewer cross-pressures than their Glasgow counterparts helped to explain why Belfast's politics were unstable while Glasgow's were not.

Consociational Theory

Consociational theory was developed by Arend Lijphart in reaction to what was seen as a sociological bias in pluralist theory.[56] According to Lijphart, social divisions by themselves did not necessarily condemn regimes to instability. Otherwise, he argued, how could one account for stability in states like Belgium, Switzerland, Austria, or the Netherlands—none of which, in his view, possessed cross-cutting social cleavages? While Lijphart accepted that certain social and political conditions were more conducive to consociational democracy than others, he claimed that the only essential conditions were the presence of strong political elites who were willing to accommodate each other and who could win their followers' support for the resulting bargain. While the design of consociational institutions could vary, they included four basic features: (1) a grand coalition, an executive inclusive of all the state's main subcultures; (2) proportional representation for the state's subcultures in public institutions, including the legislature and bureaucracy; (3) group autonomy, allowing subcultures to be self-governing where possible; (4) minority vetoes, at least when vital interests were affected.

Consociational theory was first applied to Northern Ireland by Lijphart himself in 1975, although consociational thinking was implicit in the Sunningdale Agreement of 1973. Lijphart was pessimistic about the prospects for consociational democracy, claiming that it was 'unworkable'.[57] The key problem in his view was the absence of support for it among Protestants.[58] However, he added that Northern Ireland also lacked a number of conducive conditions: rather than being divided into a number of groups none of which could govern by itself, Northern Ireland had a (Protestant) majority that was 'capable of exercising hegemonic power'; Protestants were normatively attracted to the Westminster majoritarian tradition and rejected continental power-sharing norms; there was no overarching national consensus.[59]

By the mid-1990s Lijphart was more confident about the prospects for consociationalism, and claimed that it was the only 'viable option' for Northern Ireland.[60] Rather than being 'unworkable', he now argued that it was wrong to conclude that power-sharing 'cannot be successful'. His new optimism was due to his observation that the British government now appeared committed to power-sharing and that none of Northern

Ireland's political parties was seriously proposing 'a return to majoritarianism'.[61]

Consociational theory has also been applied to Northern Ireland by Brendan O'Leary and me.[62] While broadly supportive of Lijphart's claim that a Northern Ireland government should be constructed on consociational principles, we have been critical of some of his arguments. One problem with traditional consociational research is its tendency to treat political systems as closed entities. This has led to a focus on endogenous factors when explaining conflict, and a stress on internal institutions, modelled on the traditional 'Westphalian' state, when proposing prescriptions. This focus limits the explanatory and prescriptive power of consociational theory when applied to conflicts like Northern Ireland's, which have been influenced by exogenous as well as endogenous factors, and where satisfactory prescriptions require institutions that transcend state frontiers.

In our view, an important reason why unionists refused to share power with nationalists was not because they were committed normatively to the Westminster model of government but because, as British nationalists, they preferred the default of direct rule from Westminster to the risk of power-sharing with Irish nationalists. Direct rule also helped to block what Lijphart calls a 'self-denying prophecy', a decision by elites to share power because the alternative is chaos and deepening violence. London paid the costs of the conflict, and the British army helped to prevent it reaching Bosnian levels of violence. Even if unionists had embraced consociationalism, this would not have sufficed for nationalists, who also demand institutions linking Northern Ireland with the Irish Republic. Agreement was reached in 1998 on a consociational government and North–South institutions in part because London made it clear to unionists that the default to a settlement was no longer unalloyed direct rule from Westminster but, instead, deepening Anglo-Irish cooperation in the governance of Northern Ireland. Unionist flexibility was facilitated by an IRA decision to declare a ceasefire and by the Irish government's preparedness to drop formal irredentist claims in return for a settlement.[63]

Integrationist Theory

The classical pluralist accounts described earlier are explanatory in nature. However, there is a branch of pluralist theory that has an important normative and prescriptive dimension. This branch can be described as integrationist, as it seeks to transform divided societies into integrated ones. Integrationists, like pluralists, attribute conflict to the salience of divisive identities, such as those based on ethnicity or race, and the absence of cross-cutting identities, such as those based on class. However, integrationists believe that cross-cutting identities can be constructed, if the correct policies are followed. Such policies include combating the divisive appeals of self-interested ethnic elites through the mobilization of organizations in civil society that promote transcendent identities; integration in schools, workplaces, and residential neighbourhoods; an end to discrimination; and the removal of economic inequality through economic growth and/or distribution.

Integrationism was advocated in one of the earliest books on Northern Ireland politics, written in 1961,[64] and it has been a theme of a number of works since then.[65] One complication, however, is that integrationists in Northern Ireland are themselves divided: there are some who support an integrated Ireland and some who support an integrated United Kingdom.[66] Others are post-nationalists who back the process of European integration in the belief that it will contribute to cross-cutting divisions by creating new functional allegiances across state boundaries and a new European identity that both communities in Northern Ireland can embrace.[67]

Integrationists are extremely sceptical of consociational theory and have launched a vigorous critique of it.[68] Consociationalists are accused of exaggerating the depth and resilience of social divisions, and of downplaying the capacity of humans to develop new identities. From the integrationist perspective, consociational institutions often worsen matters by strengthening the position of those sectional elites who are responsible for division in the first place. Because consociational institutions are thought to entrench and deepen division, they are seen not simply as undesirable, but also as unstable and ultimately unworkable.

The integrationist critique of consociationalism is popular among academics specializing in the Northern Ireland conflict. Several of them oppose the British government's long-standing commitment to consociational institutions, and criticize the central part these play in the Good Friday Agreement. Anderson and Goodman claim that the consociational model at the heart of the Agreement has 'very serious defects', over-emphasizes 'the primacy and the permanency of ethnic divisions', and 'actively excludes other perhaps more fruitful social categories, other bases of political mobilisation such as gender and class which cross-cut ethnic divisions'.[69] Wilford condemns consociational theory as conveying a 'rather bleak view of humanity' and as threatening to cast divisions in 'marble'.[70] He endorses an alternative strategy of promoting 'pluralistic rather than monolithic thinking' through ending discrimination in the workplace and educational integration.[71] Dixon criticizes consociationalism as 'elitist' and 'segregationist' and recommends mass participation and social integration as a more appropriate way forward.[72] In a well-cited article that rejects consociational prescriptions for Northern Ireland and South Africa, Rupert Taylor condemns Lijphart's 'uncritical acceptance of the primacy and permanency of ethnicity', argues that divisions in the two cases are constructed by self-interested elites, and calls for 'economic growth and the removal of discrimination' as an alternative strategy for conflict resolution.[73]

To these academic critiques can be added partisan attacks from both nationalists and unionists: Irish republican Kevin Rooney claims that the Agreement's consociational institutions have 'put an end to the prospects for overcoming [Ireland's] divisions and institutionalise[d] the differences between Catholics an Protestants'; the leading unionist Robert McCartney criticizes the same institutions as 'dysfunctional', 'undemocratic', and 'impermanent'.[74] Their alternatives, of course, are diametrically opposing.

Linkage Theory

One problem with much political science work on ethnic conflict is that it puts an exaggerated stress on endogenous factors. As John Whyte has pointed out, this stress is an important feature of the general academic literature on Northern Ireland.[75] There is an important body of work, however, that has been undertaken at the interface between comparative politics and international relations and that emphasizes the role of exogenous factors in the Northern Ireland conflict. This can usefully be described as 'linkage' theory because it focuses on the linkages between exogenous pressures and internal political developments in Northern Ireland.

Linkage theories are a rather mixed bag. They range from some of the worst 'scholarship' on the Northern Ireland conflict to some of the best. In the former category are works that attribute much of the conflict to funding for paramilitary groups from rogue states and diasporas,[76] as well as partisan accounts that attribute the conflict exclusively to 'perfidious Albion' or to the Irish Republic's irredentism'[77] In the latter category are a number of books that, while acknowledging the importance of internal factors, take the position that the conflict cannot be explained without reference to the actions of both the British and Irish states. An influential short book by the lawyers Tom Hadden and Kevin Boyle, published in

1985, falls into this category.[78] So does a more substantive volume by Joseph Ruane and Jennifer Todd, published in 1996.[79] In our various works on Northern Ireland Brendan O'Leary and I have also emphasized that the conflict cannot be explained adequately without recourse to British and Irish nation- and state-building failures.

Adrian Guelke has gone beyond the role of Britain and Ireland. In a book published in 1988 he argued that the violence and constitutional stalemate in Northern Ireland was crucially shaped by the international norm of self-determination.[80] In his view, the international perspective that Northern Ireland is illegitimate, a legacy of colonialism, is an important factor underlying unionist insecurity and republican aggressiveness. Guelke has also done important work on linkages between South Africa's conflict and Northern Ireland's, and has claimed that events in the former influenced developments in the latter.

The most ambitious example of linkage theory is Frank Wright's *Northern Ireland: A Comparative Analysis*.[81] For Wright, Northern Ireland is best understood as an 'ethnic frontier', a site of contested sovereignty between the British and Irish national communities. In an ethnic frontier, conflict is crucially affected by the actions of external powers beyond the frontier. If one external power intervenes to side with an internal protagonist, then the other will also seek external help, compelling a dramatic escalation in conflict. Wright holds an unstable regional environment responsible for the ferocity of past and present conflicts in the Balkans, Cyprus, and Lebanon.[82] The relative stability of Belgium and Switzerland, by contrast, flows from a tradition of non-interference and restraint by larger neighbours who have avoided intervention on behalf of their co-ethnics. When ethnic communities in a frontier zone are locked in conflict, the best that can be hoped for, according to Wright, is that interested external powers will cooperate with each other to contain the conflict rather than siding purely with their co-nationals. Northern Ireland's most benign feature, in Wright's view, was that the British and Irish governments, particularly since 1985, enjoyed amicable and cooperative relations. His prescription was that this cooperation should be consolidated into full-blown British and Irish joint authority over the region.

The British and Irish states remain unquestionably the most influential exogenous actors in the Northern Ireland conflict. In recent years, however, academics have also pointed to the impact of Europe and the United States. In a number of accounts, which overlap with the integrationist accounts discussed earlier, European integration is seen as promoting multiple or post-national identities in place of the old nationalist–unionist polarities.[83]

Intellectuals who are sympathetic to Irish nationalism put forward a variant of this: European integration will erode the identity of unionists in a way that will promote a united Ireland.[84] One unionist writer has argued that European integration is having a negative impact: it is facilitating Anglo-Irish cooperation over Northern Ireland and, by eroding traditional notions of state sovereignty, weakening the Union.[85] Other, more impartial, observers agree that European integration is diluting state sovereignty, but see this as a useful development that creates the space for imaginative institutional arrangements suited to the needs of nationally divided societies like Northern Ireland.[86]

A number of scholars have focused on the role of the United States, which is generally thought to have grown in importance after the Clinton administration assumed power in 1992.[87] Even before this, the US government was credited with persuading London to embrace a policy of power-sharing devolution in 1979 and to sign the Anglo-Irish Agreement in 1985.[88] Irish American pressure groups are said to have played an important role in persuading London to implement far-reaching employment equity legislation in 1989.[89] Clinton's administration, it has been argued, played a crucial part in the IRA's decision to declare a ceasefire in 1994,[90] and Clinton's delegate George Mitchell is widely seen as having contributed to the successful outcome of the inter-party negotiations that produced the Good Friday Agreement. While the United States is usually seen by unionists as biased against them, one commentator notes that Clinton had a good relationship with UUP leader David Trimble and that the president's last-minute assurances helped convince Trimble to sign the Good Friday Agreement.[91]

Settler Colonial Theory

A final prominent comparative approach to the Northern Ireland conflict is based on settler colonial theory. As O'Leary and I have argued, settler societies are normally extreme examples of plural societies, and the fact that Ireland, and later Northern Ireland, was a site of settler colonialism helps to explain the intensity of divisions there.[92] The legacy of the settlement of Ireland contributed to the prevalence of segregation, endogamy, and segmented labour markets. The initial act of dispossession bequeathed a legacy of inequality that continues to poison inter-group relations. The parallels between the establishment of a hegemonic control system by the dominant settler group in Ireland, and later Northern Ireland, and dominant settler control systems in South Africa, Algeria, and Rhodesia help to explain the focus of several works by comparativists.[93]

Three of these works are especially noteworthy. Ian Lustick has compared French state-building failures in Algeria with British state-building failures in Ireland. In both cases, he claims, the large-scale introduction of settlers into the two regions fundamentally disrupted a prerequisite for successful state-building: the elicitation of loyalties from the newly acquired area. At several crucial junctures, such as the Treaty of Limerick in 1691 and the Act of Union in 1801, Protestant settlers intervened to obstruct conciliatory gestures by the state towards natives.[94] This helps to explain why, when Catholic mass mobilization occurred in the late nineteenth century it took off in a separatist direction.

Don Akenson's historical research emphasizes the important fact that Ulster's Protestant settlers were religiously inspired, like the Afrikaners who settled southern Africa and the Jews who settled Palestine. All three groups, Akenson argues, saw themselves as 'chosen peoples' who had a biblical covenant with God. This helped to explain Ulster Protestants' sense of superiority to Catholics, their willingness to discriminate, their endorsement of endogamy, their cohesiveness, their intransigence, their rejection of ecumenism, and their attachment to their soil, which they saw as a promised land. Akenson is careful to note that, while religion was crucial for Protestants, it is now a much less important influence.

Ronald Weitzer, who compares Northern Ireland with Zimbabwe, is concerned with the coercive dimensions of state power in divided societies with histories of settler rule. He shows that dominant settler groups can maintain control over sometimes much larger native populations through the construction of a highly sectarian security apparatus. With obvious relevance to contemporary Northern Ireland and contemporary Zimbabwe, Weitzer claims that substantive democratization—after a transition—requires a radical overhaul of inherited security structures.[95]

Weitzer argues that Zimbabwe at independence lacked a democratic political culture and a strong civil society. It had a regime that wanted to retain the repressive character of the security apparatus inherited from Rhodesia for use against its new (Ndebele) enemies. The result was that the transition from white minority rule to majority rule, while it increased democracy, did not create a liberal democracy. The new (British) regime that took over Northern Ireland in 1972 was much more willing than its Harare counterpart to transform the police into a professional and impartial agency. However, it was impeded, on the one hand, by opposition to reform from a strong Protestant civil society and, on the other, by a Catholic minority that was strong enough to resist strengthened security measures. The result was that the British engaged in limited reforms that did not go far enough.

It is worth noting that these accounts are different from the partisan nationalist portrayal of Ireland as a colony. In the latter Ireland is seen as exploited by outsiders—British imperialists. The existence of profound internal divisions in the colony are downplayed. Settlers, to the extent that they are acknowledged, are portrayed as the dupes of metropolitan forces without their own interests or identity. There is an inference, although often delivered *sotto voce*, that those who are descended from settlers have less legitimacy than natives, and even, in the view of extremists, that they should be repatriated. The above accounts, by contrast, emphasize that Northern Ireland has important *endogenous* divisions based on the historic distinction between settlers and natives. Britain is not the only obstacle to a resolution of the conflict: the different identities and interests of settlers and natives are also factors. Following from this, none of these authors, unlike partisan nationalists, thinks the conflict can be resolved simply by Britain's withdrawal.[96] These differences are sometimes overlooked by unionist sympathizers who (incorrectly) regard any portrayal of Protestants as settlers as a nationalist argument and as implying a demand that they be discriminated against or repatriated.[97]

The Chapters

This collection builds on the rich legacy of comparative work on Northern Ireland. It assesses Post-Agreement Northern Ireland from a comparative perspective. The first set of chapters is general and theoretical, and is focused on consociational and/or integrationist theory. Rupert Taylor (Chapter 2) delivers a sustained critique of the consociational institutions in the Agreement from an integrationist perspective. He argues that a stable peace requires the rejection of the approach taken in the Agreement and, instead, the construction of a common society through integrated schools, residences, and workplaces, and through the organization of groups in civil society that are dedicated to eroding ethno-national divisions. He favours a 'non-sectarian democratic society . . . in a united "New Ireland"'.

Brendan O'Leary (Chapter 3), by contrast, defends the Agreement's consociational institutions. He notes that the Agreement also contains federal and confederal institutions covering all of Ireland and linking Ireland with Britain, and argues that both the internal and external dimensions were necessary parts of a durable settlement given the identities and aspirations of nationalists and unionists. O'Leary's chapter is wide-ranging in scope, stressing, in contrast to the positions taken by Arend Lijphart and

Donald Horowitz, the advantages of the particular proportional electoral system used in Northern Ireland, and pointing to the dangers that Britain's tradition of parliamentary sovereignty poses to stable agreements between Britain and Ireland. He argues that Northern Ireland could and should have become a federacy as well as having consociational governance.

Like Taylor, but for different reasons, Donald Horowitz (Chapter 4) is critical of the consociational aspects of the Agreement. He views the 'grand coalition' executive at the heart of the Agreement as unwieldy because it includes the extremes, particularly Sinn Féin. He regards a number of commitments in the Agreement as maximalist, and believes this will rebound, when the commitments are not delivered, to the advantage of militants. Horowitz prefers, for Northern Ireland and elsewhere, what he calls an 'incentives' approach. The likeliest and most stable coalition resulting from this is one that includes moderates and excludes militants.

In my chapter (Chapter 5) I take issue with the integrationist or 'nation-building' approach to the Northern Ireland conflict. The problem with this is that there are two national communities in Northern Ireland, and no sign that either of them is prepared to accept the other's identity or state. What is needed, therefore, are political institutions, like those in the Agreement, that cater to the bi-national nature of Northern Ireland's society.

Feargal Cochrane (Chapter 6) addresses the integrationist complaint that academics focus too much on political elites and not enough on civil society. He explores the role that a large number of peace and conflict resolution organizations have played in Northern Ireland. An important conclusion, which is at odds with integrationist thinking, is that many of these organizations are as divided as political elites along national lines, and are committed to a solution that accommodates both communities rather than to one that transcends them.

In the case-study section of the collection, Northern Ireland is compared with conflicts occurring throughout Europe, Africa, North America, the Middle East, and other parts of Asia. Antony Alcock (Chapter 7) compares Northern Ireland with a number of European conflict zones. His chapter, as discussed earlier, is an example of how unionist intellectuals use the comparative method. It can also be seen as an example of linkage theory: Alcock argues that unionists were able to accept the all-Ireland institutions in the Good Friday Agreement in the context of similar developments in other parts of the European Union. Michael Keating (Chapter 8) compares Northern Ireland with western Europe's other hotspot, the Basque Country. Like Alcock he links both regions with the process of European integration. His view is that, as this promotes a move away from the traditional notion of single identities and sovereign nation-states towards the idea of multiple identities and shared sovereignty, it offers a potential way out of both conflicts.

It may appear inappropriate to compare Northern Ireland with prosperous and non-violent Canada. As Sid Noel (Chapter 9) shows, however, Canada's relative tranquillity was not inevitable but owes much to the development of consociational practices by its English and French Canadian elites. Noel notes that if consociationalism is to work in Northern Ireland, its elites must also embrace a consociational bargain, a desire to compromise. He sees limited evidence of this, and is sceptical of the Agreement's prospects. Noel's chapter is a useful reminder that it is possible to support consociationalism normatively, while recognizing that it remains a difficult system to operate, particularly in sites of profound polarization.

Guelke, who compares Northern Ireland with Cyprus, Puerto Rico, Corsica, East Timor, and Sri Lanka, puts forward a version of linkage theory (Chapter 10). In his view, the fact that Northern Ireland is a partitioned part of an island helps to explain why the international community tends to favour a united Ireland. This is because there is an international norm that islands, as natural units, should be under one jurisdiction. International support for the Agreement can be explained, in Guelke's view, by its inclusion of all-island political institutions. Any attempt to weaken these will result in reduced international support.

One of the major obstacles to the consolidation of the Agreement is the issue of paramilitary weapons. This is tackled by Kirsten Schulze (Chapter 11), who argues that Northern Ireland has a lot to learn from how the Lebanese handled this problem. Schulze sees the inclusion of all groups, including militants, as the key to a peaceful transition. This perspective, shared by O'Leary and me, is directly at odds with Horowitz's, which is that the inclusion of militants is destabilizing and should be resisted. In a chapter that compares Northern Ireland and South Africa (Chapter 12), Padraig O'Malley squarely rejects the claim of Irish republican militants that their position is analogous to South Africa's ANC. He also claims that those who negotiated South Africa's settlement influenced their Northern Ireland counterparts. This is another example of linkage between Northern Ireland and the outside world.

The collection ends with a comparison between Ireland and Palestine –Land of Israel by Sammy Smooha (Chapter 13). Smooha's chapter examines the political consequences of different settlement patterns in the two cases. It is an example of the use of settler colonial theory to explain conflict and conflict resolution. Smooha argues that Jews have settled Palestine–Land of Israel in sufficient strength to establish a strong independent state in part of the area (pre-1967 Israel), although their attempt to incorporate the rest (the West Bank and Gaza) by settlement has failed. As a result, partition has become the most feasible way to resolve the Jewish–Palestinian conflict. In Ireland, by contrast, the position of British settlers (Protestants) is said to be much weaker than their Jewish counterparts. The Protestants are weak demographically, lack international legitimacy, are not supported by Britain, and are faced with a confident Irish nationalism. As a consequence, Smooha argues that the historical trend points to Britain's withdrawal and an end to the partition of Ireland as the most likely form of conflict resolution.

NOTES

1. J. Hewitt, cited in T. Nairn, *The Break-Up of Britain* (London: Verso, 1981), 224.
2. R. Doyle, *The Commitments* (New York: Vintage Books, 1989), 9, cited in B. Dooley, *The Fight for Civil Rights in Northern Ireland and Black America* (London: Pluto Press, 1998), 6.
3. R. Pearson, cited in R. Kearney, *Postnationalist Ireland* (London: Routledge, 1997), 76. Pearson thought that the tendency to see Northern Ireland as peculiar would change as a result of the end of the cold war and the outbreak of several conflicts in eastern Europe.
4. J. Darby, cited in J. Whyte, *Interpreting Northern Ireland* (Oxford: Oxford University Press, 1990), 196.
5. Nairn, *The Break-Up of Britain*, 222. Nairn noted, to his credit, that Northern Ireland was becoming less peculiar.
6. The Report of the Alliance Commission on Northern Ireland, cited in Whyte, *Interpreting Northern Ireland*, 199.
7. A. Guelke, *Northern Ireland: The International Perspective* (Dublin: Gill & Macmillan, 1988); A. Lijphart, Review Article, 'The Northern Ireland Problem: Cases, Theories, and Solutions', *British Journal of Political Science*, 5 (1975), 83–106; I. Lustick, *State-Building Failure in British Ireland and French Algeria* (Berkeley: Institute of International Studies, 1985); R. Rose, *Governing Without Consensus: An Irish Perspective* (London: Faber & Faber, 1971); F. Wright, *Northern Ireland: A Comparative Analysis* (Dublin: Gill & Macmillan, 1987).
8. I will be exploring this topic more fully in a future journal article.
9. The use of parallels by partisans is not limited to Northern Ireland. It is a

widespread practice. Quebec nationalists, for example, described themselves in the early 1970s as 'the White Niggers of America'. See P. Vallières, *White Niggers of America* (Toronto: McClelland & Stewart, 1971). The comparison identified them with progressive movements for civil rights in the United States and decolonization in Africa and Asia, and it identified Canada's English minority as akin to Deep South racists and imperialists. In case the point was missed, Quebec's Anglophones were labelled as 'Westmount Rhodesians', after a part of Montreal dominated by wealthy members of their community.

10. For a readable account of the ways in which Northern Ireland's Catholics and America's blacks have compared their plights, see Dooley, *The Fight for Civil Rights.*

11. American blacks appear to accept the analogy. US Congressman Donald Payne, one of the most influential black politicians in Congress, told the *Sunday Times* recently that 'there are many parallels between the situation of Catholics in Northern Ireland and the situation the black community faced in the United States'. He confirmed that he would be present at Drumcree in July 2000 to observe the Orange Order's attempt to march through the Catholic Garvaghy Road area. The *Sunday Times* suggested that Martin Luther King's daughter Bernice would also be there. 'King Daughter may Observe Drumcree', *Sunday Times*, 18 June 2000.

12. *The Need for New and Acceptable Policing in Northern Ireland,* Hearing before the Committee on International Relations, House of Representatives, One Hundred Sixth Congress, First Session, 22 Apr. 1999, serial no. 106–16 (Washington, DC: 1999), 11 and 13.

13. 'Clinton Refuses to Back Blair's Deal for RUC', *Guardian*, 25 May 2000. The words in quotation marks were spoken by a senior administration official closely involved with the Northern Ireland peace talks. They reflect this official's view of the president's position.

14. Much of what I have to say about the analogy between South Africa and Northern Ireland is derived from reading Adrian Guelke's excellent work on the subject. See A. Guelke, 'The Political Impasse in South Africa and Northern Ireland: A Comparative Perspective', *Comparative Politics* (Jan. 1991), 143–62; 'The Peace Process in South Africa, Israel and Northern Ireland: A Farewell to Arms?', *Irish Studies in International Affairs*, 5 (1994), 93–106; 'The Influence of the South African Transition on the Northern Ireland Peace Process', *South African Journal of International Affairs*, 3/2 (1996), 132–48; 'Comparatively Peaceful: The Role of Analogy in Northern Ireland's Peace Process', MS, 1998.

15. Guelke, 'Comparatively Peaceful', 3.

16. M. Farrell, *Northern Ireland: The Orange State* (London: Pluto Press, 1976), 93–4.

17. Guelke, 'The Political Impasse', 147.

18. 'Mandela's IRA Remarks Criticised', *Irish Times*, 21 Oct. 1992.

19. John Hume, *A New Ireland: Politics, Peace and Reconciliation* (Boulder, Colo.: Roberts Rinehart, 1996), 117.

20. 'Hume Likens Unionists to Afrikaners', *Irish Times*, 19 June 2000. According to Ruth Dudley-Edwards, Hume was misquoted (*Sunday Independent*, 25 June 2000).

21. In the same paragraph in Hume's book where he refers to the need for a unionist de Klerk, he puts forward the conventional nationalist position that partition is at the root of Northern Ireland's problems: 'There are parallels between the South African situation and our own. If the solution to the problem in South Africa had been to draw a line on the map, create a small white state, with two whites to every black person, and to make the rest of South Africa independent would there ever have been the possibility of peace? Would not the whites have been forced to discriminate totally against the black minority in order to ensure that it never became a majority? This is precisely what happened in Ireland, and we are still living with the consequences.'

22. Guelke, 'The Influence of the South African Transition', 140.

23. Guelke, *Northern Ireland*.

24. The comments from Maudling, Callaghan, and Hurd are cited in J. McGarry and B. O'Leary, *Explaining Northern Ireland: Broken Images* (Oxford: Blackwell, 1985), 312–13.

25. The constitutions of various communist states, including that of the USSR, included the right of republics to secede. However, these were 'sham' rights and were not meant to be taken seriously. The Canadian Constitution now includes provision for a province to leave. The federal government is required to negotiate with the government of Quebec, or any province, that wins a 'clear majority' in a referendum that has a 'clear question' on secession. If the two parties negotiate in good faith, and the negotiations fail, the province is entitled to seek international recognition as an independent state. An important aspect of Canada's provision for secession is that it is judge-made, that is, it was inserted into the constitution by the courts, not politicians. This is an ironic example of Canadian judges invoking American-style judicial activism to reach a very un-American decision.

26. See Ch. 5 of this volume.

27. Nationalists often refer to bigoted Protestants as '*black*' and the Protestant-dominated RUC as '*black* bastards'. Nationalist politicians must have some difficulty explaining this to their allies in the US civil rights movement and the South African government.

28. B. Faulkner, *Memoirs of a Statesman* (London: Weidenfeld & Nicolson, 1978), 157.

29. H. Roberts, *Northern Ireland and the Algerian Analogy: A Suitable Case for Gaullism?* (Belfast: Athol Books, 1986).

30. Queen's University Belfast Ulster Unionist Association, pamphlet (Belfast: Ulster Unionist Association, 1989).

31. See H. Roberts, 'Sound Stupidity: The British Party System and the Northern Ireland Question', in J. McGarry and B. O'Leary (eds.), *The Future of Northern Ireland* (Oxford: Clarendon Press, 1990).

32. McGimpsey was referring to Articles 2 and 3 of the Irish Constitution; *Irish Times*, 29–30 Oct. 1990. An Irish nationalist could respond that the two cases—the Sudetenland and Northern Ireland—are similar in that both flout the norm of self-determination. Large numbers of Irish and Germans were left on the wrong side of new borders because they were the weaker parties in peace negotiations.

33. Unionists also remain concerned, as is well known, about issues relating to policing reform, prisoner release, and the decommissioning of paramilitary weapons.

34. 'If the recognition of Croatia, Bosnia and the other states of the former Yugoslavia was wrong—if we were bounced into it—why is that now the basis on which we foresee a settlement being made? Recognition was wrong then and it is still wrong today.' Cited in D. Conversi, 'Moral Relativisim and Equidistance—British Attitudes to the War in the Former Yugoslavia', in T. Cushman and S. Meštrović (eds.), *This Time we Knew: Western Responses to Genocide in Bosnia* (New York: New York University Press, 1999), 257. I am grateful to Daniele Conversi for drawing this to my attention.

35. I. Paisley Jr., 'Kosovo and Ulster—The Alarming Parallel', *Belfast Telegraph*, 28 Apr. 1999.

36. A. Noble, 'Popery, NATO and the Yugoslav War: Our Analysis Vindicated!', located at *http://www.ianpaisley.org/article.asp?ArtKey=nato*

37. British and Irish Communist Organization, *Against Ulster Nationalism* (Belfast: Athol Books, 1977).

38. See Ch. 10 of this volume.

39. S. King, 'Partition Back in Vogue', *Belfast Telegraph*, 13 May 1999.

40. Guelke, 'The Influence of the South African Transition', 143–4; 'English Fascists to Join Loyalists at Drumcree', *Observer*, 2 July 2000.

41. See Ch. 5 of this volume.

42. 'Marching Orders: Ulster "Apartheid" Criticised', *Guardian*, 25 Apr. 2000.

43. 'Smyth Urges Support Ensure Electoral Gains', *Irish Times*, 25 Mar. 2000. Unionists and their sympathizers commonly describe republicans as 'fascists'. Take this recent statement from Ruth Dudley-Edwards: 'I've hated the fascist strain in Irish republicanism since my Dublin childhood. My paternal grandmother lived and breathed hatred of Britain and worship of its enemies: until her death in 1956 she had a photograph of Hitler at the end of her bed. She even wrote "Sinn Féin" on the ballot-paper if it had no candidate standing'; 'Trimble on the Wire', *Belfast Telegraph*, 19 May 2000.

44. Guelke, 'The Influence of the South African Transition', 145.

45. 'You are Fools to Believe IRA, Robinson Tells MPs', *Belfast Telegraph*, 17 May 2000.

46. Kevin Cullen, 'Boston, South Africa Figure in Irish Road to Peace', *Boston Globe*, 17 May 2000.

47. One effect of this was that integrationist opponents of the Agreement, such as Robert McCartney MP, shifted their arguments against the Agreement to the fact that it allowed Sinn Féin into government before the IRA had decommissioned its weapons rather than because it provided for power-sharing devolution.

48. Traditionally support for decentralization has been much higher in Scotland than in Wales. As a consequence, while Scotland received a Parliament with law-making powers and the (limited) ability to raise taxes, Wales received an Assembly with power to pass only secondary legislation (administrative regulations) and no money-raising powers.

49. Ch. 8 of this volume.

50. McGarry and O'Leary, *Explaining Northern Ireland*. For a sample of recent work that examines Northern Ireland from a comparative perspective, see the collection of essays edited by M. Cox, A. Guelke and F. Stephen, *'A Farewell to Arms?' From 'Long War' to Long Peace in Northern Ireland* (Manchester: Manchester University Press, 2000).

51. According to Eric Nordlinger, the cross-pressures account of political stability was 'probably the explanatory hypothesis most widely accepted among American political scientists'; *Conflict Regulation in Divided Societies* (Cambridge, Mass.: Harvard University Press, 1972), 93.

52. S. M. Lipset, *Political Man* (London: Hutchinson, 1960).

53. R. Rose, *Governing without Consensus* (London: Faber & Faber, 1971).

54. E. Aunger, *In Search of Political Stability: A Comparative Study of New Brunswick and Northern Ireland* (Montreal: McGill–Queen's University Press, 1981).

55. I. Budge and C. O'Leary, *Belfast: Approach to Crisis* (London: Macmillan, 1973).

56. A. Lijphart, 'Consociational Democracy', *World Politics*, 21 (1969), 207–25.

57. Lijphart, Review Article, 'The Northern Ireland Problem', 105.

58. Ibid., 99.

59. Ibid., 100.

60. A. Lijphart, 'The Framework Document on Northern Ireland and the Theory of Power-Sharing', *Government and Opposition*, 31/3 (1996), 268.

61. Ibid. 274.

62. J. McGarry, 'A Consociational Settlement for Northern Ireland?', *Plural Societies*, 20 (1990), 1–21; B. O'Leary, 'The 1998 British–Irish Agreement: Consociation Plus', *Scottish Affairs*, 26 (1999), 1–22; B. O'Leary, 'The Limits to Coercive Consociationalism in Northern Ireland', in R. Rhodes (ed.), *The International Library of Politics and Comparative Government: United Kingdom* (Aldershot: Ashgate, 2000); B. O'Leary and J. McGarry, *The Politics of Antagonism: Understanding Northern Ireland* (London: Athlone Press,

1996); B. O'Leary, 'Afterword: What is Framed in the Framework Documents?', *Ethnic and Racial Studies*, 18 (1995), 862–72.

63. For more details, see J. McGarry, 'Political Settlements in Northern Ireland and South Africa', *Political Studies*, 46/5 (Dec. 1998), 865–70.

64. D. Barritt and C. Carter, *The Northern Ireland Problem: A Study in Group Relations* (Oxford: Oxford University Press, 1961).

65. For example, see D. Smith and G. Chambers, *Inequality in Northern Ireland* (Oxford: Oxford University Press, 1991); C. Irwin, *Education and the Development of Social Integration in Divided Societies* (Belfast: Queen's University, 1991); E. Gallagher and C. Worrall, *Christians in Ulster, 1968–1980* (Oxford: Oxford University Press, 1982).

66. For an Irish nationalist account, see G. FitzGerald, *Towards a New Ireland* (London: Charles Knight, 1972). For a unionist account, see A. Aughey, *Under Siege: Ulster Unionism and the Anglo-Irish Agreement* (Belfast: Blackstaff Press, 1989).

67. Elizabeth Meehan is one such Europeanist. She argued in her inaugural lecture at Queen's University in Belfast in 1992 that European integration was having the desired effect: 'a new kind of citizenship is emerging [in Europe] that is neither nationalist nor cosmopolitan but which is multiple in enabling the various identities that we all possess to be expressed, and our rights and duties exercised, through an increasingly complex configuration of common institutions, states, national and transnational interest groups and voluntary associations, local or provincial authorities, regions and alliances of regions'. Cited, approvingly, in Kearney, *Postnationalist Ireland*, 84.

68. For a general discussion of this critique, see A. Lijphart, *Power-Sharing in South Africa* (Berkeley: University of California, Institute of International Studies, 1985), 106–8.

69. J. Anderson and J. Goodman, 'Nationalisms and Transnationalism: Failures and Emancipation', in J. Anderson and J. Goodman (eds.), *Dis/Agreeing Ireland: Contexts, Obstacles, Hopes* (London: Pluto Press, 1998), 21–2.

70. R. Wilford, 'Inverting Consociationalism? Policy, Pluralism and the Post-Modern', in B. Hadfield (ed.), *Northern Ireland: Politics and the Constitution* (Buckingham: Open University Press, 1992), 31.

71. Ibid. 41.

72. P. Dixon, 'The Politics of Antagonism: Explaining McGarry and O'Leary', *Irish Political Studies*, 11 (1996), 137–8. Also see his 'Consociationalism and the Northern Ireland Peace Process: The Glass Half Full or Half Empty?', *Nationalism and Ethnic Politics*, 3/3 (Autumn 1997), 20–36.

73. R. Taylor, 'A Consociational Path to Peace in Northern Ireland and South Africa', in A. Guelke (ed.), *News Perspectives on the Northern Ireland Conflict* (Aldershot: Avebury, 1994). Both Taylor and Dixon like the South African constitution that was adopted after 1999, that is, after it had been stripped of a number of consociational features that were part of a transitional

constitution in operation between 1994 and 1999. See Dixon, 'Consocia-tionalism and the Northern Ireland Peace Process', 32–3. The problem with the current constitution, however, is that it seems to have produced a one-party system for the foreseeable future. It is difficult to see how this, which bears some comparison with the Stormont regime, would suit Northern Ireland.

74. K. Rooney, 'Institutionalising Division', *Fortnight* (June 1998), 21–2; R. McCartney, 'Devolution is a Sham', *Observer*, 20 Feb. 2000. For a similar unionist perspective, see D. Kennedy, 'Evidence is Growing that Agreement did not Work', *Irish Times*, 16 Feb. 2000.

75. See Whyte, *Interpreting Northern Ireland*, 194–205.

76. See J. Holland, *The American Connection: US Guns, Money and Influence in Northern Ireland* (Swords: Poolbeg Press, 1987); C. Sterling, *The Terror Network: The Secret War of International Terrorism* (New York: Holt, Rinehart & Winston, 1981).

77. These partisan accounts are dissected in McGarry and O'Leary, *Explaining Northern Ireland*, pt. i, chs. 1–4.

78. K. Boyle and T. Hadden, *Ireland: A Positive Proposal* (London: Harmonds-worth, 1985).

79. J. Ruane and J. Todd, *The Dynamics of Conflict in Northern Ireland: Power, Conflict and Emancipation* (Cambridge: Cambridge University Press, 1996).

80. Guelke, *Northern Ireland*.

81. Wright, *Northern Ireland: A Comparative Analysis*.

82. Ibid., 276–7, 282–3, and 285.

83. See n. 67 above. Kevin Boyle has expressed a belief that the 'Europeanization of both islands . . . will force a reassessment of all relationships on these islands and in particular of the two principal influences on the present tragedy of Northern Ireland, "Britishness" as an historical integrating force and the reac-tive tradition of Irish separatism', K. Boyle, 'Northern Ireland: Allegiances and Identities', in B. Crick (ed.), *National Identities: The Constitution of the United Kingdom* (Oxford: Blackwell, 1991), 69, 78. Boyle and his colleague Tom Hadden have since tempered their Euro-enthusiasm. See K. Boyle and T. Hadden, *Northern Ireland: The Choice* (Harmondsworth: Penguin, 1994). Richard Kearney and Robin Wilson argue that European integration will allow Northern Ireland's citizens to evolve beyond nationalism and unionism. They envisage Europe developing into a federation of regions, including Northern Ireland, which will foster allegiances 'both more universal and more particular than the traditional nation-states', 'Northern Ireland's Future as a European Region', reproduced in Kearney, *Postnationalist Ireland*, 79. Cathal McCall claims that European integration has the potential to erode unionism and nationalism in Northern Ireland, particularly in the absence of sectarian violence, 'Postmodern Europe and the Resources of Communal Identities in Northern Ireland', *European Journal of Political Research*, 33 (1998), 406.

Rupert Taylor writes in Ch. 2 of this volume that 'increasing European integration has led to the erosion of absolutist conceptions of national sovereignty [and there] has been an erosion of ethno-nationalism on both sides, a fading of Orange and Green, in favour of a commonality around the need for genuine structures of democracy and justice'. Also see J. Goodman, *Nationalism and Transnationalism: The National Conflict in Ireland and European Union Integration* (Aldershot: Avebury, 1997).

84. FitzGerald, *Towards a New Ireland*, 111–12. A Cambridge economist, Bob Rowthorn, argues that closer economic cooperation between Northern Ireland and the Irish Republic in the context of the European Union will lead unionists to shift their loyalties from London to Dublin. B. Rowthorn, 'Foreword', in R. Munck, *The Irish Economy* (London: Pluto Press, 1993). In Ch. 13 of this volume Sammy Smooha claims that the option of a united Ireland 'will be less and less resisted' by unionists 'as Ireland, a member of the prospering European Union, [comes to] enjoy economic growth, expand its welfare services, and secularizes'.

85. D. Kennedy, 'The European Union and the Northern Ireland Question', in B. Barton and P. Roche (eds.), *The Northern Ireland Question: Perspectives and Policies* (Aldershot: Avebury, 1994), 177. Kennedy, a unionist who is hostile to Dublin's growing role in Northern Ireland, argues that Anglo-Irish cooperation would have been almost impossible outside the European Union: 'the experience of working together in the institutions of the Community, particularly at Council of Minister and senior diplomat and official level, was slowly transforming the relationship . . . The patron–client pattern was dissolved; in the new circumstances British ministers and diplomats could see their Irish counterparts as clever partners in Europe. Without this transformation it is almost impossible to see how Dublin–London relations could have been transformed as they were between the mid-seventies and the mid-eighties.'

86. 'Anglo-Irish Relations: Entente Cordiale', *The Economist*, 28 Nov. 1998; J. McGarry, 'Globalization, European Integration, and the Northern Ireland Conflict', in M. Keating and J. McGarry (eds.), *Minority Nationalism and the Changing International Order* (Oxford: Oxford University Press, 2001). Michael Keating makes a similar argument in his contribution to this volume, Ch. 8.

87. A. Wilson, *Irish America and the Ulster Conflict 1968–1995* (Washington, DC: Catholic University of America Press, 1995); 'From the Beltway to Belfast: The Clinton Administration, Sinn Féin, and the Northern Ireland Peace Process', *New Hibernia Review*, 1/3 (1997), 23–39; 'The Billy Boys Meet Slick Willy: The Ulster Unionist Party and the American Dimension to the Northern Ireland Peace Process, 1993–1998', *Irish Studies in International Affairs*, 11 (Autumn 2000), 121–137; A. Guelke, 'The United States, Irish Americans and the Northern Ireland Peace Process', *International Affairs*, 72/3 (1996), 521–36; 'Northern Ireland: International and North/South Issues', in W. Crotty and

D. Schmitt (eds.), *Ireland and the Politics of Change* (London: Longman, 1998); R. MacGinty, 'American Influences on the Northern Ireland Peace Process', *Journal of Conflict Studies* (1997), 31–50; J. O'Grady, 'An Irish Policy Born in the USA', *Foreign Affairs* (May–June 1996), 2–7.

88. Wilson, 'From the Beltway', 23; MacGinty, 'American Influences', 33; Guelke, 'The United States', 531–2. Also see Guelke, *Northern Ireland*, 147.

89. Guelke, 'The United States', 528.

90. Ibid., 534; MacGinty, 'American Influences', 34; O'Grady, 'An Irish Policy', 5; Wilson, 'From the Beltway', 32.

91. Wilson, 'The Billy Boys'.

92. McGarry and O'Leary, *Explaining Northern Ireland*, 333.

93. D. Akenson, *God's Peoples: Covenant and Land in South Africa, Israel and Ulster* (Ithaca, NY: Cornell University Press, 1992); P. Clayton, 'Religion, Ethnicity and Colonialism as Explanations of the Northern Ireland Conflict', in D. Miller (ed.), *Rethinking Northern Ireland: Culture, Ideology and Colonialism* ((New York: Longman, 1998), 40–54; I. Lustick, *State-Building Failure in British Ireland*; M. MacDonald, *Children of Wrath: Political Violence in Northern Ireland* (Oxford: Polity Press, 1986); D. Miller, 'Colonialism and Academic Representation of the Troubles', in Miller (ed.), *Rethinking Northern Ireland*, 3–39; B. Schutz and D. Scott, *Natives and Settlers: A Comparative Analysis of the Politics of Opposition and Mobilisation in Northern Ireland and Rhodesia* (Denver, Colo.: University of Denver, 1974); R. Weitzer, *Transforming Settler States: Communal Conflict and Internal Security in Northern Ireland and Zimbabwe* (Berkeley: University of California Press, 1990).

94. William of Orange's original Treaty of Limerick, which was conciliatory towards Irish Catholics, was converted, at the insistence of settlers, into the penal system. Pitt's proposal to link the Union of 1801 with Catholic emancipation was also blocked by Protestant settlers, with help from King George III.

95. Weitzer, *Transforming Settler States*, 1. I have been told by reputable sources that two academic works importantly influenced the Patten Commission, which delivered its report on policing reform in Northern Ireland in September 1999. One was *Policing Northern Ireland* (Belfast: Blackstaff Press, 1999), by Brendan O'Leary and me, and the other was a book by Weitzer, *Policing under Fire: Ethnic Conflict and Police–Community Relations in Northern Ireland* (Albany: State University of New York Press, 1995).

96. While arguing for the usefulness of comparing Algeria and Ireland against unionist accounts which deny any similarities, Ian Lustick does not accept the arguments of 'troops out' advocates that the Algerian analogy means the British should withdraw from Northern Ireland.

97. P. Dixon, 'The Politics of Antagonism', 133.

Part I

General and Theoretical Perspectives

2

Northern Ireland: Consociation or Social Transformation?*

RUPERT TAYLOR

Generally, the search for a solution to conflict in 'deeply divided societies' has been and continues to be influenced by consociational thinking. In deeply divided societies the strength of consociationalism is its claim to be grounded in the concrete reality of ethno-national politics. It is maintained that intractable conflict must be explained in terms of the force of ethno-national movements, and that the best way forward rests on accommodating, at elite level, the conflicting identities. This is to be achieved through constitutional engineering in which collective group structures are granted equality and autonomy.[1]

John McGarry has put the position clearly: 'The consociationalist argument is that particularly in certain contexts—deeply divided societies, where divisions are longstanding and when there is intra-group violence—it is more realistic to accept that different groups will continue to exist than to seek the "deconstruction" of group ties.'[2] The emphasis is on the need to recognize pre-existing and durable divisions, and there is a refusal to accept that the idea of integration is a useful prescription; it being claimed, for example, that 'exposure may cement group solidarity rather than defuse it'.[3] Thus, consociationalism is a means of regulating conflict, not transforming it.

Consociationalism has been developed with empirical rigour in the Northern Irish case, notably by John McGarry and Brendan O'Leary, who stress the need for 'concrete analysis of concrete situations'.[4] They maintain that the concrete 'is composed of national, ethnic and religious identities' and 'the conflict is fundamentally rooted in ethno-national antagonism' 'between two communities with different national interests'.[5] And therefore the relevance of consociationalism to Northern Ireland is self-evident. This, it is claimed, is a reality that the British government has, over time, since direct rule, come around to accepting.[6]

The 1998 Belfast Agreement, which approved a new Assembly for Northern Ireland and various confederal dimensions (notably a reciprocal North–South Ministerial Council), is clearly consociational in that it rein- forces the belief in the centrality of ethno-national politics. The institu- tionalization of ethno-nationalism is solidified in arrangements whereby the 108 members of the new Assembly are required to 'register a designa- tion of identity—nationalist, unionist or other', primarily to ensure that key decisions are taken on a 'cross-community basis', either by parallel con- sent or by a weighted majority.[7] Decisions requiring 'cross-community support' include election of the chair of the Assembly, the first minister and deputy first minister, standing orders, and budget allocations.[8] The new Northern Ireland Assembly has, however, had an inauspicious beginning, with David Trimble, as first minister, having secured only a wafer-thin majority on the unionist benches of the Assembly, and with problems of executive-formation given disagreement over the decommissioning of weapons held by the Irish Republican Army.[9] With anti-Assembly forces needing only a handful of 'defections' from the Ulster Unionist Party to block legislation, the outlook is far from rosy. Is this really where peaceful change is going to come from? Is this the best way forward?

Contrary to the prevailing consensus, this chapter argues that in fact consociationalism should not form the basis for present or future policy action in Northern Ireland. Instead, it is advanced that a social transfor- mation approach, which is concerned to transform the conflict by pro- moting participatory democracy and challenging ethno-nationalism, holds the most promise for peaceful change. It is maintained that attention must turn to the actions of inclusive pro-democracy movements in society which seek to create new relationships of social interaction that transcend divisive political boundaries. First, though, it is necessary to show how consociationalism falls short in confronting the question of social change.

Reading the Future

Consociationalism reads the future, to the extent that it does so, with a crude teleological certainty; consociationalism is a vehicle for the transi- tion initially to elite-level democracy and then to a more open form of democracy. For it is maintained that over the course of time ethno- nationalist forces will become less virulent and salient, so that the prospects for democracy increase. In reality, how does this work? It is neither obvious nor logical that ethno-nationalism can be cured by prescribing more of it through constitutional engineering. There is no prima facie case to suppose that this will occur. Such a process cannot be assumed, but must be explained—unfortunately, it is not.

In fact, consociationalism is not greatly interested in offering a theoretical understanding of social change; rather, consociationalists are primarily concerned to present a synchronic model crafted for state-sponsored planning. As such the consociational position is not prepared to look beyond the existing 'facts', beyond the 'concrete realities', to criticize the 'facts', to consider how they are produced by political processes 'and contain the potential of becoming something different from what they are'.[10] This might be considered unremarkable if the facts that consociationalists present were incontrovertible, but they are not. The facts of ethno-nationalism are more asserted than proved; there has been little, if any, attempt to probe existing levels of ethno-national consciousness empirically, to unravel the extent to which people subscribe to ethno-nationalism as opposed to other forms of identity politics, such as, most relevantly, civic nationalism, or beyond this to analyse the extent to which there are changes over time.[11] Instead what has happened is that ethno-nationalism is taken as an object of the environment, deriving its meaning as a reflex of the social system; it is not seen to be a choice made by people, but a property of society which transcends their agency. As such consociationalism has much in common with anti-Enlightenment thought in that it takes a rather constrained view of human nature.

In any event, to many of its adherents consociationalism is vindicated by its ability to outclass liberal and Marxist readings of conflict in deeply divided societies. Principally, it is argued that both liberalism and Marxism over-emphasize the economic and material foundations of conflict and cannot come to terms with the importance and durability of ethno-national solidarities. There is no doubt that both liberalism and Marxism are confronted by serious challenges, with glaring disjunctures in analysis. In fact, in general, as Barrington Moore has remarked, liberalism and Marxism are doctrines, which have 'in good measure ceased to provide explanations of the world'.[12] Consociationalists, however, present hostile and reductive readings of these positions, which lead them to fail to appreciate the significance of liberalism's and Marxism's core commitment—the commitment to the transformation of human existence.

Consociationalism gives overly economistic readings of how liberalism and Marxism understand social change; they are presented in terms of liberal economic materialism and Marxist materialism.[13] To reduce an understanding of social action to the calculation of the rational self-interested

agent, or to economics, is, however, to offer a diminished view of what liberalism and Marxism have offered and can offer; it is to portray them
devoid of their Enlightenment vision of how society can be changed for the
better by human will. The essence of liberalism is 'an awareness of the value
of freedom and of the human worth of the individual'.[14] And Marxism does
not take material forces as 'the sole determinant of consciousness', but is
concerned to consider the active self-making of society.[15]

The point that consociationalism has not grasped, but that has been central to both liberalism and Marxism, is that human freedom is a power, a
Promethean force; and as such it is not something to be limited to ethno-
national aggregates and inter-elite institutional structures. J. G. Merquior's
Western Marxism (1986) makes the point that 'whenever the concept of freedom . . . ceases to be mainly social and political, and becomes "anthropo-
logical" instead, stressing attributes of mankind rather than actions by
concrete individuals, illiberal elements seem bound to arise'.[16] This is precisely the problem with consociationalism's emphasis on ethno-nationalism.
For, given that concern is centred on ethno-national group motivations and
not on the actions of people as members of general political society, consociationalism does not go far enough in recognizing how the status quo can
be transformed through the living activities of action, speech, and thought
that seek to abolish the illusions of permanence that stand in the way of
freedom.[17]

By reducing the dynamic nature of human action to the common
denominator of ethno-nationalism, the consociational position displaces
the question of human freedom and action and is ill prepared to grasp the
dynamics of social change, of 'transformational impetus'.[18] There is a need
to recognize, far more than consociationalism does, people's ability 'to
undo what we have done', 'to start new and unending processes'; to recognize that 'Action is, in fact, the one miracle-working faculty of man.'[19]

Consider, in this regard, the South African case, another deeply divided
society where for many years consociationalism was on the political
agenda. For years social scientists talked about 'the impossibility of a liberal
solution' for South Africa,[20] and apartheid ideologues maintained that 'the
liberal vision of a common society open to all . . . [was a] pipe-dream.
There is nothing, they would argue, in the 300 years of . . . [South African]
history to indicate that such an end is possible.'[21] And yet in 1994, after over
forty years of National Party rule, South Africa fully joined the global wave
towards liberal democracy. How can this be explained? Many people have
talked of the South African transition from apartheid to democracy as a
'miracle'.[22] And in a sense it was, in that it reveals that people do have the

'gift to "perform miracles", that is, to bring about the infinitely improbable and establish it as reality'.[23]

Among the social forces that made for peace, for creating the new South Africa, were the innovative actions of an ever increasing network of progressive movements, institutions, non-governmental organizations, and associations (which included churches, trade unions, civics, and women's groups) engaged in a 'war of position' against apartheid rule, and mainly aligned to the African National Congress. This network of anti-apartheid organizations created an alternative space outside distorted and limited binary racial thinking, seeking to undercut the apartheid state's reification of 'race' and 'ethnicity', and promote the idea of a common society.[24] This pushed the conflict away from a 'black'–'white' racial form towards a non-racial perspective. The non-racial position 'was a matter of analysis, in other words we've misunderstood, we've misdiagnosed, the nature of the problem if [we] see this as white versus black'; rather it was increasingly understood that the enemy was the unjust apartheid system.[25]

Various campaigns, projects, and activities for change not only directly resisted apartheid policies, but sought to challenge group boundaries and group thinking, and play an important role by endeavouring to live the future non-racial democratic South Africa prior to the statutory end of apartheid. And this fed through to affect the agenda-setting process, the policy-making process, and the constitutional settlement, which opted for consensual democracy, not consociational democracy. Roelf Meyer, the (National Party) government's chief negotiator in the constitutional negotiation process, acknowledged that 'One's image of the conflict certainly changed over a period of time . . . it's true that in the eighties, there developed in my own mind a more non-racial image.'[26]

In sum, apartheid was defeated by a large and well-organized non-racial opposition which worked to gradually transform the black–white nature of the South African conflict and make democracy—outside the disabling limitations of consociationalism—a practical proposition. In South Africa more and more people decided and chose to cooperate actively to transform society, and, in doing so, transform themselves. This practice remained ahead of theory; as Jeremy Cronin of the South African Communist Party recognized, 'Often the practice of the [anti-apartheid] network was far in advance of the predominant paradigms of change—liberalism and classical Marxism being inappropriate to our struggle.'[27] What happened was that there was a synchronized solidarity around a vision of a non-racial and common South Africa which involved all kinds of people and opinions, and without this, as Ebrahim Rasool, the African National

Congress's leader in the Western Cape, stated, 'we may have had a situation in which we would not have got the struggle off its black and white track'.[28]

By analogy, what are the prospects for a similar process of social transformation in Northern Ireland? To what extent are there movements concerned to advance new action, new dialogue, and new thinking that challenge sectarianism and work to erode the 'Orange'–'Green' nature of the Northern Irish conflict? Is there a momentum towards a vision of a united new Ireland? John Whyte, author of *Interpreting Northern Ireland* (1990), believed that for the idea of a united Ireland to reach the stage of negotiation would require 'some miracle',[29] but, as the South African case shows, 'miracles' happen, or at least they can be created.

Creating a New Ireland

In Northern Ireland the direction of social change is being strongly influenced by the demographic situation; significantly, the Catholic population in Northern Ireland has—according to census data—risen from 35 per cent in 1971 to 42 per cent in 1991 (in Belfast from 31 per cent to 43 per cent), and this may lead to a united Ireland 'within three decades'.[30] Thus, the constitutional reunification of Ireland looms large on the horizon; all the more so given the economic forces pushing for a 'single island economy' (especially in the context of European Union politics),[31] and noteworthy here is the fact that 'in the early 1990s per capita GDP in the South rose above the level in Northern Ireland'.[32]

Given the reintroduction of single transferable vote–proportional representation at local council level in 1973, and other amendments to electoral laws, the demographic changes point towards a shifting balance of power within Northern Ireland. Already, given the reality of declining unionist majorities, a form of voluntary coalition, 'partnership government', has evolved between the Social Democratic and Labour Party (SDLP) and Ulster Unionist Party (UUP) at elected local government level. Typically this entails 'the rotation of the chair/vice chair positions and committee chairs from both political parties, proportionate distribution of committee members and sharing of representation on external public bodies'.[33] As the number of majority councils where one political party holds the overall majority of seats has declined, the number of councils following 'partnership government' has increased; by 1998 twelve councils were following this practice, most notably Belfast and Derry.[34] This development has led to 'a greater propensity to transfer votes *across* the political divide (between

SDLP and UUP) in power sharing councils', and is likely to result in increased powers to local government.[35] Importantly, these power-sharing initiatives at local government level are party-political, and as such are forms of consensual democracy and not consociational democracy.[36]

More generally, outside the formal political arena a recent survey concluded that 'most people in Northern Ireland want to live together rather than apart',[37] and a recent study by John Darby noted that 'the number and quality of concrete cross-community contacts appears to be increasing'.[38] Consider the following social trends: in the post-war era the number of mixed Protestant-Catholic marriages has risen from just 1 per cent to over 10 per cent; there is now a number of cross-community housing projects; and the extent of integrated education has widened.[39] In fact, while 'right up to the early 1980s there was little contact between pupils or teachers in Protestant and Catholic schools . . . Currently about a third of primary schools and a half of post-primary schools are involved in contact schemes.'[40] At present there are twenty-eight integrated schools in Northern Ireland (in 1990 there were ten), and at tertiary level Queen's University Belfast and University of Ulster are non-sectarian. Moreover, there has been a rise in the number of cross-community reconciliation and contact schemes concerned to break down sectarian boundaries, there have been increasing ecumenical moves by the churches, and the trade union movement has been pursuing a number of anti-sectarian programmes.

In Northern Ireland today there are about 5,000 voluntary and community groups; their annual turnover of £400 million is equal to about 6 per cent of Northern Ireland's gross domestic product, and with some 65,000 volunteers and 30,000 paid workers they represent 5 per cent of the workforce, that is 'more than are employed in agriculture'.[41] And in recent years, among a significant number of these groups, a considerable amount of strategic alliances and networking has occurred. As *A Citizen's Inquiry* (1993) noted, 'because of the nature of Northern Irish politics and the democratic deficit in which they are played out, some of the brightest talents have chosen to put their energies into the voluntary sector rather than into formal politics'.[42] Here, out of the limelight, important changes have been and are occurring; a 'politics of civil society' is emerging, composed of voluntary associations, non-profit agencies, community organizations, and activists.[43]

The most noteworthy bodies, which are working to break down Orange and Green stereotypes and transform the conflict into a less destructive and negative form, include the Corrymeela Community, established in 1965, and the Community Relations Council, created in 1990, which has been involved in a District Council Community Relations Programme, whereby community relations officers have been appointed in all twenty-six local district councils to counter sectarianism on a cross-party basis.[44] It is also the case that in recent years women's movements, such as the Northern Ireland Women's Coalition, formed in 1996, have taken a more proactive role in promoting reconciliation.[45]

Alongside the key agencies working for reconciliation, the Opsahl Commission of 1992–3 and subsequently the work of the think-tank Democratic Dialogue, founded in 1995, have promoted inclusive political dialogue and are clear attempts through 'deliberative action and creative politics' to 'define a new plural space in civil society to which all citizens have access'.[46] This is an agenda pursued by an increasing number of activists in a variety of organizational forms—and includes human rights work to promote universalist principles of justice.[47] Significantly, the European Union's Special Support Programme for Peace and Reconciliation sees itself as concerned to promote 'the space and resources to construct new visions for the future'.[48]

A major study of peace and conflict resolution organizations in Northern Ireland, while noting that such organizations and non-governmental organisations in a wider sense needed to develop a more sophisticated strategic approach, found that 'The attitude of many of these groups with regard to addressing the conflict is governed by a desire to see a broadening of political dialogue and an inclusion of civil society in the debate.'[49] In fact, there are indications of a broader vision and practice emerging. Collaborative projects involving the political, business, and trade union spheres have been initiated with, for example, the Confederation of British Industry, the Irish Congress of Trade Unions, and the Northern Ireland Council for Voluntary Action moving to take a more proactive position.

In particular, in recent years (since 1996) a new form of participation promoting active citizenship has emerged in partnerships. Funded in large part by the European Union peace package (over £40 million), and based on the European model of social partnership and dialogue, partnerships involve three equally weighted elements: the voluntary–community sector; local councillors; and representatives from the trade unions, business, and statutory sectors.[50] Partnerships involve 'actual decision-making on key issues including policy creation and allocation of finances', and today there are twenty-six district partnership groups, involving over 600 people in decision-making.[51] Moreover, there is an ever increasing number of formally established partnerships, such as several area-based partnerships through the Making Belfast Work programme; vision-setting partnerships (in Derry and Belfast); and the urban initiative partnerships (in Springvale and Shankill). Altogether, as Paul Sweeney, head of secretariat of the Northern Ireland Partnership Board, has observed, 'we are witnessing an important sea change, a fundamental shift in the nature of civic responsibility and a popular demand for new models of participatory democracy'.[52]

All these new organizational forms and projects indicate that ethno-nationalist politics will not be as important in the future as in the past. These developments are working to establish democratic politics, often where there have been none; to transform public life by introducing a wider vision. They point the way to the type of society Northern Ireland will become in the future. Already it makes no sense to talk of two monolithic mutually antagonistic ethno-national blocs within Northern Ireland.

More than ever before unionist 'ideology contains not only people who advocate alternative political tactics and strategies, but people who disagree fundamentally about who they are and where they want to go'.[53] There is an emerging 'civic unionism' in which unionism is seen 'as a political and not an ethnic or cultural ideology', being more concerned with citizenship than with self-determination.[54] In fact, as Robin Wilson, of Democratic Dialogue, has observed, there is a 'growing detachment of capital-u Unionism from those [dynamic] forces within civil society—particularly the social partners and the voluntary sector'.[55]

On the other hand, classical Irish nationalism has come to rely on arguments which—in the context of the end of the cold war and European integration—are now simply outdated.[56] The end of the cold war has pushed traditional republican thinking to reassess fundamentally the reasons for the British presence in Ireland, whereas increasing European integration has led to the erosion of absolutist conceptions of national sovereignty. This has led to new thinking, to developing an unarmed political strategy, to exploring alternative definitions of republicanism that embrace civic inclusivity and a new discourse of 'Freedom, Justice and Peace'.[57]

Thus, there has been erosion of ethno-nationalism on both sides, a fading of Orange and Green, in favour of a commonality around the need for genuine structures of democracy and justice to be established. In Northern Ireland, as new organizational forms and projects take root, and the old understandings start to lose their substance and coherence, identity politics have become more open and fluid.[58] And with this there has come a dawning recognition that the conflict has been rooted in an unjust social order, not ethno-nationalism; that the main cause of conflict has been the lack of civil rights, widespread discrimination, and socio-economic inequalities.[59] In sum, there is a diversity of progressive forces emerging which would have been hard to envisage when the troubles were at their height in the early 1970s. Furthermore, this is not just the case with regard to developments within Northern Ireland, but also with respect to North–South cross-border relations. There has been a significant growth in the number of cross-border networks and alliances, especially within the voluntary sector and with North–South business partnerships.[60]

At present, however, all these developments are generally hidden from view and remain uncharted. They have been obscured, in general, by an inability of social scientists to look beyond the 'state' and 'market',[61] and, in particular, by the elite-level focus of consociationalism. Nonetheless, there is a growing movement to build 'cross-community networks based on overlapping interests and concerns',[62] to rethink and transcend national-ism and unionism, and create a common society. And the more that demo-cratic practices are extended across North–South boundaries, the more that ethno-nationalism (which has been held in place by these very bound-aries) is undermined.[63] Cumulatively, and increasingly so, these social dynamics point towards a non-sectarian democratic society that will ulti-mately find expression in a united new Ireland—a new Ireland with an inclusive notion of citizenship (where the definition of what it means to be Irish is broadened to include northern Protestants) that would be guaran-teed by a bill of rights. This vision of a new Ireland is prefigured in the New Ireland Forum Report, the position of the New Ireland Group, and SDLP and Sinn Féin discourse around a stable and peaceful new Ireland; already, in the words of John McGarry and Brendan O'Leary, 'The key macro-policy of nationalist politicians and militants is an agreed or united Ireland which would transcend sectarianism.'[64]

Conclusion

The social transformation approach clearly projects a vision of the future that is different from that of consociationalists, and one to be realized along a very different path. In fact, from this perspective the best way forward lies in advocating the transformation of the conflict in the opposite direction from that advocated by consociationalists; to be concerned to transform the conflict, not regulate it; to extend democracy and challenge ethnicity. Instead of taking ethno-national group identity as the social base for polit-ical development, attention should focus on the formation and actions of wider and all-embracing pro-democracy (i.e. pro-people) movements in society—those movements that cross-cut social divisions, and challenge and erode the clash of opposing ethno-nationalisms and create new relationships of mutuality through networking and debate.

Thus, in the Northern Ireland context the social transformation approach advocates the development of a democratic, non-sectarian politics. In particular, attention should focus at macro level on encouraging participatory democracy, building progressive North–South cross-border relations, and securing an all-Ireland bill of rights (incorporating anti-discrimination and fair employment measures); while at micro level support should be given to promoting non-sectarian initiatives within civil society that are concerned to advance democracy and justice (for example, by encouraging integrated education and housing).

The social transformation perspective gives a deeper understanding than that of consociationalism because it does not overlook the significance of people's ability to change their world, to transform the conditions of human existence. Consociationalism fails to see society as an active subject; it does not fully confront the question of human freedom and action. Consociationalism limits understanding and the potential for people to create their own future, not only in that it sees things in ethno-national terms regardless of the actual state of people's factual histories and consciousness, but also in that it fails to identify the evolving orientations of people, simply bypassing a diachronic focus on the process and politics of subject formation. The key differences between consociationalism and social transformation can be summarized as in Table 2.1.

The major difference, of course, is that consociational arrangements work with and solidify intracommunal networks, rather than being concerned to promote intercommunal association. Thus, in Northern Ireland

TABLE 2.1. *Consociationalism versus social transformation*

	Consociationalism	Social transformation
Central concepts	Ethno-nationalism	Human freedom and action
Rooted in	A sociology of social system	A sociology of social action
Objective	Conflict regulation Segregation	Change in conflict structures Integration
Relation to change	Status quo orientated Synchronic	Change orientated Diachronic
Target	Elite politicians Elite democracy	People Participatory democracy

the consociational agenda has consciously sought to solidify communal division, and British policies have come to be informed by notions of equality based on segregation, as opposed to simply promoting integration. The new Assembly is the latest example of such a 'politics of accommodation', but it does not furnish a convincing solution. Instead of attempting to encourage participatory non-sectarian democratic politics, the new Assembly is underpinned by an elite-level ethno-national mode of organization (while the Belfast Agreement provides for a consultative civic forum, its role is bound to be heavily constrained by the overall consociational bias[65]). The problem is that there is no good reason to suppose that the promotion of ethno-national pluralism will lead to the deflation of ethno-nationalism and create a non-sectarian democratic society. Thus, as a recent *Fortnight* editorial put it, 'It could be that the institutionalized sectarianism of the Assembly will make permanent the catholic/nationalist versus protestant/unionist paradigm.'[66] More and more people in Northern Ireland are, however, looking forward to a time when they do not have to be either Orange or Green, Protestant or Catholic, unionist or nationalist. The commitment to consociationalism postpones this eventuality.

NOTES

* The author is grateful for responses to a draft version of this chapter from: Heribert Adam, James Anderson, Paul Carmichael, John Coakley, Carol Coary Taylor, Jacklyn Cock, Paul Dixon, Neville Douglas, Anthony Egan, Anthony Gallagher, Adrian Guelke, Donald Horowitz, Colin Knox, Barbara McCabe, David McCrone, Michael MacDonald, John McGarry, Jens Meierhenrich, Paul Mitchell, Gerard Murray, Liam O'Dowd, Shane O'Neill, Robin Whitaker, Rick Wilford, and Robin Wilson.

1. A. Lijphart, *Democracy in Plural Societies: A Comparative Exploration* (New Haven: Yale University Press, 1997).
2. J. McGarry, 'Political Settlements in Northern Ireland and South Africa', *Political Studies*, 46/5 (1998), 860 n. 25.
3. J. McGarry and B. O'Leary, 'Five Fallacies: Northern Ireland and the Liabilities of Liberalism', *Ethnic and Racial Studies*, 18/4 (1995), 848.
4. J. McGarry and B. O'Leary, *Explaining Northern Ireland: Broken Images* (Oxford: Blackwell, 1995), 167.
5. Ibid. 167, 306; McGarry and O'Leary, 'Five Fallacies', 855.
6. B. O'Leary, 'The Conservative Stewardship of Northern Ireland, 1979–97: Sound-Bottomed Contradictions or Slow Learning?', *Political Studies*, 45/4

(1997), 663–76. Also see A. Lijphart, 'The Frameworks Document on Northern Ireland and the Theory of Power-Sharing', *Government and Opposition*, 31/3 (1996), 267–74.

7. *The Belfast Agreement: An Agreement Reached at the Multi-Party Talks on Northern Ireland*, Apr. 1998 (Cm. 3883), Strand One, para. 6 and 5(d) (available online at *www.nio.gov.uk/agreement.htm*). Also see B. O'Leary, 'The Nature of the Agreement', John Whyte Memorial Lecture, 26 Nov. 1998, Queen's University Belfast.

8. Northern Ireland Act 1998, c. 47 (available online at *www.hmso.gov.uk/acts/ acts1998/19980047.htm*).

9. R. Wilson, 'Making the Agreement Stick: Prospects for Peace in Northern Ireland', *Renewal*, 7/1 (1999), 20–9.

10. Consider B. Moore, *Political Power and Social Theory* (Cambridge, Mass.: Harvard University Press, 1958).

11. This is not to deny that many attitude surveys have been undertaken in deeply divided societies, but to emphasize that they rarely look beyond the facts. Consider R. Taylor and M. Orkin, 'The Racialisation of Social Scientific Research on South Africa', *South African Sociological Review*, 7/2 (1995), 43–59; J. Anderson and I. Shuttleworth, 'Sectarian Readings of Sectarianism: Interpreting the Northern Ireland Census', *Irish Review*, 16 (1994), 74–93.

12. B. Moore, 'The Society Nobody Wants: A Look beyond Marxism and Liberalism', in B. Moore and K. H. Wolff (eds.), *The Critical Spirit: Essays in Honor of Herbert Marcuse* (Boston: Beacon Press, 1967), 418.

13. The leading example is McGarry and O'Leary, *Explaining Northern Ireland*.

14. H. Kuper, 'Commitment: The Liberal Scholar in South Africa', in P. van den Berghe (ed.), *The Liberal Dilemma in South Africa* (London: Croom Helm, 1979), 30.

15. G. Friedman, *The Political Philosophy of the Frankfurt School* (Ithaca, NY: Cornell University Press, 1981), 37.

16. J. G. Merquior, *Western Marxism* (London: Paladin, 1986), 29.

17. Consider H. Arendt, *The Human Condition* (Chicago: University of Chicago Press, 1958); S. Wolin, *Politics and Vision: Continuity and Innovation in Western Political Thought* (Boston: Little, Brown, 1960).

18. Consider N. Elias, 'Towards a Theory of Social Processes', *British Journal of Sociology*, 48/3 (1987), 355–83.

19. Arendt, *The Human Condition*, 246.

20. See, for example, van den Berghe (ed.), *The Liberal Dilemma in South Africa*.

21. A. Paton, *Hope for South Africa* (London: Pall Mall Press, 1958), 54. Alan Paton was a leading member of the South African Liberal Party (1953–63).

22. P. Waldmeir, *Anatomy of a Miracle: The End of Apartheid and the Birth of the New South Africa* (London: Viking, 1997).

23. H. Arendt, 'Freedom and Politics', in D. Miller (ed.), *Liberty* (Oxford: Oxford University Press, 1991), 79.

24. R. Taylor, A. Egan, A. Habib, J. Cock, A. Lekwane, and M. Shaw, *Final Report: International Study of Peace/Conflict Resolution Organisations—South Africa* (ISPO–South Africa), University of the Witwatersrand, Johannesburg (1998).

25. Interview with Laurie Nathan, former national director of the End Conscription Campaign, by R. Taylor and M. Shaw, for ISPO–South Africa, Cape Town, 26 Mar. 1998.

26. Interview with R. Taylor and A. Habib, for ISPO–South Africa, Pretoria, 9 June 1998.

27. Interview with R. Taylor and J. Cock, for ISPO–South Africa, Johannesburg, 19 Jan. 1998.

28. Interview with N. Farooqui, for ISPO–South Africa, Cape Town, 30 Sept. 1998.

29. J. Whyte, *Interpreting Northern Ireland* (Oxford: Clarendon Press, 1990), 215.

30. McGarry and O'Leary, *Explaining Northern Ireland*, 403. A recent political attitudes survey found that 36 per cent of Protestants believe that a united Ireland is 'quite likely' or 'very likely' within the next two decades; R. Wilford and R. MacGinty, 'Drop in Support for the Union', *Belfast Telegraph*, 22 Feb. 2000, 13 (available online at *www.belfasttelegraph.co.uk/archive*).

31. G. Quigley, *Northern Ireland: A Decade for Decision* (Belfast: Northern Ireland Economic Council, 1992).

32. J. Haughton, 'The Dynamics of Economic Change', in W. Crotty and D. E. Schmitt (eds.), *Ireland and the Politics of Change* (London: Longman, 1998), 30 and see p. 28, table 2.1.

33. C. Knox, 'The Emergence of Power Sharing in Northern Ireland: Lessons from Local Government', *Journal of Conflict Studies*, 16/1 (1996), 13.

34. C. Knox and P. Carmichael, 'Making Progress in Northern Ireland? Evidence from Recent Elections', *Government and Opposition*, 33/3 (1998), 372–93.

35. Knox, 'The Emergence of Power Sharing', 21.

36. For further clarification of the differences between consensual and consociational democracy, see A. Lijphart, *Patterns of Democracy: Government Forms and Performance in Thirty-Six Countries* (New Haven: Yale University Press, 1999).

37. T. Hadden, C. Irwin, and F. Boal, 'Separation or Sharing? The People's Choice', *Fortnight*, 356 (Dec. 1996), suppl.

38. J. Darby, *Northern Ireland: Managing Difference* (London: Minority Rights Group, 1995), 25.

39. J. Whyte, 1993, 'Dynamics of Social and Political Change in Northern Ireland', in D. Keogh and M. H. Haltzel (eds.), *Northern Ireland and the Politics of Reconciliation* (Cambridge: Woodrow Wilson Center Press and Cambridge University Press, 1993).

40. A. Gallagher, 'Dealing with Conflict: Schools in Northern Ireland', *Multicultural Teaching*, 13/1 (1994), 13.

41. T. Philpot, 'The Price of Peace', *Community Care* (16–22 Oct. 1997), 18–19.

42. A. Pollock (ed.), *A Citizen's Inquiry: The Opsahl Report on Northern Ireland* (Dublin: Lilliput Press, 1993), 90.

43. N. Porter, *Rethinking Unionism: An Alternative Vision for Northern Ireland* (Belfast: Blackstaff Press, 1996), 202–3.

44. J. Hughes and C. Knox, 'For Better or Worse? Community Relations Initiatives in Northern Ireland', *Peace and Change*, 22/3 (1997), 330–55. Also visit the Corrymeela Community online at *www.corrymeela.org.uk* and the Community Relations Council at *www.community-relations.org.uk*

45. Y. Galligan, E. Ward, and R. Wilford (eds.), *Contesting Politics: Women in Ireland, North and South* (Boulder, Colo.: Westview Press, 1998). Northern Ireland Women's Coalition home page: *www.niwc.org*

46. Porter, *Rethinking Unionism*, 203. See *Reconstituting Politics*, Democratic Dialogue Report no. 3 (Belfast: Democratic Dialogue, 1996); Democratic Dialogue home page: *www.dem-dial.demon.co.uk*

47. Consider, for example, the work of the Committee on the Administration of Justice (home page at *http://ourworld.compuserve.com/homepages/Comm_Admin_Justice*).

48. Northern Ireland Council for Voluntary Action (NICVA), *Partners for Progress: The Voluntary and Community Sector's Contribution to Partnership-Building* (Belfast: NICVA, 1996), 4.

49. F. Cochrane, *Final Report: International Study of Peace/Conflict Resolution Organisations—Northern Ireland* (ISPO–Northern Ireland), University of Ulster (1998).

50. NICVA, *Partnerships—A View from Within: The Voluntary/Community Sector Experience of Involvement in District Partnerships* (Belfast: NICVA, 1997); NICVA, *Building Peace, Piece by Piece* (Belfast: NICVA, 1997).

51. T. Hennessy and R. Wilson, *With All Due Respect: Pluralism and Parity of Esteem*, Democratic Dialogue Report no. 7 (Democratic Dialogue: Belfast, 1997), 8.

52. NICVA, *Making Partnerships Work* (Belfast: NICVA, 1996), 5. Also see J. Hughes, C. Knox, M. Murray, and J. Greer, *Partnership and Governance in Northern Ireland: The Path to Peace* (Dublin: Oak Tree Press, 1998).

53. F. Cochrane, *Unionist Politics and the Politics of Unionism since the Anglo-Irish Agreement* (Cork: Cork University Press, 1997), viii.

54. P. J. Roche and B. Barton (eds.), *The Northern Ireland Question: Myth and Reality* (Aldershot: Avebury, 1991), viii. Also see Porter, *Rethinking Unionism*.

55. R. Wilson, 'Listen to the People', *Fortnight*, 337 (Mar. 1995), 5.

56. M. Cox, 'Bringing in the "International": The IRA Ceasefire and the End of the Cold War', *International Affairs*, 73/4 (1997), 671–93.

57. P. Shirlow and M. McGovern, 'Language, Discourse and Dialogue: Sinn Féin and the Irish Peace Process', *Political Geography*, 17/2 (1998), 171–86. Also consider G. Adams, *Selected Writings* (Dingle, Co. Kerry: Brandon, 1997).

58. Recent attitude surveys suggest 'shades of grey now merge with the exclusive black and white nation-state relations in Northern Ireland'; N. Douglas, 'The Politics of Accommodation, Social Change and Conflict Resolution in Northern Ireland', *Political Geography*, 17/2 (1998), 226. Consider, for example, the Northern Ireland Life and Times Survey, available online at *www.qub.ac.uk/nilt*

59. This is shown in McGarry and O'Leary, *Explaining Northern Ireland*, 195, table 5.5.

60. See J. Anderson and J. Goodman (eds.), *Dis/Agreeing Ireland: Contexts, Obstacles, Hopes* (London: Pluto Press, 1998).

61. Consider L. M. Salamon and H. K. Anheier, 'The Civil Society Sector', *Transaction: Social Science and Modern Society*, 34/2 (1997), 60–5.

62. J. Ruane and J. Todd, *The Dynamics of Conflict in Northern Ireland: Power, Conflict and Emancipation* (Cambridge: Cambridge University Press, 1996), 313.

63. J. Anderson and D. Hamilton, 'Transnational Democracy versus National Conflict: Resolving Conflict in Ireland', Centre for Transnational Studies paper (1998), University of Newcastle.

64. McGarry and O'Leary, *Explaining Northern Ireland*, 192. Also see J. Hume, *A New Ireland: Politics, Peace and Reconciliation* (Boulder, Colo.: Roberts Rinehart, 1996).

65. Northern Ireland Act 1998, sect. 56. Similarly, cross-border dimensions are recognized in the Belfast Agreement (notably the North–South Ministerial Council), but they are under-developed and hostage to the internal consociational aspects of the Agreement.

66. Editorial, 'Out of Step', *Fortnight*, 372 (July–Aug. 1998), 5.

3

Comparative Political Science and the British–Irish Agreement

BRENDAN O'LEARY*

The British–Irish Agreement of 1998 was an exemplary constitutional design for an ethno-nationally divided territory over which there were rival claims to its sovereignty, ethnically polarized party and paramilitary blocs, and no reasonable prospects of peaceful integration within one civic nationalist identity.[1] Internally it was a consociational settlement. Externally it established confederal relationships, and prefigured imaginative federalist relationships and a novel model of double protection: of a minority that might become a majority, and a majority that might become a minority.[2] If this Agreement is not implemented in full, and the past tense in the first two sentences indicates my current expectations, a debate will arise over whether flaws in its design were the principal factors explaining its partial failure. This chapter is partly written in anticipation of that debate. By contrast, if the Agreement is fully implemented, albeit outside its scheduled timetable and its own agreed procedures, it will become an export model for conflict regulators—indeed it is already acquiring this status even for unpromising places, such as Kashmir.[3] If such full implementation materializes I will be extremely pleased, but this chapter may nevertheless serve the function of appraising the Agreement's novelties, possible design flaws, and possible pertinence for political scientists.

This chapter's reflections, driven by the Agreement, are threefold. First, political scientists have been too prone to recommend solely internal regulatory systems for managing ethno-national conflicts, and have thereby failed to recognize that successful ethno-national engineering not only can, but also should, address controversial sovereignty and self-determination disputes. But sovereignty disputes can have overlooked dimensions. Territory is not the be-all and end-all. States with parliamentary sovereignty, such as the United Kingdom, make it extremely difficult to entrench autonomy, i.e. to create constitutional predictability for 'federacies', and that makes such states unreliable partners in international treaties. The peculiarity of the United Kingdom's doctrine of parliamentary sovereignty is that it renders the constitutionalization of an ethno-national agreement uncertain because it remains revisable in the same manner as normal legislation.[4] Secondly, the prescriptions about electoral systems of the most able, high-minded, and comparatively informed political scientists in the field of conflict regulation have been overly committed either to one system of proportional representation—as in the case of Arend Lijphart—or to (sometimes wholly inappropriate) integrationist devices of a majoritarian kind—as in the case of Donald Horowitz. Thirdly, the novel dual premiership, designed by the major moderate parties, the Social Democratic and Labour Party (SDLP) and the Ulster Unionist Party (UUP), in the heat of the negotiations, has arguably proved to be its major institutional weakness.

A Distinctive Consociation and its External Features

The Agreement fulfilled and superseded its predecessor, the Anglo-Irish Agreement of 1985.[5] It was internally consociational, meeting all four of the criteria laid down by Arend Lijphart:[6]

Cross-community executive power-sharing. This was manifest in:

- the quasi-presidential dual premiership, elected by a concurrent majority of unionists and nationalists in the Assembly, and expected to preside over
- the inclusive grand coalition ten-member executive council of ministers—whose portfolios were allocated according to the d'Hondt procedure.

Proportionality norms. These were evident in:

- the d'Hondt procedure used to determine the composition of the Cabinet—which resulted in five unionists (three UUP, two Democratic Unionist Party (DUP)) and five nationalists (three SDLP and two Sinn Féin) holding ministries between November 1999 and February 2000;
- the electoral system (the single transferable vote in six-member districts) used to elect the Assembly;
- the d'Hondt procedure used to allocate assembly members to Committees with powers of oversight and legislative initiative; and

- existing and additional legislative provisions to ensure fair and representative employment, especially throughout the public sector, and the promise of a representative police service.[7]

Community autonomy and equality. This was evident in:

- the official recognition of the political identities of unionists, nationalists, and others, notably in the Assembly's cross-community consent procedures;
- the decision to leave alone the existing separate but recently equally funded forms of Catholic, Protestant, and integrated schooling;
- the official outlawing of discrimination on grounds of political or religious belief;
- the replacement of an oath of loyalty to the Crown with a pledge of office for ministers;
- the establishment of a Human Rights Commission tasked with protecting individual equality and liberty, and—I believe—reasonable groups rights;
- the entrenchment of vigorous equality provisions in Section 75 of the Northern Ireland Act (1998);[8]
- the promise of better legislative and institutional treatment of the Irish language and Ulster Scots—both of which became languages of record in the Assembly; and
- the promise of a Civic Forum, and participatory norms of governance, to facilitate the representation of voices that might not be heard purely through electoral or party mechanisms.[9]

Veto rights for minorities and mutual veto rights. These were evident in:

- the legislative procedures in the Assembly which required 'key decisions' to be passed either with a concurrent majority (under the 'parallel consent' procedure) or with a weighted majority (a 60 per cent majority including the support of at least 40 per cent of registered nationalists and registered unionists);
- the mutual interdependency of the first minister and deputy first minister; and of the Northern Ireland Assembly and the North–South Ministerial Council; and
- the legal incorporation of the European Convention on Human Rights and Freedoms and (the promise of) other legal enactments to give Northern Ireland a tailor-made bill of rights.

This was therefore a consociational settlement, perhaps unparalleled in its liberal democratic and institutional detail. But the Agreement was not just consociational, and departed from Lijphart's prescriptions in some respects. It had critical external institutional dimensions. It was made with the leaders of national, and not just ethnic or religious, communities (unlike most previously existing consociations), and was prompted by the cooperation of two governments of sovereign states over a disputed territory. It was endorsed by (most of) the leaders of most of the political parties in both parts of Ireland and (most of) the led in two jointly conducted referendums across a sovereign border. It was the first consociational settlement endorsed by a referendum that required concurrent majorities in jurisdictions in different states.

The Agreement established a devolved government. Non-devolved powers remained with the Westminster Parliament and the secretary of state for Northern Ireland, who continues to be appointed by the UK premier. The devolved government—executive and legislature—had full competence for economic development, education, health and social services, agriculture, environment, and finance (including the local Civil Service), though plainly it was constrained by both UK and European Union (EU) budgetary and other policies in these domains. The form of devolved government envisaged few limits on Northern Ireland's capacity to expand its autonomy. Through 'cross-community agreement' the Assembly was entitled to agree to expand its competencies; and, again through such agreement, and with the consent of the UK Secretary of State and the Westminster Parliament, the Assembly was empowered to legislate for any currently non-devolved function. The security functions of the state, policing and the courts, were not devolved, but they could be in principle. Maximum feasible autonomy[10] was therefore within the scope of the local decision-makers. A convention may have arisen in which the secretary of state and Westminster 'rubber-stamped' the legislative measures of the Assembly.[11] Indeed public policy in Ireland, North and South, might eventually have been made without direct British ministerial involvement.

For these and other reasons I maintain that, had the Agreement been fully implemented and developed, Northern Ireland would have become a clear specimen of what Daniel Elazar has called a 'federacy'.[12] A federal relationship exists where there are at least two separate tiers of government over the same territory, and when neither tier can unilaterally alter the constitutional capacities of the other. Such a relationship is a necessary element of a federal system, but whether it is sufficient is controversial. Normally a federation has sub-central units that are co-sovereign with the centre throughout most of the territory and population of the state in question. Plainly it would be premature and controversial to call the new United Kingdom a federation. But any system of constitutionally entrenched autonomy for one region makes the relationship between that region and the centre functionally equivalent to a federal relationship, and so, following Elazar, I call such a region—and its relationships with the centre and the centre's relationships with it—a federacy.

Through standard legislative majority rules the Assembly was empowered to pass 'normal laws' within its devolved competencies, though there was provision for a minority, of thirty of the 108 Assembly members, to trigger procedures that required special majorities. The passage of controversial legislation, i.e. 'key decisions', including the budget, automatically required these special procedures demonstrating cross-community support. Two rules were designed for this purpose: *parallel consent*, a majority that encompasses a strict concurrent majority of nationalists and unionists; and *weighted majority*, a majority among those present and voting that has the support of 60 per cent of members including the support of 40 per cent of nationalist members and 40 per cent of unionist members. There was also one super-majority rule, which was not explicitly concurrent, cross-community, or consociational. The Assembly was entitled by a two-thirds resolution of its membership, to call an extraordinary general election before its statutory four-year term expired. This was agreed by the parties, after the Agreement, in preference to a proposal that the secretary of state should have the power to dissolve the Assembly—a sign of the local parties' commitment to increasing their self-government rather than accept continuing arbitration from Westminster.

This distinctive devolved consociation—or consociational federacy as it would and should have become—was not a solely internal settlement, and that was multiply important. A strong conventional wisdom characterized the post-1945 political science of ethno-national questions. Taking its cue from public international law and realist international relations, it opposed changing the political borders of sovereign states; and on prudential or 'stabilitarian' grounds it feared irredentism and was sceptical of secessionist national self-determination.[13] For a long time 'external' self-determination, in law and political science, was accepted solely as a once-only right of colonial territories[14]; and this cautious reluctance to embrace national self-determination was reinforced by the received history of international relations, which was astringently critical of externally driven minority group rights regimes of the kind promoted by the League of Nations.[15]

The Agreement was, in part, a striking qualification of this wisdom. It contained agreed procedures on how a border might be changed, or rather abolished. The border in question, across the island, of Ireland is over 80 years old, the result of the Westminster Parliament's decision to partition

Ireland in 1920. The Agreement accepted the legitimacy of an irredentist aspiration: the desire of the Irish nation in both parts of Ireland to unify in one state, though the realization of that aspiration was made conditional upon the consent of majorities in both current jurisdictions in Ireland, and the recognition of the aspiration was accompanied by the removal of an irredentist territorial claim-of-right that had previously been embedded in the Irish Constitution. The Agreement, like the negotiations which preceded it, contained a recognition by the United Kingdom of the right of the people of Ireland, North and South, to exercise their self-determination to create a united Ireland if that was their wish.[16] The United Kingdom has never officially recognized Northern Ireland as a colonial territory, but its willingness to employ the language of self-determination in the making of the Agreement was an interesting departure. In addition, the Agreement promised to establish elaborate cross-border institutional arrangements explicitly seen by several nationalist parties as mechanisms to facilitate national reunification. Lastly, the Agreement contained features of an externally protected minority rights regime. The subtlest part of the Agreement was its tacit 'double protection model'—laced with elements of co-sovereignty, it was designed to withstand major demographic and electoral change. Under the Agreement the UK and Irish governments promised to develop functionally equivalent legal protections of rights, collective and individual, on both sides of the present border. In effect the Agreement promised protection to Northern Irish nationalists now on the same terms that would be given to Ulster unionists should they ever become a minority in a unified Ireland. National communities, British or Irish, were to be protected whether they were majorities or minorities, and whether sovereignty over the territory rested with the United Kingdom or the Republic—whence my expression 'double protection'. In the Agreement the two governments affirmed that

whatever choice is freely exercised by a majority of the people of Northern Ireland, the power of the sovereign government with jurisdiction there shall be exercised with rigorous impartiality on behalf of all the people in the diversity of their identities and traditions and shall be founded on the principles of full respect for, and equality of, civil, political, social and cultural rights, of freedom from discrimination for all citizens, and of parity of esteem and of just and equal treatment for the identity, ethos and aspirations of both communities.

If the conventional wisdom of post-war political science was correct, all these linkages, between an internal consociational settlement and a raft of measures that envisaged the possibility of a transformation in borders and of sovereignty regimes, should have been the key sources of instability in the Agreement, raising expectations among a national minority and arousing deep fears among the local national majority. The collapse in 1974 of the Sunningdale settlement, which had linked another internal consociational settlement to all-Ireland institutions, seemed amply to confirm the wisdom of post-war political science. For nearly ten years after the collapse of the Sunningdale settlement it was an axiom of faith among UK policy-makers that an internal consociational agreement—power-sharing—should be reached without an external agreement—an Irish dimension. Alternatively, it was held that an internal agreement should precede an external agreement.[17] This thinking was, however, reversed in the making of the Anglo-Irish Agreement.[18] Recognizing that the absence of an Irish dimension facilitated republican militancy, the UK and Irish governments established an intergovernmental conference, giving the Irish government unlimited rights of consultation on the making of UK public policy on Northern Ireland, while encouraging the Northern Irish parties to come to agree internal power-sharing. This combination of external and internal arrangements and incentives, 'coercive consociation', was, predictably, unacceptable to unionists, in the short term. But since they could not destroy the Anglo-Irish Agreement, through strikes, paramilitarism, civil disobedience, or conventional parliamentary tactics, unionists eventually came to negotiate an internal settlement in return for the modification of what they regarded as deeply unsatisfactory external arrangements. The fact that unionists were formally free to negotiate away the Anglo-Irish Agreement, replacing it with a successor Agreement with most of the same provisions, was an essential element in the making of the Agreement.

Northern nationalists certainly had their expectations raised by the making of the Agreement, and unionists certainly had, and still have, anxieties about the Agreement's external dimensions, but both the making of the 1998 Agreement and its stalling in 2000 suggest that the post-war wisdom of political science needs some revision. Consociational arrangements can be effectively combined with cross-border regimes, which enable a change in sovereignty, without engendering massive instability. True, the 'no unionists', who rejected the Agreement, did not like its external features, but they focused their rhetorical fire on the prospects of gunmen getting into (the internal) government, terrorists being released early from gaol, the failure to secure the decommissioning of (republican) paramilitaries' weapons, and on those parts of the Agreement which implied the full equality of nationalists with unionists within Northern Ireland. By contrast the 'yes unionists' trumpeted some of the external aspects of the

Agreement—pointing out, correctly, that the Agreement had led to changes in the Irish Republic's Constitution, which now required the active consent of majorities in both parts of Ireland before Irish unification could materialize, and claiming that they had 'negotiated away' the Anglo-Irish Agreement of 1985. 'Yes unionists' defended the cross-border institutions as minimal rational functional cooperation between neighbouring states, and observed, correctly, that the North–South Ministerial Council, unlike the Council of Ireland of 1974, contained no all-Ireland parliamentary body; and that they had succeeded in trimming down the ambitious cross-border institutions advocated by the Irish government, the SDLP, and Sinn Féin—the number of functional jurisdictions and the powers of (some) cross-border bodies were curtailed by the unionist negotiators. In short, and unlike 1974, the primary unionist concerns with the Agreement, which materially contributed to its suspension, cannot reasonably be said to have been with its external dimensions.

Consociation with Matching Confederations

The Agreement's meshing of internal and external institutions marked it out as novel in comparative politics, and some of its subtle external balancing elements explain why unionists were less concerned by the Agreement's external features than they were with the Sunningdale Agreement. The argument which follows assumes that confederations exist when political units voluntarily delegate powers and functions to bodies that can exercise power across their jurisdictions. Two such confederal relationships were established under the Agreement: the North–South Ministerial Council and the British–Irish Council.

The first confederation was all-Ireland in nature: the North–South Ministerial Council (NSMC). It was intended to bring together those with executive responsibilities in Northern Ireland and in the Republic. What was intended was clear. Nationalists were concerned that if the Assembly could outlast the NSMC, it would provide incentives for unionists to undermine the latter. Unionists, by contrast, were worried that if the NSMC could survive the destruction of the Assembly, nationalists would seek to bring this about. The Agreement was a tightly written contract with penalty clauses. Internal consociation and all-Ireland external confederalism went together: the Assembly and the NSMC were made 'mutually interdependent'; one could not function without the other. Unionists were unable to destroy the NSMC while retaining the Assembly, and nationalists were not able to destroy the Assembly while keeping the NSMC.[19]

The NSMC satisfactorily linked northern nationalists to their preferred nation-state, and was one means through which nationalists hoped to persuade unionists of the attractions of Irish unification. Consistently with the Agreement the Irish government agreed to change its Constitution to ensure that the NSMC, and its delegated implementation bodies, would be able to exercise island-wide jurisdiction in those functional activities where unionists were willing to cooperate. The NSMC was intended to function much like the Council of Ministers in the European Union, with ministers having considerable discretion to reach decisions, but remaining ultimately accountable to their respective legislatures. The NSMC was to meet in plenary format twice a year, and in smaller groups to discuss specific sectors (say, agriculture or education) on a 'regular and frequent basis'. Provision was made for the Council to meet to discuss matters that cut across sectors, and to resolve disagreements. In addition, the Agreement provided for cross-border or all-island 'implementation' bodies.

The scope of these North–South institutions was somewhat open-ended. The Agreement, however, required a meaningful Council. It stated that the NSMC 'will' (not 'may') identify at least six matters, where 'existing bodies' will be the appropriate mechanisms for cooperation within each separate jurisdiction, and at least six matters where cooperation will take place through cross-border or all-island implementation bodies. The latter were subsequently agreed to be inland waterways, food safety, trade and business development, special EU programmes, the Irish and Ulster Scots languages, and aquaculture and marine matters. The parties further agreed on six functional areas of cooperation—including some aspects of transport, agriculture, education, health, the environment, and tourism—where a joint North–South public company was established.[20]

The NSMC differed from the Council of Ireland of 1974, and not just in name. The name change was significant: a concession to unionist sensibilities even though the reference to the 'North' is more nationalist than unionist. There was no provision for a North–South joint parliamentary forum but the Northern Assembly and the Irish Oireachtas[21] were asked 'to consider' developing such a forum. Nationalists wanted the NSMC established by legislation from Westminster and the Oireachtas—to emphasize its autonomy from the Northern Assembly. Unionists wanted the NSMC established by the Northern Ireland Assembly and its counterpart in Dublin. The Agreement split the differences between the two positions. The NSMC and the implementation bodies were brought into existence by British–Irish legislation, but during the transitional period it was for the Northern executive and the Republic's government to decide, by agreement, how cooperation should take place, and in what areas the North–South institutions should cooperate. Once agreed, the Northern Ireland Assembly was unable to change these agreements—except by cross-community consent.

The Agreement linked Ireland, North and South, to another confederation, the European Union. It required the NSMC to consider the implementation of EU policies and programmes as well as proposals under way at the European Union, and made provisions for the NSMC views to be 'taken into account' at relevant EU meetings. The signatories to the Agreement promised to work 'in good faith' to bring the NSMC into being. There was not, however, sufficient good faith to prevent the first material break in the timetable scheduled in the Agreement occurring over the NSMC—but this was evidently a by-product of the crisis over executive formation and decommissioning. The signatories were required to use 'best endeavours' to reach agreement and to make 'determined efforts'—language that echoed that used in the Anglo-Irish Agreement of 1985—to overcome disagreements over functions where there is a 'mutual cross-border and all-island benefit'.[22]

If the Agreement is fully implemented, the new constitutional confederalism may be underpinned by economic rationality. As the Republic's Celtic Tiger continues to expand, Northern Ireland's ministers and citizens, of whatever background, might see increasing benefits from North–South cooperation. And as the European Union continues to integrate, there will be pressure for both parts of Ireland to enhance their cooperation, given their shared peripheral geographical position, and similar interests in agriculture and tourism, and in having regions defined in ways that attract funds.[23]

A second weaker confederal relationship was established by the Agreement, affecting all the islands of Britain and Ireland. Under the new British–Irish Council the two governments of the sovereign states, all the devolved governments of the United Kingdom, and all the neighbouring insular dependent territories of the United Kingdom, can meet, agree to delegate functions, and may agree common policies. This proposal met unionists' concerns for reciprocity in linkages—and provided a mechanism through which they might in future be linked to the United Kingdom even if Northern Ireland becomes part of the Republic.

Unionists originally wanted any North–South Ministerial Council to be subordinate to a British–Irish, or East–West, Council. This did not happen. There was no hierarchical relationship between the two councils. Two textual warrants suggest that the NSMC was more important and far-reaching than its British–Irish counterpart. The Agreement required the establishment of North–South implementation bodies, leaving the formation of east–west bodies a voluntary matter; and stated explicitly that the Assembly and the NSMC were interdependent, making no equivalent status for the British–Irish Council.

The development of this confederal relationship would be stunted if the Irish government was reluctant to engage in a forum where it may be outnumbered by seven other governments—of Westminster, Scotland, Wales, Northern Ireland, Jersey, Guernsey, and the Isle of Man—but rules would presumably develop to ensure the joint dominance of the governments of the sovereign states. The British–Irish Council may yet flourish as a policy formulation forum, if the UK's devolved governments choose to exploit it as an opportunity for intergovernmental lobbying and alliance-building, or to build alliances with the Irish government on European public policy—which would give impetus to federalist processes.

Consociation with Matching Federalist Possibilities

The Agreement opened other external constitutional linkages for Northern Ireland, one within the United Kingdom, and another possibility with the Republic, which held federalist promise.

Within the United Kingdom the Agreement seemed the penultimate blow to centralist unionism already dented by the 1997–8 referendums and legislative Acts establishing a Scottish Parliament and Welsh National Assembly.[24] But did the Agreement simply fall within the rubric of 'devolution within a decentralized unitary state'? Arguably not. The United Kingdom is composed of two unions: that of Great Britain and that of Great Britain and Northern Ireland. The constitutional basis of the latter is distinct.

The nature of devolution in Northern Ireland was not closed by the 1998 Northern Ireland Act; an open-ended mechanism to expand autonomy existed—albeit with the consent of the secretary of state and the approval of Westminster. No such open-ended provision was granted to the Scottish Parliament or the Welsh Assembly. Maximum feasible autonomy while remaining within the Union was feasible, provided there was agreement to that within the Northern Assembly.

The Agreement, unlike Scottish and Welsh devolution, was embedded in a treaty between two states, based on the United Kingdom's recognition of Irish national self-determination. The United Kingdom officially acknowledged that Northern Ireland has the right to join the Republic, on the basis of a local referendum, and it recognized, in a treaty, the authority of Irish national self-determination throughout the island of Ireland. The Agreement's institutions were brought into being by the will of the people of Ireland, North and South, and not just by the people of Northern Ireland (recall the interdependence of the NSMC and the Assembly). In consequence, under the Agreement, the United Kingdom's relationship to Northern Ireland, at least in international law, in my view, had an explicitly federal character: Northern Ireland had become a federacy. The Westminster Parliament and executive could not, except through breaking its treaty obligations, and except through denying Irish national self-determination, exercise power in any manner in Northern Ireland that was inconsistent with the Agreement. This interpretation was made by the author and others immediately after the Agreement was made. Plainly the suspension of the Assembly in February 2000 showed that the United Kingdom's authorities did not feel constrained by its reasoning, a point to which I shall return.

The Agreement also opened federalist avenues in the Republic—one of the most centralized states in Europe. The NSMC was seen by nationalists as the embryonic institution of a federal Ireland. This stepping stone theory was most loudly articulated by 'no unionists', but they were not wrong to surmise that many nationalists saw the NSMC as 'transitional'. Sinn Féin said so; so did Fianna Fáil.

The Irish government and its people did not abandon Irish unification when they endorsed the Agreement. Instead it became 'the firm will of the Irish nation, in harmony and friendship, to unite all the people who share the territory of the island of Ireland, in all the diversity of their identities and traditions, recognizing that a united Ireland shall be brought about only by peaceful means with the consent of a majority of the people expressed, in both jurisdictions in the island' (from the new Article 3). The amended Irish Constitution therefore officially recognizes *two* jurisdictions that jointly enjoy the right to participate in the Irish nation's exercise of self-determination. Unification is no longer linked to 'unitarism', and is compatible with either confederation or federation.

Irish unification cannot be precluded because of present demographic and electoral trends—which have led to a steady rise in the nationalist share of the vote across different electoral systems.[25] The unification envisaged in the redrafted Irish Constitution is, however, now different. It no longer has anything resembling a programme of assimilation. Respect for 'the diversity of . . . identities and traditions' connects with both consociational and con/federal logic. The Republic is bound to structure its laws to prepare for the possibility of a con/federal as well as a unitary Ireland. Northern Ireland is a fully recognized legal entity within the Irish Constitution, and its elimination as a political unit is no longer a programmatic feature of *Bunreacht na hÉireann*.[26]

Externally Protecting the Agreement

The two states not only promised reciprocity for the protection of present and future minorities, but also created two intergovernmental devices to protect those communities. The most important was the successor to the Anglo-Irish Agreement, namely the new British–Irish intergovernmental conference, which guarantees the Republic's government access to policy formulation on all matters not (yet) devolved to the Northern Assembly or the NSMC.[27] Unionists claimed that they had removed the 1985 Anglo-Irish Agreement in return for conceding a North–South Ministerial Council. This claim was exaggerated. Under the new Agreement the Irish government retains a say in those Northern Irish matters that have not been devolved to the Northern Assembly, as was the case under Article 4 of the Anglo-Irish Agreement, and, as with that agreement, there will continue to be an intergovernmental conference, chaired by the minister for foreign affairs and the Northern Ireland secretary of state, to deal with non-devolved matters, and it will continue to be serviced by a standing secretariat. The new Agreement, moreover, promises to 'intensify co-operation' between the two governments on all-island or cross-border aspects of rights, justice, prisons, and policing (unless and until these matters are devolved). There is provision for representatives of the Northern Assembly to be involved in the intergovernmental conference—a welcome parliamentarization—but they will not have the same status as the representatives of the governments of the sovereign states. The Anglo-Irish Agreement fully anticipated these arrangements.[28] Therefore, it is more accurate to claim that the Anglo-Irish Agreement was fulfilled rather than deleted.

Formal joint sovereignty of the two states over Northern Ireland was not established, but the governments guaranteed the Agreement, and embedded it in an international treaty. Irish officials had been wary since the early 1990s of trading likely irreversible constitutional changes—transformations of Articles 2 and 3 of the Constitution—in exchange for institutions that might share the same fate as the Sunningdale settlement. That is why they argued that the Agreement as a whole should be embedded in a treaty. Together with the fact that the Agreement had been endorsed in double referendums, the official Irish belief, and the Irish nationalist belief, was that the Agreement, like Northern Ireland's constitutional choice between membership of the United Kingdom and of the Republic, rested on the consent of the Irish people, through the joint act of self-determination of the North and South. The UK government would not have power to do anything that was not legitimate under the Agreement's procedures.

It has become apparent that the UK government, eventually, did not share this understanding. The New Labour government acted in classic Diceyan fashion in suspending the Northern Assembly and the UK side of the NSMC, using the doctrine of parliamentary sovereignty to arrogate to itself the power of suspension—which had not been granted to it in the making of the Agreement, nor in its (UK) legislative enactment in the 1998 Northern Ireland Act.

The constitutional meanings of the suspension—not evident in most of the contributions to the debates over the power of suspension that occurred in the House of Commons and the House of Lords—are highly significant. The UK government's officials knew that suspension would breach the formal Agreement, because in the summer of 1999, when both governments contemplated a suspension mechanism, the United Kingdom proposed to the Irish side that the treaty that was about to be signed by the two governments should be amended to make it compatible with suspension. No such amendment was made. The United Kingdom's justification of the suspension was that it was necessary to save the first minister, David Trimble. His threat to resign because the Irish Republican Army (IRA) had not delivered on decommissioning would become operative in an environment in which 'yes unionists' no longer commanded an absolute majority of the registered unionists in the Assembly—and therefore, it was feared, he could not in future have been resurrected as first minister. This reasoning was false: the Assembly, by weighted majority, was entitled to pass any measure to amend its current rules for electing the dual premiers, and to send this measure to Westminster for statutory ratification. So, in short, there were mechanisms within the Agreement under which Trimble could have regained the position of first minister. But even if the UK's reasoning had been correct, the suspension was both an unconstitutional and a partisan act. It was unconstitutional in Irish eyes because the suspensory power had not been endorsed with cross-community consent through the negotiation of the Agreement, or in the referendums, or in the United Kingdom's legislative enactment of the Agreement. It was also partisan because neither the Agreement, nor the Mitchell Review of the Agreement, required Sinn Féin to deliver material decommissioning by the IRA on the basis of a deadline set by the leader of the UUP. The sole agreed deadline for decommissioning required all political parties to use their best endeavours to achieve full decommissioning by 22 May 2000, two years after the endorsement of the Agreement in the referendums.

One of the relevant passages of the Agreement referred to procedures for review if difficulties arose across the range of institutions established on the entering into force of the international treaty between the two governments: 'If difficulties arise which require remedial action across the range of institutions, or otherwise require amendment of the British–Irish Agreement or relevant legislation, *the process of review will fall to the two Governments in consultation with the parties in the Assembly. Each Government will be responsible for action in its own jurisdiction*' (my italics). The italicized passages, read in conjunction with the Agreement as a whole, suggest that the UK government was obligated formally to consult the parties in the Assembly and the Irish government over obtaining any power of suspension, and that any remedial action required the joint support of the two governments, especially as regards their treaty. That each government would be 'responsible for action in its own jurisdiction' was not taken by the Irish side to mean that the Westminster Parliament had unilateral discretion to alter, amend, suspend, or abolish the institutions of the Agreement. It merely meant that for agreed remedial action there would not be joint sovereignty but rather parallel legislative procedures to be followed in each state.

The central purpose of the United Kingdom's agreement to delete Section 75 of the Government of Ireland Act of 1920, and of the Irish state's agreement to modify Articles 2 and 3 of the Irish Constitution, had been to show that both states were engaged in 'balanced' constitutional change, confirming that Northern Ireland's status as part of the United Kingdom or the Republic rested with its people alone, and to facilitate the establishment of institutions in Northern Ireland that were rooted in local popular consent. The United Kingdom's Diceyans have obviously interpreted the United Kingdom's deletion of Section 75 of the Government of Ireland Act as meaningless because in their eyes Parliament's sovereignty remains intact even when it removes a statutory statement which says it remains intact. Irish negotiators obviously should have been more careful: the United Kingdom's 'constitution' is Ireland's British problem. Had the Agreement fully bedded down, perhaps Northern Ireland's status as a federacy would have developed the status of a constitutional convention—the United Kingdom's mysterious functional poor relation of constitutionality. But it was not to be.

The act of suspension has four constitutional messages. First, it has made it plain that every aspect of the Agreement is vulnerable to Westminster's doctrine of parliamentary sovereignty. Everything in the Agreement—its institutions, its confidence-building measures, the promise that Irish unification will take place if there is majority consent for it in both parts of Ireland—is revisable by the current Westminster Parliament, and any future Parliament, irrespective of international law, or the solemn promises made by UK negotiators in the run-up to, and in the making of, the Agreement. No UK parliamentarian can look an Irish nationalist or republican in the eye and say that Northern Ireland's status as part of the United Kingdom, and its institutional arrangements, ultimately rest upon the consent of its people. By its actions the Westminster Parliament has affirmed that it regards its sovereignty as unconstrained by the Agreement. Had it sought and obtained the assent of the Northern Assembly—by cross-community consent—to its possession of the power of suspension that would have been a different matter. It did not. Even if the secretary of state's motives were entirely benign—and that has been questioned—his decision to obtain the power of suspension destroyed the assumptions of nearly a decade of negotiation.

Secondly, the suspension will spell out to official Irish negotiators, and Northern nationalists, the necessity, in any new round of negotiations, of entrenching Northern Ireland's status as a federacy, perhaps in the same manner as the United Kingdom's courts are instructed to make European law supreme over law(s) made by the Westminster Parliament, through full domestic incorporation and entrenchment of the relevant treaty. Without such protection the Agreement cannot be constitutionalized consistently with both the Agreement and the exercise of Irish national self-determination, North and South. This will require Ireland's negotiators to require Westminster to repeal the suspension Act and to declare that its sovereignty is circumscribed by the Agreement.

Thirdly, unionists themselves must consider the constitutional consequences of suspension. If the 'yes unionists' embrace the Diceyan reading of the doctrine of parliamentary sovereignty, as some plainly do, then they may one day suffer the consequences of the sword they urged Westminster to deploy. What Westminster does on unionists' behalf today it can take from them tomorrow—on exactly the same basis. Under the doctrine of parliamentary sovereignty the Union rests not on the consent of its component parts, but rather on Westminster's say-so: Westminster is free to modify the Union in any way it likes, for example, through full-scale joint sovereignty over Northern Ireland with the Republic, or through expelling Northern Ireland from its jurisdiction.

Lastly, the suspension spells a very blunt warning to the Scottish Parliament and the Welsh Assembly and supporters of these devolved institutions—bodies that were created with smaller proportions of popular support and lower electoral turnouts than their Northern Irish counterpart. Sovereignty, in Westminster's eyes, remains indivisibly in its possession: even under 'modernizing' New Labour, Westminster remains the site of the supreme sovereign, the unconstitutionalized Crown-in-Parliament.

Electoral Systems and Consociational Design

Elections to the 108-member Assembly used a proportional representation (PR) system, the single transferable vote (STV) in six-member constituencies—though the Assembly was entitled, by cross-community consent procedures, to advocate change from this system. The Droop quota in each constituency was therefore 14.3 per cent of the vote, which squeezed the very small parties, or, alternatively, encouraged them to form electoral alliances.[29] Thus the smaller of the two loyalist parties, the Ulster Democratic Party (UDP), led by Gary McMichael, won no seats in the first Assembly election. Very small parties, which can gather lower-order preferences from across the unionist and nationalist blocs, such as the Women's Coalition, showed that this system need not preclude representation for small parties among the 'others'.

This system of voting is not what Arend Lijphart recommends for consociational systems: he is an advocate of party-list PR systems, principally because he believes that they help make party leaders more powerful, and better able to sustain inter-ethnic consociational deals.[30] Lijphart also argues for party-list PR, rather than STV, because it allows for a high district magnitude (enabling greater proportionality), is less vulnerable to gerrymandering, and is simpler for voters and organizers—arguments to be addressed shortly.

Those who would like to see David Trimble in greater control of the UUP, a pro-Agreement party with a strong anti-Agreement minority in its ranks, may have hankered after Lijphart's preferred form of PR. But whether party-list PR in itself would have helped Trimble overcome resistance to the Agreement within his party ranks may legitimately be doubted. The Northern Ireland case suggests that modification of the consociational prescriptive canon is in order. Had a regionwide party-list system been in operation in June 1998, the UUP would have ended up with fewer seats, and with fewer seats than the SDLP, and, in consequence, the implementation of the Agreement would have been even more problematic. This is because under party-list PR the UUP's seat share would have been much closer to its vote share, whereas under STV the party benefited from transfers which took its seat share significantly beyond its first-preference vote share (see Table 3.1). There is a further and less contingent counsel against party-list systems in consociational systems where the relevant ethnic communities are internally democratic, rather than sociologically monolithic. A region-wide party-list election gives incentives to dissidents to form their own parties, or micro parties. In 1998 a party-list system would have fragmented and shredded the UUP's support more than actually transpired. Hardliners under party-list systems have every reason to form new parties knowing that their disloyalty will penalize the more moderate parties they leave behind, but will not necessarily reduce the total vote and seat share of their ethno-national bloc. Hardline conduct will cost little to their bloc. This objection to Lijphart's favoured prescription is not merely speculative. The 1996 elections to the Northern Ireland Peace Forum used a mixture of a party-list system and reserved seats. Party proliferation and the erosion of the UUP first-preference vote were some of the more obvious consequences.[31]

The single transferable vote, of course, does not guarantee party discipline, as multiple candidates for the same party in a given constituency may present, tacitly or otherwise, slightly different emphases on party commitments. I suggest, however, that the STV system, combined with higher effective thresholds than under most forms of party-list PR, makes it more likely that parties will remain formally unified, and therefore better able to make and maintain consociational deals. In any case, neither party-list PR nor STV has automatic consequences for central party leadership control over their candidates. At the very least the prescriptive superiority of the party-list system for enhancing the capacity for party leaders to make and sustain consociations is unproven, and Lijphart's consistent counsel in this respect should be modified.[32]

Let me briefly address Lijphart's second-order arguments for party-list PR instead of STV. I have already argued implicitly in favour of the higher thresholds that exist in STV with six-member districts than in region-wide list PR (where the district magnitude might be as high as 108). That is because, other things being equal, I favour restraining party fragmentation in preference to achieving allegedly 'better' proportionality, and I favour reducing the number of players necessary to sustain a consociational coalition. Secondly, and contra Lijphart, I maintain that STV, legislatively enacted with uniform district magnitudes, and implemented by an independent electoral commission tasked to create uniform electorates, is no more vulnerable to gerrymandering than regional party-list PR. I concede that STV is only suitable for numerate electorates, but otherwise its complexities are not especially mysterious—no more so than the formulae used for achieving proportionality in party-list systems. Try discussing d'Hondt, Hare, and Sainte-Laguë in public bars!

The operation of STV in Northern Ireland suggests a corrective not only to Lijphart's prescriptions, but also to Donald Horowitz's favoured remedies for moderating ethnic conflict. STV has the great merit of encouraging 'vote-pooling':[33] in principle, voters were able to use their lower-order preferences (transfers) to reward pro-Agreement candidates at the expense of anti-Agreement candidates.[34] In this respect STV looks tailor-made to achieve the 'inter-ethnic' and 'cross-ethnic' voting favoured by Horowitz, a strong advocate of institutional and policy devices to facilitate conflict reduction.[35]

Consistent, however, with his general anti-consociational premises, Horowitz believes that the STV system damages the prospects for inter-ethnic cooperation because the relatively low quota required to win a seat in six-member constituencies (14.3 per cent) makes it too easy for hardline parties and their candidates to be successful.[36] He also thinks that the Agreement's other institutions, biased towards the key consociational partners (nationalists and unionists), compound this effect by weakening the prospects of cross-ethnic parties, such as the Alliance, which he believes impairs the long-run chances of conflict reduction.

The Northern Ireland case, and the limited working of the Agreement so far, in my view suggests some normative and empirical challenges to Horowitz's reasoning—even if he may be right to be sceptical about the general stability of consociational systems. Horowitz would generally prefer the use of the alternative vote (AV) in single-member constituencies in Northern Ireland, as elsewhere, because its quota (50 per cent plus one) would deliver strong support to moderate ethno-national and cross-ethnic candidates. His reasoning is that the high threshold requires parties (and candidates) to moderate their appeals in search of lower-order preferences. The problem with this prescription is straightforward. The outcomes it would deliver would be majoritarian, disproportional, both within blocs and across blocs, and unpredictably so.[37] The outcomes would, additionally, have much more indirectly 'inclusive' effects than STV.

Let me justify this argument specifically. In some of Northern Ireland's existing constituencies, none of which is gerrymandered, there would be unambiguous unionist and nationalist majorities. In these constituencies the use of the AV would lead to the under-representation of local minority voters, and to local fiefdoms. Preference transfers in such constituencies would be more likely to occur within blocs rather than across blocs. Secondly, while candidates who could not expect to win a majority of first-preference votes would have to seek support for lower-order preferences under AV, it would not be obvious that their best strategy would be to seek lower-order preferences across the ethno-national divide because the imperative of staying in the count would dictate building as big an initial first- and second-preference vote tally as possible.[38] Lastly, and most significantly, it is reasonable to believe that AV would never be agreed by hardline parties tempted to enter a consociational settlement because they would sensibly believe it would be likely to undermine their legislative success. Since the 1998 Agreement was made possible by encouraging 'inclusivity', by facilitating negotiations which included Sinn Féin (the party that had supported the IRA) and the Progressive Unionist Party (PUP) and the UDP (the parties that had supported the Ulster Defence Association and the Ulster Volunteer Force), it would have been perverse for their leaders to have agreed an electoral system which would have minimized the seat-winning prospects of their newly moderated hardline parties.

Indeed STV arguably worked both *before and after* the Agreement to consolidate the Agreement's prospects. To begin with it helped to moderate the policy stance of Sinn Féin. After its first phase of electoral participation in elections in Northern Ireland in the 1980s, and in the Republic in the latter half of the 1980s, the party discovered that it was in a ghetto. Its candidates in some local government constituencies[39] would pile up large numbers of first-preference ballot papers, and then sit unelected as a range of other parties' candidates would go past them to achieve quotas on the basis of lower-order preferences. They received very few lower-order preferences from SDLP voters. However, once the party moderated its stance, once it promoted the IRA's ceasefire(s), and became the champion of a peace process and a negotiated settlement, it found that both its first-preference vote and its transfer vote (and seats won) increased. These rewards would not have been delivered by any other widely used voting system that I know of.

The constitutional design argument that can be extracted from this story is this: once there has been party fragmentation within ethno-national blocs, STV in multi-member districts ($M \geq 4$) can assist accommodating postures and initiatives by parties and candidates, both intra-bloc and inter-bloc. The corollary is that STV's positive effects apply best to already polarized and pluralized party systems in ethno-nationally divided territories. If there has been no prior history of ethnicized party polarization within a state, or no deep pluralization of parties within ethno-national blocs, then the merits of STV's implementation may be doubted on Horowitzian grounds. This reflection raises what may be the key problem with Horowitz's electoral integrationist prescriptions: they apply best to forestalling or inhibiting ethnic conflict; they seem much less effective remedies for cases of developed, protracted, and intense ethnic and ethno-national conflict. Horowitz's integrationist prescriptions may be most pertinent at the moment of formation of a competitive party system—but once party formation and pluralism have occurred, there will be few agents with the incentives to implement Horowitz's prescriptions, and if a third party or outside power did so, it would be a provocation to the less moderate parties and would therefore most likely reignite ethno-national tensions. The normative objection that can be levelled against Horowitz's position is that, in the run-up to a power-sharing bargain, proportionality norms better match parties' respective bargaining strengths and their conceptions of justice than do majoritarian systems, even majoritarian systems with artificial distributive requirements. Once party pluralism has already occurred, some form of proportionality is more likely to be legitimate than a shift to strongly majoritarian systems (such as AV), which will be seen, correctly, as deliberate electoral gerrymandering. Likewise, systems with ad hoc distributive requirements will always be (correctly) represented as gerrymanders—albeit well-intentioned.

Perhaps it is necessary to add that these arguments are narrow and qualified. STV is no panacea; it is not enough on its own to facilitate ethno-national conflict regulation; and it may not be appropriate everywhere. But I maintain that it can help to promote accommodative moves, and to consolidate consociational deals in ways that regionwide party-list systems and the AV system in single-member constituencies cannot.

There has been some empirical confirmation of the merits of STV since the Agreement was made. Vote-pooling occurred within the first Assembly elections—as we can surmise, to an extent, from actual counts,[40] as Geoffrey Evans and I can confirm from a survey we helped design,[41] and as unpublished work on actual counts by Paul Mitchell of Queen's University, Belfast, also suggests. In short, *some* of the SDLP's and Sinn Féin's voters found it rational to reward David Trimble's UUP for making the Agreement by giving its candidates their lower-order preferences, and so helped them against Ian Paisley's DUP and Robert McCartney's United Kingdom Unionist Party (UKUP). Likewise, *some* of the UUP's and the

PUP's voters transferred their lower-order preferences to pro-Agreement candidates within their own bloc, among the others, and among national-ists. (Of course, transfers also took place amongst the 'no unionists'—and between 'yes' and 'no unionists'.) In our survey approximately 10 per cent of each bloc's first-preference supporters gave lower-order preference sup-port to pro-Agreement candidates in the other bloc. Within-bloc rewards for moderation also occurred: Sinn Féin won lower-order preferences from SDLP voters, and the PUP had candidates elected on the basis of transfers from other candidates.

Table 3.1 reports the outcome of the June 1998 elections to the Assembly. The proportionality of the results was evident, both with respect to blocs and with respect to parties. But the deviations in seats won compared to the first-preference vote primarily benefited the pro-Agreement parties. The UUP was the principal beneficiary of the transfer of lower-order prefer-ences, taking its seat share (25.9 per cent) significantly above its first-preference vote share (21.3 per cent)—though these lower-order prefer-ences came from voters who voted 'no' as well as those who voted 'yes' to the Agreement, as was evident in ballot papers and in our survey.[42] The Women's Coalition was the most widespread beneficiary of lower-order preferences, winning two seats despite a very low first-preference vote share. Its inclusive orientation towards both republicans and loyalists meant that the transfer process assisted it more than the Alliance, as its successful can-didates won transfers from every party, whereas the Alliance's appeal for lower-order preferences was more confined to middle-class SDLP and UUP voters. The net transfers by voters to the pro-Agreement candidates, though not as significant as had been hoped, performed one very important task. They converted a bare 'anti-Agreement' majority of the first-preference vote (25.5 per cent) within the unionist bloc of voters into a bare 'pro-Agreement' majority (27.7 per cent) among seats won by unionists, a result that was essential for the (possible) stabilization of the Agreement. The data are suggestive: STV may be helpful both in achieving vote-pooling and in providing moderating incentives within a consociational system.

The Northern Ireland Act and the Northern Ireland (Elections) Act 1998 opened one novelty in the practice of STV in Ireland. Both Acts left it open to the secretary of state to determine the method of filling vacancies: this may be done through by-elections or substitutes, or through whichever method the secretary of state deems fit. By-elections, used in the Republic of Ireland and hitherto in Northern Ireland, are anomalous in a PR sys-tem.[43] A candidate who wins the last seat in a six-member constituency and who subsequently resigns or dies is unlikely to be replaced by a candidate of the same party or persuasion in a by-election—which would then become the equivalent of AV in a single-member constituency. The Northern Ireland Assembly (Elections) Order of 1998 has provided for a system of alternatives, or personally nominated substitutes, with a provision for by-elections if the alternatives system fails to provide a substitute. The disproportionality possibly induced by by-elections—and with consequent unpredictable ramifications for the numbers of registered nationalists and unionists and the operation of the cross-community rules—needed to be engineered out of the settlement, and it was a good sign that the parties cooperated with this concern in mind.

TABLE 3.1. *Party performances in 1998 Assembly election*

Political parties	Seats	First preference vote (%)	Percentage of seats
SDLP	24	22.0	22.2
Sinn Féin	18	17.7	16.6
Other nationalists	—	0.1	—
Total nationalists	42	39.8	38.8
UUP	28	21.0	25.9
PUP	2	2.5	1.8
UDP	—	1.2	—
Other 'yes unionists'	—	0.3	—
Total 'yes unionists'	30	25.0	27.7
DUP	20	18.0	18.5
UKUP	5	4.5	4.6
Other 'no unionists'	3	3.0	2.8
Total 'no unionists'	28	22.8	25.9
Alliance	6	6.4	5.5
Women's Coalition	2	1.7	1.9
Others	—	1.3	—
Total others	8	9.4	7.4

The Dual Premiership

Among its institutional novelties the Agreement established two quasi-presidential figures, a dyarchy.[44] The first minister and deputy first minister were to be elected jointly under the parallel consent rule. Presidentialism in essence is an executive that cannot be destroyed by an assembly except through impeachment. The dual premiership has presidential characteristics because it should be almost impossible to depose the two office-holders, provided they remain united as a team, until the next general election.

The first and the deputy first minister were to be elected together by the *parallel consent procedure*, an idea that flowed out of the making of the Agreement which required propositions to have the support of a majority of parties, including parties representing a majority of nationalists and of unionists. The rule gave very strong incentives to unionists and nationalists to nominate a candidate for one of these positions that was acceptable to a majority of the other bloc's members in the Assembly. In the first elections for these posts in *designate* or *shadow* form, pro-Agreement unionists in the UUP and the PUP, who between them had a majority of registered unionists (thirty out of fifty-eight), voted solidly for the combination of David Trimble of the UUP and Seamus Mallon of the SDLP. Naturally so did the SDLP, which enjoyed a majority among registered nationalists (twenty-four out of forty-two). (The 'no unionists' voted against this combination, while Sinn Féin abstained.)

The rule practically ensures that a unionist and a nationalist share the top two posts, and that the post-holders be acceptable to a majority of both blocs—pure concurrent majoritarianism. The Agreement and its UK legislative enactment, the Northern Ireland Act (1998), made clear that the two posts had identical symbolic and external representation functions;[45] indeed they have identical powers. Both were to preside over the Executive Committee of Ministers, and have a role in coordinating its work: the sole difference is in their titles.[46] Their implicit and explicit coordinating functions, as approved by the Shadow Assembly, were elaborated in February 1999. There was to be an Office of the First and Deputy First Ministers. It was to have an Economic Policy Unit, and an Equality Unit, and was tasked with liaising with the North–South Ministerial Council, the British–Irish Council, the secretary of state on reserved and excepted UK powers, EU–international matters, cross-departmental coordination, and so on.

The prime-ministerial dyarchy was to be quasi-presidential, because, unlike executive presidents (and unlike most prime ministers), neither the first nor the deputy first minister formally appointed the other ministers to the Executive Committee—save where one of them is a party leader entitled to nominate the ministries to which his party is entitled. Posts in the Executive Committee were to be allocated to parties in proportion to their strength in the Assembly, according to a mechanical rule, the d'Hondt rule.[47] The rule was simple in its consequences: any party that won a significant share of seats and was willing to abide by the new institutional rules established by the Agreement was to have a reasonable chance of access to the executive, a subtle form of Lijphart's 'grand coalition government'. It was a voluntary grand coalition because parties were free to exclude themselves from the Executive Committee, and because no programme of government had to be negotiated before executive formation. The design created strong incentives for parties to take their entitlement to seats in the executive because, if they did not, they would go either to their ethno-national rivals or to rivals in their own bloc. The rules did not, however, formally require any specific proportion of nationalists and unionists.[48]

This dual premiership critically depended upon the personal cooperation of the two holders of these posts, and upon the cooperation of their respective majorities (or pluralities—under the weighted majority rule). The Northern Ireland Act (1998) reinforced their interdependence by requiring that 'if either the First Minister or the deputy First Minister ceases to hold office, whether by resignation or otherwise, the other shall also cease to hold office' (Article 14(6)). This power of resignation was in fact to be strategically deployed twice, by both elected office-holders.

In the summer of 1999 Seamus Mallon of the SDLP resigned as deputy first minister (designate), complaining that the UUP were 'dishonouring' the Agreement and 'insulting its principles' by insisting upon the prior decommissioning of paramilitaries' weapons before executive formation.[49] He did so to speed an intergovernmental review of the implementation of the Agreement. The constitutional question immediately arose: did Mallon's resignation automatically trigger Trimble's departure from office, and require fresh elections to these positions within six weeks? The initial presiding officer's answer to this question was that it did not, because the Assembly was not yet functioning under the Northern Ireland Act.[50] This answer was accepted, and in November 1999 Mallon's resignation was rescinded with the assent of the Assembly with no requirement that the two men would have to restand for office.

Shortly afterwards David Trimble was to use the threat of resignation—helping thereby to precipitate the suspension of the Assembly in February 2000. He wrote a post-dated letter of resignation to the chairman of his party, who was authorized to deliver it to the secretary of state if Sinn Féin failed to achieve IRA movement on the decommissioning of its weapons—in the form of 'product'—within a specified period after the UUP had agreed to full-scale executive formation, and the initiation with full plenitude of all the Agreement's institutions. As we have seen, the fear that this resignation would become operative was the proximate cause of the UK secretary of state's decision to suspend the Assembly: Peter Mandelson believed that without a 'yes unionist' first minister capable of winning the support of a majority of registered unionists, and with all UUP ministers likely to resign their portfolios, no workable executive would be available.

How should we appraise the executive design in the Agreement? The special skill of the designers–negotiators was to create strong incentives for executive power-sharing and power division, but without requiring parties to have any prior formal coalition agreement—other than the institutional agreement—and without requiring any party to renounce its long-run aspirations. The dual premiership was designed to tie moderate representatives of each bloc together, and to give some drive towards overall policy coherence. The dual premiership was intended to strengthen moderates in both camps and to give them significant steering powers over the rest of the executive. The d'Hondt mechanism ensured inclusivity, and was carefully explained to the public as achieving precisely that.[51] Distinctive coalitions could form around different issues within the executive, permitting flexibility, but inhibiting chaos (given the requirement that the budget be agreed by cross-community consent). In these respects and others the Agreement differs positively from the Sunningdale experiment of 1973.

Yet the executive, and the dual premiership in particular, has proven unstable—and for reasons that go beyond the holders' personalities. Two reasons mattered: the precariousness of the 'yes unionist' majority bloc, and the potency of the resignation weapon available to each premier. Arguably this inter-moderate party deal was a weak spot in institutional design: had the first and deputy first premiership been allocated according to the d'Hondt procedure, and had parties which threatened not to take up their executive seats simply lost access to executive power, then there would have been very strong incentives for the executive to be sustained, especially if the UK secretary of state had decided to take a hands-off approach to any threats of non-participation in the executive. This procedure would also have meant that no suspension could have been justified on the grounds that it was necessary to 'save' David Trimble's chances of returning to the position of first minister—though that excuse was not valid, as I have already argued.

Using the d'Hondt rule to allocate the dual premierships, with the same Mitchell-inspired ministerial oath of office—perhaps modified by a rule that one premiership had to go to the unionist party with the highest number of seats and the other to the nationalist party with the highest number of seats— would, however, have had the consequence of making more likely the future passage of hardline party leaders, such as Paisley or Adams, to such positions. That, of course, was one motivation behind the construction of the dual premiership by the moderates. However, the prospect feared by the moderates may not have spelled disaster: the prospect of such high office might have further moderated the stances of the respective hardline parties. It is a heretical thought.

What was definitely not foreseen was that failure to timetable the formation of the rest of the executive immediately after the election of the premiers would precipitate a protracted crisis of executive formation. If the Agreement is rebuilt, amendments to the Northern Ireland Act (1998) could be adopted by the UK Parliament, or by the Assembly, that would be consistent with the Agreement, to prevent any recurrence of this type of crisis. In future candidates for first and deputy first minister could be obliged to state the number of executive portfolios that will be available, and the formation of the executive should be required immediately after their election. That would plug this particular constitutional hole. It may, however, be unnecessary. It is unlikely that future candidates for first and deputy first ministers will agree to be nominated without a firm agreement from their opposite number on the number of portfolios and the date of Cabinet formation.

The crisis of executive formation which dogged the implementation of the Agreement between June 1998 and November 1999 arose for political and constitutional reasons. Politically it arose shortly after the Agreement was made because David Trimble insisted that Sinn Féin deliver some IRA decommissioning before its members would take their seats in the Executive Committee: 'no government before guns' became his party's slogan. Under the text of the Agreement Trimble had no warrant to exercise this veto:

- no one party (unless it enjoys a majority within one bloc) can veto another party's membership of the executive—though the Assembly as a whole, through cross-community consent, may deem a party unfit for office (it has not done so);
- the Agreement did not require decommissioning before executive formation on the part of any paramilitaries or of any parties connected to them—though it did require parties to use their best endeavours to achieve the completion of decommissioning within two years, that is, by 22 May 2000;
- any natural reading of the Agreement mandated executive formation as the first step in bringing all the Agreement's institutions 'on line'.

Trimble rested his case on a letter he received from the UK premier on the morning of the Agreement, indicating that it was Tony Blair's view that decommissioning 'should begin straight away'. Commmunications from UK premiers do not, of course, have the force of law (outside the ranks of New Labour). But Trimble's real concern was to appease critics of the Agreement within his own party—his negotiating team split in the making of the Agreement, a majority of his party's Westminster members opposed the Agreement, and his new Assembly party contained critics of the Agreement.

Trimble was initially facilitated in exercising a tacit veto by the UK and Irish governments who were sympathetic to his exposed position, and he also took advantage of the fact that the SDLP did not make the formation of the rest of the executive a precondition of its support for the Mallon–Trimble ticket for deputy first minister and first minister. The SDLP did so because it wished to shore up Trimble's political position. One flexible provision in the Agreement gave Trimble time to stall. The Agreement stated that there must be at least six 'Other Ministers', but that there can be 'up to' ten. The number of ministries was to be decided by cross-community consent, and that gave an opportunity to delay on executive formation. It would be December 1998 before the parties reached agreement on ten ministries after the UUP abandoned its demand for a seven-seat executive in which unionists would have had an overall majority.

In mid-November 1999 it looked as if the crisis over executive formation would finally be resolved. The UUP accepted that the running of the d'Hondt procedure to fill the Cabinet could occur after the *process* of decommissioning began—with the IRA appointing an interlocutor to negotiate with the International Commission on Decommissioning— while actual decommissioning, consistent with the text of the Agreement, would not be required until after executive formation. Senator George Mitchell, in concluding his Review of the Agreement and with the consent of the pro-Agreement parties, stated that 'Devolution should take effect, then the executive should meet, and then the paramilitary groups should appoint their authorised representatives, all on the same day, in that order.' This was an honourable resolution to what looked like becoming a funda-mental impasse—though the Ulster Unionist Council fatefully rendered it problematic. To get its support its leader offered the previously cited post-dated resignation letter to become operative within a specified period that had not been negotiated under the Mitchell Review. As we all know, the IRA did not deliver, at least not in the way that Secretary of State

Mandelson believed was required; suspensory powers were obtained and used; and the Agreement remains only partially fulfilled at the time of composition. Had the Agreement been followed to the letter, the parties in the Assembly could have determined by cross-community consent that Sinn Féin and the PUP were not fit for office because they had not used their best endeavours to achieve comprehensive decommissioning. That avenue was not deployed, and the governments of the two sovereign states are presently doing their best to put Humpty-Dumpty together again. Suspension did not save David Trimble from the wrath of his party, 43 per cent of whom voted for a stalking-horse, the Reverend Martin Smyth. He remains leader of the UUP but bound by a party mandate for reformation of the executive that neither the UK government nor republicans seem likely to deliver. The 'yes unionists' have failed decisively to rout the 'no unionists', partly through mismanagement, and partly through lack of preparation of their base for the changes the Agreement required. But their failure was made even more likely by the republican position on decommissioning. Republicans seem locked in a ghetto of insecurity—determined that, at best, the decommissioning of their weapons be the last or joint last act of implementation—which merely compounds the insecurity of 'yes unionists'. The republican determination to avoid a major internal split—while accepting minor splinters in their movement— proved too much for the unionist moderates, who lived with a split in their ranks in making the Agreement but sought to repair it in its implementation. So near, and yet, right now, so far.

Conclusion

The normative political science of this analysis is, I hope, clear. Consociational and confederal devices provide the best repertoires to address largely bicommunal ethno-national disputes where a sovereign border has separated a national minority living in its homeland from its kin state, and where the descendants of a historically privileged settler colonial portion of a *Staatsvolk* cannot, or are refused permission to, control the relevant disputed territory on their own. Such devices are capable of being constructed with and without guidance from constitutional designers—though plainly diffusion of institutional repertoires through political science and law is now part of global life. Comprehensive settlements, after inclusive negotiations, which incorporate hardliners looking to come in from war or political isolation, and that address the identities, interests, and ideological agendas of all parties, are likely to produce complex, inter-linked institutional ensembles that look vulnerable. Referendums may, however, assist their legitimization and the consolidation of the pre-agreement pacts. Preferential voting in the STV mode both enables cross-ethnic vote-pooling and benefits hardliners willing to become less hardline. Double protection models offer imaginative ways to make possible changes in sovereignty less threatening, both now and later. But where any bloc is divided over the merits of such a settlement, and where its leaders respond more to the threat of being outflanked than they do to the imperative of making the new (tacit) cross-ethnic coalition work, it may prove impossible to implement the agreement. These agreements are precarious—but they are infinitely better than their alternatives—fighting to the finish, or the panaceas proposed by partisan or naive integrationists. And sometimes they work; this one is not yet definitively dead.

NOTES

* I would like to thank Chris McCrudden and John McGarry for their critical comments on this chapter. They are not responsible for its final form. I would also like to thank Shelly Deane and Simone Lewis for their research assistance.

1. The Agreement has many names (Belfast, Stormont, Good Friday) and though my preference is to call it the British–Irish Agreement I will refer simply to the Agreement, shorthand for *Agreement Reached in the Multi-Party Negotiations*, 10 Apr. 1998 (n.p.), 30. My preferred description, the British–Irish Agreement, occasions difficulty because that is the technical title of the treaty that was intended to ratify and protect the Agreement.

2. B. O'Leary, 'The Nature of the Agreement', *Fordham Journal of International Law*, 22 (1999), 1628–67; B. O'Leary, 'The Nature of the British–Irish Agreement', *New Left Review*, 233 (1999), 66–96.

3. S. Bose, 'Kashmir: Sources of Conflict, Dimensions of Peace', *Survival* 41 (1991), 149–71. Also, this would make a nice counterpoint to the export experience of the 'Westminster model'. See A. F. Madden, '"Not for Export": The Westminster Model of Government and British Colonial Practice', in N. Hillmer and P. Wigley (eds.), *The First British Commonwealth: Essays in Honour of Nicolas Mansergh* (London: Cass, 1980).

4. C. McCrudden, 'Northern Ireland and the British Constitution', in J. Jowell and D. Oliver (eds.), *The Changing Constitution* (Oxford: Clarendon Press, 1989).

5. Details of the latter can be found in B. O'Leary and J. McGarry, *The Politics of Antagonism: Understanding Northern Ireland* (London: Athlone Press, 1996), ch. 6.

6. A. Lijphart, *Democracy in Plural Societies: A Comparative Exploration* (New Haven: Yale University Press, 1977).

7. J. McGarry and B. O'Leary, *Policing Northern Ireland: Proposals for a New Start* (Belfast: Blackstaff Press, 1999).

8. C. McCrudden, 'Equality and the Good Friday Agreement', in J. Ruane and J. Todd (eds.), *After the Good Friday Agreement: Analysing Political Change in Northern Ireland* (Dublin: University College Dublin Press, 1999); C. McCrudden, 'Mainstreaming Equality in the Governance of Northern Ireland', *Fordham International Law Journal*, 22 (1999), 1696–1775; C. McCrudden, J. McGarry, and B. O'Leary, 'Equality and Social Justice: Explaining the Agreement, Part 4', *Sunday Business Post*, 10 May 1998.

9. McCrudden, 'Mainstreaming Equality in the Governance of Northern Ireland'.

10. The Assembly was prohibited from legislating in contravention of the European Convention on Human Rights, EU law, modifying a specific entrenched enactment, discriminating on grounds of religious belief or political opinion. It could not 'deal with' an excepted power except in an 'ancillary way'—which roughly meant that it might not enact laws which modify UK statutes on excepted matters (e.g. the Crown). These prohibitions reflected the Agreement's consociational character, its European context, and the fact that Northern Ireland was not becoming an independent sovereign state.

11. One material change flowed from the UK's legislative enactment of the Agreement. The Assembly was entitled to expand its autonomy but only with regard to *reserved* (not *excepted*) matters. Reserved matters, importantly, include the criminal law, criminal justice, and policing.

12. D. Elazar, *Exploring Federalism* (Tuscaloosa: University of Alabama, 1987), 7. See also pp. 63–65.

13. See the discussion in M. Lind, 'In Defence of Liberal Nationalism', *Foreign Affairs*, 73 (1994), 87–99.

14. L. Buchheit, *Secession: The Legitimacy of Self-Determination* (New Haven: Yale University Press, 1978), 16–19; A. Cassese, *The Self-Determination of Peoples: A Legal Reappraisal* (Oxford: Clarendon Press, 1995), 71 ff.

15. J. Mayall, *Nationalism and International Society* (Cambridge: Cambridge University Press, 1990), ch. 4.

16. In the Joint Declaration for Peace, a joint UK and Irish prime-ministerial statement made at Downing Street, the United Kingdom first publicly indicated its intention to make this recognition: 'They [the British government] accept that such agreement may, as of right, take the form of agreed structures for the island as a whole, including a united Ireland achieved by peaceful means on the following basis. The British Government agree that it is for the people of the island of Ireland alone, by agreement between the two parts respectively, to exercise their right of self-determination on the basis of consent, freely and concurrently given, North and South, to bring about a united

Ireland if that is their wish. They reaffirm as a binding obligation that they will, for their part, introduce the necessary legislation to give effect to this, or equally to any measure of agreement which the people living in Ireland may themselves freely so determine without external impediment'; 15 Dec. 1993. See J. McGarry and B. O'Leary, *Explaining Northern Ireland: Broken Images* (Oxford: Blackwell, 1995), app. A, 409.

17. The position of the United Kingdom's policy-makers was reinforced by the conviction that it would be very difficult to persuade the Republic to change Articles 2 and 3 of its Constitution, or that the price of doing so would be too high for the United Kingdom and unionists.

18. B. O'Leary, 'The Anglo-Irish Agreement: Statecraft or Folly?', *West European Politics*, 10 (1987), 5–32.

19. The Agreement did not mention what would happen if the United Kingdom suspended the Assembly—because the Agreement did not give this power to the Westminster Parliament.

20. The Agreement provided an annex that listed twelve possible areas for implementation. These were: agriculture (animal and plant health); education (teacher qualifications and exchanges); transport (strategic planning); environment (protection, pollution, water quality, waste management); waterways; social security–social welfare (entitlements of cross-border workers and fraud control); tourism (promotion, marketing, research and product development); EU programmes (such as SPPR, INTERREG, Leader II, and their successors); inland fisheries; aquaculture and marine matters; health (accident and emergency measures and related cross-border issues); and urban and rural development.

21. This is the collective name in Gaelic for the two chambers of the Irish Parliament, *Dáil Éireann* and *Seanad Éireann*.

22. The possibility of a unionist minister refusing to serve on the Council appeared likely given that unionist parties which opposed the Agreement, especially the DUP, were eligible for ministerial portfolios, but participation in the NSMC was made an 'essential' responsibility attaching to 'relevant' posts in the two administrations ('relevant' meant, presumably, any portfolio a part of which is subject to North–South cooperation). This left open the possibility that a politician opposed to the North–South Council might take a seat on it with a view to wrecking it. *But* ministers were required to establish the North–South institutions in 'good faith' and to use 'best endeavours' to reach agreement. Since these requirements were presumably subject to judicial review, it was unlikely that overt wreckers would be able to take part in the North–South Council for long.

23. E. Tannam, *Cross-Border Cooperation in the Republic of Ireland and Northern Ireland* (Basingstoke: Macmillan, 1999).

24. R. Hazell and B. O'Leary, 'A Rolling Programme of Devolution: Slippery Slope or Safeguard of the Union?', in R. Hazell (ed.), *Constitutional Futures: A*

History of the Next Ten Years (Oxford: Oxford University Press, 1999). The formation of an English Parliament would be the last blow.

25. B. O'Leary, 'More Green, Fewer Orange', *Fortnight*, 12–15 and 16–17 (1990); McGarry and O'Leary, *Explaining Northern Ireland*, ch. 10; B. O'Leary and G. Evans, 'Northern Ireland: La Fin de Siècle, the Twilight of the Second Protestant Ascendancy and Sinn Féin's Second Coming', *Parliamentary Affairs*, 50 (1997), 672–80.

26. *Constitution of Ireland* (Dublin: Government Stationery Office, 1937, as amended).

27. The other, less immediately important protective body, was the British–Irish Council. If Irish unification ever occurred, the Republic's government would find it politically impossible not to offer the British government and unionists reciprocal access in the same forum.

28. B. O'Leary and J. McGarry, *The Politics of Antagonism: Understanding Northern Ireland* (London: Athlone Press, 1996), chs. 6–7.

29. The Droop quota used in STV is (total vote/$N+1$) $+1$, where N = number of Assembly members to be elected.

30. A. Lijphart, 'Electoral Systems, Party Systems and Conflict Management in Divided Societies', in R. Schrire (ed.), *Critical Choices for South Africa* (Cape Town: Oxford University Press, 1990).

31. G. Evans and B. O'Leary, 'Frameworked Futures: Intransigence and Inflexibility in the Northern Ireland Elections of May 30 1996', *Irish Political Studies*, 12 (1997), 23–47; G. Evans and B. O'Leary, 'Intransigence and Flexibility on the Way to Two Forums: The Northern Ireland Elections of 30 May 1996 and Public Opinion', *Representation*, 34 (1997), 208–18.

32. My co-researcher John McGarry and I used to assume the prescriptive superiority of the party-list system. See e.g. J. McGarry and B. O'Leary (eds.), *The Future of Northern Ireland* (Oxford: Oxford University Press, 1990), 297. Facts and reflection have made me reconsider the merits of STV. See e.g. B. O'Leary, 'The Implications for Political Accommodation in Northern Ireland of Reforming the Electoral System for the Westminster Parliament', *Representation*, 35 (1999), 106–13; and B. O'Duffy and B. O'Leary, 'Tales from Elsewhere and an Hibernian Sermon', in H. Margetts and G. Smyth (eds.), *Turning Japanese? Britain with a Permanent Party of Government* (London: Lawrence & Wishart, 1995).

33. D. Horowitz, *Ethnic Groups in Conflict* (Berkeley: University of California Press, 1985), 628 ff.

34. This option was also open to anti-Agreement voters, but more unlikely for those with transitive preferences: DUP and United Kingdom Unionist Party (UKUP) voters are unlikely to give their lower-order preferences to republican Sinn Féin, should that party ever choose to stand for elections.

35. Horowitz, *Ethnic Groups in Conflict*; D. Horowitz, 'Ethnic Conflict Management for Policymakers', in J. V. Montville (ed.), *Conflict and*

Peacemaking in Multiethnic Societies (Lexington, Mass.: Heath, 1989), 115; D. Horowitz, 'Making Moderation Pay: The Comparative Politics of Ethnic Conflict Management', in Montville (ed.), *Conflict and Peacemaking in Multiethnic Societies*; D. Horowitz, *A Democratic South Africa? Constitutional Engineering in a Divided Society* (Berkeley: University of California Press, 1991).

36. Personal conversations with Donald Horowitz during his period as a STICERD distinguished visiting professor at the London School of Economics, 1998–9.

37. No electoral system can guarantee certainty of outcomes, and in a sense it would be undemocratic if it could. The predictability of an electoral system's operation which I commend here is that which gives voters and party leaders reasonable cues as to how they should cast their ballots and conduct their campaigns in accordance with their preferences.

38. It may be that AV's presumptively moderating effects would materialize better in multi-ethnic political systems with no actual or potentially dominant group and many heterogeneous and polyethnic constituencies—a situation that does not describe Northern Ireland.

39. STV has been used in local government elections in Northern Ireland since 1973, and in the European parliamentary elections since 1979. Interestingly, the hardline unionist Ian Paisley has been most successful in the three-member district used to elect Northern Ireland's MEPs; in the more proportional five- or six-member local government constituencies the DUP has not fared as well.

40. R. Sinnott, 'Centrist Politics Makes Modest but Significant Progress: Cross-Community Transfers were Low', *Irish Times*, 29 June 1998.

41. G. Evans and B. O'Leary, 'Northern Irish Voters and the British–Irish Agreement: Foundations of a Stable Consociational Settlement?', *Political Quarterly*, 71 (2000), 78–101.

42. Ibid.

43. M. Gallagher, 'Does Ireland Need a New Electoral System?', *Irish Political Studies*, 2 (1987), 27–48.

44. In current work with others I am examining the other novel dimension of the executive designed in the Agreement—the d'Hondt procedure for the allocation of ministerial portfolios.

45. A Foreign Office official recounted to me how this fact had to be patiently explained to all British embassies and consulates who were inclined to take the titles of first and deputy more seriously than they should have: confidential discussion, London, Feb. 2000.

46. The Northern Ireland Act (1998) enabled the top two ministers to hold functional portfolios, Clause 15(10).

47. O'Leary, 'The Implications for Political Accommodation in Northern Ireland of Reforming the Electoral System for the Westminster Parliament'; O'Leary, 'The Nature of the Agreement'.

48. That was temporarily changed: in the course of the crisis over executive for-
    mation in the summer of 1999 the secretary of state introduced a new rule
    requiring that a well-formed executive consist of at least three designated
    nationalists and three designated unionists. On 15 July 1999, in a handwritten
    note to the initial presiding officer, the secretary of state introduced an addi-
    tional standing order to the running of d'Hondt, namely 'On the completion
    of the procedure for the appointment of Ministers (designate) under this
    Standing Order, the persons appointed shall only continue to hold Ministerial
    office (designate) if they include at least three designated Nationalists and
    three designated Unionists.' This order, authorized under the Northern
    Ireland (Elections) Act 1998, in my view was a breach of the letter of the
    Agreement by the UK government. Given that the parties had agreed that the
    executive should consist of ten ministers (in addition to the first and deputy
    first ministers) the standing order, in effect, gave power of veto to both the
    UUP and the SDLP over executive formation (because each party was entitled
    to three positions on the basis of its strength in seats). The standing order was
    introduced in a hurry to stop executive formation leading *either* to an all-
    nationalist executive as actually transpired—given the decision of the UUP to
    fail to turn up to the Assembly when the process of executive formation was
    triggered, and the decision of the 'no unionists' not to take their designated
    ministerial entitlements—*or* to an executive in which there would have been
    no pro-Agreement unionists (see the *Official Report of the New Northern
    Ireland Assembly*, Belfast, 15 July 1999, 317–37). This panic measure, intro-
    duced for high-minded motives, subtly changed the executive incentive struc-
    tures agreed by the SDLP and the UUP in the negotiation of the Agreement.
    The standing order was rigidly consociational, but it was not negotiated by the
    parties, was not endorsed in the referendums, and encouraged moderates to
    over-bargain, knowing that they could veto executive formation. Insecure
    moderates as well as hardliners can be troublesome agents. My perspective
    here may be at odds with that of Donald Horowitz (personal conversations).
49. See statement by the Deputy First Minister (Designate), *Official Report of the
    Northern Ireland Assembly, Belfast*, 15 July 1999, 325.
50. 'Members will recall that the First Minister (Designate) and the Deputy First
    Minister (Designate) were elected, and I use the common parlance, "on a
    slate", when we were in a post-devolution situation. That means that under
    the Northern Ireland Act, both positions would fall when one resigned, but
    the remaining individual would remain in a caretaker capacity for up to six
    weeks. Before the end of that period the Presiding Officer would call for a fur-
    ther election. However, we are still functioning under the Northern Ireland
    (Elections) Act for these purposes and, therefore, the position of the First
    Minister (Designate), as I understand it—and you have simply asked me for
    an immediate view—is unchanged. It is possible that some Standing order, or
    other arrangement, may already be on the way, but I have no knowledge of it.'

Official Report of the New Northern Ireland Assembly, Belfast, 15 July 1999, 326–7.

51. 'The purpose is to ensure confidence across the community . . . so that people know that their parties will, if they receive a sufficient mandate in the election, have the opportunity for their Members to become Ministers and play their part in the Executive Committee'. House of Commons, Official Report, vol. 319, 18 Nov. 1998, col. 1023.

4

The Northern Ireland Agreement: Clear Consociational, and Risky

DONALD L. HOROWITZ*

The Agreement consummated in Belfast on Good Friday of 1998 is extraordinary in three respects. It is mainly consociational, it is coherent, and it is maximal in its commitments. Few constitutional plans that emerge from a lengthy process of negotiation exhibit such clear and single-minded direction.

The Agreement is consociational, in that it contemplates a grand coalition, an executive constituted by proportional representation, government on the basis of inter-group consensus rather than majority rule, and a certain degree of group autonomy.[1] Consociational agreements are very rare in severely divided societies. They are preferred by minorities because they provide guarantees against majority rule, but opposed by majorities for the same reason. It requires some special conditions to overcome these typically divergent preferences. Even when these obstacles have been overcome, the divergent interests of majorities and minorities may reassert themselves later, thus rendering such agreements vulnerable to being undone, as the consociational Cyprus Constitution of 1960 was overthrown by the Greek side within a year. All the more reason to see the Belfast Agreement as exceptional.

The Agreement also has a large measure of coherence. With a couple of exceptions, it is not merely consociational but consistently so. The exceptions relate to the electoral system and the requirement of Stormont legislators to identify themselves as unionist, nationalist, or 'other'.[2]

To achieve proportional representation of groups in parliament, consociational theory generally advocates adoption of list system proportional representation.[3] The negotiators, however, chose the single transferable vote (STV),[4] a preferential system that can impair group proportionality by permitting the election of legislators on the basis of second or subsequent preferences.

The negotiators also embraced a provision for weighted majorities—a guarantee that legislation affecting group interests would not pass unless it commanded the assent of a majority of all legislators plus majorities of unionist legislators and of nationalist legislators or 60 per cent of all legislators plus 40 per cent of legislators of each group.[5] By requiring members of the Assembly to designate their affiliations, the Agreement goes beyond what advocates of consociationalism generally recommend.[6] The requirement disadvantages those legislators who do not identify themselves by group affiliation and thus do not qualify for inclusion among those whose support is needed to form part of a weighted majority.

These exceptions notwithstanding, the Agreement contains strongly interlocking consociational provisions regarding the inclusion in government of all parties with significant support, the constitution of the executive and chairs of legislative committees, respect for group cultures and affiliations, and rejection of majority decision-making. The coherence of the Agreement is unusual, especially in view of the multiplicity of participants in the meetings that produced it. A process of negotiation could be expected, in the ordinary course of events, to produce bargaining over provisions to be included. The exchange of incommensurables might, if successful, give rise to an agreement based on a number of different principles reflecting the varying preferences of parties to the negotiations, principles accepted in part in return for the acceptance of other principles. In Fiji, for instance, the search for an accommodative constitution in a deeply divided society led to a mélange of provisions, some based on consociational principles, some based on the creation of electoral incentives to inter-ethnic conciliation (using a preferential system called the alternative vote), and some based on purely majoritarian principles.[7] The far more internally consistent arrangements agreed in Belfast require explanation.

The clear and maximal commitments of the Agreement are also unusual. The Good Friday Agreement is surely a constitution. At moments of constitutional decision, political decision-makers in most severely divided societies resort to purposeful ambiguity with respect to the most serious problems that divide them. They do this for three reasons. First, they do not wish to create enduring and festering sources of dissatisfaction by purporting to resolve issues in a clear and decisive way, so that shortfalls in delivery will soon be visible. Secondly, agreement on the constitution is not the end of the struggle for advantage, and a victory that cannot be won today but may be won tomorrow can be accommodated by an ambiguous formulation that suits all sides. Thirdly, if the process by which they create their constitution is based on negotiation between leaders of the respective groups, the bargaining in which they engage involves splitting the difference or the exchange of incommensurables. The Malaysian constitutional negotiations of 1956 exemplify the sort of ambiguity that emerges from this process. The Malays were recognized as entitled to a 'special position' as the indigenous people, but Chinese and Indians were entitled to have their 'legitimate interests' respected.[8] Similarly ambiguous formulations were shaped regarding divisive linguistic, religious, and educational issues. The Northern Ireland Agreement, by contrast, is a model of clarity.

The Agreement commits the parties to 'parity of esteem' for the two traditions, to proportional inclusion of Catholics and Protestants in public bodies, and to self-determination for the people of Northern Ireland as they decide (by repeated iterations of Ernest Renan's daily plebiscites on national allegiance[9]) whether to remain in the United Kingdom or to join the Irish Republic.[10] So scrupulous and transparent is the Agreement about respecting the national conscience of the two peoples whom it takes to constitute Northern Irish society that it exempts legislators from any declaration of loyalty to the current sovereign as a condition of political office. It requires merely an oath to discharge one's office faithfully.[11] Rarely, if ever, has a constitutional document been so explicit about the conditional character of sovereignty and national allegiance, even when—indeed, particularly when—these were issues central to groups in conflict. Here, too, the exceptionalism of the Agreement stands out.

If the Good Friday Agreement is conspicuous in the clarity of its pluralistic commitments, nowhere is that more true than in the provisions for inclusion of all parties in the executive on a proportional basis. In practice, this implies an unequivocal commitment to include Sinn Féin in government, as its share of seats was anticipated (correctly, as the 1998 elections showed) to qualify it for inclusion in the Cabinet. The spectrum of those entitled to be included in government by virtue of the Agreement thus runs the gamut from those who deny the legitimacy of the regime whose offices they will inhabit—and whose denial was so explicit during the negotiations that they failed to advance serious proposals for any Stormont government—to those for whom it is regarded as an act of treachery to sit with them. This is consociationalism to the maximum degree.

After an agreement is consummated, its contours often begin quickly to seem natural, even foreordained. Alternative possibilities appear increasingly remote. Obstacles that stood in the way are regarded as less important than they may have been. Yet the exceptionalism of the Northern Ireland Agreement—its consociational character, its coherence, and its unequivocal, maximal commitments—is palpable. The entitlements it creates and the issues it purports to resolve at a stroke are the very things that ethnic groups in severely divided societies struggle over: who is to be included in government and on what terms, to what extent and in what directions will group claims be acknowledged officially, in what spheres will groups be entitled to proportional representation, which group's symbols and attachments will be recognized as legitimate. To each of these keenly contested questions, the Good Friday Agreement provides a straightforward answer.

The Agreement raises several insistent questions: What alternatives to consociation might have been available to the negotiators? How was the Agreement consummated? What are the likely consequences for the politics of ethnic conflict of an agreement with the contours of the Belfast Agreement? The remainder of this essay takes these questions up in order, giving shorter shrift to some than to others.

Approaches to Inter-Group Conciliation

The consociational approach is a widely advocated but rarely adopted approach to reducing inter-ethnic conflict. Another approach, increasingly recommended but also only rarely adopted, is not based on any requirement that all parties to a conflict be included in government or that group guarantees be provided in advance. Instead, it rests on the provision of incentives for inter-group accommodation.[12]

Where the incentive approach is pursued, political parties and leaders who pursue conciliation are rewarded. The main mechanism is an electoral system that induces political parties to rely for their margin of victory on the votes of members of groups other than their own. Such incremental votes will not be forthcoming unless the party seeking them takes moderate positions on matters of inter-group conflict and then behaves moderately while in office, lest it risk losing the support of such marginal voters at the next election. Parties are still ethnically based; but, if the incentives to seek votes across group lines are strong enough, multi-ethnic coalitions of moderate parties of the respective groups may form to exchange the votes of their supporters in various constituencies. If ethnically based party A cannot win a seat in a constituency on the votes of members of group A alone, but needs votes from group B to prevail, it may align itself with party B to secure those votes. In a different constituency, party B may need votes of members of group A to win the seat. This mutually beneficial exchange may form the basis of a pre-electoral coalition of parties moderate enough to secure marginal votes across group lines and able to compromise while in office. The compromising middle coalition then acts to fend off the uncompromising parties on its flanks. The compromises induced in this way form the basis of inter-group accommodation, but without the inclusion of all parties in government. Rather, parties of the moderate middle, which find the exchange of votes easier to accomplish, are likely to form a government.

This approach stands in contrast to the consociational approach, which is based on complete inclusion of all segments of all groups (for groups are assumed to be solidary rather than divided),[13] on rejection of majoritarian principles, and on provision of extensive guarantees. The incentives approach assumes that the compromising inter-ethnic middle will be opposed on the ethnic flanks but that, if it follows the incentives skilfully, it will continue to hold a parliamentary majority. Seeking votes from more than one group, the compromisers typically guarantee little at the outset but produce accommodative policies as they go along. They understand that the conflicting claims of the respective groups cannot be put to rest in a single blow, and they recognize that the compromises are not fully satisfying for the groups in conflict. The claims of groups in conflict tend, after all, to be incompatible. Ethnically based flank parties survive by espousing mutually exclusive group claims and opposing the attempts of the middle to provide partial satisfactions to all sides.

Some multi-ethnic states have stumbled across apt institutions to encourage inter-ethnic moderation of this kind, and a few have begun to explore more deliberate measures to build in incentives to accommodation. Often these measures are embodied in the electoral system chosen to induce parties to behave moderately or risk defeat. For national executive offices, territorial distribution of votes may be required, so that victorious candidates need the largest number of votes plus a stated minimum percentage in various localities or regions. If the various groups are unevenly distributed across the territory, a distribution formula may make it impossible for candidates to win the election on the votes of their group alone. The alternative vote, a preferential electoral system that requires a majority, rather than a mere plurality, for election, may have the same effect.[14] If, in a heterogeneous constituency, a candidate cannot reach the 50 per cent-plus-one threshold on the first-preference votes of his or her own group, it becomes necessary to appeal for second and subsequent preferences across ethnic lines. Whatever the precise method, the result of vote transfers across group lines is to induce politicians to behave moderately on ethnic issues and, if moderation becomes rewarding, to produce a pre-electoral coalition of moderates.

Consociational theory, by contrast, assumes that parties reach government on the votes of members of their own ethnic group alone. It does not contemplate pre-electoral coalitions across group lines or assume that the need for inter-group vote transfers is an engine of moderation and compromise. Rather, it relies on statesmanship to produce compromise after elections, and indeed it mandates a compulsory post-election grand coalition as a central feature of a consociational regime. In this way, the consociational approach sacrifices majoritarian principles—government and opposition—whereas the incentives approach aims at a governing multi-ethnic coalition and an opposition consisting of ethnically based parties. The incentives approach is consistent with majoritarian principles, but it aims to prevent majorities and minorities from breaking perfectly along ethnic lines and thereby to prevent ethnic majorities from dominating minorities.

Both consociational and incentive-based institutions are difficult to adopt. Those countries that most need conflict-reducing institutions are precisely the ones that are least likely to adopt them. Politicians who benefit from the pursuit of ethnic claims have no reason to transform the conflict-prone environment in which they thrive. Majorities are especially unwilling to adopt institutions that require them to share power with minorities. It is not surprising, then, that conflict-reducing measures are often adopted when outsiders have an important part to play in deliberations on new institutions. The Dayton Accord set up a strongly consociational regime for Bosnia, at the behest of the United States, and incentive-based institutions were recommended by a Fiji Constitution Review Commission chaired by a New Zealander.[15]

Both approaches have their supporters. Consociational guarantees are particularly attractive to minorities and therefore unattractive to majorities. There has been a recent growth of interest in incentive-based approaches,[16] but the fact that they do not meet the desire of minorities for protection that is guaranteed makes their adoption problematic. This is one reason why Northern Ireland went in a consociational direction, despite the fact that certain conditions—especially the ability to create heterogeneous constituencies and a differentiation of parties into those of moderate and those of more extreme disposition—might provide an excellent foundation for incentive-based institutions. After all, half of the eighteen Assembly constituencies consist of at least 30 per cent Catholic and 30 per cent Protestant voters; and, of these, two consist of at least 40 per cent Catholic and 40 per cent Protestant voters. There was some suggestion before the election that 'pro-Agreement parties'—mainly the Social

Democratic and Labour Party (SDLP) and the Ulster Unionist Party (UUP)—might exchange preferences under the STV system that was adopted. An alternative vote system might actually have made such exchanges more exigent and rewarding. But guarantees were more attractive. These are themes I shall return to at a later point.

Learning from Experience

In 1976 a political scientist with much experience of Northern Ireland declared that the unique feature of the Northern Ireland conflict was that it had no solution.[17] Many others, inside and outside Northern Ireland, have long been pessimistic about making progress on the conflict, much less executing a far-reaching agreement designed to put much of the conflict, and certainly its violent features, to rest. Similar pessimism is frequently expressed about apparently intractable ethnic conflicts elsewhere. The Northern Ireland Agreement confounds pessimism, especially of the sort that consigns ethnic antagonists to the desserts justly earned by those who cannot forget the past, people who are thought to be prisoners of ancient enmities whose causes are shrouded in the mists of time.[18]

In confounding clichés like these, the Agreement—any agreement—is an altogether good thing. Severely divided societies have intractable problems, compounded by the frequently zero-sum quality of the claims and by an array of grievances, passions, and prejudices. But this does not mean that progress on such problems is impossible.

The Agreement goes further, however. It also falsifies the predictions of those who think that occasions for comprehensive settlements of issues of inter-group conflict are rare and that there was little in the situation of Northern Ireland in 1998 to produce a ripe moment for a sweeping agreement. Moreover, the framers of the Agreement overcame the obstacles inherent in a process of negotiation, in which the asymmetrical preferences of majorities and minorities, expressed in the course of bargaining, could be fulfilled only by an exchange likely to produce a mixed package of provisions, perhaps along the lines previously described for Fiji.

Explaining the consummation of the Northern Ireland Agreement in the face of the obstacles posed by a negotiation format is a formidable task. The parties did overcome the obstacles, and in this sense the Agreement is a remarkable feat. In a separate study, I have undertaken to provide a more comprehensive explanation for the Agreement,[19] and I shall not reiterate the details here. Suffice it to say that consummation of the Agreement was facilitated by three conditions: the declining majority of unionists, the conversion of the negotiating process into a forum with some special characteristics, and the previous experience Northern Ireland had had with attempts to settle the conflict.

Protestants are still a majority in Northern Ireland and will be for a considerable time to come, although their relative numbers are declining due, among other things, to emigration. (The majority of Ulster Protestants who study in England are thought not to return.[20]) Differential rates of voter turnout and the support some Protestants give to multi-ethnic parties such as the Alliance Party and the Women's Coalition reduce the potential unionist share of the vote further. In the 1998 elections to the Assembly that followed the referendum ratifying the Agreement, unionist parties secured just half of the total vote. Unionists have begun to see themselves, as nationalists have long seen themselves, as a minority in need of protection.

Only one other feature of the explanatory schema requires mention here: the part played by Northern Ireland's previous experience with conciliatory proposals. The last experience Northern Ireland had had with a devolved parliamentary regime was the power-sharing government of 1973–4, constituted pursuant to the Sunningdale Agreement of December 1973. Sunningdale envisioned a power-sharing coalition of moderate unionists, moderate nationalists, and the inter-ethnic Alliance Party. The chief minister, Brian Faulkner, was the leader of what was then the Official Unionist Party, and his deputy was the leader of the SDLP, Gerry Fitt. On each flank there was bitter opposition to the coalition. Even before the government was formed, Faulkner was able to carry only a bare majority in favour of it in his party's council. Many unionists had opposed admission of nationalists to government altogether, and Sinn Féin regarded it as inadmissible for nationalists to sit in any Northern Ireland government at all. Under the weight of these attacks and a variety of contentious constitutional issues, especially the North–South Council that was ultimately to give the Irish Republic a role in Northern affairs, the government did very poorly in the UK parliamentary elections of February 1974, losing eleven of the twelve Northern Ireland seats at Westminster to anti-Sunningdale candidates. By May, its majority faltering, especially on the unionist side, the government fell.

Following the failure of Sunningdale, unionists, nationalists, and the governments of the United Kingdom and the Irish Republic attempted periodically to agree upon the contours of a new constitutional dispensation for Northern Ireland. Recollections of the failure of the 1973–4 regime were never far from the surface. Over time, the SDLP leadership became convinced that two elements would be required for a durable settlement. The first was an external or Irish Republic dimension, which had already featured in the Council of Ireland agreed at Sunningdale. The second was the incorporation of Sinn Féin in negotiations and in the regime that was to emerge from the negotiations. Since my concern is the internal arrangements (Strand One of the Agreement), I shall not dwell on the reasons for or shape of the North–South and East–West arrangements contained in Strands Two and Three, respectively, but concentrate instead on Strand One.

SDLP leader John Hume and his colleagues had begun talks with Sinn Féin in 1988; these accelerated in the 1990s. The SDLP leaders became convinced that Sinn Féin was serious about a constitutional approach to Northern Ireland's problems. If this were true, it might be possible to wean the Irish Republican Army (IRA) from its violent approach.

More pertinent for present purposes were the lessons the SDLP took from the failure of the power-sharing government in 1974. A Sunningdale-style government of the moderate middle, comprising only those parties inclined to compromise, was, SDLP leaders believed, inadequate to create political stability in Northern Ireland. With Sinn Féin on the outside, there would be continued violence and a party disposed to make compromise difficult by accusing the SDLP of surrendering the interests of the nationalist community in the North. Furthermore, the SDLP minority at Stormont would face the unionist majority alone. It would be preferable if its position could be augmented by a more even distribution of Protestant and Catholic legislators. By the time of the Brooke–Mayhew talks of 1991–2 the SDLP had set its face decisively against any dispensation that did not include Sinn Féin (and, by implication, loyalist parties connected to Protestant paramilitaries as well). The SDLP also wanted a regime based on guarantees of decision-making authority for the two communities, rather than majoritarian processes.

Partly because the SDLP would not assent to proceeding on any other basis, the British and Irish governments, having themselves met with Sinn Féin, increasingly framed their proposals on the basis of an aspiration to include everyone. Gradually and fitfully, the proposals advanced by the two governments also presupposed an inclusive regime and a set of guarantees surrounding political decision-making that amounted to consociationalism. The Framework Document of 1995 proposed an executive panel of three members (which, by predictable electoral strength, would have two Protestant members and one Catholic member). Each member would have a veto.[21] (This proposal was a revised version of one submitted by the SDLP at the Brooke–Mayhew talks earlier in the decade.) Committee chairs would be appointed by proportional representation of all parties, rather than constituted by the majority. In the 1998 Agreement, the panel mutated into a jointly elected, two-person chief executive, and proportional appointment of committee chairs was expanded into proportional selection of Cabinet ministers as well.

The SDLP's bitter experience with majoritarian Stormont parliaments, and then with the less than fully inclusive power-sharing government of 1973–4, led the SDLP leadership to conclude that only a thoroughly inclusive regime, replete with consociational guarantees, could succeed. By the 1990s there was a sense among SDLP leaders and, to some extent, among others as well that everything else had been tried and failed. Proposals that were advanced in the 1990s increasingly reflected such views, which account, in considerable measure, for the final, consociational shape of the 1998 Agreement.

Power-Sharing, Centre Version

There is some ground to think that the SDLP diagnosis of the failure of 1973–4 was misconceived. To be sure, the Sunningdale experiment was a government of the middle, and it proved to be insufficiently strong to withstand the pressures that it faced. But neither the absence of the extremes in government nor the absence of consociational guarantees was responsible for the fall of the power-sharing government of 1974. Rather, it was the accumulation of a series of formidable constitutional issues that were put on the Faulkner government's plate in 1974 and the division among unionists that led to that government's downfall. Neither causal condition would have been altered by an inclusive, consociational regime.

I said earlier that governments that attempt to bridge ethnic differences typically find ambiguous, compromise formulas to deal with the many contentious, fundamental ethnic issues they face. They also try not to face these issues all at once. The Faulkner power-sharing government had not been afforded this luxury. In December 1973, the Irish and British governments stated that a majority of the people of Northern Ireland, but only such a majority, could effect a change in the status of Northern Ireland— that is, could choose for Northern Ireland to accede (or not) to the Irish Republic. At the same time, it was agreed that a Council of Ireland would be set up at an unspecified future date and that it would have the power to take 'executive decisions' of an unspecified sort. Unionists who were fearful of a united Ireland were supposed to be mollified by the majority consent language of both governments. Instead, their fears were enhanced by the intention to set up the Council of Ireland and, within a couple of weeks thereafter, by the decision of an Irish court that Dublin's declaration of the requirement of majority consent for a change in status was a mere 'statement of policy' rather than a durable constitutional commitment. The power-sharing experiment, opposed by many unionists to begin with, was made more difficult by the simultaneous intrusion of major ethno-constitutional issues regarding self-determination and the future role of the Irish Republic in Northern Ireland affairs.

The combination of these issues and a unionism divided about power-sharing overwhelmed the government in 1974. The fact that the 1973–4 government was merely a coalition of the middle and thus insufficiently inclusive was not the source of its disintegration. Had that government been more inclusive, it might actually have fallen sooner. Consociational guarantees would not have saved it. Given divisions among unionists, the Faulkner government was vulnerable to accusations that it made excessive concessions on the issues it faced.

The one thing that might have shored up the power-sharing regime would have been a different electoral system. The Stormont Assembly of 1973 was elected on the basis of the STV, which opens the possibility that candidates who do not receive enough first-preference votes to meet the quota (or threshold) required to win a seat may meet the quota on the basis of second or subsequent votes transferred from those whose first-preference candidates have already met their quota. Such transfers could come from supporters of parties representing the same ethnic group or a different group. Inter-ethnic vote transfers would ordinarily go only to candidates who were moderate on ethnic issues. But, although it is a preferential system, STV is unlike alternative voting, which requires a majority threshold for victory, a requirement that can induce parties to look across group lines for the majority necessary to win a constituency. STV in multi-member constituencies makes it relatively easy for a candidate to reach the threshold of victory on first preferences. To win a seat in a five-member constituency, for instance, the quota is only 16.67 per cent of the total vote. Consequently, candidates of large parties often do not need to rely on vote transfers; and, if they do, they may still reach the quota on the basis of transfers from those voters of their own ethnic group whose first preferences have gone to a different ethnically based party of the same group. In the 1973 Northern Ireland elections, an insignificant number of voters transferred votes to candidates across group lines.[22]

Had there been in place in 1973 an electoral system that created more powerful incentives for moderate parties to transfer votes of their supporters to moderate candidates of other groups, the parties of the middle might have had a stronger electoral foundation and a more secure parliamentary majority. Although the government of 1973–4 was intended as a coalition of the three moderate parties, the electoral system did not make it particularly rewarding for those parties to cooperate before, rather than after, the election.

Ironically enough, the 1973 STV electoral system was carried forward into the 1998 Agreement. Some small parties might have done better under a list-proportional representation electoral system, had one been adopted in 1998, but STV had considerable support from nearly all parties. No one at the negotiations argued for a different electoral system, designed to promote inter-group political cooperation in the electoral process. STV was the strongly preferred system. The only serious question debated in 1998 was the size of the multi-member STV constituencies.

As in 1973, there were few vote transfers across group lines in the 1998 Assembly election. The vast majority of seats (ninety out of 108) were won on first preferences alone. Those candidates who did not win on first preferences generally won on preferences transferred from voters of their own ethnic group, not from transfers across group lines.[23]

An alternative version of the lessons of 1973–4 might, then, attribute the failure of the power-sharing government to an overload of fundamental issues at the outset, a unionism that was deeply divided on the basic issue of power-sharing, and an electoral system that did nothing to support parties willing to compromise as against those who staked their position on opposition to power-sharing. STV was a system perfectly compatible with the maintenance of ethnically based parties and not particularly suppotive of multi-ethnic coalitions. That is as true today as it was in 1973–4.

Ironies of the New Dispensation

While the received lessons of 1973–4 may not have been accurate, they certainly were powerfully felt. They justified a bold new departure, an inclusive regime studded with consociational guarantees and maximal commitments. Ironically enough, those who acceded to the Agreement, setting their face against a government of the moderate middle, did so at a time when conditions for a government of the moderate middle had become much more favourable than they had been a quarter of a century earlier.

Northern Ireland society had never been more ready for compromise on the issues that divide Protestants and Catholics than it was in 1998. There had been a softening of the lines of conflict. Surveys show that significant fractions of both groups are interested in living together, rather than apart, that they see members of the other group as ordinary people like themselves, rather than as demons with whom it is impossible to make peace.[24] Rates of intermarriage have increased in the territory as a whole, and especially in Belfast. Perhaps most remarkably, in a 1996 sample survey half the population refused to agree that it was 'in sympathy' with 'unionism' or 'nationalism'.[25] Only 28 and 17 per cent of the sample, respectively, indicated that it was in sympathy with either of the movements. To be sure, most people still vote by group affiliation, but it is likely that much of this ethnic voting is based on a version of prisoner's dilemma, a fear of being alone in defecting while the other side chooses not to defect. Quite clearly, in terms of attitude, Northern Ireland now has a moderate centre. Under these conditions, a successful centre government would likely be able to make inroads into the support of the parties on the ethnic flanks.

Furthermore, considerable progress has been made on the specific ethnic problems of the previous generation. Most notable among these is the problem of employment discrimination against Catholics. This issue is barely raised any longer as a collective grievance. Violence and intimidation are also both in decline. Northern Ireland has not had a face-to-face ethnic riot since 1969, and paramilitaries have been obliged to avoid civilian targets and to justify the targets that they choose, on pain of losing supporters in their own community. These are all signs of a softening conflict.

The irony is that the participants in the Belfast negotiations had set their face against a government of the moderate middle at the very moment the moderate middle had grown strong. The participants embraced the extremes when the public was repelled by the violence of the extremes.

Stretching the Spectrum

In 1998, as in 1973–4, unionism was badly divided, but Ian Paisley's Democratic Unionist Party (DUP) was not opposed in 1998, as its predecessors were in 1973–4, to sharing power with the constitutional nationalists of the SDLP. What the DUP, some members of other small unionist parties, and some members of the UUP opposed was inclusion of Sinn Féin. Had a government of the moderate middle been agreed at Belfast on Good Friday, the UUP could easily have delivered substantial majority support among Protestants. By contrast, the agreement that was reached perpetuated the appeal of rejectionist unionism. (Of course, an agreement of the middle would have left Sinn Féin outside and threatened the SDLP with the same kind of attacks to which the 1998 Agreement exposed the UUP.) Where divisions of this kind exist, those who are actively engaged in inter-group compromise must always be concerned that the concessions they make will be attacked by political competitors within their own group and that these attacks will erode their majority standing within their group.

The crisis of 1999, which concerned the decommissioning of weapons by the IRA and prevented the immediate formation of a government, was a product of these divisions among unionists. With pro- and anti-Agreement unionists divided 29–29 in the Assembly at Stormont, the admission of Sinn Féin to the Cabinet was a very risky course for the UUP leadership.

During the negotiations, UUP leaders had expressed their preference for committee rather than cabinet government and had yielded on the issue only at the end of the negotiations. In a committee system, with committee chairs allocated proportionately, any party with a significant share of seats could chair a committee, but those who held committee chairs would not need to be regarded as partners in government. Without a Cabinet, there would be no government as such, and the UUP could not be accused of sitting in the executive with Sinn Féin partners. Periodically during the negotiations, too, UUP leader David Trimble had expressed reservations about the design for a wholly inclusive regime that was being pressed on him. Presumably, the UUP leadership was drawing its own lessons from 1973–4, and it feared being outflanked, as Brian Faulkner, the leader of the power-sharing government, had been. In the end Trimble agreed to a completely inclusive dispensation, but members of his own party threatened to form a new party if the UUP entered a Cabinet with Sinn Féin without the prior decommissioning of IRA weapons.[26]

The two parties that made the greatest concessions at Belfast in 1998 were Sinn Féin, which had earlier vowed not to sit in an internal Northern Ireland Parliament but nevertheless accepted Strand One, and the UUP. But the positioning of these two parties means that the concessions they made were not symmetrical. Sinn Féin is not a middle party in danger of being accused of a sell-out and being outflanked. On the Catholic side, that position is occupied by the SDLP. The UUP, however, is very much in that position. Threatened as they are by the DUP, UUP politicians must be wary of the concessions they make, lest they become members of a minority party among Protestants. Hence the arms decommissioning compromises of 1999 and 2000 that saved the Agreement, at least temporarily.

Maximal concessions of the sort agreed on Good Friday are best made by parties that possess a monopoly of support in their own group. To be sure, the concessions themselves are likely to generate new intra-ethnic opposition, as such concessions have in Malaysia, Sri Lanka, and other severely divided societies. But the prospect for implementing such concessions is much better when those who make them enjoy a monopoly position at the outset.[27] The prospect is also better if the conceding party can compensate for losses of support on its flank by increases in votes transferred by its negotiating partner across ethnic lines. But, for reasons already stated, STV is not the best system for encouraging such exchanges.

It is possible, of course, that, for exactly the same reasons, the SDLP could not have agreed to a government of the moderate middle without enhancing Sinn Féin's position at its own expense (although a careful judgement on this would have to factor out SDLP's decade-long publicly stated commitment to including Sinn Féin). Sinn Féin's vote share has been increasing, partly at the expense of the SDLP. Younger Catholic voters are disproportionately attracted to Sinn Féin.[28] If the SDLP could not agree to a government of the middle without eroding its support, that would not necessarily mean that the UUP was in a better position to concede the issue to the SDLP. It would mean that there was, at best, a very thin and easily eroded basis for consensus. That is what the post-Agreement disruptions of 1999 reflected.[29]

The difficulties encountered in 1999 in setting up the new regime concerned only Sinn Féin's place in the executive. Since the government was not fully functioning, the difficulties did not concern the other maximal commitments that were made in the Agreement, for parity of esteem, proportional representation of groups in government bodies, complete equality across the board—the sort of issues, as I said earlier, that comprise the stuff of ongoing inter-group debate in severely divided societies. Maximal commitments of this kind, in the context of intra-ethnic flank competition, set up the parties making the commitments for a shortfall in delivery on them, as the political costs accumulate later. The weight of such a heavy agenda has not yet been felt in Northern Ireland. The benefits of reform are immediate, but the costs are cumulative.[30]

The Pitfalls of Maximalism

The consociational approach adopted in Northern Ireland raises problems of democratic theory and practice. Since it aims to incorporate in government all parties with electoral support, it raises questions about the place of government and opposition. The Good Friday Agreement envisions that Cabinet ministers will be appointed by the parties entitled to Cabinet seats, rather than by the first minister and/or deputy first minister. Whether collective responsibility for Cabinet decisions will apply under these provisions remains unclear.[31] So is the location of opposition. If most compromises are made by the middle parties, that may mean that opposition on the flanks will take place inside government rather than outside. This would be a crucial change from British and Irish constitutional conventions. The only conventional opposition, in the house itself, contemplated implicitly by these arrangements, would be provided by the small parties that are unable to meet the d'Hondt standard for a Cabinet seat: the Women's Coalition and the small loyalist parties, all of which already see themselves as forming an opposition in the Assembly, though they hold relatively few seats. There will be either a fractious Cabinet or a stunted opposition.

Since so few severely divided societies have opted for a fully consociational path, it is difficult to foresee how these issues will play out. It is certainly conceivable that the DUP and Sinn Féin, alienated by compromises devised by the UUP and SDLP, would at some point leave an inclusive government and join the opposition. If so, this would leave a government of the middle, burdened with a maximal agenda to fulfil. Each element of the agenda might furnish the opposition with more fodder. It is no accident that governments of the middle typically try to make only incremental progress on ethnic issues. Even so, such governments are fragile and vulnerable to dissolution. It is quite possible that the UUP and SDLP may come eventually to believe that less might have been more.

In so far as they try to include all parties on equal terms, consociational regimes pose serious distributive challenges. Riker's law of the minimum winning coalition[32] may not quite be a law, in the sense of an iron-clad regularity, but it does contain an important core of behavioural truth. Parties generally aim to put together support that will be victorious at a level closer to 51 per cent than to 100 per cent. If there is little distributive advantage concomitant upon victory, then the incentives to be victorious are greatly reduced. Those who design consociational constitutions rather blithely violate this law. The likely result is that, despite assurances of proportional distribution, certain parties in government will aim at disproportional distributions, thereby driving those who receive fewer rewards to the opposition, so that they may attempt to win the next election.

That is one reason why consociational governments may be frail and why, despite his best efforts, Arend Lijphart, the most dedicated proponent of consociational dispensations, was able to name only four allegedly consociational regimes in the developing world—Lebanon, Malaysia, Surinam, and the Netherlands Antilles[33]—not one of which had the grand coalition that was said to be the sine qua non of a consociational regime. Each had a coalition of parties, opposed by others, and some violated other consociational precepts as well. The creation of a multi-ethnic coalition in a severely divided society inevitably also creates ethnic opposition to the coalition's compromises. That is likely to be the case in Northern Ireland, too. The all-inclusive regime, then, may not be durable.

It is interesting to speculate more specifically on the likely consequences of compromise in Northern Ireland. In the first instance, since the UUP gave more than the SDLP did in the negotiations, the UUP will be first to feel the consequences, as other unionists make their opposition felt. But subsequent compromises may entail shortfalls in delivering on the far-reaching commitments made at Belfast in 1998. If a UUP–SDLP-led government accepts a shortfall on these, the SDLP will feel the pressure on its flank. Already the inclusion of Sinn Féin has increased Sinn Féin's legitimacy and its share of the vote significantly. In the 1998 Assembly elections, Sinn Féin received 17.63 per cent of the vote to the SDLP's 21.96 per cent. If the need for the SDLP to compromise should lead Sinn Féin into opposition, the compromises that are made would likely work to the disadvantage of the SDLP. It would be ironic in the extreme if the ultimate effect of an agreement made at a time of growing moderation of the Northern Ireland conflict were to reduce the strength of those political parties on both sides that are most inclined to compromise and increase the strength of those inclined to pursue untrammelled group interests.

NOTES

* In conducting the research that underlies this essay, I have benefited from the support of the Globalization and Democracy Program at Duke University and the Duke Center for European Studies, both of which helped fund my field research in Northern Ireland, as well as the STICERD Distinguished Visitor Programme and the Government Department of the London School of Economics, which provided a most congenial base for the research. I am particularly grateful to the United States Institute of Peace and the Harry Frank Guggenheim Foundation, under whose auspices the multi-country project on constitutional design (of which the Northern Ireland research forms a part) was conceived and funded. I benefited from the comments of John McGarry and the

able research assistanceof Ericka Albaugh and Claire Kramer at Duke and Katherine Adenay at the London School of Economics. Finally, I am pleased to record my indebtedness to Brendan O'Leary at the London School of Economics for his hospitality and for several helpful conversations on Northern Ireland. The conclusions are, however, entirely my own.

1. See B. O'Leary, 'The British–Irish Agreement: Consociation Plus', MS, London School of Economics, 13 May 1998. See generally A. Lijphart, *Democracy in Plural Societies* (New Haven: Yale University Press, 1977).
2. *Agreement Reached in the Multi-Party Negotiations* [hereafter cited as *Agreement*], 10 Apr. 1998 (n.p.), Strand One, para. 6.
3. Lijphart, *Democracy in Plural Societies*, 40, 52.
4. *Agreement*, Strand One, para. 2.
5. Ibid., para. 5(d).
6. See A. Lijphart, *Power-Sharing in South Africa* (Berkeley: University of California Institute of International Studies, 1985).
7. See Constitution (Amendment) Act 1997 of the Republic of the Fiji Islands, 25 July 1997, Articles 6(g), 50, 51, 54, 99(5). See also *Report of the Joint Parliamentary Select Committee on the Constitution*, Parliamentary Paper no. 17 (Suva: Parliament of Fiji, 1997), 17, 20.
8. See R. S. Milne, *Government and Politics in Malaysia* (Boston: Houghton Mifflin, 1967), 39–41.
9. See E. Renan, *Qu'est-ce qu'une Nation?* (Paris: Presses Pochet, 1992), 55.
10. *Agreement*, 'Constitutional Issues', para. 1(i).
11. Ibid., Strand One, Annex A.
12. For general statements, see D. L. Horowitz, *A Democratic South Africa? Constitutional Engineering in a Divided Society* (Berkeley: University of California Press, 1991), 154–60, 163–203; D. L. Horowitz, 'Ethnic Conflict Management for Policymakers' and 'Making Moderation Pay: The Comparative Politics of Ethnic Conflict Management', in J. V. Montville (ed.), *Conflict and Peacemaking in Multiethnic Societies* (Lexington, Mass.: Lexington Books, 1989); B. Reilly, 'Preferential Voting and Political Engineering: A Comparative Study', *Journal of Commonwealth and Comparative Politics*, 35/1 (Mar. 1997), 1–19. For the incentive argument in the Northern Ireland context, see D. L. Horowitz, 'Conflict and the Incentives to Political Accommodation', in D. Keogh and M. H. Haltzell (eds.), *Northern Ireland and the Politics of Reconciliation* (Cambridge: Cambridge University Press, 1993).
13. Lijphart's conceptions assume a 'coalition of the segments', Lijphart, *Democracy in Plural Societies*, 201, 205. He writes: 'The primary characteristic of consociational democracy is that the political leaders of all significant segments of the plural society cooperate in a grand coalition to govern the country' Ibid., 25.
14. See Reilly, 'Preferential Voting and Political Engineering'.

15. See *The General Framework Agreement for Peace in Bosnia and Herzegovina*, 21 Nov. 1995, Articles 1, 4, Annex 3; *Towards a United Future: Report of the Fiji Constitution Review Commission*, Parliamentary Paper no. 34 (Suva: Parliament of Fiji, 1996).

16. See e.g. Reilly, 'Preferential Voting and Political Engineering'; International Crisis Group (ICG), 'Changing the Logic of Bosnian Politics: Discussion Paper on Electoral Reform', 10 Mar. 1998; ICG, 'Breaking the Mould: Electoral Reform in Bosnia and Herzegovina', 4 Mar. 1999. Both ICG reports are located at *http://www.intl-crisis-group.org*

17. R. Rose, *Northern Ireland: Time of Choice* (Washington, DC: American Enterprise Institute for Public Policy Research, 1976), 139.

18. In the interest of clarity, I should state this is certainly not my view of the Northern Ireland conflict, or most others for that matter, but it is only a slight caricature of the views of some journalists and politicians.

19. D. L. Horowitz, 'Explaining the Northern Ireland Agreement: The Sources of an Unlikely Constitutional Consensus', MS, Aug. 1999.

20. P. Compton, 'Catholic/Non-Catholic Demographic Differentials in Northern Ireland', in W. Haug, Y. Courbage, and P. Compton (eds.), *The Demographic Characteristics of National Minorities in Certain European States* (Strasbourg: Council of Europe, 1998), 104.

21. See B. O'Leary, 'What is Framed in the Framework Documents?', *Ethnic and Racial Studies*, 18/4 (Oct. 1995), 862–72.

22. See Rose, *Northern Ireland: Time of Choice*, 78, 93.

23. B. O'Leary, 'The Nature of the British–Irish Agreement', *New Left Review*, 233 (Jan.–Feb. 1999), 66–96.

24. See J. Darby, *Northern Ireland: Managing Difference* (London: Minority Rights Group, 1995), 15, 25; K. Heskin, *Northern Ireland: A Psychological Analysis* (Dublin: Gill & Macmillan, 1980), 45.

25. G. Evans and B. O'Leary, 'Frameworked Futures: Intransigence and Flexibility in the Northern Ireland Elections of May 30 1996', *Irish Political Studies*, 12 (1997), 23–47.

26. *Irish Times*, 29 June 1998.

27. See D. L. Horowitz, *Ethnic Groups in Conflict* (Berkeley: University of California Press, 1985), 404, 425.

28. G. Evans and M. Duffy, 'Beyond the Sectarian Divide: The Social Bases and Political Consequences of Nationalist and Unionist Party Competition in Northern Ireland', *British Journal of Political Science*, 27 (1997), 71.

29. On the motion to approve UUP participation in a government, following the decommissioning compromise of November 1999, Trimble received only 58% support from his party's governing council—and then only after he pledged to resign from the Cabinet in February 2000 if progress on decommissioning of weapons was inadequate.

30. This is a formulation attributed to the late Wallace Sayre of Columbia University.

31. For a discussion of this issue, see Y. Ghai, *Implementation of the Fiji Islands Constitution* (Suva: Citizens' Constitutional Forum, 1998).
32. W. H. Riker, *The Theory of Political Coalitions* (New Haven: Yale University Press, 1962), 32–101.
33. Lijphart, *Democracy in Plural Societies*, 147–57, 201–6.

5

Northern Ireland, Civic Nationalism, and the Good Friday Agreement

JOHN MCGARRY

Civic nationalism originated with the Jacobins during the French revolution and has since been exported throughout the world. It is now the dominant form of nationalism in the Western democracies, including the United States, Australia, and France. Civic nationalists hold the view that everyone in the state, regardless of race or ethnicity, is a member of the nation and entitled to equal citizenship. The promotion of a common civic identity is thought to be indispensable to political stability. It is also seen as underpinning the social solidarity required for welfare state redistribution and for deliberative democracy.[1]

Civic nationalism is juxtaposed by its supporters with ethnic (or racial) nationalism, which restricts membership in the nation to the relevant ethnic group.[2] Ethnic nationalism is blamed for most of the human disasters that have afflicted the world in the last century, including the Holocaust, apartheid, and ethnic cleansing in the former Yugoslavia. It is also said to threaten the well-being of several Western civic democracies, including the United Kingdom, Spain, and Canada. From this perspective, the problem is the existence of lingering ethnic sentiments among national minorities, such as the Scots, Basques, and the Québécois.[3]

It is this latter tendency, for civic nationalists to be unsympathetic to the claims of national minorities, that I am concerned with in this chapter. Three common and related positions can be identified: first, that the identities of such minorities are backward-looking; second, that these identities are (more or less) superficial and malleable, the product of social inequalities, physical isolation, or manipulation by ethno-national elites rather than deeply rooted sentiment;[4] and third, that the distinctiveness of national minorities should not be granted substantive institutional recognition.[5] The political structure preferred by those who hold these views is an integrated nation-state, constructed on principles of equal citizenship. Individual rights are stressed over group rights, although some 'multiculturalist' civic nationalists are prepared to concede limited cultural and political rights to minorities as groups as long as these are consistent with a common national identity.[6] Civic nationalists are generally not prepared to recognize minorities as national minorities as they fear that this will endanger stability, social solidarity, and even state unity. It is also claimed in some accounts that any new state formed as a result of 'ethnically driven' secession would be illiberal and would mistreat its own minorities.[7]

Instead of catering to the 'distinctiveness' of national minorities, civic nationalists prefer to win such minorities over through integrationist policies. This includes the propagation of an ideology of inclusion through catch-all political parties, trade unions, and other civic associations; the banning of discrimination; the promotion of economic growth and/or redistribution; and integration in schools, workplaces, and residential neighbourhoods.

It is hardly surprising that these principles, which are embraced by liberals and Marxists, and which are dominant among American intellectuals, are popular with those who seek peace in Northern Ireland. There are in fact three distinct approaches to the Northern Ireland conflict that are consistent with the civic nationalist positions I have identified: one republican, one unionist, and a third approach that is allegedly non-partisan. In this chapter I discuss these approaches and their flaws. I argue that a settlement was unattainable in Northern Ireland while republican and unionist leaders insisted on stretching their nations over their respective (British and Irish) minorities. It was only when key actors on both sides embraced the concept of a bi-national compromise that a settlement—the Good Friday Agreement of 1998—could be reached. The chapter ends with a defence of the Agreement's institutions against its civic nationalist critics.

Northern Ireland—a Hotbed of Inclusiveness

It may appear odd to outsiders who are used to thinking of Northern Ireland as a site of ethnic (or 'sectarian') hatreds, but its intellectuals and politicians talk more about inclusion than exclusion. Three different varieties of civic inclusion have dominated intellectual and political debate.

Civic (Irish) Nationalism

The first view, the one with the longest lineage, insists on the construction of an Irish republic capable of transcending what are seen as rival sectarian identities. This position has been put forward since the 1790s, when Wolfe Tone, following the Jacobins, called on the people of Ireland 'to substitute the common name of Irishman in place of the denominations Catholic, Protestant and Dissenter'.[8] It was represented by Young Ireland in the 1840s, with its support for the 'multicultural' tricolour as the flag of an independent Ireland. In recent history a civic nationalist discourse has become hegemonic. A tolerant and pluralist 'civic' Ireland is now the expressed goal of every Irish nationalist party, including Sinn Féin.

The traditional republican position—associated with Sinn Féin for much of the past thirty years—is that sectarian division in Ireland is not the result of primordial hatreds or deep-rooted sentiments. Rather, it is seen as a consequence of Britain's historic policy of divide and rule.[9] British imperialists governed Ireland, it is claimed, by bestowing privileges on Irish Protestants. When the issue of Home Rule for Ireland arose in British politics after 1886, British Conservatives 'played the Orange card', stirring up Protestant opposition to home rule for reasons to do with partisan politics in Britain. In the face of an Irish nationalist rebellion, the British government partitioned Ireland without the formal support of a single Irish MP, Protestant or Catholic. The result was twofold, although the first is discussed more frequently than the second. On the one hand, a statelet was created in Northern Ireland with an inbuilt Protestant majority. Protestants were capable of monopolizing government as long as they stressed zero-sum politics and maintained ethnic solidarity, and this is what they did. On the other hand, partition resulted in an almost homogeneously Catholic state in the south of Ireland. For most of its history it pursued a public policy consistent with its religious make-up, elevating the position of the Catholic Church and imposing Catholic morality in the regulation of sexuality and the body. Britain's partition of Ireland, therefore, produced two sectarian identities, and made impossible the realization of Tone's civic ideal. Ireland remains partitioned in this exogenous account because Protestants continue to fear for their religious identity under Dublin rule and because of the benefits of a large British subvention.

Republicans have argued that unionism is not only superficial but also regressive. Unionists are likened, routinely, to pariah groups like the Boers of South Africa, the whites of Rhodesia, or the colons of Algeria. The unionist Orange Order is seen as similar to the Ku Klux Klan in the United

States, and connections between unionists and British or European fascist organizations are regularly highlighted. Northern Ireland's majority population is often portrayed as still operating with a seventeenth-century Ascendancy mindset while republicans, by contrast, are cast in the role of missionaries preaching Enlightenment values.[10]

Sinn Féin's position prior to the start of the current peace process was to oppose political institutions that would substantively accommodate such an identity. It was argued instead that the British state, as the chief cause of sectarianism in Ireland, should be removed by force. At that point, it was claimed, unionist chauvinism would dissipate and Protestants would come to accept their destiny as Irish people in a united Ireland. Sinn Féin insisted that a prerequisite for a settlement was a statement from the British government of its intention to withdraw from Ireland. It would not even condone a devolved Assembly and executive in Northern Ireland in the context of a united Ireland, as it believed this would prolong unionist ethnocentrism. It was prepared to accept a four-unit federal Ireland, but insisted that the northern unit be the historic province of Ulster, which included the six counties of Northern Ireland plus the overwhelmingly nationalist counties of Donegal, Monaghan, and Cavan.

More moderate nationalists, particularly in the Social Democratic and Labour Party (SDLP), argued that republican violence was counter-productive and that a united Ireland was unattainable, at least in the short term. They pressed instead for a compromise with unionists. Sinn Féin and the IRA consistently opposed such compromises, including the Sunningdale Agreement of 1973. This provided for Northern Ireland to remain part of the United Kingdom, for a power-sharing executive to be established in Northern Ireland, and for a Council of Ireland to discuss matters of common interest between the Dublin and Belfast governments. Sunningdale was largely destroyed by loyalist and unionist opposition, but it was also undermined by republicans, who waged an intensifying campaign of violence throughout its brief history.

Civic Unionism

The civic project of Irish republicans has come to be matched in recent decades by a civic unionist project. Traditionally, unionism in Ireland has been ethnic and exclusionary. While William Pitt sought to build a civic United Kingdom by linking the Act of Union with Catholic emancipation, he was frustrated by Anglo-Irish Protestants, Tories, and King George III. Some of those who opposed Home Rule for Ireland at the end of the nineteenth century did so on civic grounds, although civic unionists were more conspicuous in Britain (and in southern Ireland) than in Ulster. For most of the period between 1921 and the 1970s the dominant unionist party, the UUP, made no attempt to reach out to Catholics, although smaller (small 'u') unionist parties like the Northern Ireland Labour Party did. Northern Ireland's first prime minister, Sir James Craig, professed that he was proud to have constructed a 'Protestant parliament for a Protestant people',[11] and the UUP did not appoint a Catholic cabinet minister until its regime was on the verge of collapse in 1968.

The argument that an integrated United Kingdom, operating on civic principles, is the best solution for the Northern Ireland conflict was increasingly made by UUP politicians after the 'proroguing' of the Stormont Parliament in 1972. The transition from support for devolution to support for integration was facilitated by Enoch Powell's decision to join the party in 1974 and by James Molyneaux's accession to the leadership in 1979. In the wake of the Anglo-Irish Agreement of 1985 a number of unionist interationist organizations were formed outside conventional politics, including the Campaign for Equal Citizenship and the Campaign for Labour Representation in Northern Ireland. These took the position that if the Union was to be sold to both Catholics and Protestants, it should be detached from traditional unionist political parties, which were too closely associated with sectarianism.[12] In recent years this version of civic unionism has become most closely identified with Robert McCartney, the founder of the Campaign for Equal Citizenship and current leader of the United Kingdom Unionist Party. It is also supported by Ireland's most famous intellectual, Conor Cruise O'Brien, the Scottish journalist John Lloyd, and a number of academics, such as Arthur Aughey, Hugh Roberts, and Patrick Roche.[13] By the 1990s, it was de rigueur for politicians from all unionist parties, including even the Democratic Unionist Party (DUP), to defend an integrated United Kingdom as something that could include Catholics and even Irish nationalists.

While republicans argue that divisions in Ireland are not deeply rooted, civic unionists make the same argument about divisions in Northern Ireland. The roots of the conflict are said to lie in Britain's decision, first, to withdraw from the rest of Ireland in the face of an ethnically motivated Irish rebellion, and second, to establish a devolved parliament in Belfast, against the wishes of unionist leaders, rather than integrating Northern Ireland into the United Kingdom. The separatist mentality of northern nationalists has been explained as a result of manipulation by nationalist political parties, priests, and republican paramilitaries. It has also been encouraged, in the view of unionists, by the Republic of Ireland's irredentism, by the British government's lack of commitment to the Union and unwillingness to take on the IRA, and by the failure of the British political parties to organize in Northern Ireland, a failure that has isolated the region from Britain's civic political culture.[14]

Just as republicans claim that unionists are reactionaries, civic unionists make the same point about nationalists. For a long time the Republic of Ireland was ridiculed as a bucolic theocracy that would trample on the rights of unionists. Irish republicans, it is claimed, were 'ethnic cleansers' long before the Serbs popularized the concept, allegedly driving out a large part of the Irish Free State's Protestant population in the years after partition. Sinn Féin is regularly denounced as fascist by unionist politicians and intellectuals, particularly by unionist opponents of the Good Friday Agreement.[15]

In line with this thinking, unionists were not prepared to accommodate nationalists before 1998. They refused to countenance any political link between Northern Ireland and the Republic of Ireland, or any substantial devolution to Northern Ireland. Such accommodation, it was argued by unionist intellectuals, would not only appease Irish chauvinists, including IRA murderers, but would damage progressive elements in unionist politics and increase the popularity of chauvinistic Protestant politicians, or drive people to join loyalist paramilitaries.[16]

While republicans called for an integrated Irish nation-state, civic unionists insisted on an integrated British nation-state.[17] Concessions to separatist nationalism were not necessary to win over Catholics, from this perspective. All that was needed was for the British government to make clear its commitment to the Union and for the Republic of Ireland to abandon its irredentism.[18] Civic unionists pushed for legislation affecting Northern Ireland to be incorporated into British legislation or, if separate legislation was necessary, for it to be passed by normal parliamentary procedures rather than by Order in Council; for Northern Ireland's representation at Westminster to be increased; and for Northern Ireland to be administered in the same way as regions in Britain. Some lobbied for the main British political parties, the Conservatives and Labour, to organize in Northern Ireland. During the height of 'electoral integrationism' in the late 1980s, it was believed that this would bring two benefits: it would help to export Britain's more rational and modern political culture to Northern Ireland; and by giving the electorate the opportunity to vote for the only two parties capable of forming the British government, it would democratize rule from

London and undermine the appeal of devolution.[19] The aim of the more enthusiastic civic unionists was to replace Northern Ireland's rival sectarian identities with a transcendent British civic identity, to make the region, as Margaret Thatcher once claimed it already was, 'as British as Finchley'—her suburban London constituency.[20]

Social Transformation or 'Bottom-Up' Civic Nationalism

There is a third type of civic nationalism, whose proponents emphasize the need for Northern Ireland's society to be transformed from the bottom up. 'Transformers' typically blame Northern Ireland's divisions on factors such as social segregation, economic inequality, and ethnocentric appeals by elites in both communities. In response, they call for policies to promote social integration, for increased public spending to tackle the 'material basis' of sectarian identities,[21] and for sectarian elites on both sides to be challenged by civil society, particularly those organizations, such as trade unions or peace and conflict resolution groups, that 'cross-cut social divisions and challenge and erode the clash of opposing ethnonationalisms'.[22]

Transformers are sceptical of the integrating capacities of political institutions, even those constructed on consociational (power-sharing) principles, as it is thought that these are likely to be dominated by sectarian elites. In some accounts it is claimed that consociational institutions do more harm than good, entrenching divisions when the goal should be to overcome them. From this perspective, which is put forward by Rupert Taylor in this volume, social transformation is a prerequisite for a lasting political settlement and any attempt to create the latter without the former will be counter-productive.[23]

Because they see divisions as superficial, many transformers are optimistic about the prospects for social integration. Taylor argues that there is already evidence of increasing integration in housing and schools, and stresses that a significant number of voluntary associations are already working to break down 'Orange and Green stereotypes' and to promote a new inclusiveness.[24]

Social transformation is popular among intellectuals, particularly on the left. It is also represented in small parties from outside the ethnonational blocs, including the Alliance, Democratic Left, the Labour Party, and the Northern Ireland Women's Coalition. Transformers usually prioritize the construction of an integrated society in Northern Ireland over either a united Ireland or maintaining the United Kingdom, and many like to see themselves as post-nationalists rather than nationalists. However, some transformers lean towards a united Ireland or the United Kingdom.[25]

The Limits to Civic Nationalism in Northern Ireland

The problem with the first two approaches outlined above is a rather fundamental one: neither has any cross-community appeal or is likely to develop this in the foreseeable future. For over a century Northern Ireland has been divided electorally into two rival ethno-national blocs, and the divisions have become particularly intense during the past thirty years. While nationalist and unionist parties won an average of 82 per cent of the vote during the five elections that were held between 1973 and 1975, they have received an average of 90.6 per cent in Northern Ireland's last five elections.[26] There has been no swing voting between the two blocs, and any change in their respective share of the poll has been the result of differential birth-rates and electoral participation rates.[27] Nor have parties from outside the two ethno-national blocs shown any sign of making a political breakthrough. Rather, as the figures suggest, the 'middle ground' has been squeezed in recent decades.[28]

There are several reasons why neither ethno-national community has been prepared to accept the inclusive appeal of the other. First, these appeals have been made during a period of polarizing inter-ethnic violence. Indeed, the republican plea to Protestants to embrace 'the common name of Irishman' coincided with a violent campaign in which republicans killed and injured thousands of Protestants. Second, the constitutional goals associated with the respective positions are little different from what would be argued for on purely ethnocentric grounds. Both sides in fact interpret the civic language of their rivals as a politically correct smokescreen designed mainly for external consumption and not meant to be taken seriously by their ostensible targets. Unionists believe that what republicans, or at least the republican grassroots, are attached to is the land that unionists occupy—Ireland's fourth green field—rather than the unionists themselves. Nationalists note that unionists did not enunciate civic principles during the Stormont regime between 1921 and 1972, when they had the power to put them into practice. Civic unionism, everyone is aware, became popular only after the British government abolished Stormont and pressured unionists to accommodate nationalists. It became particularly prominent only in the late 1980's, after a series of political and international defeats for unionists, including the Anglo-Irish Agreement, which was enthusiastically endorsed by international opinion. Both sides in Ireland, then, have tended to regard the other's civic appeals in much the same way as Croats and Bosnian Muslims interpreted Slobodan Milošević's claim that he wanted to maintain a civic and inclusive Yugoslavia—as ethnic chauvinism in tactical guise.

Even if unionists and nationalists had been able to accept that the inclusive appeals of their rivals were sincere, this would hardly have sufficed to win them over. This is because, as communities with distinct national identities, neither wants to be subsumed within the other's nation-state even if they were guaranteed equal citizenship. Even moderate nationalists insist on, at a bare minimum, institutional links between Northern Ireland and the Republic of Ireland. Even moderate unionists, who are prepared to tolerate cross-border institutions in order to accommodate nationalists, insist on retaining the political link with Britain. In this, both communities are like national communities elsewhere, in Canada (Quebec), Britain (Scotland), Spain (Basques and Catalans), all of which insist on institutional accommodation of their own identity and reject attempts by their respective majorities to treat everyone as undifferentiated citizens.

While the first two versions of civic nationalism are unrealistic and unfair, the third is merely unrealistic. It is difficult to criticize social transformation as a long-term objective. However, there is no evidence that it can be achieved any time soon, and especially not outside the context of a political settlement acceptable to both sides. Transformers' optimism about the feasibility of their project stems from their belief that electoral data reflect elite politics and are not representative of a considerable consensus outside conventional politics. However, they cannot explain why, in free and open elections, only nationalist and unionist elites win, while elites that stress cross-cutting issues such as class receive only derisory support. Their belief is also in tension with the fact that turnout in Northern Ireland elections is higher than in the United Kingdom as a whole (or in Great Britain),[29] and the fact that the position of political parties on constitutional issues also broadly reflects the preferences reported in survey data.[30]

It is not even true that the constitutional goals of Northern Ireland's 'civil society', its large number of civic associations, are dramatically different from those of its political parties. The most popular civil society organizations in Northern Ireland, the Orange Order and Gaelic Athletic Association, are solidly unionist and nationalist, respectively.[31] It is the case that several, smaller, peace and conflict resolution organizations reach across the national divide and seek to promote a transcendent identity. However, just as many, according to the academic who has most closely studied them, are nationalist or unionist groups that want an honourable bi-national compromise.[32] Finally, contrary to Taylor's argument in Chapter 2, there is no clear indication that the two communities desire to mix socially. Even if there was, it is not clear that this would obviate the need for, or be incompatible with, a political settlement that accommodated both groups.[33]

Faced with the reality of a society polarized along ethno-national lines, the British and Irish governments have sought a bi-national compromise and they have been supported in this by the moderate nationalists of the SDLP and by Alliance. Such a compromise—the Good Friday Agreement—was reached in 1998 because leading republicans and unionists took some, albeit reluctant, steps away from their respective integrationist positions.

From National Integration to Bi-National Compromise

A compromise did not come about because the attachment of republicans to a united Ireland or unionists to the United Kingdom weakened. Rather agreement was reached because events made it clear that first preferences were unattainable, at least in the short term.

Republicans' path to a settlement began with the Hume–Adams talks of 1988–94, when the SDLP leader sought to convince Sinn Féin that its strategy of violence was counter-productive, alienating not just unionists, but Britain and potential supporters in Irish America. A learning curve, aided by the vehemence of loyalist attacks on republicans in the early 1990s, increased republicans' respect for the resilience of unionism and for its independence from metropolitan manipulation. It was also clear that the military struggle had resulted in stalemate, and that it was compromising Sinn Féin's electoral strategy. At the same time republicans' faith in constitutional politics increased because of support from an increasingly interventionist United States administration and because of demographic change that favoured Catholics. The rising Catholic share of the population and a corresponding increase in Sinn Féin's vote helped to convince its leaders that they could exercise meaningful influence within Northern Ireland. It also allowed them to sell compromise to their followers while claiming that a united Ireland had been postponed rather than cancelled.

The volte-face by David Trimble's UUP resulted from several related factors. After a brief fling with integration in the late 1970s, the British government made it increasingly clear that this was no longer an option. Indeed, after 1985 the government indicated that unalloyed direct rule was not on offer either. Unionists had always considered this preferable to the risks of a settlement with nationalists. In the Anglo-Irish Agreement of 1985, however, Britain gave the Republic of Ireland a role in policy-making in Northern Ireland, while offering to reduce this in the event of an agreement on devolution between nationalists and unionists. The default to compromise shifted from direct rule from Westminster to London–Dublin cooperation in the governance of Northern Ireland, with the danger, from the unionist perspective, that this would be consolidated and extended in the absence of agreement between the Northern Ireland parties. There was no immediate movement. At first, unionists thought they could destroy the Agreement by protest, although it proved impervious to this. There was also hope that the Agreement could be resisted or turned back while the Conservatives were in power in London, and particularly during the 1992–7 Parliament when the Conservative government depended on unionist support in the House of Commons. The UUP began to negotiate seriously with the SDLP and Sinn Féin only following Labour's landslide victory in 1997 and Tony Blair's signal that he was committed to achieving a settlement by May 1998.

Another factor that induced unionist flexibility was the increasing Catholic share of the population and the matching increase in support for nationalist parties, particularly Sinn Féin. This trend underlined that time was not on the side of unionist negotiators. The rising nationalist vote also undercut the integrationist argument that nationalism was superficial. It showed not only that civic unionism was falling on deaf Catholic ears, but that the continuing failure to accommodate nationalists was squeezing moderates.[34] Unionist intellectuals, including Paul Bew, an adviser to David Trimble, switched subtly from the integrationist position that any accommodation of nationalists was a boon to Protestant sectarianism to the argument that a (minimalist) accommodation of nationalism was necessary for peace and the erosion of extremism.[35] The changing demography also undermined traditional unionist opposition to power-sharing. As advisers to the UUP pointed out in the wake of the Agreement, with the nationalist share of the population continuing to increase, unionists might soon be 'grateful' they had agreed to mandatory power-sharing.[36]

The case for integration with Britain was also undercut by the Labour government's decision in 1997 to devolve power to a Scottish parliament and Welsh assembly. Integrationists in Northern Ireland had resisted an assembly in Belfast partly on the grounds that it would create a political distinction between Northern Ireland and Britain. They had insisted in their rhetoric that Northern Ireland be treated the same as Scotland and Wales. The government's 'devolution all round' package made it easier for unionist moderates to embrace it and to sell it to their followers. Moreover, as the Scottish and Welsh devolution packages were asymmetrical, reflecting the desire of Scots for more radical decentralization, it became easier to accept, or at least more difficult to argue against, a *sui generis* package suited to Northern Ireland's peculiar needs, including mandatory power-sharing and cross-border political institutions.

Finally, UUP leader David Trimble's decision to negotiate was facilitated by the novel flexibility of republicans. It would have been impossible for Trimble to negotiate with Sinn Féin if the IRA had not declared a ceasefire in 1994, although Trimble did not enter comprehensive negotiations until three years later. The IRA ceasefire also ushered in loyalist ceasefires and the participation of two refreshingly flexible loyalist parties in the political negotiations. Their presence acted as a crucial cushion for Trimble against DUP accusations that his involvement in talks jeopardized the Union.

In the 1998 Agreement both republicans and unionists stepped away from previous absolutisms. Sinn Féin dropped its insistence that a settlement should include a British withdrawal and a united Ireland. Under the Agreement these matters were to be left to Northern Ireland's electorate to decide, by simple majority, at an unspecified point in the future. Sinn Féin also agreed that a referendum be put to voters in the Irish Republic proposing the amendment of clauses in the Irish Constitution that expressed sovereignty over Northern Ireland. The UUP accepted that the United Kingdom must substantively accommodate the identity of Northern Ireland's nationalists. It agreed that a united Ireland could come about as soon as a majority in Northern Ireland wanted. Both sides settled on the compromise of power-sharing devolution and new political institutions linking both parts of Ireland (and Ireland with Britain) over integration into their respective nation-states. The compromise represented evolution from the fixation of both sides with the Westphalian sovereign state. While both used to claim that *their* nationalism was progressive and the other's was reactionary, in the Agreement they acknowledged that both unionism and Irish nationalism should enjoy 'parity of esteem'.

The Good Friday Agreement's Consociational Institutions and Northern Ireland's Refuseniks

The consociational institutions at the heart of the Good Friday Agreement have been criticized from all three integrationist positions described earlier. In this final section I address these criticisms.

Two broad and related objections are raised. The first is that, instead of resolving the conflict, these institutions promote sectarianism and division, and entrench existing identities. Republican dissidents, including the 32 County Sovereignty Movement and Republican Sinn Féin, argue that they 'institutionalize' division.[37] Unionist rejectionists, such as the civic unionist intellectual and politician Robert McCartney, label the provisions for power-sharing 'divisive'.[38] Transformers in Democratic Left and Alliance, two small parties outside the ethno-national blocs, criticize it as a 'pact' between the dominant sectarian political parties against the 'others' who are trying to transcend difference.[39] In Chapter 2, Taylor claims that its consociational institutions 'solidify intracommunal networks' when the goal should be to promote 'intercommunal association'.

Second, it is argued that the consociational institutions are inherently unstable. Both republican and unionist opponents of the Agreement point to its 'inauspicious beginnings',[40] including the fact that it was rejected by nearly half of the unionist electorate and that it took until December 1999, nineteen months after the settlement was signed, before a power-sharing executive could be established. Critics seized on the temporary suspension of the executive in February 2000 and ongoing disputes over the decommissioning of paramilitary weapons, policing reform, and which flag to fly over public buildings to support their position.[41] Robert McCartney's (wishful) thinking is typical of rejectionist opinion: he argues that the Agreement's power-sharing institutions are 'impermanent', 'dysfunctional', and 'unworkable', and that it is only a matter of time before the 'macabre parody of real democracy' is brought to a halt by its 'inherent defects and weaknesses'.[42]

In a sub-version of this argument, several unionists claim that it is the Agreement's imposition of a 'Grand Coalition' executive model that explains its instability.[43] This is because such a coalition provides for the inclusion of Sinn Féin. It is implied here that if the mandatory Grand Coalition model was dropped, unionists would be open to establishing a voluntary coalition with the moderate SDLP. Such an executive, it is claimed, would be more likely to agree on a collective programme of government and would be more in keeping with British parliamentary traditions. The view that Sinn Féin's inclusion in government destabilizes the Agreement is not restricted to unionist partisans. It is shared by a prominent impartial intellectual, Donald Horowitz, who makes this argument in Chapter 4 of this volume.

My position is that these criticisms are invalid. The claim that the Agreement promotes sectarianism flows from a distorted view of what sectarianism is. There is a basic inability in the above accounts to distinguish, on the one hand, between policies that promote injustice and incite conflict between groups and, on the other hand, policies that are designed to promote equitable settlements and better inter-group relations.[44] Only the former can properly be described as sectarian.

The Good Friday Agreement falls squarely into the latter category. It promotes mutual respect and peaceful coexistence between groups, principles that are the polar opposite of sectarianism and division. As integrationists on both sides acknowledge when questioning the Agreement's stability, it cannot work unless there is intercommunity cooperation. Its central institutions have been deliberately crafted to rule out ethnocentric policies. This is clear in three crucial areas. First, to be elected first minister or deputy first minister requires 'parallel consent', support from a majority of the Assembly plus a majority of both nationalist and unionist Assembly members. This is a formula that effectively guarantees one post for each community and requires each of them to suggest a moderate candidate acceptable to the other side. Second, key legislation cannot be passed unless it is supported by a majority in the Assembly and by at least 40 per cent of nationalists and unionists. Third, each community's favoured institution has been made interdependent. Nationalists cannot undermine the Northern Ireland Assembly in the hope that the North–South Ministerial Council (NSMC) will remain intact, and unionists cannot destroy the NSMC and retain the Assembly. Both communities are required to work both institutions.[45]

The Agreement not only stresses equality ('parity of esteem') between nationalists and unionists, it also offers protection to individuals, including those who regard themselves as neither unionist nor nationalist. Each minister is required under the Agreement to behave in a non-partisan way towards the citizens of Northern Ireland: 'to serve all the people of Northern Ireland equally, and to act in accordance with the general obligations on government to promote equality and prevent discrimination'.[46] The Agreement provides for the entrenchment of the European Convention of Human Rights in Northern Ireland law, which will make it easier for citizens to bring cases against authorities; a new Northern Ireland Human Rights Commission; a Bill of Rights for Northern Ireland; and a new statutory Equality Commission. The British government is also committed to creating a statutory obligation on public authorities in Northern Ireland 'to promote equality of opportunity in relation to religion and political opinion; gender; race; disability; age; marital status; dependants; and sexual orientation'. Public bodies are to be required to draw up statutory schemes indicating how they will implement their obligations.

The criticism that the Agreement entrenches existing identities is directed at a requirement that members elected to the Assembly register as 'unionists', 'nationalists' or 'others'. This was enacted to provide a veto for the nationalist minority (and a future unionist minority, should one materialise): the passage of important measures requires the support of a majority in the Assembly and the support of at least forty per cent of both registered nationalist and unionists. One effect of this is hat it previleges nationalist and unionists over 'others'. Arguably, it creates a minor incentive for voters to support nationalist or unionists, or for elected members to register as nationalists or unionists, as members from these groups will count more than 'others'. It also has the effect of pre-determining, in advance of election results, that nationalists and unionists are to be better protected than 'others'.

It should be noted, however, that privileging a particular group of members or pre-determining beneficiaries in advance of elections is not recommended by consociationalists, even if, as in this case, the pre-determined groups have constituted almost all of the electorate for the past century.[47] What consociationalists prefer is that minority vetoes be implemented in ways that do not specify which groups are to be protected. One alternative in Northern Ireland would have been to require a weighted majority, say seventy per cent of the Assembly's members, big enough to protect *any* sizable minority. The Agreement's designers rejected this on the reasonable grounds that it would have facilitated the destruction of the settlement by a minority of chauvinists opposed to compromise. This alternative, that is, would have helped to resolve one of the two objections discussed above (the Agreement institutionalizes existing identities) but exacerbated the other (the Agreement is unstable). Another option would have been to require for the passage of key legislation not only a certain proportion of nationalist and unionist votes, but also the same proportion of votes from 'others'.[48]

In a number of other respects the Agreement's institutions are more conducive to the emergence of new parties, including parties that are neither unionist nor nationalist, than is the Westminster system. The Assembly uses a proportional representaion–single transferable vote (PR–STV) electoral system, which allows parties to win seats with a much smaller threshold than is normally required under single-member plurality.[49] As a result, voters in Assembly elections are less likely than voters in Westminster elections to consider voting for a new party a waste of time. By allowing for the ranking of preferences, PR–STV also provides an opportunity for non-communal or transcommunal voting on lower preferences.[50] In this respect, also, it is more conducive to extra-bloc voting than its Westminster counterpart. Under the Agreement, any party, not just the existing parties or nationalist or unionist parties, is entitled to seats in the executive if it meets the quota established by the d'Hondt system. Because the executive is constituted proportionately, a party is entitled to membership in government with a much smaller share of seats in the legislature than is normally required in the Westminster system. This means that new parties have a better chance to promote their visibility, influence public policy, and further demonstrate to their supporters that voting for them is a meaningful exercise.[51]

In addition, the Agreement establishes a Civic Forum alongside the elected Assembly. This institution will be made up of representatives of organizations from outside conventional politics. It presents an opportunity for those who do not feel represented by conventional political parties to have their voices heard, and has no counterpart elsewhere in the UK, including in the new devolved regimes in Scotland and Wales. If all these institutional features are considered in balance, it shows that while the Agreement recognizes nationalist and unionist identities, it does not preclude the development of other identities.

More important than any of these features, however, is what can be called the 'consociational paradox'. The paradox is that the institutional accommodation of rival groups and an extensive period of cooperation between them is more likely to transform identities in the long run than any of the integrationist options discussed earlier. This is what happened in the Netherlands, where a long period of power-sharing between Catholics and Protestants eroded the salience of divisions to a point where consociational institutions were no longer necessary.[52] Already there is evidence, which should not be exaggerated, that Northern Ireland's Agreement has produced non-traditional alliances across communal lines. In the election of June 1998 pro-Agreement groups appear to have engaged in intercommunal transfers to maximize the number of pro-Agreement politicians in the Assembly.[53] If the Agreement is consolidated, there is much greater likelihood of debate on socio-economic and related issues than in the political vacuum that preceded devolution.

It is this increased possibility of what transformers call 'normal' politics that explains why many of them (including Alliance, Democratic Left, the Northern Ireland Women's Coalition, and numerous peace and conflict resolution organizations) support the Agreement, while retaining misgivings about some of its provisions. For these groups it is not a choice, as Rupert Taylor puts it in this volume, of 'consociation *or* social transformation'. Rather, it appears to be a matter of 'consociation and social transformation' or even 'consociation and then social transformation'.

It is difficult to dispute the integrationist claim that post-Agreement Northern Ireland is unstable, although much of the reason for this instability is continuing adherence to unworkable integrationist positions on both sides. On the republican side, militant dissidents justify their continuation of the armed struggle, which produced the atrocity of Omagh in August 1998, on the grounds that the Agreement sets back the achievement of an integrated Ireland. The fear of losing members to these dissident factions has curtailed Sinn Féin's ability to make the compromises that are necessary to make the Agreement work, and both the dissidents' actions and Sinn Féin's hesitancy have posed problems for pro-Agreement unionists. On the unionist side, the Trimble leadership is threatened by rejectionists, who appear to believe that a compromise with nationalists (or with republicans) is not necessary.[54]

The proper way to assess the Agreement's contribution to stability, however, is not to contrast contemporary Northern Ireland with societies that are not divided, but to contrast it with pre-Agreement Northern Ireland. By this standard, the Agreement stands up remarkably well. Northern Ireland has widely accepted constitutional arrangements for the first time. The Agreement has helped to consolidate ceasefires by the region's main paramilitary organizations. 1999, the first full year since the Agreement was reached, is the only year in the last thirty-one in which no soldier or police officer has been killed. The Northern Ireland Tourist Board recently reported that tourist spending levels in 1999 set a record, and that the number of visitors was up 11 per cent over the previous year.[55]

Sinn Féin's expulsion from the power-sharing executive would more likely result in catastrophe than improved stability. The remarkable moderation of republicanism since the 1980s, is closely linked to the Sinn Féin leadership's argument that gains can be secured through constitutional politics. Expulsion from the executive would undermine the party's constitutionalists and lead to a reradicalized Sinn Féin or a seepage of support to dissident republican groups. In any case, the unionist idea of a voluntary coalition with the SDLP would only work if the SDLP agreed, and there is little prospect of this. The SDLP understands the electoral consequences of colluding with unionists to expel Sinn Féin. It has also been committed for the past decade to bringing Sinn Féin into constitutional politics.

Many unionist rejectionists know that the exclusion of Sinn Féin is tantamount to scrapping the Agreement, which is why they suggest it. Horowitz's objection to Sinn Féin's presence on the executive is more puzzling as it is in stark tension with his best-known thesis—that the incentive of winning political office is the key to inducing moderation. Horowitz argues elsewhere that political leaders in ethnically divided societies should be required to appeal across ethnic lines if they are to win office, and he suggests complex electoral systems to achieve this.[56] However, moderation can also result from intra-bloc movement, from ultras moving towards the positions of moderates. This is precisely what has happened in Northern Ireland as Sinn Féin, to the chagrin of republican dissidents, has expanded its support by shifting to positions once associated with the SDLP and the Republic's Fianna Fáil. Following the logic Horowitz has employed elsewhere, barring Sinn Féin from the Northern Ireland executive (or the Republic's governing coalition, as has been suggested by a number of commentators) would reduce its incentive to moderate.

The Agreement's fragile compromise may not survive. If it fails, however, the most logical alternative is not one of the integrationist options considered earlier, but something that looks like the current compromise. Until politicians agreed to work an Agreement Mark 2, the most likely and most desirable scenario is that Northern Ireland would be governed by both London and Dublin, acting in increasingly close cooperation. In fact, one way to stabilize the Agreement against its most potent opponents, the large body of unionist rejectionists, is for the two governments to make clear that the alternative is increased London–Dublin cooperation in the governance of Northern Ireland. This would involve reapplying the logic of the Anglo-Irish Agreement, which as I have argued, played a role in securing unionist support for the 1998 Agreement in the first place. If enough unionists come to support the Agreement, and it is consolidated, the threat posed by republican dissidents should dissipate.

If, in the event of the Agreement's collapse, it proves impossible for London and Dublin to get agreement at the Northern Ireland-wide level, they should opt instead to promote decentralization, a radical increase in powers for those local governments that are prepared to share power along consociational lines. This would put pressure on the chauvinists, who would be presented with a choice of cooperating with their rivals or losing any say in local decision-making. The experience gained in sharing substantial power at the local level would help to breed a new generation of politicians who could then go on to share power at the regional level.[57]

Conclusion

The case of Northern Ireland suggests a number of serious problems with what I have identified as a civic nationalist approach to conflict resolution in nationally divided societies. One is that the choice is not always the stark one depicted in many accounts, between civic nationalism and ethnic nationalism. Rather, it is often between two projects, both of which claim to be civic. This is the case not only in Northern Ireland. In Canada, Quebec nationalists offer what they describe as a civic nationalism based on Quebec, while Canadian nationalists counter this with a civic project based on Canada. In Spain, Catalans and Basques offer up civic nationalisms based on their respective territories while Spaniards offer an alternative based on Spain. In the United Kingdom, Scottish nationalists promote their brand of inclusive nationalism in competition with a British variety. It is not always easy for impartial liberals to pick between these rival projects, claims by partisans notwithstanding.

Another problem is that appeals that are made in civic language are often seen by the targeted minority as ethnocentrism in politically correct garb, an impression that is not always correct but often is. In Northern Ireland both sides make civic appeals, but these are decoded as merely shrewd forms of sectarianism by the other side. In Canada, also, while both Anglo-Quebeckers and Quebec nationalists describe their own nationalisms as civic, each sees the other's as ethnic.[58]

If we leave suspicions about sincerity aside, it is also clear that civic nationalism, even in its multicultural variant, is incompatible with the substantive institutional recognition that national minorities want. These seek more than to be treated as equal individuals within someone else's nation-state or to be given a limited form of cultural recognition on a par with immigrant (Muslim or Buddhist) minorities. They want far-reaching institutional recognition of their national identity, their precise demands varying from place to place.[59]

The failings of civic nationalism help to explain why projects that are civic in their language are often ethnically homogeneous in their support base, as in Northern Ireland and Quebec. This in turn causes confusion about what sort of nationalism we are dealing with. Some academic observers, with their minds on the inclusive appeals of a particular nationalist elite, describe its nationalism as civic. Others, observing the same nationalism but focusing on the followers or rejecting the sincerity of the project's leaders, label it as ethnic.[60]

Finally, I have argued that the substantive institutional recognition of national minorities does not entrench antagonistic identities. Rather, it is likely to bring out the benign characteristics of rival identities and to marginalize chauvinists more effectively than unwanted inclusion projects. It also offers the prospect that an overarching consensus can be developed. This is not to say that multinational political settlements always succeed. Minorities may well seek to widen their autonomy, and perhaps to secede. However, the forcible inclusion of minorities is no guarantee of stability either.

NOTES

1. As John Stuart Mill wrote, 'Free institutions are next to impossible in a country made up of different nationalities. Among a people without fellow-feeling, especially if they read and speak different languages, the united public opinion, necessary to the workings of representative government cannot exist'. J. S. Mill, *Utilitarianism, On Liberty, Considerations on Representative Government* (London: Everyman, 1993), 392. For the importance of civic nationalism to the welfare state, see D. Miller, *On Nationality* (Oxford: Oxford University Press, 1995).

2. The distinction between civic and ethnic nationalism is made, among others, by Michael Ignatieff, *Blood and Belonging: Journeys into the New Nationalisms* (London: Viking, 1993) and by William Pfaff, *The Wrath of Nations: Civilization and the Furies of Nationalism* (New York: Simon & Shuster, 1993). Others make a similar distinction using different terms. Hans Kohn distinguishes between Western and Eastern nationalisms, 'Western and Eastern Nationalisms', in J. Hutchinson and A. Smith (eds.), *Nationalisms* (Oxford: Oxford University Press, 1994), 162–5. David Hollinger writes about post-ethnic and ethnic nationalism, in *Postethnic America* (New York: Basic Books, 1995). Thomas Franck distinguishes civic nationalism from tribal nationalism, in 'Tribe, Nation, World: Self-Identification in the Evolving International System', *Ethics and International Affairs*, 11 (1997), 164. Charles Taylor distinguishes patriotism from nationalism, in 'Nationalism and Modernity', in R. McKim and J. McMahan (eds.), *The Morality of Nationalism* (New York: Oxford University Press, 1997), 40. Francis Fukuyama distinguishes between civic

nationalism and 'cultural' or 'ethno-linguistic' nationalism, in 'Don't Do it Britannia', *Prospect*, May 2000, 21–4.

Others authors discuss the civic–ethnic distinction but in a critical way. See R. Brubaker, 'Myths and Misconception in the Study of Nationalism', in M. Moore (ed.), *National Self-Determination and Secession* (Oxford: Oxford University Press, 1998), 257–60; M. Moore, 'Nationalism', in *UNESCO Encyclopedia* (forthcoming); W. Kymlicka, 'Modernity and Minority Nationalism: Commentary on Thomas Franck', *Ethics and International Affairs*, 11 (1997), 171–6. My chapter belongs to this second category.

3. Pfaff sees minority nationalisms in general as ethnic (*The Wrath of Nations*). Ignatieff argues that Quebec nationalism is ethnic (*Blood and Belonging*). Fukuyama sees both Quebec and Scottish nationalism as 'cultural' or 'ethno-linguistic' ('Don't Do it Britannia').

4. The view that national and ethnic identities are malleable is especially popular among post-modernists, including many (ex-)Marxists who used to insist on the essentialist nature of class. Many of them divide the academic world into those who, like themselves, understand that identities are constructed and those who think that they are primordial and unchanging (This is the gist of Rupert Taylor's contribution to this volume). In fact, however, no modern social scientist dissents from the view that identities are constructed and contingent. Even the anthropologist Clifford Geertz, who is most regularly attacked for a primordialist position, made no such claim (see C. Geertz, 'Primordial and Civic Ties', in J. Hutchinson and A. Smith (eds.), *Nationalism* (Oxford: Oxford University Press, 1994), 29–34). The real division today is not between those who think identities are manipulable and those who think they are permanent, but between those who think it is relatively easy to engineer identity change and those who believe that this is difficult, particularly in violently polarized societies. As David Miller, who belongs in the former camp, argues, there should be 'a *stronger* sense of the malleability of such [cultural] identities, that is, the extent to which they can be created or modified consciously' (D. Miller, *Market, State and Community: The Foundations of Market Socialism* (Oxford: Oxford University Press, 1989), 237). For the latter perspective, see J. McGarry, 'Political Settlements in Northern Ireland and South Africa', *Political Studies*, 46/5 (1998), 853–70.

5. Many Canadian civic nationalists, taking their lead from the late Pierre Trudeau, refuse to recognize the province of Quebec as a 'distinct society' in the Constitution. It is feared that such recognition will strengthen those who believe that the Québécois constitute their own nation and that it will detract from the vision that is dominant among English-speaking Canadians of Canada as a civic nation of 'equal individuals and equal provinces'. The issue, which was the focus of intense debate between 1987 and 1990, almost resulted in the break-up of Canada. The government of Quebec followed English Canada's failure to recognize Quebec's distinctiveness with a referendum in 1995 that proposed

sovereign Quebec. The sovereigntist side lost the referendum by an extremely narrow margin. 49.4% voted in favour and 50.6% voted against.

6. Civic nationalism comes in multiculturalist and assimilationist ideal types. The former is compatible with respect for the culture of minorities and resembles the practice of 'multiculturalism' in the United States, Australia, and Canada. The latter requires ethnic minorities to embrace the culture of the dominant group, and is associated with the republican approach used in France.

7. One of the reasons given by some Canadian nationalists for opposing the secession of Quebec is that a separate Quebec would be less liberal than Canada and would discriminate against its Anglophone minority, its native minorities, and women.

8. Cited in B. O'Leary and J. McGarry, *The Politics of Antagonism: Understanding Northern Ireland* (London: Athlone Press, 1996), 92.

9. According to K. Rooney, 'the divisions in Ireland are artificial . . . created and maintained by Britain to enable it to rule its last colony . . . There is absolutely no natural basis for the divisions between catholics and protestants. We are the same race, speak the same language, and share the same history'. See K. Rooney, 'Institutionalising Division', *Fortnight* (June 1998), 21.

10. See Ch. 1 of this volume.

11. To be fair to Craig, his statement was made in response to de Valéra's boast that he had constructed a Catholic state in the South.

12. While the campaign for 'equal citizenship' was publicly committed to non-sectarianism, its stress was on removing inequality between the British citizens of Northern Ireland and those in Great Britain rather than inequality inside Northern Ireland.

13. See A. Aughey, *Under Siege: Ulster Unionism and the Anglo-Irish Agreement* (Belfast: Blackstaff Press, 1989); H. Roberts, 'Sound Stupidity: The British Party System and the Northern Ireland Question', in J. McGarry and B. O'Leary (eds.), *The Future of Northern Ireland* (Oxford: Oxford University Press, 1990); P. Roche and B. Barton (eds.), *The Northern Ireland Question: Myth and Reality* (Aldershot: Avebury, 1991).

O'Brien joined McCartney's United Kingdom Unionist Party and was elected under its banner to the Northern Ireland Forum in 1996. In his memoirs he expresses support for a non-sectarian united Ireland. See C. C. O'Brien, *Memoir: My Life and Themes* (London: Profile Books, 1998), 439–47. His current position seems to be that any civic nationalism will do as long as it is genuinely civic.

14. Roberts, 'Sound Stupidity'.

15. See Ch. 1 of this volume.

16. P. Bew and H. Patterson, 'Scenarios for Progress in Northern Ireland', in McGarry and O'Leary (eds.), *The Future of Northern Ireland*.

17. Before devolution in 1997 and the Good Friday Agreement in 1998, some unionists argued that the United Kingdom was a multinational state rather

than a nation-state. This was clearly true in the social sense, but it was not true in the political institutional sense. There was no substantive institutional accommodation of the national identity of Scots, Welsh, or Irish nationalists. There is now, but only as a result of devolution to Scotland and Wales and the Good Friday Agreement.

18. See P. Roche, 'Northern Ireland and Irish Nationalism', in J. Wilson Foster (ed.), *The Idea of the Union: Statements and Critiques in Support of the Union of Great Britain and Northern Ireland* (Vancouver: Belcouver Press, 1995), 133. See also J. Oliver, 'Constitutional Uncertainty and the Ulster Tragedy', *Political Studies*, 59/4 (1988), 427–36.

19. The fact that the ability to vote for the major British parties did little to under-cut the Scots' desire for devolution appears not to have occurred to electoral integrationists.

20. For Irish republicans, the claim that Northern Ireland was 'as British as Finchley' appeared as daft as John Cleese's observation that his grandfather had died 'fighting to keep China British'. See A. McIntyre, 'We, the IRA, have Failed', *Guardian*, 22 May 1998. There are parts of Margaret Thatcher's auto-biography which suggest that, despite her famous soundbite, she shared McIntyre's view.

21. Rupert Taylor approvingly cites Henry Patterson as claiming that the accom-modation of the minority's national identity in the Anglo-Irish Agreement was a poor substitute for dealing with the 'material basis of Catholic griev-ance', in 'A Consociational Path to Peace in Northern Ireland and South Africa?', in A. Guelke (ed.), *New Perspectives on the Northern Ireland Conflict* (Aldershot: Avebury, 1994), 171 n. 13.

22. See Taylor, p. 47 in this volume.

23. Taylor argues that the Good Friday Agreement's consociational institutions work in the 'opposite' way to what is needed and that they could well 'make permanent the Catholic–nationalist versus Protestant–unionist paradigm'. See Ch. 2 in this volume. Anderson and Goodman share Taylor's perspective. They worry that the institutions may have achieved the 'opposite of supersed-ing national conflict'. J. Anderson and J. Goodman, 'North–South Agendas for Dis/Agreeing Ireland', in J. Anderson and J. Goodman (eds.), *Dis/agreeing Ireland: Context, Obstacles, Hopes* (London: Pluto Press, 1998), 233.

24. See Ch. 2. N. Douglas makes the same point in 'The Politics of Accom-modation, Social Change and Conflict Resolution in Northern Ireland', *Political Geography*, 17/2 (1998), 220 and 222.

25. Taylor sees social transformation as creating the conditions for a 'non-sectarian' and peaceful united Ireland. See Ch. 2.

26. Within the nationalist bloc, moreover, the republican (radical nationalist) share of the vote has been increasing. In its first five election campaigns (1982–7) Sinn Féin won an average of 37.3% of the nationalist vote. In its last five campaigns (1996–9) its average increased to 41%. These figures have

been calculated from the electoral data provided by Nicholas Whyte, *http://www.explorers.whyte.com*

The trend within the unionist bloc is more difficult to measure, as both major unionist parties have been equally intransigent for most of the period. There is some evidence, however, that the UUP's increased moderation in recent years has cost it electoral support to the advantage of the DUP.

27. The rising nationalist share of the electorate, from 24.1% in the 1973 election to the Northern Ireland Assembly, to an average of 32.5% in seven elections between 1982 and 1989 and 39.8% in five elections between 1996 and 1999, has nothing to do with the conversion of unionists. It is the result of Sinn Féin's participation in electoral politics since 1982, a higher electoral-participation rate by Catholics and an increase in the Catholic share of the population. See B. O'Leary and J. McGarry, *The Politics of Antagonism: Understanding Northern Ireland* (London: Athlone Press, 1996), 192; B. O'Leary and G. Evans, 'Northern Ireland: La Fin de Siècle, the Twilight of the Second Protestant Ascendancy and Sinn Féin's Second Coming', *Parliamentary Affairs*, 50 (1997), 672–80.

28. While the most important of the middle-ground parties, the Alliance Party of Northern Ireland, averaged 8.4% of the vote in its first five (Northern Ireland-wide) election campaigns (1973–5), it averaged only 6% in its last five election campaigns (1997–9). During the last two regional elections in 1996 and 1998 the total vote of parties outside the ethno-national blocs (Alliance, the Northern Ireland Women's Coalition, and the Labour Party) amounted to only 8.4% on both occasions. See J. McGarry, 'European Integration, Globalization and the Northern Ireland Conflict', in M. Keating and J. McGarry (eds.), *Minority Nationalism and the Changing International Order* (Oxford: Oxford University Press, 2001).

29. Turnout in local government and European elections is consistently higher than in the rest of the United Kingdom, despite the fact that Northern Ireland's local governments have fewer powers than Great Britain's, and that Northern Ireland has more elections. Turnout in elections to the Northern Ireland Forum in 1996 (64.7%) and Assembly in 1998 (68.6%), was higher than in the 1999 elections to the Scottish Parliament (59%) and Welsh Assembly (45%). Only in Westminster elections is turnout lower in Northern Ireland (67.4% in 1997 and 69.8% in 1992) than in Great Britain (71.4% and 77.9% respectively). Some of the variance here can be explained by the use of the single-member plurality system (SMP) for Westminster elections but not for the other elections. Given the absence of swing voters in Northern Ireland, SMP makes results fairly predictable, which can dampen enthusiasm for voting. For more details on differential electoral turnout between Northern Ireland and Great Britain, see McGarry, 'Globalization, European Integration and the Northern Ireland Conflict'.

30. For survey data ranging from the 1960s to 1980s, see E. Moxon-Browne, 'National Identity in Northern Ireland', in P. Stringer and G. Robinson (eds.), *Social Attitudes in Northern Ireland: The First Report* (Belfast: Blackstaff Press, 1991). For data from the early 1990s, see K. Trew, 'National Identity', in R. Breen, P. Devine, and L. Dowds (eds.), *Social Attitudes in Northern Ireland* (Belfast: Appletree Press, 1996), table 1.

31. See F. Cochrane's contribution to this volume. In addition, Shane O'Neill observes that 'even politically active feminists in Northern Ireland seek to be recognized as one of the national communities by women from the other traditions . . . most feminists freely acknowledge the political primacy of the national struggle . . . The same point might be made about activists in the gay and lesbian communities.' See S. O'Neill, 'Mutual Recognition and the Accommodation of National Diversity: Constitutional Justice in Northern Ireland', MS, 1999, 6.

32. Cochrane, Ch. 6 of this volume.

33. It may be true, as Taylor says, that the 'extent of integrated education has widened', but it has widened to only 3% of the school-age population. Taylor cites a survey reported by Tom Hadden that indicates 'most people in Northern Ireland want to live together rather than apart', but Hadden has also argued that the 'major trend' in housing since 1971 has been for both communities to 'congregate in areas where they feel safer and less exposed'. See K. Boyle and T. Hadden, *Northern Ireland: The Choice* (Harmondsworth: Penguin, 1994), 33. Finally, Taylor cites an article from John Whyte in support of his claim that 'there are now a number of cross-community housing projects'. However, in this article, Whyte actually claims that 'residential segregation is increasing'. See J. Whyte, 'Dynamics of Social and Political Change in Northern Ireland', in D. Keogh and M. Haltzel (eds.), *Northern Ireland and the Politics of Reconciliation* (Cambridge: Cambridge University Press, 1993), 115. Whyte also makes clear 'the adamant opposition of unionists to any kind of united Ireland', a conclusion Taylor overlooks or chooses to ignore (ibid. 107).

34. Addressing critics of the Agreement at the UUP's annual conference in 1999, David Trimble asked if their preferred alternatives had managed to stem Sinn Féin's growing vote, or if there was an alternative plan on how to achieve this (*Irish Times*, 14 Oct. 1999).

35. Paul Bew and his colleagues Henry Patterson and Paul Teague called for the establishment of cross-border institutions as a 'symbolic fig leaf' to nationalists (P. Bew, H. Patterson, and P. Teague, *Northern Ireland: Between War and Peace* (London: Lawrence & Wishart, 1997), 214). These intellectuals deserve considerable credit for this shift.

36. 'Shock Report has UUP Reeling', *Irish Examiner*, 20 June 2000.

37. See Rooney, 'Institutionalising Division'. Rooney worries that the Agreement, by establishing institutions that 'celebrate difference', has 'put an end to the prospects for overcoming these divisions'. For other republican critiques of

the Agreement, see R. O'Bradaigh, 'Deal Means British Rule will be Strengthened', *Irish Times*, 13 May 1998, and the various articles by A. McIntyre, 'Why Stormont Reminded me of "Animal Farm"', *Sunday Tribune*, 12 Apr. 1998; 'Inside their Minds', *The Times*, 17 Aug. 1998; 'We, the IRA, have Failed'.

38. R. McCartney, 'Devolution is a Sham', *Observer*, 20 Feb. 2000.
39. Spokespersons for Democratic Left and the Alliance Party have criticized the Agreement, respectively, as a pact 'between the two dominant sectarian and tribal blocs' and as emphasizing 'two communities' rather than all the people who share 'common values and principles'. P. J. McLean, 'Five Reasons why Socialists should Say Yes to the Deal', *Irish News*, 9 May 1998, and P. McGarry (no relation), 'Why the Agreement may Fail', *Belfast Telegraph*, 16 Sept. 1999.
40. The phrase is Taylor's (Ch. 2 in this volume).
41. D. Kennedy, 'Evidence is Growing that Agreement did not Work', *Irish Times*, 16 Feb. 2000, and P. Roche, 'A Stormont without Policy', *Belfast Telegraph*, 30 Mar. 2000. The title of Kennedy's article suggests that he thought the Agreement was already a thing of the past.
42. McCartney, 'Devolution is a Sham'.
43. Kennedy, 'Evidence is Growing that Agreement did not Work', and Roche, 'A Stormont without Policy'.
44. Some civic nationalists appear unable to appreciate the difference between ethnic cleansing and apartheid, on the one hand, and power-sharing between groups on the other. Thus when Brendan O'Leary and I expressed our support for consociationalism in *Explaining Northern Ireland* (Oxford: Blackwell, 1995), one critic wrote that our views could be seen as 'condoning . . . ethnic cleansing'. See P. Dixon, 'The Politics of Antagonism: Explaining McGarry and O'Leary', *Irish Political Studies*, 11 (1996), 139. For a perspective that appears to equate the defence of the rights of multicultural minorities with the policies of the apartheid state in South Africa, see L. Piper, 'Whose Culture? Whose Rights? A Critique of Will Kymlicka's Multicultural Citizenship', Paper presented at the IPSA XVIII World Congress, Quebec City, 1–5 Aug. 2000.
45. For an analysis of the Agreement, see the series of articles by C. McCrudden, J. McGarry, and B. O'Leary in the *Sunday Business Post* (Dublin), 'Answering Some Big Questions', 19 Apr. 1998; 'Dance of the Ministries', 26 Apr. 1998; 'All-Ireland Bodies at Work', 3 May 1998; 'Equality and Social Justice', 10 May 1998; 'The Heart of the Agreement: A Bi-national Future with Double Protection'. For an analysis of the Agreement, see B. O'Leary, *The British–Irish Agreement: The Second Peace by Ordeal* (provisional title) (Oxford: Oxford University Press, forthcoming).
46. The Agreement, 36 (c).
47. See A. Lijphart, 'Self-Determination versus Pre-determination of Ethnic Minorities in Power-Sharing Systems', in W. Kymlicka (ed.), *The Rights of Minority Cultures* (Oxford: Oxford University Press, 1995).

48. There would have to be appropriate safeguards here to prevent rejectionist unionists or nationalists registering as 'others' in order to prevent the passage of legislation.

49. This helps to explain why the Westminster Parliament is dominated by two parties, while the new Northern Ireland Assembly is dominated by four. A PR–party-list electoral system with Northern Ireland as one constituency would be even more facilitative of new parties. However, before integrationists rush for this option, they should consider that the fragmentation of the party system that it would give rise to might not necessarily have 'integrating' effects. PR–party list would also put more power in the hands of the political elites that integrationists often hold responsible for the conflict. Some of the disintegrative consequences of PR–party list could be mitigated if a threshold was established which parties would have to surpass before winning seats. However, while a threshold, say 5%, might keep the 'lunatic' fringe from winning seats, it might also ruin the prospects of the 'sensible' fringe, including integrationist parties like Democratic Left and Alliance.

    The potential of PR to facilitate the emergence of non-unionist and non-nationalist parties was recognized by the Unionist government of Northern Ireland in 1929 when they abolished PR because of the danger that it would lead to the emergence of smaller parties, some of which might stress non-constitutional issues. The reintroduction of PR by the British government in 1973 did not have the effect of breaking the nationalist–unionist mould that its backers hoped it would. However, this was due to the popularity of the nationalists and unionist blocs rather than the deficiency in the electoral system.

50. See Ch. 3.

51. There is an argument for making the executive even more inclusive by extending its size. A larger executive, constituted by the d'Hondt mechanism, would give a seat to the Alliance Party and might in future give seats to other small parties. Alternatively, the executive could be constituted by the Sainte-Laguë mechanism, which is more advantageous for small parties than d'Hondt. See McGarry and O'Leary, *Explaining Northern Ireland*, 373–5.

52. A. Lijphart, *Democracy in Plural Societies* (New Haven: Yale University Press, 1977).

53. See R. Sinnott, 'Centrist Politics Makes Modest but Significant Progress: Cross-Community Transfers were Low', *Irish Times*, 29 June 1998, and G. Evans and B. O'Leary, 'Northern Irish Voters and the British-Irish Agreement: Foundations of a Stable Consociational Settlement?', *Political Quarterly*, 71 (2000), 78–101.

54. Ironically, the Real IRA and unionist rejectionists are working allies: both claim that a bi-national compromise is unstable, while being jointly responsible for making it so.

55. 'Peace Boosts Tourism Figures', BBC News, 10 Feb. 2000, *http://news.bbc. co.uk*

56. See D. Horowitz, *A Democratic South Africa: Constitutional Engineering in a Divided Society* (Berkeley: University of California Press, 1991), 177–83.

57. This suggestion is also made by Sid Noel in Ch. 9 in this volume. Simon Jenkins, a journalist, has argued that power-sharing at the Northern Ireland level is unworkable and that the alternative should be decentralization to local governments. See S. Jenkins, 'A Song for Ireland', *The Times*, 19 Mar. 1999.

58. Michael Ignatieff, an Anglophone Quebecker, denounces Quebec nationalists as ethnic nationalists. See his *Blood and Belonging*, ch. 4. Daniel LaTouche, a Francophone Quebecker, denounces Anglophone Quebeckers as ethnocentric and Francophobic (see his 'Globalization in a Very Small Place: From Ethnic to Civic Nationalism in the Age of the Internet', in Keating and McGarry, *Minority Nationalism and the Changing International Order*. The rival views held by the 'two solitudes' can be seen in the reaction to a famous— infamous in English Canada—speech by the separatist premier of Quebec, Jacques Parizeau, on the night in Oct. 1995 when he narrowly lost a referendum on sovereignty the separatist premier of Quebec. Parizeau blamed the defeat on 'money and the ethnic vote', that is, on the fact that while Francophones split 60–40 for and against sovereignty, Anglophones (traditionally wealthy Quebeckers) and recent immigrants (the ethnics) voted homogeneously against it. In the English Canadian Press the incident was taken as conclusive proof that Parizeau was an ethnic chauvinist. For many Francophones, however, Parizeau was merely confirming what they already suspected—that it was non-Francophones who behaved tribally.

59. For more on the distinction between the aspirations of immigrants and minority nations, see W. Kymlicka, *Multicultural Citizenship* (Oxford: Oxford University Press, 1995).

60. Will Kymlicka describes Quebec nationalism as civic because he focuses on the dominant civic nationalist language and policies of Québécois political leaders. See W. Kymlicka, 'Modernity and Minority Nationalism', 173–4. Ignatieff sees it as ethnic because of its support base and because he thinks Quebec nationalists are motivated by ethnocentrism. See Ignatieff, *Blood and Belonging*, ch. 4.

6

Unsung Heroes? The Role of Peace and Conflict Resolution Organizations in the Northern Ireland Conflict

FEARGAL COCHRANE*

For the past two decades non-governmental organizations (NGOs) have played an increasingly important role in progressive social change throughout the world. In three recent centres of political conflict, Northern Ireland, South Africa, and Israel–Palestine, a diverse array of peace–conflict resolution organizations (P–CROs) were involved to some degree within the political process, prior to, during, and after the establishment of major peace agreements and ceasefires. This essay inquires into the structure and behaviour of such groups in Northern Ireland, and asks what their role in the peace process has been and what impact they have had on civil society more generally. The text will make use of research, recently carried out by me as part of the International Study of Peace/Conflict Resolution Organizations (ISPO). The ISPO project is the first major, internationally comparative effort to analyse the nature, role, and impact of NGOs engaged in some aspect of peace–conflict resolution activity across four regions of recent political conflict. With the (sometimes stuttering) movements towards peace in 1993–4 of South Africa, Israel–Palestine, and Northern Ireland, we set out to investigate the role played in the peace process by these conflict resolution and community development groups within the NGO sector and to examine the contribution they have made to civil society.

The Development of the Peace–Conflict Resolution Organization Sector

It is impossible to understand contemporary political issues in Northern Ireland without acknowledging the role that history has played. The devel-

opment of the NGO sector and the P–CROs that evolved out of it is no
exception. The fall of the local, unionist-dominated administration at
Stormont in 1972 and the introduction of direct rule from Westminster
was *the* key turning-point in the development of NGO activity in Northern
Ireland.

It is ironic (in view of the focus of this essay on P–CROs) that when sectarian violence increased in the early 1970s, one of the first noticeable
forms of community organization was the creation of the main parami-li-
tary groupings within nationalist and unionist urban areas, particularly in
Belfast and Derry. While the Irish Republican Army (IRA) had not formally gone out of existence prior to the outbreak of political conflict in
1969, it had become moribund and inactive. The IRA split at the beginning
of 1970, with the emergence of the Provisional IRA, which advocated a
more intensive military campaign against British administration and
sought to act as defenders of Catholics in areas of Belfast who were being
burned out of their homes and intimidated by loyalists. On the unionist
side, the Ulster Volunteer Force (UVF) had formed in 1966, while the
Ulster Defence Association, a larger grouping of urban working class
Protestants, emerged in September 1971. This acted as an umbrella organization, bringing together a range of Protestant vigilante groupings such
as the Loyalist Association of Workers and Shankill Defence Association, in
response to a desire for more coordinated action against the Provisional
IRA and attacks on Protestant civilians. Many of the activists within the
P–CRO sector in Northern Ireland today are veterans of this period, and
some became involved in paramilitary activity at this time. The 'single-
identity' loyalist community development group Ulster Community
Action Network (UCAN) (Londonderry) has its roots within the UDA,
while the 'cross-community' reconciliation organization Women Together
for Peace was formed in reaction to the rise in sectarian violence in the
early 1970s.

It may seem to be a paradox that many of those who are today engaged
in reconciliation and/or conflict resolution activity were themselves once
actors in that same conflict. The explanation for this anomaly is that the
type of people who are now attracted to rebuilding their communities in
the late 1990s were also the people who were anxious to defend those communities in the early 1970s. In that sense, therefore, the formation of both
sets of paramilitary groupings was an act of community organization identical in motivation, though differing substantially in ideology, activities,
and outcomes, to the community development initiatives and conflict resolution organizations that exist today.

The effective permanence of direct rule (from 1972 until the recent Good Friday Agreement of April 1998, and subsequent restoration of devolved authority in December 1999) has had a major impact on the development of the NGO sector and the peace and conflict resolution organizations that evolved out of it. The introduction of what was, in effect, government by remote control, left a democratic deficit in the region. No longer responsible for public policy or delivering services, the main political parties contented themselves by indulging in a destructive critique of government policy and one another. The seemingly endless procession of elections throughout the 1970s and 1980s, together with attempts to massage the political stalemate via inter-party talks, saw an emphasis being placed upon the constitutional future of Northern Ireland, while pressing social and economic issues slipped down the policy agendas of most parties. Crucially, politics within Northern Ireland became disconnected from the process of day-to-day government. As political power and responsibility transferred from the political parties to unelected quangos and the Northern Ireland Office (a branch of the Civil Service which effectively carries out many of the duties previously discharged by the Stormont government), there was a corresponding brain drain within the political class. It became increasingly difficult after 1972 for the parties (especially on the unionist side) to recruit members and activists, with much of the talent seeking alternative avenues for making a positive contribution to their communities, such as through business or voluntary sector activity. This trend was recognized by the Opsahl Report in 1993, when it commented that:

because of the nature of Northern Irish politics and the democratic deficit in which they are played out, some of the brightest talents have chosen to put their energies into the voluntary sector rather than into formal politics. This further underlines the importance of the voluntary sector and its potential contribution to the search for a settlement and the process of reconstruction that would need to follow it.[1]

The introduction of direct rule in 1972 had differing impacts upon unionist and nationalist politics and on the evolution of the community-based organizations that emerged within the region. Nationalist opposition to the Stormont regime had led to the development of a range of self-help groups such as the Credit Union (an alternative low-interest bank run by the community) and campaigning organizations epitomized by the civil rights movement. Consequently, when the edifice of government disappeared in 1972, there was already an infrastructure of community-based

organizations in place. This was not the case within the unionist population, the majority of whom had looked to Stormont, rather than the NGO
sector, for political and economic leadership.

The absence of an administration at Stormont encouraged fracturing
within unionist politics and the beginning of a reassessment by the
Protestant working class about their alliance with the middle class. Prior to
1972 unionism was relatively easy to understand; it was about preserving the
Stormont administration, which was always, of course, a unionist administration. In that sense the political project was about self-preservation.
However, after Stormont's collapse, and the rise in politically motivated violence that surrounded the period, things seemed much more complex. The
existence of separate unionist parties all competing for the same votes
encouraged each unionist party to differentiate itself from the others by
offering an alternative vision of the future. Crucially, with respect to the
development of NGOs and community activism within Protestant politics,
the introduction of direct rule in 1972 began the process of revisionism
within working-class loyalism, and gradually led to a re-evaluation of its
relationship with the unionist political elite. While the nationalist community had never developed a psychological attachment to the Stormont
administration, or looked to it for political or social leadership, and had consequently developed a tradition of community activism and self-help, this
was not the case within unionist politics. The majority of unionists regarded
Stormont as *their* government and looked to it for leadership. There was not
the same tradition of self-organization within the unionist community for
the simple reason that for the majority of the time they had had an under-
developed critique of the political system, a condition reinforced, of course,
by their perception that the nationalist community was trying to destroy that
system. Table 6.1 illustrates the manner in which the end of the Stormont
administration in 1972 acted as a fulcrum for Catholic and Protestant relationships with the 'state'.

From 1972, therefore, having previously regarded themselves as socially,
culturally, and politically (if not economically) superior to their Catholic
neighbours, the Protestant working class had to deal with a pervasive sense
of failure. One consequence of this sentiment within working-class unionism has been a desire to provide its own leadership through community
activism and self-help initiatives. Since 1972 there has been no tier of government in Northern Ireland that unionists could look to for leadership,
while such leadership that was given was characterized by failure and
negativity. Those who adhered to this view felt the need to play 'catch-up'
with the Catholic community. This trend within working-class unionism

TABLE 6.1. *Political trends before and after 1972*

Years	Catholic–nationalist	Protestant–unionist
1920–72	History of community activism	Little history of community activism
	Looked inwards for resources and leadership	Looked to Stormont for resources and leadership
	Politically fractured	Politically united
	Low community morale	High community morale
1972–2000	Sense of more equitable political and economic administration	Sense of less fortunate political and economic administration
	Better community morale	Deteriorating community morale
	More united politically	Less united politically
	Growth in community activism	Accelerated growth in community activism

turned full circle with the emergence of the 'fringe' loyalist parties the Progressive Unionist Party (PUP) and Ulster Democratic Party following the ceasefires of 1994. Apart from being former loyalist paramilitaries, many of the leading figures within both of these parties have also been very active within the NGO sector, particularly in single-identity community development work. To that extent, a line can be drawn through loyalist paramilitarism, community activism, and political representation in the peace process.

The development of the P–CRO sector within Northern Ireland is a consequence of the unique historical political and economic conditions experienced by the region during the period. The democratic deficit, together with the experience of economic deprivation within Catholic and Protestant working-class areas, led to a politicization around socio-economic issues, which in turn provided the infrastructure for P–CROs to develop in response to the political conflict.

The social consequences of the community conflict which exploded in 1968–9, such as changing housing patterns caused by increased segregation, and the displacement of refugees burned or intimidated out of their homes, scattered many people to areas with few community resources or facilities. As a result of this dislocation, people were forced to fall back on their own means, and many established groups within their areas to lobby for community development. While some of these were purely social or economic in nature, others were politically militant. Paradoxically, therefore, many 'self-help' initiatives often precluded any formal community development from state agencies. 'No-go' areas were formed, most famously in 'Free Derry', which came to be dominated not by community workers but by paramilitaries on both sides. The rise in sectarian violence that accompanied the breakdown of the state forced people to take positions of leadership and control within their own areas. Vigilante groups were formed in Belfast, while ad hoc relief centres and transport systems were set up to assist people who had been forced out of their homes. Community action developed, therefore, in response to political crisis and not merely economic necessity. The evolutionary experience of the NGO sector in Northern Ireland is therefore unique, as it was linked organically into the parallel realities of political instability and politically motivated violence.

The unequal pattern of economic development within the Catholic and Protestant communities during the Stormont administration, and the disruption of unionist economic control after 1972, were also crucial to the development of community-based initiatives within the two communities. Table 6.2 illustrates the differential patterns of economic development within the Catholic and Protestant communities before and after 1972.

TABLE 6.2. *Patterns of economic development*

Years	Protestant–unionist	Catholic–nationalist
1920–72	Control of local economy	Little economic power
	Good level of education	Low qualifications
	Well trained for needs of local economy	Badly trained for needs of local economy
	Good socio-economic networks	Bad socio-economic networks
	Dominant stereotype	Inferior stereotype
1972–2000	Loss of economic control through modernization	Growth in economic power owing to greater public sector jobs
	Loss of dominant economic position owing to legislative reform	Strengthening economic position owing to legislative reform
	Rising insecurity at loss of economic dominance	Lessening of alienation owing to to rise in economic opportunity

From the creation of Northern Ireland in 1920 until the introduction of direct rule in 1972 the Protestant middle class exerted a firm grip on the region's economy. They dominated all aspects of private-sector manufacturing industry and finance, and controlled the large public-sector companies, as well as being the major influence within agricultural and business organizations. During this period the Protestant population had better educational qualifications than the majority of Catholics, were better trained for industrial and business occupations, and crucially were better connected than their Catholic counterparts. Within such an environment, retaining economic control was facilitated by its self-reproducing character:

with property, skills, networks of contacts and influence transmitted intra-familially and therefore intracommunally. The new firms in the 1950s and 1960s sought out the areas with the best infrastructure—in practice Protestant dominated—for economic reasons . . . Hiring practices typical of the period—taking existing workers' relatives or shop stewards' references, preferring ex-servicemen, advertising first in the immediate neighbourhood, stressing the 'right' attitude to authority—ensured that Protestants rather than Catholics would be hired.[2]

The introduction of direct rule in 1972 had a dramatic effect on the Northern Ireland economy. While the Protestant-controlled private sector steadily declined (especially the traditional industries of shipbuilding, engineering, and textiles), a massive increase took place in public-sector spending. The pattern from the 1970s and through the 1980s was for contraction in small, family-owned companies and an expansion in public-sector employment with external investment from Britain and elsewhere. This trend took place in an atmosphere of rising unemployment, which rose from 9 per cent in 1979 to 18 per cent in 1986. The political implications of the changing nature of the Northern Ireland economy are clear. The transition from a dominant locally owned private sector to externally owned businesses and a strong public sector which was no longer controlled by a unionist government at Stormont dramatically reduced Protestant domination of the economy.

This trend was accompanied by Catholic demands for fair employment practices, which in turn saw legislation being introduced by the British government in an attempt to achieve greater equality. The Fair Employment Act was passed in 1976, making direct discrimination in private and public employment illegal, and the Fair Employment Agency was established to promote equality of opportunity and examine individual cases of abuse. This was replaced in 1989 by the more effective Fair

Employment Commission, which has been very active in tackling cases of discrimination in employment. These have dealt mostly (though not exclusively) with Catholic grievances.

It has been difficult for unionists not to interpret these reforms as an attack upon the Protestant community. Their experience of political and economic reform since 1972 has largely been a negative one, generating a sense of injustice and alienation within working-class Protestant communities that has become translated into a desire for community activism. This sense of social exclusion is embodied by the following summary of feelings expressed by Protestant community workers at a seminar on Belfast's Shankill Road in 1994.

The opinion of many within the Protestant working class is that the adverse, socio-economic circumstances confronting them have been ignored by everyone (except when it suits)—the Protestant middle class, the media, the government, the politicians. The remarkable growth of community organizations over the past twenty-five years is a sign that ordinary people realise they have to confront their social and economic circumstances themselves.[3]

This sense of social exclusion within the Protestant working-class community, which had been growing since 1972, combined with their perception of political failure to produce a self-help ethos within many urban areas in Belfast and Derry. The radicalization taking place at the community level led to the rapid formation of self-help community development organizations and the type of activity that had been going on within Catholic areas for decades before.

The background to the evolution of the NGO sector in Northern Ireland was clearly influenced, therefore, by the political and economic circumstances that surrounded it. The emergence of P–CROs was similarly influenced by the context of the political conflict that emerged in the region after 1968.

One of the most interesting questions when studying community action within an area of protracted social conflict is to ask, when and why did groups form? Did they emerge at a particular time following a specific event in the conflict, or was the relationship between violence and peace groups less direct? In Northern Ireland there are examples of P–CROs forming as a direct 'gut' response to particular acts of violence. The Peace People, for example, formed in 1976 following the killing of two children in a road accident involving members of the Provisional IRA. Similarly, Enniskillen Together, a cross-community reconciliation organization, was set up after the Remembrance Day bombing in the town by the Provisional

IRA in 1987. Families Against Intimidation and Terror (FAIT) was another group that formed as a direct result of a 'punishment attack' by the IRA in 1989. However, there are many other P–CROs that have emerged in Northern Ireland in a less explicit manner, owing to a concern about the general growth in sectarianism, or economic and social hardship within a particular community. There is no clear pattern here, other than the fact that 'battalions' of P–CROs have emerged in Northern Ireland over the last thirty years, either as a direct or as an indirect by-product of the political conflict in the region.

The initial motivation for the establishment of P–CROs in Northern Ireland mirrors the complexity of the groups themselves. While some formed in response to a particular violent event and pursued a single-issue human rights focus, such as FAIT, others emerged because of a gradual sense that their defined community was losing out, economically, socially, or culturally. Yet others evolved out of existing organizations or those that had recently become defunct. In this sense, the initial focus and objectives of the P–CRO were often linked closely to the circumstances of its birth. UCAN (Londonderry) is a good example of a typical urban single-identity group, with its central focus being simply an operational extension of its birth. UCAN emerged in the early 1970s out of the UDA as a working-class Protestant alliance committed to reviving the loyalist cultural and economic position in urban centres of Northern Ireland. UCAN (Londonderry) was formed in 1995 as an offshoot of this organization, committed to improving the economic and social conditions of the Protestant working-class community in the Waterside area of Londonderry.

The central focus of community development groups, therefore, such as UCAN (Londonderry) or Dove House Resource Centre in Derry, and single-issue human rights groups such as FAIT or the Peace Train, is very well defined (and is sometimes self-defining) and differs from other organizations studied such as Quaker House or the Ulster People's College. These organizations tend to have a looser and more adaptable focus, responding to what they see as changing community needs, rather than lobbying against a pre-identified set of issues or grievances.

While some organizations such as Women Together formed in response to a general decline in community relations and subsequent upsurge in sectarian violence, others had a more focused approach, though this remained within the parameters of the symptoms and products of the conflict rather than addressing its inherent political or historical causes. The Committee on the Administration of Justice, for example, was formed in 1981 as a civil rights organization with a particular focus on the criminal justice system.

The general background to its birth relates to the deteriorating political situation in the early 1980s and the difficulties presented to the British government of devising and operating legislative procedures for dealing with politically motivated violence within a human rights context.

The emergence of the Peace Train organization in 1989 again illustrates the way in which a specific by-product of the conflict (in this case the blowing-up of the Belfast to Dublin railway line by the IRA), rather than its inherent causes, was the dynamic behind group formation. When one of the organization's former activists was asked to explain the factors that motivated such a diverse collection of individuals to come together at this particular time and on this particular agenda, it was claimed that its genesis was the product of an emotional gut feeling, rather than an intellectual reaction to an intractable political problem. People from a wide variety of political and cultural persuasions came together simply because: '*there was something inherently appalling* about the IRA (which espoused Irish unity), repeatedly blowing up the one physical link between Northern Ireland and the Irish Republic'.[4]

Diagnoses and Cures

It is clear that there are a lot of groups within Northern Ireland engaged in peace and conflict resolution activity. However, it is also apparent that these organizations have a variety of viewpoints on the conflict and how it should be resolved. The first point to make is that the vast majority of P–CROs in Northern Ireland have been formed in response to the *symptoms* of the political conflict in Northern Ireland rather than its *causes* or perceived causes, whether those symptoms took the form of an escalation in politically motivated violence, a sense of communal deprivation, or a belief that a defined community was losing out, politically, socially, culturally, or economically. While single-identity groups and cross-community organizations clearly defined *the community* in different ways, the motivation for establishment was often identical.

It is significant that most of the P–CROs active in Northern Ireland have a very under-developed view of the conflict and the possible approaches to resolving it. The groups fall into two broad categories, of having either a behavioural or a structural view of the conflict (described below), but this exists in a rather general and vague sense. At one level it seems very odd that groups who are active as P–CROs should avoid developing a coherent analysis of the conflict's causes—other than in the most primitive sense.

There are two reasons that explain this apparent anomaly. First, many of the people who were drawn to these organizations were motivated by the symptoms of the conflict, which of course are real, tangible, and terrible, rather than its causes, which may be political, historical, and invisible. As it was the effects of the conflict rather than its underlying causes that impacted upon people in their everyday lives, it is understandable that P–CROs evolved in response to these and have mobilized around them, whether that involved campaigning against the use of plastic bullets by the Royal Ulster Constabulary, or against paramilitary punishment beatings and intimidation of the civilian population. It is also the case, of course, that the effects of the conflict are much easier to tackle than the causes, as they are often more visual and self-contained. As a consequence, the goals and objectives of many P–CROs were developed to address the effects of violence and the human costs of the conflict.

The second reason why P–CROs emerged in response to the effects of the conflict is a practical one. The desire of many of them to broaden their support often prevented them from developing a coherent analysis of the causes of conflict. To have presented such an argument would inevitably have meant making value-judgements about 'who was to blame' for it, and thus very quickly to make enemies of one side or the other. In addition, as P–CROs will often attempt to gain support for their goals by trying to attract as wide a constituency as possible, they will often try to appear non-partisan, non-political, or apolitical. They may consciously seek to include Protestant and Catholic, unionist and nationalist, loyalist and republican, in their membership, or even on their management committees. The effect of this is that they are constrained within certain limitations, in terms of both their analysis of the political conflict and the nature of their activities. To move away from the central focus of the organization, or to attempt to broaden that focus by moving from the specific to the general, could risk creating internal animosities or splits within the group.

Within Northern Ireland most of the analysis of the P–CRO sector is kept at a general level. Statements such as 'We have all suffered from the conflict' are typical. In practically every case the P–CROs do not see the conflict as being the sole responsibility of the paramilitary organizations. Most see it as being a wider issue of community mistrust and sectarianism, where the paramilitary groups are the product of, rather than causes of, the conflict.

During the last thirty years of P–CRO activity in Northern Ireland two alternative views of the conflict have evolved. The first is a behavioural analysis and the second is a structural analysis. The behavioural analysis argues that the conflict is, at its most fundamental, a product of dysfunctional human relationships, a consequence of a negative stereotyping of the 'other' community and a lack of contact and communication with that 'other' community to break down the myths and distrust that provide the fuel for conflict. The structural analysis, on the other hand, believes that the conflict is a consequence of fundamentally separate national identities and a political system that has fostered the separate development of two communities.

These opposing approaches to analysing the conflict have led to two different views on how it should be resolved. Those who subscribe to the behavioural model argue for reforms that will increase contact between the two communities, such as the provision of children's holidays, or political seminars to facilitate dialogue between unionists and nationalists. This sees the creation of better community relations and cross-community reconciliation as being the key to conflict resolution in Northern Ireland. Those who adhere to the structural model suggest that large-scale changes have to be made in the structure of society for the conflict to be resolved, such as reform of the political system and other social and economic modes of organization.

Of course, single-identity groups within the nationalist and unionist communities had radically different attitudes to the structural problems causing the conflict. Thus, for unionists it was a political system that was squeezing the life out of their community and trying to extinguish their cultural tradition, while for nationalists it was the partition of Ireland and the malign interference of Britain in Irish politics. It has to be stressed that the adoption of either of these models by the P–CRO is often unconscious and is not clear-cut. Quite often elements of behavioural and structural approaches will be held simultaneously by individuals and organizations. Such philosophical double-think may be inconsistent or anomalous, but it exists nonetheless. Perhaps the explanation lies in the fact that unlike in other regions, such as South Africa or Israel–Palestine, P–CROs in Northern Ireland are often broad coalitions driven by pragmatic alliances and focused on the symptoms of the conflict, rather than cohesive movements committed to clear ideological goals, such as ending apartheid or Israeli occupation.

Unsurprisingly, considering the diversity of organizations that exist in Northern Ireland, attitudes among P–CROs concerning the causes of political conflict in Northern Ireland reflect those of the general society. However, it is possible to detect a number of common themes. These centre around the desire to bring 'ordinary people' into the political process and to supplement attempts by the political elites to reach a historic compromise, with contributions from other sections of civil society. There is a strong belief within the P–CRO sector that the formal political process and the actors within it have failed to produce a viable settlement and have excluded the ordinary people from exerting their influence. Consequently, there is a desire to see a broadening of the political dialogue and an inclusion of civil society in the political debate.

As explained at the beginning of this chapter, three types of conflict resolution activity are carried out in Northern Ireland. One approach is to engage in cross-community activity; a second is to work on an inter-community basis, that is, separately with both sides of the community on the basis of their common socio-economic interests. The third approach is single-identity work within one community. The main focus of such groups is to redress what they regard as economic and social deprivation within their own defined communities, as a first step towards decreasing sectarianism or tackling more contentious political or cultural issues. However, with single-identity organizations there is a major question of where the internal capacity-building of such groups stops and the inter-community conflict resolution element begin? Are these P–CROs actually engaging in a conflict resolution strategy, or simply producing better-educated bigots?

It is clear that P–CRO attitudes to the causes of political instability and inter-ethnic violence are often determined by practical realities, the focus of its activities, and the nature of its constituency. Thus, a cross-community reconciliation group will invariably possess a different organizational view from a single-identity community development group. In both cases the make-up of participants and the focus of activity will often determine the general attitude to questions surrounding the political conflict. For example, single-identity groups such as UCAN (Londonderry) and Dove House Resource Centre take a structural approach to the conflict, albeit from opposite ends of the political spectrum. From these perspectives the problem is based on flawed political structures and the incompatible goals of two distinct ethno-national communities. As one person remarked, 'There is the British and there is the Irish, and never the twain shall meet.'[5] Similarly, a single-issue human rights group such as FAIT that concentrates on paramilitary punishment attacks would take the view that the conflict centres around 'the terrorists', while a community development group from an interface area of Belfast such as the Springfield Inter-Community Development Project would adopt a much less judgemental strategy. Cross-community reconciliation organizations such as Women Together advocate a more behavioural model, arguing that politically motivated violence is a consequence of the creation of negative stereotypes and could be tackled through cross-community contact and communication. It would be accurate to say that single-identity and most conflict resolution P–CROs adopt a structural definition, while most of the cross-community and reconciliation groups fit more neatly within the behavioural model. It is important to emphasize that many groups demonstrate features of both approaches, sometimes simultaneously. As suggested above, such inconsistency reflects the fact that these organizations are not driven by ideology but by a more pragmatic agenda.

The structural model often emphasizes one or more of the following variables: that two separate national identities exist within Northern Ireland; that the political system is based upon sectarian division; that a zero-sum equation exists whereby any gain for one bloc will automatically be a loss for the other; that the two communities are demographically and physically divided; that the historical evolution of Northern Ireland plays a central role in the conflict and must be addressed in any conflict resolution strategy; and that structures of separation in the social and cultural fields such as religion, education, music, and sport all underpin and reinforce communal division and conflict. Groups that conform to the behavioural model are more likely to emphasize the contact hypothesis; the need for communication and dialogue within and between the two main communities; the need to address economic deprivation and the social, political, and cultural causes of community alienation; and the need to tackle sectarianism at both the individual and group levels.

The one uniting factor that binds all P–CROs together in Northern Ireland is the emphasis on the present and future rather than the past. There is a clear effort to concentrate on how to move out of the conflict, rather than to come to any definitive conclusions about why it exists or what its underlying causes might be. However, once again this poses the question whether P–CROs can actually contribute to resolving a conflict if they consciously avoid an organizational view regarding its causes and dynamic forces.

These structuralist and behaviourist attitudes displayed by the P–CROs studied, parallel the wider academic debate surrounding the dynamics of the Northern Ireland conflict and possible approaches to managing or resolving it. There are those who argue, on the one hand, that the rival ideologies of Irish nationalism and Ulster unionism can be transcended through behaviourist mechanisms such as greater contact, communication, dialogue, and new modes of thinking. Others take the structural perspective that these rival ideologies are separate and antithetical identities which cannot be integrated but must be recognized and accommodated through political mechanisms such as consociationalism. This debate is ongoing within the academic community, and is reflected by several contributions within this volume. I will address the impact that the P–CRO sector has had on this argument in the next section.

Contributions of Peace–Conflict Resolution Organizations to the Peace Process

For the last thirty years of politically motivated conflict in Northern Ireland, P–CROs have tirelessly mined the seam of hope and dialogue within an atmosphere of increasing polarization and sectarianism. Countless people have joined such organizations and given generously of their time and energy, often for little material reward, while some have paid for such involvement with their lives. Hundreds of millions of pounds have been poured into this sector over the period by successive British governments and lately by the European Union, to fund a plethora of community reconciliation and community development projects. It seems reasonable, therefore, to ask whether all of this activity and effort has had any effect on the nature of the conflict and the society within which that conflict takes place.

During the last six years Northern Ireland has experienced a peace process which, on 10 April 1998, culminated in a historic political agreement between unionists and nationalists. The hard question to ask is, did the activity of the P–CRO sector influence the development of the peace process, and if so in what ways? Alternatively, would the peace process have happened anyway, regardless of the work that these organizations have carried out over the last thirty years?

It would be accurate to say that the P–CRO sector has not had a direct impact upon the peace process in Northern Ireland. It is ironic perhaps to recognize that the major turning-points that have moved the political process forward have often been violent events rather than peaceful ones. The most obvious example of this was the Shankill bombing of 23 October 1993, when an IRA man killed himself and nine civilians in a no-warning bomb on Belfast's Shankill Road. The following weekend loyalist paramilitaries retaliated, killing seven people in the Rising Sun bar at Greysteel. At this point Northern Ireland seemed to many who were living there to be looking into a Bosnian-style abyss of civil war and large-scale sectarian violence. The political process had stalled with the recent failure of multi-party talks between the main 'constitutional' parties, and the vacuum was being filled by paramilitary violence. At that moment the work of P–CROs seemed to count for little. It was the prospect of descending into that abyss that galvanized the British and Irish governments into further activity, leading within a few months to the signing of the Downing Street Declaration on 15 December 1993.

The major impact of P–CROs has not been direct, therefore, but indirect. The last thirty years of activity have had a gradual effect on the terms of political debate and have introduced the inclusivist NGO philosophy into the political arena. It is very difficult to point to a single P–CRO and claim that it has had a significant effect on the direction of the peace process. It would be fair to say that the NGOs that have had the greatest impact have not necessarily been those with the highest public profiles. Ironically, it has been the small-scale local initiatives and the work of the 'unsung heroes' that has turned out to be the most lasting and effective. The larger demonstrations and public vigils organized by groups such as the Peace People in the late 1970s failed to develop and could not sustain momentum, because they lacked a sense of strategic purpose or direction. However, such groups *were* extremely valuable as an emotional safety-valve to display community opposition to violence.

Indirectly, the NGO sector generally has been extremely influential in the peace process. The work of the sector over the last thirty years has encouraged debate, and provided the opportunity for community activists to come forward and form an extra tier of progressive leadership within civil society generally and in the political process in particular. This has included providing an avenue for former paramilitaries to enter the political process via community activism. One person explained this transformation in the following way: 'I think so many people went into the Maze prison and found God and sought forgiveness, and one or two of them went in and found sociology and politics, and which are the people who have come forward and are useful now? It's not the God-squad ones!'[6] The growth of the NGO sector in Northern Ireland has provided the space for such people to grow, and some on both the republican and loyalist sides have now entered mainstream politics.

At least four of the political parties involved in negotiating the Good Friday Agreement of 10 April 1998 have been substantially influenced by community sector politics, and many of these people have been elected to the Northern Ireland Assembly set up in June to implement the

Agreement. Perhaps the most obvious of these is the Northern Ireland Women's Coalition, whose members have been substantially drawn from the NGO sector. While the Women's Coalition has struggled to obtain significant electoral support, it has attempted to infuse the political process with the NGO values of inclusiveness, dialogue, and tolerance. It has to be admitted, of course, that many within the political process in Northern Ireland remain immune from the charms of such ideas. Nevertheless, there is tangible evidence that the ideas and ethos promoted by the NGO sector have impacted directly on the political structures of Northern Ireland.

The Civic Forum is an aspect of the Good Friday Agreement which is often forgotten in the publicity that accompanies high-profile issues such as new cross-border bodies and weapons decommissioning, yet this is an integral part of the Agreement which was actively promoted by the Women's Coalition and the NGO sector generally. This is a revolutionary idea in terms of Northern Ireland politics, as it is a non party-political structure which gives institutional recognition to the other stakeholders in civil society, and is envisaged as acting as a resource for the explicitly polit-ical lower chamber. It is unlikely that the Civic Forum would have been created without the intellectual contribution made by the NGO sector over the duration of the conflict.

At a more general level it is unlikely that the negotiations that led to the Good Friday Agreement would have ended successfully without the con-tributions made by the loyalist parties and the Women's Coalition. If we accept this point, then we also have to accept the fact that the P–CRO sec-tor and the wider civil society within which it is located were pivotal to the success of the peace process.

Returning to the argument concerning the integration or accommoda-tion of unionist and nationalist identities, the findings from this study of the P–CRO sector may contribute to the debate. The first point to make is that 'civil society' is not a homogeneous beast in Northern Ireland with coherent political objectives, as was the case in South Africa and to a lesser extent in Israel–Palestine. While some P–CROs are working to erode the traditional political identities represented by unionism and nationalism, just as many (if not more) are committed to accommodating these alternative identities and establishing mechanisms that will allow them to coexist peacefully. It is clear that those P–CROs who argue that sectarian divisions between the 'two communities' can be broken down and transcended by a new post-nationalist citizenship would fall mainly within the cross-community category. Those adopting the more structural approach that the 'two community' model is mutually exclusive tend to be single-identity in nature. To repeat the opinion of one such organization: 'There is the British and there is the Irish and never the twain shall meet.'

However, the signing of the Good Friday Agreement on 10 April 1998 would suggest otherwise. The two communities did meet, and the activity of the P–CRO sector played a significant part in this success. Some critics of the settlement argue that it has institutionalized the sectarian divisions within Northern Ireland and that the communities have not met, but continue to dance uneasily around one another. This point will be addressed shortly.

There is a paradox here. While much of civil society, including the larger groups such as the business sector, trade unions, and the churches, is articulating a philosophy based on post-nationalism and on the possibility of a new citizenship that would end sectarianism and bring the two communities together, it appeared to embrace a settlement that did the reverse, that recognized the 'two community' model and constructed political institutions around that reality. For example, within the new Northern Ireland Assembly members have to designate themselves as being either 'unionist', 'nationalist', or 'other', and contentious decisions are now being taken through the means of a sectarian headcount.

It is curious that, while some observers who are opposed to consociationalism see its application in Northern Ireland as being a step backwards in the search for a lasting settlement (including authors within this volume), few of the P–CRO groups or civil society activists are adopting the same attitude. In fact, many of these people from within the P–CRO sector who would also adhere more to the behavioural rather than structural school became involved in the independent 'yes' campaign during the referendum on the Good Friday Agreement.

It might seem anomalous that civil society activists who believe in the transitive capacity of unionism and nationalism should embrace a settlement that seems to do the opposite, namely, that enshrines and highlights the 'two communities' model, rather than attempting to break it down or reconcile it. Perhaps the explanation for this is contained in a deeper understanding of the nature of the Agreement. At one level the Good Friday Agreement is located firmly within consociational theory, as explained above. However, simply because the new Assembly recognizes the reality of an ideological division between unionism and nationalism, and builds in structures to reflect this reality, it does not follow that such divisions will remain set in stone forever. To take a neighbouring example, who would argue that the nature of the Labour and Conservative Parties in Britain today is the same as it was in the early 1980s when Thatcherism and democratic socialism stalked the land? While the labels are the same and people may still categorize themselves as being in one camp or the other, the meaning of this, and the character of the parties and their interactions with one another, have changed enormously during the last twenty years. This evolution was not prevented simply because both sides were defined in an oppositional and adversarial relationship to one another. It is entirely possible, therefore, to see unionism and nationalism being transcended *in substance* through the Good Friday Agreement, whatever labels are used to delineate the sides. This explains why P–CROs and civil society groups with structural or behavioural perspectives (or both) can accept the Agreement with equal enthusiasm. It reflects the existing ideological divisions within Northern Ireland without cutting off the possibility that these may transform and evolve in the years to come. If the Agreement is implemented as intended and begins to work, it is possible to envisage a new form of politics emerging within Northern Ireland which is based on pragmatism rather than ideology. If the executive does begin to function effectively and becomes responsible for delivering services, balancing budgets, and prioritizing public spending plans, it is conceivable that the politicians and the people who support them will become concerned with more immediate social and economic issues rather than the wider ideological debate. If politics starts to become a battle over resources rather than identities, it is possible that some form of class-based politics could evolve, with informal coalitions being made across traditional party lines. Over time, as cross-border cooperation increases and the relationship between Northern nationalism and Britain becomes less contested, it is possible that the whole nature of the unionist and nationalist blocs will alter beyond recognition. Questions about what it means to be British or Irish may become increasingly confused, especially if adherents do not feel their political and cultural identities to be threatened.

All of this, of course, is for the future. The question of whether the existing ideological divisions represented by unionism and nationalism will be eroded and replaced by new forms of political allegiance will only be answered in the years to come. The Good Friday Agreement recognizes the reality of political divisions in Northern Ireland as they exist today. It does not, as some opponents of consociationalism would suggest, preclude the eventual erosion of those divisions over time. That P–CROs and civil society activists have been able to recognize this and embrace the Agreement from both structural and behavioural perspectives illustrates perhaps that the air is fresher in the real world than in the theoretical wind tunnel.

Conclusion

This chapter has demonstrated that P–CROs are woven into the fabric of Northern Ireland society and are just as much a product of the region's historical evolution as the paramilitary groups that many of them were established to oppose. It is also clear that the universe of organizations is extremely complex and diverse, incorporating groups with a wide range of activities and ideological objectives.

While the positive impact of this activity over the last thirty years has been less apparent than the negative effects of political violence, it is reasonable to conclude that the P–CRO sector in Northern Ireland has had a considerable indirect impact on the development of the peace process, by creating new social forces within which politics has taken place. In addition to promoting an inclusivist ethos that was slowly adopted by the political elites, P–CROs provided the opportunity for individuals to move out of paramilitary activity into community activism and eventually, via political parties such as Sinn Féin, the PUP, and the Northern Ireland Women's Coalition, into mainstream political activity and a direct (and positive) impact on the peace process. It remains to be seen whether the Good Friday Agreement will survive, and whether unionists and nationalists within Northern Ireland will be able to continue the difficult task of building peace within a deeply divided society. However, while many obstacles remain, the efforts to do this will be significantly advanced by the activity and commitment of the P–CRO sector within Northern Ireland.

NOTES

* I wish to thank Professor Seamus Dunn, director of the Centre for the Study of Conflict at the University of Ulster and leader of the Northern Ireland ISPO team, for his work, advice, and leadership on this research project.
1. A. Pollak, *A Citizen's Inquiry: The Opsahl Report on Northern Ireland* (Dublin: Lilliput Press, 1993), 90.
2. J. Ruane and J. Todd, *The Dynamics of Conflict in Northern Ireland* (Cambridge: Cambridge University Press, 1996), 153.
3. *Ulster's Protestant Working Class: A Community Exploration*, Island Pamphlet no. 9, (Belfast: Island Publications, 1994), 13, 15.
4. Interview with leading member of the Peace Train, 15 Feb. 1997; my italics.
5. Interview with UCAN spokesperson, 17 Mar. 1997.
6. Interview with Northern Ireland civil servant, 16 Apr. 1997.

Part II

Comparative Case-Studies

7

From Conflict to Agreement in Northern Ireland: Lessons from Europe

ANTONY ALCOCK

In 1994 the Northern Ireland conflict appeared intractable. Each of the protagonists had gone as far as they could go, it seemed, without renouncing fundamental principles. The historical origins of the Irish Republic meant that it could not abandon the minority community in the North without reneging on its very foundations. However, it had no card to play to persuade the majority in the North to accept unification—no economic inducements, no cultural attractions. It was precisely the absence of cogent arguments for unification that left violence as the only alternative. The British government, on the other hand, could not withdraw from Northern Ireland as long as the majority wished to remain with Britain.[1] Yet four years later a settlement was reached and endorsed by referendum by 71 per cent in Northern Ireland and 96 per cent in the Republic. It was widely and warmly welcomed in the rest of Britain, the European Union, and the United States, with the opposition in Northern Ireland largely restricted to unionists. In this chapter, I examine the questions that the settlement sought to address, and how it compares with models of conflict management in other divided communities in Europe.

Background to Conflict: Irish Irredentism

After the First World War, while Irish nationalists sought complete separation and independence from Britain, the British government preferred a united Ireland in close association with the Crown. Northern unionists believed that the latter solution would only be temporary: ultimately Ireland would break away. They wanted to keep their Protestant-controlled industries, based on shipbuilding and textiles, within the extensive free trade area of the British empire, with its markets and sources of raw materials.[2] It was thought that the nationalist demand for tariff autonomy under home rule or independence would spell ruin 'since it would condemn them to a protectionist regime that would expose them to retaliatory discrimination in the world outside, offering them as recompense only the impoverished agrarian Irish hinterland'.[3] The British government's answer, in the 1920 Government of Ireland Act, was to establish two Parliaments, one in Dublin, the other in Belfast, with the hope that discussions between them would eventually bring about unification.

This did not occur. British evacuation of Southern Ireland, the 1921 Anglo-Irish Treaty introducing partition, and civil war in the South between pro- and anti-Treaty forces made the break inevitable, if not immediate. A boundary treaty signed in 1925 between London and Dublin and registered with the League of Nations seemed to seal partition as a permanent reality.

The forces of Irish irredentism were too strong, however. In 1932 Éamon de Valéra, an opponent of the 1921 Treaty, came to power. In 1937, under his leadership, a new Irish Constitution was adopted in which Dublin laid formal claim to Northern Ireland. Article 2 of the new Constitution declared, 'The national territory consists of the whole island of Ireland, its islands and territorial seas', while Article 3 declared that 'Pending the reintegration of the national territory, and without prejudice to the right of the Parliament and Government established by this Constitution to exercise jurisdiction over the whole of that territory, the laws enacted by that Parliament shall have the like area and extent of application as the laws of [the Irish Free State] and like extraterritorial effect.'

There are other such irredentist claims in the world. Thus, for example, in the Argentine Constitution of 1994 Article 1 of the Transitional Provisions states that

The Argentine Nation ratifies its legitimate and essential sovereignty over the Malvinas, South Georgia and South Sandwich Islands, and the corresponding maritime and insular areas, as an integral part of the national territory. The recovery of these territories and the full exercise of sovereignty over them, while respecting the way of life of their inhabitants in accordance with the principles of international law, are a permanent objective that can never be renounced by the Argentine people.

The 1987 Constitution of South Korea is utterly unambiguous in stating that the territory of the Republic 'shall consist of the Korean peninsula and its adjacent islands', and that the Republic 'shall seek unification and shall formulate and carry out a policy of peaceful unification based on the principles of freedom and democracy'. Both the People's Republic of China (Beijing) and the Republic of China (Taipei) agree there is only one China, and that in principle the eventual mutual goal is reunification. The only difference is that, whereas Taipei seeks reunification only by peaceful means, Beijing has refused to renounce the use of military force to obtain it. In western and central Europe the only direct claim is that of Spain to Britain's Dependent Territory of Gibraltar. This claim is not written into the Spanish Constitution.

Less direct and more aspirational, the Preamble of the 1949 German Constitution called upon the entire German people 'to accomplish, by free self-determination, the unity and freedom of Germany'. Thus, 'filled with the resolve to preserve its national and political unity', the German people living in the *Länder* of the former Federal Republic acting 'also on behalf of those Germans to whom participation was denied' (most notably in the Democratic Republic) adopted a transitional Constitution in 1949 which would become invalid 'on the day when a Constitution adopted in a free decision by the German people comes into force'.[4]

In Ireland de Valéra did not stop at merely announcing a claim. An economic boycott of the North was ordered. Force to regain the North was ruled out only on the grounds that it would fail, and not for any moral reason.[5] The effects of the claim and the boycott on relations between Northern Ireland and the Irish Free State, and on intercommunity relations in the North were disastrous. The claim served unilaterally to denounce the 1925 Boundary Agreement between Britain and the Free State and brought the position of Northern Ireland as part of the United Kingdom into question yet again. For most unionists it was perceived as legitimizing the terrorism of the Irish Republican Army (IRA), which indeed began a campaign early in 1939, including in mainland Britain. It brought to an abrupt halt any reconciliation that might have developed after nationalist MPs elected to the Northern Ireland Parliament had ended their policy of abstention in 1925. The siege mentality of the unionist community, never far below the surface in view of suspicions about British governments' commitment to the Union (suspicions reinforced by the refusal of Britain's main political parties to campaign in the province), were revitalized. Unionists believed themselves justified in considering nationalists potential if not actual agents of a foreign power. They acted accordingly, using their majorities, particularly in local councils, in regard to the distribution of jobs and housing, in a way perceived by nationalists as outright discrimination. Not, of course, that the same measures were not pursued in councils with nationalist majorities against unionists.

For over fifty years the British and Irish governments and Northern nationalists argued that the articles were merely aspirational. Even some unionists began accepting this thesis, although their numbers diminished sharply as the province became increasingly involved in crisis after 1969. Unsurprisingly, therefore, there was great indignation among unionists when the Irish government signed the 1975 Helsinki Final Act, Basket One, Section A (iii) of which stated: 'The participating states regard as inviolable all one another's frontiers as well as the frontiers of all the states in Europe and therefore they will refrain now and in the future from assaulting these frontiers. Accordingly they will also refrain from any demand for, or act of seizure and usurpation of part of or all of the territory of any particular state.'[6]

Given the belief that the Irish government, or at least certain members of it, were responsible for arming the militant wing of the IRA in 1970,[7] unionists were hardly mollified by the explanation that a territorial claim was compatible with the Helsinki Final Act provided it was pursued by peaceful means.[8] The transformation of the IRA's militant wing into the Provisional IRA, the increasing savagery of republican terrorism, and the use of the Republic's territory by the Provisional IRA to mount attacks in the North widened the gulf between unionists and Dublin.

However, it was not until 1990 that the 'aspiration' thesis was put to the test. As a result of a challenge to the 1985 Anglo-Irish Agreement, the chief justice of the Irish Supreme Court ruled that the integration of the national territory was a constitutional imperative rather than an aspiration, and that Article 2 was a claim of legal right.[9]

The irredentist claim had an effect in one other serious way. After Westminster prorogued Stormont in March 1972 on the grounds that the unionist government had lost control of the security situation, British policy was to bring about a government in Northern Ireland to which the nationalist community could give support. This, it was hoped, would cut the ground from under the Provisional IRA, and if Provisional IRA terrorism stopped, there would be no need for loyalist terrorism. The British government's solution was institutionalized power-sharing between political parties representing the unionist and nationalist communities. But the unionist community rejected overwhelmingly the idea of power-sharing, arguing that it was dishonest to require power-sharing when it was the policy of one of the partners sharing power to dissolve the framework within which that power was shared. Fears about the nationalist minority were augmented by the Irish Republic's territorial claim.

Furthermore, power-sharing was not a traditional British form of government except in wartime. Unionists were the majority; they expected, as in Britain, that the majority should rule. Nevertheless, in 1973 the British government held elections for a power-sharing government to take office in Northern Ireland. Some members of the Ulster Unionist Party (UUP), the nationalist Social Democratic and Labour Party (SDLP), and the non-sectarian Alliance Party formed a power-sharing executive at Stormont. Its tenure of office, however, was brief. The unionist community split, with more anti-power-sharing unionists being elected, including the Revd Ian Paisley's Democratic Unionist Party (DUP), than those in favour of power-sharing. A general strike by the Protestant working class led to the collapse of the experiment in May 1974, three months after a Westminster election had confirmed the strength of unionist opposition to power-sharing. Unsurprisingly, two further attempts to create a power-sharing government, in 1975 and 1982, also failed, largely, though not exclusively, because of unionist opposition.[10]

London soon realized that if terrorism was one problem, the fact that unionists hostile to power-sharing would always be in a majority in any provincial assembly was another. The question of how to overcome these twin problems came to dominate British government thinking on Northern Ireland. The answer was the Anglo-Irish Agreement of November 1985, a kind of London–Dublin condominium,[11] signed between Mrs Margaret Thatcher, the British prime minister, and Dr Garret Fitzgerald, the Irish Taoiseach. Mrs Thatcher hoped to gain Irish support against the Provisional IRA (which was using the territory of the Republic to store arms and prepare attacks against the North) by allowing the Irish Republic a consultative role in the government of Northern Ireland. Dublin's role extended to human rights, security policy, justice, and public appointments. The two governments were to meet regularly in an intergovernmental conference. This was to be serviced by a permanent secretariat established at Maryfield, outside Belfast. What was extraordinary was that unionists were not consulted at all (provoking the resignations of both Mrs Thatcher's treasury minister and close political friend Ian Gow, and a future president of the Irish Republic, Mrs Mary Robinson, from the Irish Labour Party), and the Agreement was imposed on them. To unionists, Thatcher's initiative— unprecedented in relations between two sovereign states—was treasonous. Worse, Dr Fitzgerald's period as Taoiseach ended soon after, and he was replaced by Charles Haughey of Fianna Fail, a hardline nationalist. As a minister in the early 1970s, Haughey was believed to have been one of those in the Irish government behind the arming of the Provisional IRA.[12]

The much-hoped-for cooperation against the Provisional IRA never materialized. Far from promoting peace and stability in Northern Ireland by reconciling the two communities, all the Agreement did was increase unionist distrust of the British government in London to the point of hatred, while confirming the Republic as an enemy state. The abolition of the Agreement therefore became a key objective of unionist policy.

Irredentism in Europe and its Consequences

So far the argument is that irredentism on the part of the Irish Republic played a key role in preventing good relations between Northern Ireland and the Irish Republic and between the two communities in Northern Ireland. This thesis is confirmed by experiences elsewhere in Europe.

The most striking example of satisfactory minority relations following abandonment of a territorial claim may be seen in the Åland Islands, where a 97 per cent Swedish-speaking majority enjoys considerable autonomy together with measures to preserve the Swedish identity of the islands, and of the islanders. The Islands had been Swedish until 1809, when they were ceded to Russia. When Finland declared its separation from the collapsing Russian empire in 1917, it claimed the Islands as a successor state to Russia, but Sweden also sought to regain them. The issue was referred to the League of Nations. In 1921 it decided in favour of Finland, but urged Sweden and Finland to negotiate a far-reaching autonomy for the area. Upon the establishment of arrangements satisfactory to the islanders, Sweden dropped its claim to the Islands. Since then the area has been a model for majority–minority relations.

Another example of the removal of doubt over the territorial destiny of an area leading from a situation of crisis to a generally satisfactory solution can be seen in the case of South Tyrol. At the time of the 1946 De Gasperi–Gruber Agreement, which left South Tyrol with Italy, the Austrian government failed to renounce the region. This, coupled with vociferous Tyrolese (North and South) claims that the situation was only temporary, enabled the Italian government to take advantage of the doubts about the territorial destiny of the province to grant only a very restricted autonomy to an area where Italians were in the minority.

Thus, for example, the province of South Tyrol, with its two-thirds German-speaking majority, was joined to that of Trento, practically 100 per cent Italian, to create the region Trentino–Alto Adige, where Italians were in a two-thirds majority. With very few exceptions, legislative power came to lie in the hands of an Italian-dominated regional Assembly, composed of the representatives of the two provinces, rather than with the provincial legislators. Even where provinces had legislative authority, this was useless as financial resources were controlled by the Italian state. Power-sharing was required at regional and provincial level. Although it appeared that all administrative posts in South Tyrol were to be filled on the basis of ethnic proportions, this was rejected in regard to state and semi-state sectors operating in the province, such as the postal and rail services, a rejection upheld by the Constitutional Court. South Tyrolese protests were ignored, and terrorism began—first to separate South Tyrol from Trento, and then, more seriously, from Italy. And when the Austrian government was thought to be turning a blind eye to terrorists operating from its soil, the Italian government vetoed 1968 talks between Vienna and the European Community (EC).[13]

What led to a satisfactory solution of the South Tyrol question was three things. First, with the Austrian State Treaty of May 1955, the boundaries of the country were laid down as those of 1 January 1938 (that is, without South Tyrol) and these boundaries were guaranteed by the United States, the Soviet Union, Great Britain, and France. This removed the element of doubt about South Tyrol's territorial destiny and paved the way for talks on the revision of the autonomy statute. Secondly, the talks involved not only the Austrian government (with North Tyrolese as part of the delegation) and the Italian government, but also the representatives of the majority German-speaking community, the South Tyrolese People's Party (Südtiroler Volkspartei). Thirdly, Austria agreed that when the revisions to the autonomy statute had been fulfilled, it would declare the dispute (technically over the implementation of the De Gasperi–Gruber Agreement) closed.

The result of the tripartite talks was to give the South Tyrolese almost all of what they wanted. Most of the legislative powers of the region were transferred to the two provinces, and ethnic proportionality was applied to all-state and semi-state bodies operating in South Tyrol. South Tyrol was also to receive fixed allocations from the state's sectoral budgets.[14] Within twenty years the province had become one of the richest in Italy, with massive inward investment mostly directed at year-round tourism, and with generous aid from the EC's Common Agricultural Policy. Unemployment was almost the lowest in Italy; terrorism more or less died out; and following the collapse of the Soviet empire and the rise of ethnic tensions in eastern Europe, the South Tyrolese model of autonomy was extensively studied by the new regimes and their hopeful minorities.

While South Tyrol is a story of success, doubts over territorial destiny have had catastrophic results in Cyprus. In 1960 an independent republic was created from the former British colony following six years of revolt by elements of the Greek Cypriot majority (80 per cent of the population) and intercommunal strife between them and the Turkish minority (18 per cent). A prime cause of the strife was the hostility of the Turks to the declared aim of the Greeks, *enosis*, or union with Greece. Aware of the treatment of Turks in mainland Greece, the preferred option of the Turks was partition of the island. Nevertheless, the Greek and Turkish Cypriots were forced by the United States, Britain, Greece, and Turkey to accept a power-sharing Constitution. This entrenched a number of safeguards such as a right for both groups to veto key legislation. Civil service posts were to be filled in the ratio of seven Greeks to three Turks.

This was seen as undemocratic by the Greek Cypriot majority, whose leader, Archbishop Makarios, sought to change the Constitution in 1963. The Turks, believing this to be but a preliminary step to *enosis*, refused to support it. The liberal use of vetoes soon put an end to the running of the state, particularly in regard to the fixing and collecting of revenue, and the regime collapsed. Intercommunal strife resumed. The Turks retreated to their ghettos, and United Nations troops attempted to keep the two communities apart. In 1974 the Greek military government in Athens attempted to regain popularity by overthrowing Makarios and implementing *enosis*, but this was met by a full-scale invasion of Cyprus by Turkey. It seized the north-eastern part of the island, amounting to 37 per cent of its territory, thus establishing the *de facto* partition sought by Turkish Cypriots from the beginning.

Similarly, in eastern Europe the Hungarian minorities in Romania, Slovakia, and the Voivodina province of Serbia have been regarded as potential sources of irredentism, potentially seeking to restore the pre-First World War boundaries of the Kingdom of Hungary. With the collapse of communism and ethnic nationalism rampant in its place, there were ample grounds for mutual mistrust. Budapest accused its neighbours of discriminating against the Hungarian language and the right to use Hungarian given names and place names. Budapest's neighbours were alarmed by the claim of the Hungarian prime minister, Josef Antall, in 1993 to speak for all 15 million Hungarians, only 10.4 million of whom actually lived in Hungary.[15] However, much of the reason for the mistrust was removed when in 1995 Hungary signed a treaty with Slovakia and in 1996 with Romania. Under these treaties the parties announced in broadly similar terms, and referring to the Helsinki Final Act, that they respected their common boundaries and territorial integrity. They confirmed that they had no territorial claims on each other and would not raise any such claims in future.[16]

In Northern Ireland, as in these other cases, political stability required an end to external irredentism. Unionists made it clear to both the British and Irish governments that there could be no agreement in Northern Ireland unless Articles 2 and 3 of the Irish Constitution were eliminated or amended to remove their imperative nature. For nationalists, if ground would have to be given on Articles 2 and 3 to satisfy unionists, then the sense of the unity of the Irish people which the articles expressed would need to be recaptured elsewhere. The answer lay in the development of cross-border cooperation between North and South in Ireland, along the lines of such cooperation that already existed in the European Community and had already been mooted in previous Anglo-Irish negotiations since the outbreak of the 'Troubles'.

Nine months after the fall of Stormont in March 1972 Britain and the Irish Republic had become full members of the European Community. Over the next twenty-five years, while Northern Ireland remained under direct rule from Westminster, western Europe was transformed. The Community assumed a large number of economic powers at the expense of the member states, and the number of member states increased to fifteen. Less obvious, but of great importance for Northern Ireland, were two developments. One was the rise in the fortunes of regional and cultural minorities, no longer seen as a threat since all national frontiers were recognized, Northern Ireland being the exception. Instruments such as the 1992 Council of Europe's European Charter for Regional or Minority Languages, led to enhanced teaching of minority languages and to their expansion in media and the public administration. The Charter has now been signed by eleven of the European Union's members including Britain. Six countries in eastern Europe have also signed the Charter.

The other development, also based on frontier stability, was the rise of European regionalism and cross-border cooperation. If before 1972 only Germany, Austria, and Switzerland were federal states and Italy a regional state, by 1998 Belgium had become a federal state, Spain a devolved state, while Britain was about to become one. The existence of so many regions, provinces, and cantons with legislative, executive, and financial powers enabled most of them to proceed to the next stage in the process of European integration, namely, cross-border and trans-frontier cooperation. Their philosophy was that in many border areas not all problems could—or indeed should—be solved by inter-state foreign policy; there was a need for a lower-level foreign policy where decisions could be taken by local politicians and civil servants.

A precedent was set in 1972 when seven regions from four countries founded the organization Arge-Alp (Arbeitsgemeinschaft (Working Community) Alps). The regions were Bavaria (West Germany), North Tyrol, Vorarlberg (Austria), South Tyrol, Trento, Lombardy (Italy), and Graubünden (Switzerland). By 1990 they had been joined by Salzburg (Austria), St Gallen, Ticino (Switzerland), and Baden-Württemberg (West Germany). The aim was to develop common policies in agriculture, transport and communication, cross-border national parks, and the environment.[17] Within twenty years the numbers of Arges and similar concentrations had increased to six,[18] covering the borders between France and Spain, France and Switzerland, and extending to east European countries, and dealing also with flood prevention, cartography, waste disposal, education, and culture. The Arges operate on the principle that their work remains in the hands of regional politicians answerable to regional parliaments. Decisions are therefore taken by consensus by the heads of region at their annual meeting.[19]

Taking formal note of the advance of regionalism, in May 1980 the Council of Europe adopted the Madrid Outline Convention on Transfrontier Cooperation between Territorial Communities or Authorities. The participating states agreed to promote cross-border cooperation, including the right of local and regional authorities to make agreements with their neighbouring foreign opposite numbers in the fields of competence as laid down by domestic laws. The European Community's Maastricht Treaty on European Union of February 1992 provided for the establishment of a Committee of the Regions as a new Community institution. Although the Committee was only consultative, this was the first time the Community had recognized the existence of local and regional government and admitted that these had a place—perhaps through the principle of subsidiarity—in the construction of Europe. So far over 100 regions have set up offices in Brussels to keep in touch with developments, lobby for contracts and aid, and put pressure on national delegations.

A further step in European regionalism has been the opportunity for sub-national regions to make agreements with a state, as occurred with the 1982 Netherlands–Flanders Language Union Treaty.[20] And when the Yugoslav Federation collapsed in 1990 and Slovenia and Croatia became independent, no questions were raised about their standing in the Arge Adria group of regions.

It did not escape the promoters of European regionalism that its development could be used to promote economic, social, and cultural links, if not political unification, of ethnic groups separated from their kin by frontiers. With regard to the Tyrolese, separated by the 1919 Treaty of St Germain, an attempt was made in the early 1990s by the Italian provinces of South Tyrol and Trento together with the Austrian province of North Tyrol to create the Autonomous European Region of Tyrol (AERT). The promoters sought harmonization of legislative and executive powers and social organization in the three provinces, something that would have required considerable constitutional change in Austria and Italy. In a draft statute prepared by experts in 1995, it was proposed that the AERT would exercise its powers in relation to fourteen matters of common interest including transport and communications, energy, the environment, health, tourism, agricultural improvements, trade promotion, handicrafts, fairs and markets, cross-border national parks, culture, leisure and sport, and scientific and technological research.

As it happened, these proposals came up against the hostility of both the Austrian and the Italian governments. Vienna pointed out that North Tyrol would be overstepping its competence in regard to a number of sectors, and that a province did not have the right to cede powers to an inter-state body. Rome feared that the proposals would arouse nationalism. A suggestion that overwhelmingly German North and South Tyrol were the nucleus of the AERT and if necessary could take decisions by majority rather than consensus was also a matter of concern for the overwhelmingly Italian-speaking province of Trento. The whole matter has been set aside for the moment, as has constitutional reform in Italy.[21]

In fact the application in Ireland of cross-border cooperation designed to link a divided people followed hard on the heels of the establishment of Arge-Alp, although there is no evidence that the former was influenced by the latter. The Sunningdale Agreement of December 1973 proposed a Council of Ireland in which a Council of Ministers and Consultative Assembly would be given executive, harmonizing, and consultative functions, with decisions to be taken by unanimity in the Council, in regard to such issues as tourism, transport, agriculture, and electricity. The experiment failed. Moderate unionists might have been prepared to accept harmonization functions for the Council, but no unionist would accept a body which could tell a Northern Ireland Assembly what to do. Statements by the SDLP that the Council would produce a dynamic that could lead to an agreed single state for Ireland, and the requirement that power be shared, contributed to a general unionist hostility to the Agreement. Following the Ulster Workers' Council strike, the power-sharing executive collapsed in May 1974 after only five months in office.[22]

The theme was resumed in the 1995 Framework Documents when the British and Irish governments proposed a North–South institution with executive, harmonizing, and consultative powers. Executive powers were to apply to sectors involving a natural or physical all-Ireland framework, EC programmes and initiatives, marketing and promotion activities abroad, and culture and heritage. Harmonizing powers were to apply to aspects of agriculture and fisheries, industrial development, consumer affairs, transport, energy, trade, health, social welfare, education, and economic policy. These aspects included such matters as training and advisory services, research, mutual recognition of teacher qualifications, and cross-border provision of hospital services. The governments also expected that there would be consultation on a 'a wide range of functions'.[23]

Unionists rejected these proposals out of hand as bringing about Irish unification at the economic, even if not at the political, level. Nevertheless, the Framework Documents provided the theoretical basis for the governmental and all-party talks which began in June 1996 and ended in the Agreement of 10 April (Good Friday) 1998. The talks themselves covered three strands: Strand One: the internal governance of Northern Ireland (i.e. the Assembly); Strand Two: North–South relations (i.e. cross-border bodies); and Strand Three: east–west (i.e. British–Irish relations—Articles 2 and 3 of the Irish Constitution).

There were also two important subcommittees. One involved decommissioning. The British and Irish governments had arranged for an international commission, under General John de Chastelain of Canada, to prepare means and procedures for the decommissioning of terrorist weapons. The other dealt with so-called confidence-building measures and included a large variety of issues such as prisoners, police, justice, the Irish language, human rights, and economic and social development. The problem for the governments was how to get the unionists to negotiate with Sinn Féin, the political wing of the IRA, without prior decommissioning at the same time as bringing Sinn Féin into the political process by getting it to subscribe to a code of principles prepared by Senator George Mitchell of the United States along with two colleagues. All parties had to subscribe to these principles as a condition for admission to the talks.[24] It was not until September 1997 that this problem was overcome and issues were substantively addressed.

Articles 2 and 3 of the 1937 Irish Constitution. Whereas the unionist and Alliance parties wanted to get rid of the territorial claim to the North enshrined in Articles 2 and 3 of the Irish Constitution for the reasons mentioned above, the Irish government and people were concerned that if the claim was removed, people living in the North and considering themselves Irish would no longer be able to claim Irish citizenship and receive Irish passports. Thus a form of words had to be found which, while abandoning the claim to the political unity of the island as a whole, or perhaps reduced it to aspirational terms, maintained the unity of the Irish people as a whole. This was achieved in the new version of the articles:

Article 2. It is the entitlement and birthright of every person born in the island of Ireland, which includes its islands and seas, to be part of the Irish nation. That is also the entitlement of all persons otherwise qualified in accordance with law to be citizens of Ireland. Furthermore, the Irish nation cherishes its special affinity with people of Irish ancestry living abroad who share its cultural identity and heritage.

Article 3. (1) It is the firm will of the Irish nation, in harmony and friendship, to unite all the people who share the territory of the island of Ireland, in all the diversity of their identities and traditions, recognizing that a united Ireland shall be brought about only by peaceful means with the consent of a majority of the people, democratically expressed, in both jurisdictions in the island. Until then, the laws enacted by the Parliament established by this Constitution shall have the like area and extent of application as the laws enacted by the Parliament that existed immediately before the coming into operation of this Constitution. (2) Institutions with executive powers and functions that are shared between those jurisdictions may be established by their respective responsible authorities for stated purposes and may exercise powers and functions in respect of all or any part of the island.[25]

The new version of the articles is thus a success for the unionists. The principle of consent has been written into the Irish Constitution. That consent has to be achieved democratically 'in both jurisdictions', that is, separately, thus on the one hand implying recognition of Northern Ireland, and on the other invalidating the simplistic traditional Irish nationalist view of self-determination, namely, that since everyone on the island was Irish the Irish people as a whole on the island should vote on whether the island should be united or divided politically. Further, in Article 1 of the Constitutional Section of the Agreement the Irish government explicitly recognized Northern Ireland as an integral part of the United Kingdom.[26] On the other hand, the British government agreed to repeal the 1920 Government of Ireland Act.[27] This had been sought by the Irish government on the grounds that it amounted to a British territorial claim since under that Act the ultimate responsibility for the future of Northern Ireland lay with the Westminster Parliament rather than with its people, by consent. This issue was not a problem for the UUP since the principle of consent had already been enshrined in the 1973 Sunningdale Agreement and the 1985 Anglo-Irish Agreement. However, Section 1(2) of the Government of Ireland Act defined Northern Ireland, and there was also some concern over whether the Westminster Parliament's authority to leg-islate for Northern Ireland might be affected. British legal opinion was that domestic law did not require any general definition of the territorial extent of Northern Ireland, and that Parliament's authority to legislate for Northern Ireland was not affected.[28]

With the withdrawal of the Republic's territorial claim to the North, the only territorial claim remaining in western and central Europe is that of Spain to Gibraltar, ceded to Britain in the 1713 Treaty of Utrecht. The with-drawal of the Irish claim has not, however, meant that the issue of the ter-ritorial destiny of Northern Ireland has gone away. Indeed, according to the Agreement, if it appears likely to the secretary of state that a majority of voters in Northern Ireland wished to form part of a united Ireland he or she could order the holding of a poll to ascertain the wishes of the Northern Ireland population. However, should such a poll fail, seven years would have to elapse before a similar poll was held.[29] The first draft of the Agreement had proposed a period of five years.[30] This was opposed by the unionist negotiators and extended to seven years on the grounds that in effect this would keep a politically destabilizing issue almost permanently on the agenda. The issue of a border poll and the issue of consent which it underpins are unique in Europe. On the other hand, the withdrawal of the claim—and the Agreement as a whole—might provide an incentive for unionists to create a political, economic, and social climate that would encourage as many of those perceived to be in the other community as pos-sible to accept that Northern Ireland should remain part of Britain for the foreseeable future. Above all, the withdrawal of the claim removed a major objection to power-sharing by unionists.

The Northern Ireland Assembly

If nationalists were to be given cross-border bodies to convey the sentiment of Irish unity, Northern Ireland required an Assembly with legislative, administrative, and financial powers. It was agreed that the Assembly should have 108 members, with six elected from each of the eighteen Westminster constituencies. Elections to the Assembly were to be by proportional representation.[31] The Assembly was to exercise legislative and executive authority in relation to the six existing Northern Ireland gov-ernment departments, Agriculture, Economic Development (including Tourism), Education, the Environment (including Transport), Finance, and Health and Social Security, with the possibility of taking on responsibility for other matters,[32] such as European affairs and equality. These departments were to be run by committees of the Assembly, filled in proportion to party strengths with powers of scrutiny, policy development, and consultation. Security, however, was to remain the responsibility of Westminster.[33]

The ministries were to be allocated to parties on the basis of the d'Hondt system (with reference to the number of seats held by each party in the Assembly). The largest party would provide the province's first minister, and the second-largest party the deputy first minister. All the ministers would constitute an Executive Committee to agree a programme with an agreed budget. All the ministers were required to take a pledge of office, which, among other things, contained a commitment to non-violence and exclusively peaceful and democratic means in exercising office, to participate in the preparation of a programme of government, and to operate within the framework of the programme agreed.[34]

There are three unusual features concerning the operation of the Northern Ireland Assembly, compared to similar situations elsewhere in Europe. First, while there was institutionalized power-sharing in Cyprus and South Tyrol, in Northern Ireland this took the form of a government of all the major parties rather than that of a formal coalition government and opposition.

Secondly, there was the voting system, which provided for not one but two methods of reaching a decision. Decisions were to be taken by majority voting, except for key decisions, which were to require cross-community consensus. To make this possible, members were required to give a declaration of identity—nationalist, unionist, or other.[35] Such key decisions included the election of the chair (speaker) of the Assembly, and the first minister and deputy first minister; approval of standing orders; and approval of the budget and its allocations, as well as when a 'petition of concern' was brought by at least thirty Assembly members. These key decisions had to be taken either by parallel consent—a majority of those present and voting including a majority of the unionist and nationalist designations present and voting, or a weighted majority of 60 per cent of members present and voting, including at least 40 per cent of each of the nationalist and unionist designations present and voting.[36] The setting of a low threshold in the latter alternative centred round the fear among both governments, the UUP, the SDLP, and the small parties that the Assembly could become gridlocked, and ultimately destroyed, if parties who might wish to destroy it (the DUP and Sinn Féin being the leading suspects) could win enough seats to continually prevent decisions from being taken. They might then be able to breach normal thresholds of 75 per cent or 66 per cent. This fear would not be unfounded.

Thirdly, there was the question of challenging the constitutionality of legislation. In Cyprus, under Article 6 of the 1960 Constitution, legislation considered discriminatory by the minority (that is, Turkish) community could be challenged before the Constitutional Court by the (Turkish) vice-president. In South Tyrol, according to Article 56 of the Autonomy Statute, if a bill was considered prejudicial to the equality of the two language groups, a majority of the councillors of one language group could ask for separate voting. If this was not granted or if the bill was approved despite two-thirds of the language group in question voting against, a majority of that group could contest the law before the Constitutional Court. In the meantime the appeal had no suspensive effect, so that the democratic will of the majority continued in force until a negative decision by the Court. In Britain the highest court of the land is the House of Lords, but there was no provision for legislation by the Assembly to be referred to it. Curiously enough the same lack of ability to appeal to a higher court was thought to be a major weakness of the former Stormont regime.[37] Instead there is provision for the appointment of a special committee to examine and report on whether a measure or proposal for legislation is in conformity with equality requirements including the European Convention of Human Rights or any (future) Northern Ireland bill of rights. The Assembly would then consider the report of this committee, and determine the matter in accordance with the cross-community consent procedure. Referral to the committee would be at the behest of the executive or the relevant departmental committee, voting on a cross-community basis. However, where there was a petition of concern, the Assembly would have to vote to determine whether the issue should be subject to this special procedure, and if the vote failed to achieve a cross-community parallel consensus, the special procedure would have to be followed.[38]

Cross-Border Cooperation

A question often asked during the negotiations was whether one should go beyond European models of cross-border cooperation. Unionists sought a minimal programme of cooperation. Indeed, for many of them cross-border arrangements were one thing; all-Ireland arrangements quite another. But the key issue was accountability, that is, decisions taken by any cross-border institution would have to require the approval of both jurisdictions, and here unionists were prepared to consider existing European models.

Nationalists sought a much wider scope. They wanted a cross-border body that could take decisions which would be implemented in each jurisdiction. They were therefore pleased with the opening proposals by the independent chairman along the lines of the Framework Documents: in seven main sectors (covering twenty-four policy fields) a North–South Ministerial Council should use 'best endeavours' to reach agreement on the adoption of common policies; in nine main sectors (covering sixteen policy fields) the Council would 'take decisions' on action for implementation separately in each jurisdiction; and in eight sectors (tourism, the environment, EU programmes, transport, inland waterways, the Irish language, trade promotion and company development, and the arts) implementation bodies would be established in which the Council could 'take decisions' on action at an all-island and cross-border level. Furthermore, the nationalists wanted cross-border bodies to be established immediately, by government legislation, even before the Assembly came into being.[39]

For unionists this was, like the Framework Documents, an attempt to bring about the economic and social unification of Ireland even if Northern Ireland remained politically part of Britain. It would not have been possible to sell such an arrangement to the unionist community in a referendum. Unionists also feared that a nationalist minister from the North and one from the Irish Republic could agree a policy that would effectively mean a united Ireland in that sector, which was why it was essential for any decision taken by a cross-border body to be answerable to both jurisdictions. They also feared that if cross-border bodies were established before the Assembly was set up, and the Assembly collapsed, for example, by nationalists either refusing to participate in it or defeating the cross-community voting arrangements envisaged, then the cross-border bodies would continue to exist but with no unionist participation. Nationalists, on the other hand, were afraid that a unionist-dominated Assembly and unionist-dominated committees of the Assembly would simply refuse to cooperate on cross-border bodies.

It was David Trimble, the UUP leader, who pointed out to sceptics in his party that a large amount of cross-border cooperation was already being carried out, particularly in the form of EU programmes such as INTERREG. These programmes were there already; they required to be carried on. A forty-three-page paper was produced detailing existing cooperation between Northern and Southern ministries and other institutions, including universities and quangos.

The negotiations resulted in a North–South Ministerial Council being established. It was to bring together those with executive (that is, ministerial) responsibilities in Northern Ireland and the Irish Republic 'to develop consultation, co-operation and action within the island of Ireland—including through implementation on an all-island and cross-border basis—on matters of mutual interest within the competence of the Administrations, North and South'. The Council was to meet in different formats—in plenaries twice a year with Northern Ireland led by the first minister and the Irish government led by the Taoiseach, and sectorally, with each side represented by the appropriate minister.[40]

It was to discuss and consult on matters of mutual interest, 'use best endeavours' to reach agreement on the adoption of common policies, and 'take decisions' by agreement on policies for implementation separately in each jurisdiction, in relevant areas within the competence of the administration, North and South.[41]

To please nationalists during the transitional period between the elections to the Northern Ireland Assembly and the transfer of power to it a 'work programme' was to be undertaken, covering at least twelve subject areas.[42] However, as part of the work programme the Ministerial Council was required to identify at least six matters where existing bodies would be the appropriate mechanism for cooperation in each separate jurisdiction, and six where cooperation would take place through agreed implementation bodies on a cross-border or all-island level. This reduction to twelve from the forty-eight subject-matters proposed originally was another success for the unionists since any expansion of this list would require the agreement of the Assembly. Equally vital for them was that accountability of the bodies was to lie with the Assembly and Oireachtas respectively, whose approval was required for decisions beyond the defined authority of those attending.[43] And important for both sides was the point that the North–South Ministerial Council (and, therefore, the cross-border bodies) and the Northern Ireland Assembly were to be mutually interdependent, and that one could not function successfully without the other.[44] The Council was to be supported by a standing joint secretariat staffed by the Northern Ireland Office and the Irish Civil Service, and was to be funded by both administrations.

Conclusion

In analysing the constitutional aspects of the Agreement, it can be concluded that it brings the management of Northern Ireland nearer to the

European mainstream. The withdrawal of the territorial claim to the North by the Irish Republic not only brought the latter into line with the Helsinki Final Act; it also made it easier for unionists to participate in a power-sharing Assembly (and indeed, as David Trimble's opponents in the UUP pointed out, this was the first time the party had formally accepted the principle of power-sharing) and in the cross-border arrangements. On the other hand, unionists were always under pressure from the threat that should there be no Agreement the British and Irish governments would go ahead and implement any cross-border arrangements they might wish, using institutions without any democratic accountability in Northern Ireland, as indeed the province had been governed since 1974.[45]

As for the cross-border arrangements themselves, they too could be said to fall within the pattern of existing European models. That a region can come to an agreement with a state is not unprecedented. The attempt to have a Council that could take decisions implementable in both jurisdictions, without ratification by the said jurisdictions, was successfully resisted by unionists. But the Northern Ireland Assembly's right of ratification extended only to sectors where Northern Ireland had powers. Only to that extent did unionists limit the effects of the 1985 Anglo-Irish Agreement. As unionists hostile to the Good Friday Agreement pointed out, while it theoretically replaced the Anglo-Irish Agreement, the Irish government operating through the British–Irish Intergovernmental Conference continued to be able to 'put forward views and proposals' on 'non-devolved Northern Ireland matters'. The Conference also provided a forum for London and Dublin to discuss 'all-island and cross-border cooperation on non-devolved issues'.[46]

The present Agreement, therefore, still provides for a foreign state to enjoy a consultative role in the management of part of the United Kingdom's national territory, and thus an unprecedented situation in European inter-state relations still remains.

Overall, from the constitutional point of view, the Good Friday Agreement was positive for unionists. They may not have attained everything they wanted, but nevertheless what they have gained is a cause for satisfaction. However, the constitutional aspects are only one part of the Agreement. Other parts relate to measures to enhance the position of the Roman Catholic minority, policing and justice, and above all, prisoners and the decommissioning of terrorist weapons. These issues, and the problems they caused for unionists, are not part of this chapter and have been analysed elsewhere.[47] But how they are settled will have no less a bearing on the success or failure of the Agreement.

NOTES

1. A. E. Alcock, *Understanding Ulster* (Lurgan: Ulster Society, 1994), 140–4.
2. P. Buckland, *A History of Northern Ireland* (Dublin: Gill & Macmillan, 1981), 5.
3. F. S. Lyons, *Ireland since the Famine* (London: Collins, 1973), 289–90.
4. German Constitution, Article 146, 1949.
5. J. Bowman, *De Valera and the Irish Question 1917–73* (Oxford: Oxford University Press, 1989), 194–8.
6. *Keesings Contemporary Archives* (London: Longmans, 1975), 27301 ff.
7. Lyons, *Ireland since the Famine*, 770–1.
8. Alcock, *Understanding Ulster*, 111.
9. K. Maginnis, *McGimpsey & McGimpsey v. Ireland* (Dungannon: privately published, 1990), 10.
10. Alcock, *Understanding Ulster*, 64–5.
11. 'Anglo-Irish Agreement', *Ireland Today*, special number (Nov. 1985).
12. Lyons, *Ireland since the Famine*, 770–1.
13. A. E. Alcock, *History of the South Tyrol Question* (London: Michael Joseph, 1970), chs. 7, 8, 10, and 433–44.
14. A. E. Alcock, *Geschichte der Südtirolfrage—Südtirol seit dem Paket 1970–80* (Vienna: Braumüller, 1982).
15. *Daily Telegraph*, 10 Feb. 1993.
16. *Treaty on Good-Neighbourly Relations and Friendly Co-operation between the Republic of Hungary and the Slovak Republic of 19 March 1995*, Article 3; *Treaty between the Republic of Hungary and Romania on Understanding, Co-operation and Good Neighbourhood of 16 September 1996*, Articles 3 and 4.
17. F. Esterbauer, *Regionalismus* (Munich: Bayerische Landeszentrale für Politische Bildungsarbeit, 1978), 137–48.
18. With the addition of Arge-Adria (1975), COTRAO (1982), Arge-Pyrenees (1983), Arge-Jura (1985), Arge-Danube (1990–1).
19. Esterbauer, *Regionalismus*, 13.
20. Y. Peeters, *Regional Contact* (Copenhagen: Foundation for International Understanding, 1988), i. 91–4.
21. P. Pernthaler and S. Ortino (eds.), *Europaregion Tirol* (Trento: Autonome Region Trentino–Südtirol, 1997), 170–1, 241–50, 291–2.
22. P. Bew and G. Gillespie, *Northern Ireland: A Chronology of the Troubles 1968–1993* (Dublin: Gill & Macmillan, 1993), 73–6.
23. The so-called Framework Documents consisted of two documents: *A New Framework for Agreement (Joint Framework Document)* and *A Framework for Accountable Government in Northern Ireland*, 22 Feb. 1995.
24. (1) To democratic and exclusively peaceful means of resolving political issues; (2) to the total disarmament of all paramilitary organizations; (3) to agree that

such disarmament must be verifiable to the satisfaction of an independent commission; (4) to renounce for themselves, and to oppose any effort by others, to use force or to threaten to use force, to influence the course or the outcome of all-party negotiations; (5) to agree to abide by the terms of any agreement reached in all-party negotiations and to resort to democratic and exclusively peaceful methods in trying to alter any aspect of that outcome with which they may disagree; (6) to urge that punishment beatings and killings stop and to take effective steps to prevent such actions.

Parties failing to live up to these standards were to be suspended from the talks. Subsequently this happened on two occasions. The Ulster Democratic Party was suspended for two weeks in Jan. 1998 after members of one of the paramilitary organizations it was presumed to represent admitted murdering two Catholics. In Feb. 1998 Sinn Féin was suspended for one week after the Provisional IRA was held responsible for the murder of a drug-dealer.

25. British–Irish Agreement, Article 2. The text is contained in *The Agreement Reached in Multi-Party Negotiations*, Cmd. 3883 (London: Stationery Office, Apr. 1998).
26. Ibid., Constitutional Issues, Annex B.
27. Ibid., Schedule 1, Article 3, and Annex A, Schedule 1, Article 1.
28. Letter of Paul Murphy (Minister of State, Northern Ireland Office) to David Trimble, 9 Apr. 1998.
29. British–Irish Agreement, Constitutional Issues, Annex A, Schedule 1, Article 3.
30. The Independent Chairmen, Draft Paper for Discussion, British–Irish Agreement, Constitutional Issues, Annex A, Schedule 1, Article 3, 7 Apr. 1998.
31. British–Irish Agreement, Strand One, Article 2.
32. Ibid., Article 3.
33. Ibid., Articles 8 and 9.
34. Ibid., Articles 14–24 and Annex A.
35. Ibid., Article 6.
36. Ibid., Article 5.
37. Alcock, *Understanding Ulster*, 63.
38. British–Irish Agreement, Strand One, Articles 11–13.
39. Ibid., Article 7 and Annexes A, B, and C.
40. Strand Two, Articles 1 and 3.
41. Ibid., Article 5.
42. Ibid., Article 8 and Annex. Agriculture (animal and plant health); education (teacher qualifications and exchanges); transport (strategic planning); environment (environmental protection, pollution, water quality, waste management); inland waterways; social security (cross-border workers, fraud control); tourism (promotion, marketing, research, product development); EU programmes (SPPR, INTERREG, Leader II, and their successors); inland fisheries; aquaculture; health (accident and emergency services and related cross-border issues); urban and rural development.

43. Ibid., Article 6.
44. Ibid., Article 13.
45. See *A New Framework for Agreement 1995* (Joint Framework Document), Article 47.
46. British–Irish Agreement, Strand Three, Article 5.
47. A. E. Alcock, *Triumph or Tragedy? The British Irish Agreement on Northern Ireland of 10 April (Good Friday) 1998 and the Crisis of Unionism* (Bolzano: European Academy, 1998).

8

Northern Ireland and the Basque Country

MICHAEL KEATING*

The Roots of Conflict

Northern Ireland and the Basque Country are the sites of the two most intractable and violent nationalist conflicts in western Europe. Both are widely regarded as anachronisms in contemporary Europe and viewed with bewilderment by outside observers. As with other such conflicts, interpretations are divided between the 'ancient hatreds' school, who emphasize deep historical continuities, and those who point to modern conditions as the critical factors. Both regions have seen peace initiatives in the late 1990s, the one modelled closely on the other. While the two cases have much in common, there are also important differences in the context, the parties in conflict, and the issues at stake. Comparing them offers much insight into theories and the dynamics of nationalist and ethnic conflict more generally. Like many other national conflicts, these ones have deep roots, but the nature of present-day alignments and conflicts was determined by the conditions of modernization, urbanization, industrialization, and political mobilization of the nineteenth and early twentieth centuries. So neither primordialist nor purely modernist accounts can explain just why these two European peripheries should have resisted incorporation into their respective states (Spain, the United Kingdom, and the Republic of Ireland) and become the scene of nationalist violence. For explanation we need to look to political factors and the evolution of social forces over the course of the last century.

The bearers of identity in both Ireland and the Basque Country go back a long way. The Basque language is unrelated to any other known idiom and has served as an important marker of differentiation, although it has retreated considerably over the centuries. Another bearer of identity is institutional, the 'historic territories' with their *fueros*, or historic rights, which the monarchs of Castile had to swear to uphold. Although *fueros* existed in many parts of Spain, as did similar privileges elsewhere in Europe, those of the Basque provinces were the most extensive and codified and lasted longer. They were not finally eliminated until the nineteenth century, and the special tax arrangement, or *concierto económico*, still exists. The Irish have been long regarded as a people apart, distinguished by language, law, and custom in the Middle Ages. From the sixteenth century they were also distinguished by religion, as the old Irish and Anglo-Normans remained loyal to Catholicism, merging in an Irish nation, while the seventeenth-century settlers, particularly in the north, retained their protestantism.[1] Since many Protestants were nonconformists, most Irish people, both Catholic and Protestant, were outside the state church and subject for many years to civil discrimination. Ireland was, like Scotland, institutionally separate even after the Union of 1801 but, unlike Scotland, governed by an English minister, maintaining a colonial dimension to the relationship.[2]

So neither area was fully assimilated into its respective state before the modern age. In the early modern era, before the arrival of nationalism as we know it, both regions were the site of a type of conservative, regionalist reaction found across much of Europe. Jacobitism, a movement in favour of the Catholic Stuart dynasty deposed in 1688, found its strongest support in Ireland and the Highlands of Scotland. It has often been confused with nationalism, especially in Scotland, but was in fact dedicated to the reconquest of all three kingdoms but with respect for the old traditions and customs of each. Carlism, a movement started in the 1830s in favour of a rival branch of the Bourbon dynasty, promised a return to 'God and the old law' (or *fueros*) and gained its strongest support in the Basque provinces (including Navarre) and Catalonia. Both Jacobites and Carlists staged periodic revolts, whose defeat was followed by efforts to extirpate the old culture and traditions that sustained them.

Nationalism, however, is another matter, the product of the modern age, and it is significant that, having moved on, neither Irish nor Basque nationalists use Jacobite or Carlist imagery and historical referents, although their opponents, especially the Northern Ireland Protestants, use their defeat as a basic historical reference. While nationalism has many precursors in Ireland, its first serious manifestation was in the rebellion of the United Irishmen in 1798, inspired by the French revolution and bringing together Catholics and Presbyterians and even a few of the Anglican ascendancy. Nationalism developed through the nineteenth century to become hegemonic by its end. Basque nationalism emerged very suddenly at the end of the nineteenth century, following the defeat of the last Carlist rising, under the inspiration of Sabino Arana. Both nationalisms, like nearly all such movements, are historical 'inventions', relying on a tendentious account of history. Arana took particular liberties with the historical record in portraying the Basques as an independent nation in a purely dynastic union with Spain,[3] while Irish nationalists looked to ancient Celtic heroes as their precursors. Anti-nationalists like to point out that neither Ireland nor the Basque Country had ever really been united except under British or Spanish rule respectively. This is merely the reverse of the nationalist teleology. Both fail to address the issue of how, why, and when nations were created and nationalism came to command broad acceptance.

Both the province of Vizcaya and north-east Ulster experienced rapid industrialization and urbanization from the mid-nineteenth century, causing massive social dislocation to formerly rural and traditional societies. Into this unstable mix was added nationalism, a doctrine that could enable people to take control of their collective destiny, or could sow further conflict and communitarian division. While in most of western Europe and North America industrialization and urbanization served, in the medium to long term, as factors of social and ethnic integration, the north of Ireland and the Basque Country more closely resembled some of the central European examples, where industrialization and urbanization sharpened communitarian conflict, notably in competition in the labour market. Yet they did so in strikingly different ways. Nationalism came to Ireland in a liberal, inclusive, and civic form, aiming to bridge communitarian divisions, but ended up exacerbating them and, with the Protestant reaction, precipitating a communitarian conflict. Basque nationalism, on the other hand, started out as an ethnically exclusive doctrine, directed against immigrant workers from other parts of Spain, but ended up much more inclusive, so that, while the Basque society is still divided between natives and immigrants and there is a linguistic division, the boundaries are very porous and there is a rather high degree of assimilation. To understand this, we need to look at the rival claims of class and nation as bases for political mobilization, and appreciate, *pace* both traditional Marxists and many scholars on ethnicity, that one does not always or necessarily triumph over the other. They can coexist in complex patterns, shaped by local circumstances and political conditions. Then we need to examine the role of violence and of politics in eroding or sustaining communitarian divisions.

Divided Communities

Northern Irish Protestants had deep traditions of hostility to, and confrontations with, Catholics, but they also had a tradition of republican
dissent which had allowed many of them to come out for the United
Irishmen in 1798, against the British and Anglican establishment.[4]
Sectarianism had already undermined the 1798 rebellion and the nineteenth century saw the triumph of the anti-Catholic tradition of
Protestantism and the growth of an inter-class Protestant coalition under
the leadership of the Orange Order and the Unionist Party, in opposition
to Irish home rule. Catholics, for their part, were organized through the
Catholic Church, which reached a modus vivendi with sectors of the
nationalist movement. So in the course of the nineteenth century the previous complex pattern of communitarian loyalties polarized into separate
and solidaristic Catholic and Protestant communities.[5] This polarization
took a specfic form in the north, when community divisions were deeper
but nationalism developed later.[6] In the later part of the century, Irish
nationalism evolved in a more primordial, exclusive direction, tied to
Catholicism and, to some extent, Gaelic revivalism [7]. Catholic societies
such as the Ancient Order of Hibernians, the Catholic Defence Society, or
the Catholic Association or Ireland, inspired by the renewal of the church,
grew. This was ever less accommodating of the Protestant tradition and,
especially, of the Presbyterians in the north. There was a strong class
dimension to politics and an active and militant labour movement in
Belfast[8] but working class solidarity gave way to sectarianism, especially
after the rise of Sinn Féin and the Irish Republican Army (IRA) at the end
of the First World War. Industrial relations were marked by divisions
within the working class and the progressive exclusion of Catholics from
the skilled trades. Sectarian conflict, coinciding almost precisely with
divisions on the national question, was thus renewed and came to dominate politics and social relations in the region. Socialism was largely
squeezed out, the Labour Party reduced to a minimal presence, and, apart
from sporadic successes, efforts to construct a cross-sectarian socialist
party have consistently failed.[9] Trade unionism was more successful than
political socialism, mobilizing cross-community support in several industrial confrontations.[10] All-Ireland and non-sectarian trade union structures were preserved against the odds and made advances in times of
peace, despite some rivalries between Irish and British bodies.[11] Yet these
proved largely ineffective at times of conflict and sectarian polarization.[12]

Far from being able to bridge the sectarian divide, they have survived only by keeping out of the major political issues in Northern Ireland.

In its early days Basque nationalism had seemed set on an analogous course. Arana, while not against industrialization on principle[13] was opposed to many of its consequences, notably the influx of non-Basque workers into the province of Vizcaya. For Arana there was a radical incompatibility between Basques and Spaniards and no possibility of assimilation. His was an ethnically exclusive and even racist philosophy, based strictly in blood lines: no one was allowed into the original Basque Nationalist Party unless all four of their family names (corresponding to their four grandparents) were Basque. The language was revered as a mark of identity only as long as it served to exclude outsiders, and Arana was fiercely opposed to the idea that incomers should learn it, going so far at one point as to say that, if the immigrant workers learned Basque, then the Basques would have to find themselves some other language. In 1894, while his focus was still on Vizcaya rather than the larger Basque Country, he wrote:

If we had to choose between a Vizcaya populated by *maketos* [immigrants] speaking only Basque, and a Vizcaya populated by Vizcayans who only spoke Castilian, we would without doubt opt for the latter . . . If we put on one side the complete and absolute death of Vizcaya, that is the extinction of its race and its language and the disappearance of all written and remembered reference to its laws and history, and on the other side an independent but *maketo* Vizcaya ruled by the laws of our fathers, possessing its own language and inheriting our history, we would opt for the former.[14]

The context for these remarks was an attack on the Catalan policy of assimilating immigrants. After Arana's death attitudes relaxed somewhat and Basque nationality was accorded on the basis of birth, residence, and assimilation, although the early exclusivist attitude has left its mark.[15] From the early twentieth century a section of the Basque bourgeoisie around Ramón de la Sota adhered to the Partido Nacionalista Vasco (Basque Nationalist Party, PNV), and the anti-industrial ethos was dropped. Attempts were then made to forge inter-class alliances, adopting the ideology of paternalism and Basque solidarity, and informed by Catholic social doctrine. Sota himself helped found and finance the Basque trade union (Solidaridad de los Obreros Vascos–Euskal Langileen Alkartarua (SOV–ELA) as an instrument to combat the socialists, and discriminated in favour of Basque workers in hiring in his factories. Yet class conflict proved too strong to permit such an ethnic alliance. The Basque bourgeoisie was more inclined to suppression than paternalism and did not hesitate to call in the Spanish army to put down workers' revolts. By 1922 SOV–ELA was staging a strike against Sota.[16] The Catalan bourgeoisie was caught in a similar bind at this time, relying on the Spanish state both for tariff protection and to keep down their revolutionary workers. Basque workers thus developed a class as well as a national consciousness, a tradition which they have retained, re-establishing their own trade unions after the transition to democracy in the 1970s,[17] in competition with the Spanish unions, which appeal more to the immigrant workers from other parts of Spain. This did not mean a return to discrimination against non-Basque workers, although cooperation with Spanish unions is limited to specific industrial issues. While in Northern Ireland status differences tend to reinforce each other, with the Catholic–nationalist community being both economically and politically disadvantaged, the Basque Country has a more complex pattern. Native Basques tend to be better off socio-economically than the immigrants, although the latter represent the 'state nationality' and natives are better represented in the autonomous regional government. The immigrant community has always been fragmented, without cultural or organizational unity,[18] and there is no organization or ideology of particularism and resistance comparable to Orangism in Northern Ireland.

Basque experiences in the twentieth century have been profoundly moulded by the Civil War, which divided the region, with the Carlists (strong in Alava and Navarre) siding with Franco. Conservative and Catholic Basque nationalists, however, were forced into an alliance with republicans and the Left, later sharing the experience of oppression and exile. The exiled PNV came under the influence of European Christian democracy, developing a more internationalist, European vision and an ideology of social solidarity. There was a wide consensus that the restoration of democracy in the 1970s should include Basque self-government, and there was little opposition to the statute of autonomy. In the case of Northern Ireland, by contrast, experiences in the twentieth century have been highly divisive. The welfare state does seem to have reconciled many Catholics to the British connection, but without engaging their emotive support. The partition of Ireland in 1922 was seen as a device to frustrate Irish Catholic aspirations, and the Stormont regime made no attempt whatever until towards its end to recognize the distinct aspirations of the Catholic community. On the contrary, the unionist leadership strove consistently to build a populist Protestant coalition, excluding the Catholics and preventing the emergence of a labour or socialist challenge from within the Protestant community.[19] The establishment of a Catholic state in the South gave force and credibility to these efforts, making Irish unity ever more elusive.

Survey data show that both regions are divided on the question of identity, but in different ways and with considerable internal differentiation by class and neighbourhood. Events have served to deepen community divisions in Northern Ireland, while in the Basque Country political leaders have, in general, sought to integrate and to defuse community tensions. In Northern Ireland Catholics see themselves as Irish while Protestants see themselves as British or from Ulster. In Rose's 1968 survey only 15 per cent of Catholics labelled themselves as British and further questions revealed that most of these used the term purely descriptively, to recognize a juridical fact, rather than as a badge of pride. Only 4 per cent of people were the product of mixed marriages, although the proportion may have risen since then as a result of secularization. The troubles since 1969 have served further to polarize the two communities, whose members are less likely to live in the same neighbourhoods or to form friendships. Since 1968 British identification among Northern Ireland Catholics and Irish identification among Protestants have fallen.[20] Yet there are considerable differences within Northern Ireland, depending on class and locational factors, from the working-class communities of Belfast, where identities are highly polarized, to the middle-class and coastal areas, where there is an easier coexistence. Figure 8.1 shows a divided community, with relatively few people choosing the middle-ground option of 'Northern Irish/sometimes Irish'.

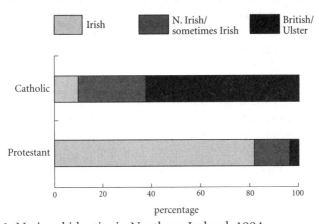

FIG. 8.1. National identity in Northern Ireland, 1994.
Source: R. Breen, 'Who Wants a United Ireland? Constitutional Preferences among Catholics and Protestants', in *Social Attitudes in Northern Ireland, Fifth Report* (Belfast: Appletree, 1996)

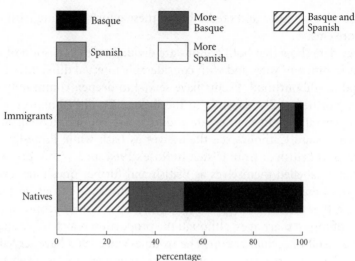

FIG. 8.2. National identity in the Basque Country, 1989.
Source: F. J. Llera, *Los Voscos y la Politica* (Bilbao: Servicio Editorial, Universidad de Pais Vasco, 1994)

Since the restoration of democracy Basque nationality has proved more assimilating than either community in Northern Ireland. Being a native is, along with being Basque-speaking, the best indicator that someone will consider the Basque Country to be a nation and be in favour of independence.[21] As Figure 8.2 shows, there is a clear distinction in national identity between immigrants and natives, with the latter much more likely to describe themselves as simply Basque and the former as simply Spanish. Yet there is a large overlapping group in the middle, who have adopted a dual identity. This is not exactly the same as the middle category in the Irish survey, but is a rough functional equivalent. When asked what are the conditions under which somebody can consider themselves Basque, the biggest response (79 per cent) in a 1989 survey was 'the desire to be Basque', followed by defence of the Basque nation and living and working in the Basque Country. Only 41 per cent considered it necessary to have been born in the Basque Country, while 36 per cent stuck with the original Aranist formula that one had to be descended from a Basque family.[22] The ascriptive criteria of birth and descent had lost considerable support since 1979, although they were stronger among supporters of nationalist parties (and by inference among natives). In a 1991 survey 62 per cent of young people declared themselves to be more Basque than Spanish and 40 per cent to be only Basque, yet 69 per cent of them, and 76 per cent of Basque-speaking youth, declared that the only condition for being Basque was the desire to be so.[23] This indicates a considerable degree of assimilation among second- and third-generation immigrants, since these form a majority among the youth, and a recognition that this is possible and desirable. Immigrants show a stronger tendency to integrate, and even gravitate to the extreme nationalist options, when they are in a local minority, as in some of the towns of Guipuzcoa, but are much less likely to do so in the large working-class housing schemes along the left bank of the Nervion in Vizcaya. Respondents to the 1989 survey were evenly divided on the question of whether native Basques have more chances to advance, although there was not a large difference between natives and immigrants on this question, and 94 per cent of immigrants were satisfied with life in the Basque Country. Since most immigrants are working-class, these figures have a class as well as an ethnic dimension, but show that there are not widespread complaints of ethnic discrimination. In particular, the establishment of an autonomous government is not seen as a factor that would disadvantage non-Basque incomers living in the region. Command of the Basque language is, not surprisingly, much more common among natives and is correlated with identity and nationalism, but there are strong social incentives for second-generation incomers to acquire it. Enrolment in school programmes taught solely in Castilian has fallen sharply, in favour especially of the option of learning in both languages.

Voting patterns show the same contrasts. In Northern Ireland nationalist parties draw exclusively from Catholics and unionist parties from Protestants (Table 8.1). Only the small Alliance Party draws support from

TABLE 8.1. *Percentage religious affiliation of party supporters, Northern Ireland, 1992*

	UUP	DUP	SF	SDLP	APNI	Other	Non	DK
Protestant	92.4	89.2			50.2	43.5	34.9	39.3
Catholic			94.8	96.2	31.2	34.4	42.6	47.1
No religion	7.1	10.4	5.2	2.9	18.7	22.1	22.5	13.6

Note: UUP, Ulster Unionist Party (mainstream unionist); DUP, Democratic Unionist Party (extreme unionist); SF, Sinn Féin (extreme nationalist); SDLP, Social Democratic and Labour Party (moderate nationalist); APNI, Alliance Party (non-sectarian).

Source: G. Evans and M. Duffy, 'Beyond the Sectarian Divide: The Social Bases and Political Consequences of Nationalist and Unionist Party Competition in Northern Ireland', *British Journal of Political Science*, 27 (1997), 47–81.

both communities. There is virtually no crossover from voters between the nationalist and unionist parties, but rather party competition takes place within the two blocks.[24]

In the Basque Country voting patterns are also inherited, showing rather little change from one election to the next, and correlated with native or immigrant status, but with much less polarization than in Northern Ireland (Table 8.2). The vote for radical nationalists of Herri Batasuna is weighted to natives, but one in ten Herri Batasuna voters is an immigrant. Euskadiko Eskerra, a breakaway group from ETA ('Basque Homeland and Liberty') which has since joined the Socialists, had an electoral profile very close to the mean. The Partido Socialista Obrero Español (the Socialists, PSOE) are overwhelmingly the party of the immigrant working class but do have a base among natives. Both the moderate nationalists of the PNV and the Spanish-oriented Partido Popular (Popular Party, PP), which share the conservative vote, draw from both communities, as does Unidad Alavesa, a party based in the province of Alava which has strong anti-nationalist traditions. This picture is confirmed by other surveys.[25] So while there is indeed a clear division between the nationalist and non-nationalist community, this does not correspond, as in Northern Ireland, to purely ascriptive characteristics.

The contrast extends also to the participation and integration of the two cases into the wider state and society. After the political demise of the Anglo-Irish gentry class, the influence of Irish–Northern Irish political and

TABLE 8.2. *Percentage composition of party support in Basque Country, 1990, by origin*

	Sample	PNV	PSOE	HB	EA	PP	EE	UA
Native A	44	57	13	64	74	47	41	50
Native B	9	8	7	12	7	2	15	8
Native C	14	6	15	14	7	15	13	4
Immigrant	34	30	65	10	12	36	31	37

Notes: Native A—born in Basque Country with two Basque parents; native B—born in Basque Country with one Basque parent; native C—born in Basque Country to immigrant parents.

PNV, moderate nationalist, Christian democrat; PSOE, socialist; HB radical nationalist; EA, nationalist, social democrat; PP, right-wing, centralist; EE, breakaway from HB; UA, provincialist, anti-nationalist.

Source: F. J. Llera, *Los Varcos y la política* (Bilbao: Servicio Editorial, Universidad de la País Vasco, 1994).

economic leaders in the public life of the United Kingdom was minimal. Basques, on the other hand, have been prominent in all the Spanish political parties, in the great industrial conglomerates, and in the banks.

Both conflicts have an internal dimension, based on community divisions, and an external one, based on nationalism and the desire for independence of the Basque Country or the reunification of Ireland. The external dimensions differ in important ways. The presence of an external reference point in the independent Republic of Ireland and the memory of partition mark the politics of Irish nationalism. While the Basque Country is also divided between two states (Spain and France) and nationalists claim Navarre, against the will of the majority of its population, there is no independent Basque state.

Casual observers sometimes postulate primordial explanations, tracing the divisions of Northern Ireland back to the seventeenth century or, in some versions, to the twelfth-century Norman invasions. In fact matters are more complex than this. Surveys on separation or irredentism are notoriously susceptible to the wording and context of the question. There is a tendency for those Catholics who, as we have seen, identify themselves as Irish to favour Irish unity, while Protestants overwhelmingly and vehemently oppose it. Yet surveys indicate that Catholics are more preoccupied with their immediate situation within Northern Ireland. Rose's 1968 survey showed 21 per cent of Catholics in favour of retaining the border and only 14 per cent in favour of immediate unification.[26] Surveys in the late 1970s confirmed that Northern Catholics were more concerned with power-sharing than reunification.[27] On a very soft question in 1995 just 53 per cent of Catholics preferred Irish unity, although only 13 per cent were opposed.[28] A 1996 survey showed 15 per cent of Catholics in favour of remaining within the United Kingdom while 34 per cent wanted to join the Republic.[29] Protestants, on the other hand, consistently come out as massively opposed to Irish unity. Other data suggest that Catholics are less likely to feel strongly nationalist than are Protestants to feel strongly unionist.[30] This may reflect a sense of realism in the Catholic community, since Irish unity is a remote prospect, but it may also show that the British state, with its more extensive welfare provisions and public services, is not automatically rejected and that Catholics will respond to initiatives to improve their immediate position. This has made Catholics much more amenable to solutions such as power-sharing or shared sovereignty which have been tried over the last twenty-five years. Yet support for Irish unity as an alternative has increased over that time, because of the intractability of the conflict and the community polarization.

Similarly, in the Basque Country one cannot read off support for independence from Basque identity, although they are related. Half of those describing themselves as nationalists in the 1989 survey wanted independence, against 12 per cent of the non-nationalists,[31] a division of opinion certainly, but not a stark polarization. Support for independence is strongest among native Basques and Basque speakers.[32] Among party supporters, those of Herri Batasuna are the only ones who come through as massively in support of independence. Experience elsewhere confirms that secession is, for most people most of the time, a rather abstract idea, often poorly understood. Given the present-day transformation of the state, the concept is less clear than ever. This does open up the possibility of other ways of accommodating national identities.

So primordialist explanations which place the roots of the conflict in the clash between two perennial cultures are of only limited utility in both cases. Identity is constantly being made and remade. Similarly, the idea that the two conflicts are a zero-sum contest over sovereignty needs to be modified. There are hardline separatists in both cases, but also a large middle group amenable to novel approaches. So we must seek political explanations for why community polarization has occurred and how it has been perpetuated, and inquire into its precise dimensions.

Moderates and Radicals

Both cases show support for nationalist options varying considerably within the nationalists' natural constituency. Nationalists in both cases are sharply divided into moderates, who seek a democratic, peaceful, and legal solution, and radicals who are linked to violent groups. At times the moderates align themselves with the non-nationalists and the state in condemning violence, while at other times they see themselves as part of a single nationalist community.

The division between the constitutional and the physical-force nationalists in Ireland goes back to the nineteenth century, but in its present form dates from the early 1970s when the constitutional nationalists reorganized themselves in the Social and Democratic and Labour Party (SDLP) and the hardline republicans gathered in Sinn Féin, the political wing of the IRA. In the Basque Country the division first appeared in the 1930s with the emergence of the militant Jagi Jagi,[33] but the current split goes back to the foundation of ETA in 1959 and, crucially, to the decision of ETA to continue its armed activity after the transition to democracy. Extreme nationalists are now grouped in Herri Batasuna, while the moderates support the PNV. Nationalists of all stripes reject the state in principle, seeing it as marked by original sin, in the partition of Ireland, and the refusal of the Spanish state during the transition to accept the principle of Basque self-determination. Nationalists played little part in the politics of Northern Ireland before the 1960s; and the PNV recommended abstention in the constitutional referendum of 1978, and then claimed that the failure of a majority of the electorate to support it rendered it illegitimate. Both the SDLP and the PNV, however, strongly reject violence and participate in the political system. The opening-up of possibilities for Catholic participation after the fall of the Stormont regime, and the democratic transition in Spain, have encouraged this, and the PNV has formed the autonomous Basque government since it was set up in 1980. These nationalist parties therefore walk a fine line between acceptance and rejection of the state, in contrast to the nationalist parties in Scotland and Catalonia, which, while not supporting the present organization of the state, do not question its legitimacy. They are also notable in recognizing the limitations posed on their aspirations by the divisions within their own societies. So the SDLP has consistently recognized that Irish unity would be possible only with the consent of the majority within Northern Ireland and through a peaceful, political process. The PNV, for their part, recognize that pressing for Basque independence would exacerbate community divisions within the Basque Country, that Navarre cannot be coerced into joining the Basque Country, and that the French Basque provinces will not come in as long as there are French and Spanish states.

Radical nationalists, for their part, have refused both recognition and participation. Theirs is an essentialist view of the nation legitimized not by popular consent but by their very fidelity to this notion. Their discourse is largely self-referential, with those who question this legitimacy being defined out of the equation. Irish republicans have traditionally argued that only the people of Ireland as a whole have the right to self-determination, refusing the Protestants a veto, but even when the Catholics have voted for compromise, as in 1922 and 1974, have refused to accept this either. Herri Batasuna has a similar ambivalent discourse, insisting on the right of self-determination of the Basques and the need for a referendum in the whole Basque Country, including Navarre and the three French provinces, although this would certainly not produce a majority for independence. Indeed the wider the Basque Country is defined, the smaller the yes vote would be. They square this circle by insisting that Basques cannot at present exercise self-determination because the context of the Spanish and French states prevents them from constituting themselves as a group.[34] So ETA must 'represent' the unrealized people; what matters is not numbers but commitment. Both Sinn Féin–IRA and Herri Batasuna–ETA have experienced a series of splits over the years, on nationalism but especially on the relative priority of the national and class questions. In 1969 the more militant nationalists broke with official Sinn Féin–IRA, which had espoused Marxism and the class struggle, to form the Provisional Sinn Féin and Provisional IRA, committed to the traditional republican goals. The Official IRA later abandoned violence and evolved into a left-wing political party without any nationalist dimension. In 1974 there was a similar split between ETA-militar and ETA politico-militar, with the latter evolving into Euskadiko Eskerra, a left-wing party that eventually merged with the Basque socialists. The ideological base of the remaining hardline parties has shifted according to circumstances. In the 1970s both stressed Marxist and left-wing themes and adopted a Third World liberationist discourse. This enabled them to stress class as well as nationalist themes and compete with the left-wing breakaway factions. It also enabled them to mobilize international left-wing opinion (including sections of the left wing of the British Labour Party) and to gain financial support and arms from communist regimes and the likes of Libya's Qaddafi. With the collapse of communism, the crisis of Marxism, and the end of decolonization, this has been de-emphasized in favour of a looser, populist discourse and a return to more narrowly nationalist themes. Since the 1970s both regions have been hit by de-industrialization, and the presence of a large number of unemployed youths creates further opportunities for radical nationalism.

The strategies of violence of the IRA and ETA bear marked similarities. In both cases one objective is to define the nationalist community itself, marking it off and differentiating it both from non-nationalists and from moderate nationalists. This is not, as the media like to say, 'mindless violence' since it does have a purpose. Nor it is intended to inflict a military defeat upon the state, since that is out of the question. Rather, it follows a political logic. The strategy of action–repression–action is aimed at provoking the state into a repressive reaction, thus cementing nationalist support. Each action is presented as being carried out in the name of the essentialist nation, or as a response to state violence. In this way, the terrorists never accept moral responsibility for the consequences of their own actions, always throwing it back to the enemy. Even discussing the morality of violence becomes futile, leading those who have had enough to break away or drop out, hence the series of fissions in the movements. In both cases, terrorism has often had the desired effect of producing an overreaction by the state, confirming the terrorists' claims about the illegitimacy of the state. A series of spectacular IRA bombing campaigns in England in the 1970s provoked an equally spectacular series of miscarriages of justice, suggesting that Irish people accused of politically motivated offences could expect nothing from British justice. It is widely believed that there was a 'shoot to kill' policy to avoid the need to bring IRA people before the courts, and the British army in Northern Ireland came to act, in many ways, as an army of occupation in the Catholic areas, abusing persons and property in the course of searches and torturing prisoners.[35] In the Basque Country government officials organized death squads, the Grupos Antiterroristas de Liberación (GAL), to seek out and assassinate alleged ETA activists in France. Of the twenty-eight killed in the early and mid-1980s at least half had no connection with ETA.

Another, highly political, strategy is to make seemingly reasonable and humane demands for the treatment of prisoners, hoping that the state will refuse and so convert the prisoners into victims. The most spectacular was the IRA hunger strikes in the 1980s, in support of demands to be treated like prisoners of war rather than common criminals. The Thatcher government played its part here according to the IRA's own script, and its obstinate refusal to concede helped Sinn Féin immeasurably.[36] Herri Batasuna has made a lot of political capital out of its campaign to have ETA prisoners serve their terms in the Basque Country, where their families could visit them, and to be eligible for normal early release. The government has insisted that this must be conditional on their renouncing their allegiance; its real fear is that, as in Northern Ireland, ETA prisoners would be under the discipline of their own commanders and less likely to repent.

While the strategies of Herri Batasuna–ETA and Sinn Féin–IRA are similar, their targets reflect the different contours of the two conflicts. Both attack the police and armed forces as well as economic targets, and both have attacked civilians. A subtle but significant difference is that, in line with Aranist tradition, ETA regards the rest of Spain as one, and has placed bombs in Catalonia as well as in Madrid, while the IRA has confined itself to attacks in England and has never staged one in Scotland or Wales.[37] Neither is explicitly sectarian in its strategy, although the IRA and other republican groups have been guilty of sectarian murders. ETA, on the other hand, kills Basques and non-Basques indiscriminately. In the late 1990s it ran a campaign of assassinations of local politicians belonging to the conservative Popular Party; in the past it has killed socialist politicians and even Basque nationalists. This results from the fact that native Basques are found on both sides of the nationalist divide. Violence is critical in this case in defining the radical nationalist community itself, in the absence of other markers of identity. The *abertzale* community becomes self-referential, justified by its own logic and consolidated by shared complicity in violence.[38] Both the IRA and the Protestant paramilitaries also use violence to maintain domination within their own communities, enforcing a rough justice and dealing with delinquents. Radical nationalists in both countries also stage mass demonstrations of intimidation, taking over the streets, but this is most common in the Basque case and is accompanied by physical attacks on peace demonstrations or counter-demonstrations. Perhaps the biggest difference in the violent dimensions of the conflict, however, is the existence in Northern Ireland of loyalist terrorism, rooted in the Protestant community and fiercely sectarian. This exacerbates the conflict but limits the ability of the IRA to take over the public square or provoke open mass conflict, which could easily result in all-out civil war.

Guerrilla insurgencies like these cannot be sustained for long without the water in which the fish can swim. Here we come to one of the most difficult aspects of the whole issue, the degree of active and passive support for political violence. At one level the issue looks clear-cut. The great mass of the population in both places rejects political violence and condemns terrorist atrocities. Yet the parties linked to the IRA and ETA have a significant support base. Sinn Féin has over the years mobilized between 20 and 40 per cent of the Catholic vote, while Herri Batasuna's support has been as high as 20 per cent and in recent years has been around 15 per cent. It is linked to an extraordinarily complex set of organizations known collectively as the Movimiento de Liberación Nacional Vasco (MLNV), including Herri Batasuna, trade unions, and womens' and youth groups. While organizations within the MLNV will avoid and evade the issue of violence, it is known that the movement as a whole is subordinate to the military strategy of ETA.

It is not always clear what degree of support for violence is implied by voting for these parties. Overt support for violence is rare, but there is a degree of passive support which prevents open condemnation and understands the political motivation of terrorism. The lack of state legitimacy, more widely felt in society including the democratic nationalist parties, helps establish something of a moral equivalence of the state security forces and the paramilitaries. A 1984 survey showed that 80 per cent of SDLP supporters opposed violence, while 70 per cent of Sinn Féin supporters defended it.[39] In the Basque Country there was widespread tolerance of ETA before the transition to democracy, but this has steadily fallen over the years. Between 1978 and 1989 the proportion of Basques considering ETA to be patriots or idealists fell from 48 to 23 per cent, with only Herri Batasuna voters considering them patriots.[40] Outright rejection of violence increased from 35 to 60 per cent between 1981 and 1989, and encompassed all shades of opinion except Herri Batasuna supporters. By 2000, just 7 per cent gave any support to the ETA violence. While supporters of the centre and right-wing Spanish parties have always condemned ETA, the fall in support has been very marked among supporters of the Socialists and the PNV, reflecting their acceptance of the new democratic order and system of autonomous government. By 1986, 80 per cent of all voters (including 80 per cent of PNV voters) disagreed that violence was necessary to achieve political aims. Herri Batasuna supporters divided almost evenly between those who did and those who did not support violence.[41] Polls almost certainly underestimate the degree of support for violence, since it is not something with which people can easily agree in the abstract. What is perhaps more important is the 'politics of the last atrocity', in which people's emotions are engaged by acts of violence, whether by the security forces or by the paramilitaries. Incidents like Bloody Sunday in Northern Ireland or the activities of the GAL can cause the security forces to lose legitimacy, which is then very difficult to regain. Terrorist attacks similarly produce waves of revulsion which may undermine support.

Electoral support for the extreme nationalist parties, however, goes beyond those who overtly espouse political violence. The maintenance of separate political and paramilitary wings of the movements helps the illusion that the two strategies are distinct and that one can support the one without the other. This allows about half the Herri Batasuna voters and a third of Sinn Féin voters to declare their opposition to political violence. The relationship between the political and paramilitary wings is by definition difficult to research. It does appear that the leadership of the IRA and Sinn Féin are the same, but that Herri Batasuna is strictly subordinated to ETA and is used by it. In both cases, the extreme nationalists have forged their own subcultures, with violence serving to mark the boundary and maintain the movement. Both are resolutely secular movements rooted in deeply Catholic societies and competing with Catholicism for social domination and the definition of the subculture. Herri Batasuna and Sinn Féin supporters are much less likely to be religious than those of the PNV and SDLP respectively.[42] This may not be a direct effect, but one mediated by age, with the young being both more secular and more militant,[43] but it does establish a social boundary and removes the moderating influence of the church, which in both cases has had a very ambivalent attitude to nationalism. In Northern Ireland Sinn Féin's support is concentrated in the working class, while the SDLP draws a cross-class electorate. The equivalent is not true in the Basque Country, except that Herri Batasuna is weaker among the highest social class.[44] Support for extreme nationalism is also concentrated geographically. Sinn Féin has traditionally had support around the border with the Republic and has built up a dominant position in the enclosed Catholic community of West Belfast. Herri Batasuna is strongest in the province of Guipuzcoa, where it is the largest single party, with 20–5 per cent of the vote and especially in the small and medium-sized towns. It is also strong in the small towns of northern Vizcaya and in some of the Basque-speaking pockets of Navarre but is weaker around Bilbao and hardly features in Alava. Apart from age, it is difficult to establish a clear profile of the extreme nationalists in both cases, except, at the risk of stating the obvious, that they are strongly separatist or irredentist, while supporters of the more moderate parties are more inclined to compromise and in any case place less stress on the national question. Sinn Féin and Herri Batasuna have established their own subcultures, rooted in social networks and families. In the cities of the Basque Country there are separate PNV and Herri Batasuna bars, the latter adorned with pictures of ETA prisoners and full of younger and more shabbily dressed people. Confrontation with the authorities helps to sustain the solidarity of these subcultures and, in Northern Ireland, allows the IRA to present itself as the defender of a community under siege. Extreme nationalists have not, generally, taken their seats in the state parliaments, which they regard as illegitimate, although occasionally they put in a symbolic appearance without taking the oath of allegiance which would allow them to participate. They do, however, participate in local government, using their position there to build up support on the ground.

Figures 8.3 and 8.4 show support for moderate and extreme nationalists in the two cases. What stands out in the Basque case is the stability in overall support for nationalist parties and in the division between the two wings. The Northern Ireland case is greatly complicated by the formation of new parties and splits in old ones, but overall the picture is very different. The total nationalist vote increases in the 1970s as Catholics become more actively involved in electoral politics and the Northern Ireland Labour Party declines, and continues to increase steadily, probably because of demographic factors, except in the election of 1979, when the non-sectarian Alliance Party did quite well among the Catholic middle classes. Republicans scored well in 1983, in the aftermath of the hunger strikes, and in 1997, when, despite the break in the IRA ceasefire, there was a widespread perception that the republicans were committed to promoting

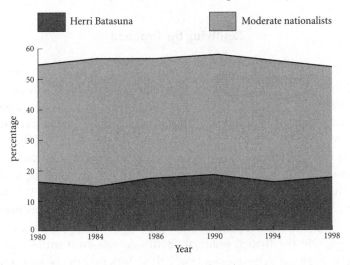

FIG. 8.3. Vote for moderate and extreme nationalists, autonomous elections in the Basque Country

peace. Herri Batasuna, now competing as Euskal Herritarrok to present a new image, similarly reversed a previous slow decline in 1998, following the ETA ceasefire and the launch of a peace process. Three of its new deputies were in gaol for terrorist offences.

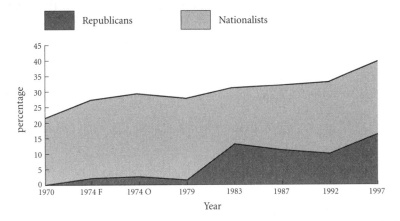

FIG. 8.4. Nationalist and republican vote, Northern Ireland, general elections, 1979–1997

Resolving the Problem

It has often been argued that nationalist politics is inherently zero-sum, since it touches on the question of sovereignty. Certainly the demand that a state surrender part of its territory is one that is not easily conceded, but its significance is quite different in the two cases. In Northern Ireland there is a precedent in the secession of the present Irish Republic, and the nationalist case can be presented as the completion of a process started in 1920. In Spain there is no precedent for secession and no existing Basque state to which the region could accede. Perhaps more importantly, the British government has no real stake in Northern Ireland. It is of no economic or strategic importance, it is not regarded by most British people as part of the homeland, and the British political parties do not even contest elections there. The most explicit statements of British lack iof interest were made in the Downing Street Declaration (1993) and the Good Friday Agreement (1998), but even when Britain guaranteed the border in 1949, it did so only as long as the Parliament of Northern Ireland wanted it. Northern Ireland has not usually been a matter contested between the British parties, and during the Stormont regime Northern Ireland affairs were isolated almost completely from British politics. Polls have shown that about half the British public favours withdrawal or Irish unity.[45] This was not always the case; before the First World War the Conservative and Unionist Party was prepared to countenance civil war to prevent a measure of Irish home rule which they believed would lead to the break-up of the United Kingdom.

The Spanish state, on the other hand, has a large stake in the Basque Country. Although no longer the economic powerhouse that it was, it is still an important industrial region, forming part of the Spanish mainland and situated on one of the two principal routes into Europe—the other route goes through Catalonia, which would certainly react to Basque independence with moves of its own. The main Spanish parties, the socialist PSOE and the conservative PP, both draw support there; indeed the PP has been steadily increasing its support in the Basque Country, recently at the expense of the provincialist Unidad Alavesa. The Spanish parties also use the Basque issue for political purposes, vying with each other to prove themselves hard on terrorism, making extravagant claims about the moderate nationalists, and seeking to use the Basque issue to stir up a Spanish nationalism within the Basque Country and in other parts of Spain. Some PSOE politicians, such as Alfonso Guerra, have sought to exacerbate divisions between immigrant and native Basques for electoral reasons, making wild allegations of discrimination unsupported by the reported experience of immigrants, and portraying the Basque government as though it were a kind of Spanish Stormont.

If the moderate nationalist demands are difficult for a state to concede, those of the extreme nationalists have, not by chance, been impossible. Moderate nationalists accept that nationality and secession are matters to be decided by consent; extreme nationalists have a transcendental conception of the nation which they feel entitled to impose against the consent of substantial minorities or even majorities. They need to stress extreme and even impossible demands in order to maintain a degree of support for their extreme methods. The states, for their part, have consistently emphasized that they cannot and will not negotiate or talk with terrorists. There is a certain element of, perhaps necessary, hypocrisy here. British governments had contacts with the IRA as early as the 1970s,[46] while the Spanish government was engaged in talks with ETA in Algeria in the mid-1980s. It is very difficult for a democratic government to accept the legitimacy of groups whose power rests upon violence; yet neither government hesitated long before beginning a dialogue after the respective militants declared ceasefires.

Until the 1970s both nationalisms were contained by overtly suppressive measures directed against the nationalities themselves. While this type of official discrimination has largely been dismantled, there are still those who consider the problem as a security one, to be dealt with by police measures. There is a long history of exceptional security laws for Ireland, although these were condemned by unionists like Dicey as a affront to the equality before the law which should prevail in a unitary state. In the 1980s and early 1990s there was a renewed emphasis on tough security measures, including restrictions on Sinn Feín, whose members could not be interviewed directly on television. Similar measures were taken in the Basque Country after the coming to power of the conservative government in 1996. The entire leadership of Herri Batasuna was gaoled for encouraging terrorism, and the party's newspaper was closed. These measures do seem to have had some effect in convincing militants that a purely military solution was not possible. Yet they have also served to give propaganda victories to the militant nationalist parties, which could portray themselves as the victims of illiberal measures of repression. The mainstream parties have been able regularly to condemn violence, and in the Basque Country there was a formal agreement, the pact of Ajuria Enea, which constituted a front against terrorism. With the parties associated with the paramilitaries gaining some 15 per cent of the vote, a strategy of isolation is at best a partial solution. Nationalists have also emphasized the political origins of violence. There is also the fact that the security forces themselves are widely distrusted by the nationalist population, not just by supporters of the extreme options. In the Basque Country policing is gradually being transferred to the Ertzainza, an autonomous force built entirely from scratch with no involvement from the Spanish national police or the Guardia Civil and who command greater legitimacy. This has not prevented the Ertzainza from eing targets of ETA attacks.

From the late 1970s there was a policy of 'criminalization' of the Northern Ireland conflict, and 'Ulsterization', in which local security forces would take over from the British army. Yet attempts to recruit Catholics into the Royal Ulster Constabulary and the Royal Irish Regiment (formerly Ulster Defence Regiment) have been an almost complete failure, since the force is so strongly associated with Protestant dominance. The British army, for its part, is seen as an instrument of British rule and not an impartial force.

One strategy compatible with liberal democracy is that of assimilation. After the fall of the unionist ascendancy Protestant leaders of various stripes in Northern Ireland proposed measures to remove discrimination against Catholics, to recognize their cultural specificity, and even to accept formal power-sharing arrangements, on condition that the Catholics accept that they were British. Similarly, people in Madrid frequently say that they would concede the Basques a large measure of self-government, if only the Basque leaders would make a forthright declaration that they were Spanish. These apparently liberal gestures merely evade the central issue of identity or assume that it can be relegated to the private realm.

A very different strategy, which recognizes the existence of separate communities and builds on them, is consociationalism, but this too raises difficulties in both cases. In Northern Ireland, where it has been tried on various occasions, it is acceptable to moderate nationalists, giving them a share in power, but not to republicans since it implies recognition of partition, of the British state, and of the province of Northern Ireland as a political unit. In the Basque Country consociationalism is a non-starter, since there are not two clearly defined communities with their own structures and leaders. The problem, rather, is a division within the Basque community.

Devolution, or home rule, on a majoritarian basis is similarly limited in its applicability. In the case of Northern Ireland, the division between the two communities means that home rule will result in domination by the Protestant majority (at least until such time as the Catholics attain a demographic majority). In the Basque Country there has been an autonomous or home rule government, with rather extensive functions since 1980, and this has greatly eased tensions. It does not, of course, satisfy extreme nationalists, for whom nothing less than a seven-province independent state will do. Nor, however, does it address the symbolic issues at the heart of the concerns of even moderate nationalists. These still regard the 1978 Spanish Constitution as illegitimate since it did not recognize the right of self-determination or the constituent power of the Basque people.

In the late 1990s a new approach emerged in both cases, associated with the moderate nationalist parties and various peace groups. These start from the premisses that:

- political violence is unacceptable and must cease permanently if a solution is to be found;
- political violence nevertheless does have political roots and cannot be dealt with merely as a criminal matter;
- any solution must bring in the electors of the extreme parties and induce the paramilitaries to lay down their weapons;
- this involves, not the isolation of the people of violence, nor attempts to divide their movements by splitting off relative moderates, but their incorporation into the political process;
- any dialogue must be without political conditions or preconceived commitments to sovereignty;
- there is an internal dimension, concerned with community relations, and an external dimension, concerned with the status of the territory within the state and the international order, and these two are connected;
- no traditional state-like solution is possible.

In Northern Ireland the initiative was taken by John Hume, leader of the SDLP, who opened a dialogue with Sinn Féin which eventually led to the IRA ceasefire. In the Basque Country this role was played by the PNV, who started talks with Herri Batasuna, against considerable opposition from the main Spanish parties, aiming to draw them into a similar peace process. In the Pact of Estella the PNV, Eusko Alkartasuna (a social-democratic nationalist party), Herri Batasuna, and the Basque post-communists agreed on a programme for more self-government, effectively replacing the alignment of Ajuria Enea (democrats versus supporters of violence) with a front of nationalists against the Spanish parties (PP and Socialists). A further pact, that of Lizarra, among the three nationalist parties, demanded the right to self-determination. Yet at the same time the PNV maintained its support for the Spanish government of the PP, which depended for its majority on the PNV, Catalan nationalists, and Canaries regionalists. This delicate tightrope held until the Basque elections of October 1998. Shortly before these ETA finally declared a ceasefire. That these processes were so similar is no coincidence, since the Basques had followed the Northern Ireland talks closely, hoping to apply the lessons at home. Both ETA and the IRA were weakened and weary after twenty years of conflict in which they had come no closer to achieving their aims and, in some ways, had made them more difficult, but both needed some political response if they were to deliver a cessation of hostilities and enter the political process. The differences between the two cases emerge again, however, when we examine the range of matters that are negotiable and the parties to the negotiations. In the Northern Ireland case, everything was left open and the Good Friday Agreement of 1998 provides explicitly for the right of the people of Northern Ireland to decide whether they will remain in the United Kingdom or join the Republic of Ireland. It leaves the question of sovereignty somewhat loose and undetermined, with its complex arrangements for cooperation involving the Northern Ireland Assembly, the British government, the Irish government, and the collection of sovereign, non-sovereign and semi-sovereign entities to be included in the British–Irish Council. It links this external dimension of the conflict with an internal settlement providing for power-sharing and the participation of all parties in government.

The PNV leadership has declared that this open-ended process is preferable to their own statute of autonomy, even though they already have, under the statute, much greater powers than the Northern Ireland Assembly is ever likely to gain. Neither of the main Spanish parties has indicated that it is prepared to go this far, insisting that any settlement must be firmly within a Spanish framework. Following the 1998 Basque elections, the PNV negotiated a formal pact in which Euskal Herritarrok gave parliamentary support to the minority PNV government. At the same time the PNV moved to a more overtly pro-independence position and renewed its attacks on the Basque statute of autonomy as an illegitimate imposition. This contrasts with the situation in Northern Ireland, where the SDLP has sought a consociational government of all parties and not a nationalist front. There is now a fear in the Basque Country that this nationalist front could alienate working-class immigrant supporters of the PSOE and produce a communitarian cleavage, which so far has largely been avoided. The breakdown of the ETA ceasefire in late 1999 left the PNV isolated and a produced a political vacuum in the Basque Country.

Another critical difference is in the number and type of actors involved. In the Basque case, Herri Batasuna has long insisted that the state must negotiate directly with ETA, an unlikely prospect and one that would serve to undermine moderate nationalism. The PNV, for its part, insists that negotiations should take place among the Basque parties, on the basis of the right to self-determination, and not with Madrid. This is equally unacceptable to the state. In Northern Ireland another track was taken with the involvement of outside parties, notably the Republic of Ireland and the United States, whose involvement increased steadily from the mid-1980s once the United Kingdom accepted that this was not a purely domestic political issue. These external brokers are absent in the Basque case.

Conclusion

Both of these conflicts are complex and multidimensional, resistant to simple stereotypes and reductionist explanations and to most of the conventional categories of political science.[47] Simple parallels are similarly difficult to draw. Yet is it their very complexity which is perhaps their strongest resemblance, and peace efforts need to start from this. The Northern Ireland peace process has attracted a great deal of attention overseas. That such a bitter and divisive confrontation can be managed says a great deal for the political process. Some Spanish observers have put this down to the traditional pragmatism and common sense of the British, ignoring the fact that one of the issues at stake is whether they are British at all. A more hardheaded view is that pragmatic and commonsensical people do not need this kind of arrangement, which is not found in other parts of the United Kingdom. The Northern Ireland Agreement is evidence, rather, of the need to negotiate, not with one's friends, but with one's enemies. In this it bears some resemblance to the pacts by which the transition to democracy in Spain was managed. Consociationalism may not be possible in the Basque Country in the absence of two clearly demarcated communities, nor is it a requirement for civil peace, but any solution will require the suspension of political competition in favour of a return to pactism. A purely nationalist front, as favoured by the PNV in recent years, is not going to achieve this; it seems merely to have convinced the radical nationalists that they do not need to make political concessions to the non-nationalist community. The Northern Ireland process also bears a similarity to decolonization experiences in which 'terrorists' become 'statesmen' overnight. The British government's attitude is now that of a colonial trustee rather than a sovereign power. This point is much less relevant in the Basque Country, which has never been a colony in any sense. In both cases, the only solution is one that abandons absolutist ideas of sovereignty and recognizes multiple identities and shared sovereignty. The process of European integration has rendered old conceptions of sovereignty redundant and, although both states have been reluctant to admit it, this idea will eventually impose itself. Both also face pressures from within. With the Scottish Parliament and Welsh Assembly the United Kingdom is transforming itself into a complex, asymmetrical, multinational state in which there are many ways and degrees of being British. This draws on old traditions of territorial accommodation and diversity. Spain, despite launching its own devolution process earlier, has come less far in recognizing this. Its history since 1714 has been one in which the statewide parties have sought to impose a unitary conception of the state on French lines. In their Declaration of Barcelona the nationalist parties of the Basque Country, Catalonia, and Galicia have called for a new model of the plurinational state, one that recognizes this vital symbolic dimension. If this were to be on offer, it would provide another key element in resolving the Basque problem, but this will require a change of mentality on the part of Spanish political elites as well as a sea change in the attitude of the radical nationalists.

NOTES

* I am grateful to Sean Loughlin, Tony Hepburn, and participants at a seminar at Queen's University, Belfast, for comments on an earlier draft. I am also grateful to Geoff Evans for advice, and to the government of the Basque Country and to Alfredo Rodriguez Gurtubay for a research visit to the Basque Country in 1998.

1. N. Canny, 'Early Modern Ireland, c.1500–1700', in R. F. Foster (ed.), *The Oxford Illustrated History of Ireland* (Oxford: Oxford University Press, 1989).
2. B. O'Leary and J. McGarry, *The Politics of Antagonism* (London: Athlone Press, 1993).
3. J. De La Granja, *El nacionalismo vasco: un siglo de historia* (Madrid: Tecnos, 1995); I. Fox, *La invención de España* (Madrid: Cátedra, 1997).
4. R. Kee, *The Green Flag* (London: Weidenfeld & Nicolson, 1972).
5. J. Ruane and J. Todd, *The Dynamics of Conflict in Northern Ireland* (Cambridge: Cambridge University Press, 1996).
6. A. C. Hepburn, 'Identity and Conflict in a Divided City-Region', in H. G. Haupt, M. G. Müller, and S. Woolf (eds.), *Regional and National Identities in Europe in the XIXth and XXth Centuries* (Amsterdam: Kluwer, 1998).

7. P. O'Mahoney and G. Delanty, *Rethinking Irish History: Nationalism, Identity and Ideology* (London: Macmillan, 1998).
8. G. Walker, *Intimate Strangers: Political and Cultural Interaction between Scotland and Ulster in Modern Times* (Edinburgh: Donald, 1995).
9. E. Rumpf and A. C. Hepburn, *Nationalism and Socialism in Twentieth-Century Ireland* (Liverpool: Liverpool University Press, 1977).
10. A. Helle, 'Shifting Loyalties: Protestant Working-Class Politics in Ulster', in P. Pasture and J. Verberckmoes (eds.), *Working-Class Internationalism and the Appeal of National Identity* (Oxford: Berg, 1998).
11. D. Fitzpatrick, 'Ireland since 1870', in Foster (ed.), *The Oxford Illustrated History of Ireland*.
12. Helle, 'Shifting Loyalties'; C. Norton, 'Trade Unions in a Divided Society: The Case of Northern Ireland', in Pasture and Verberckmoes (eds.), *Working-Class Internationalism and the Appeal of National Identity*.
13. G. Jauregui, *Entre la tragedia y la esperanza: Vasconia ante el nuevo milenio* (Barcelona: Ariel, 1996).
14. S. Arana Goiri, 'Errores catalanistas', *Bizkaitarra*, 22 Apr. 1894, repr. in S. de Pablo, J. L. de la Granja, and L. Mees (eds.), *Documentos para la historia del nacionalismo vasco* (Barcelona: Ariel, 1998).
15. G. Jauregui, 'Origines y evolución ideológica y política', in A. Elorza (ed.), *La historia de ETA* (Madrid: Tecnos, 2000).
16. J. M. Lorenzo Espinosa, *Historia de Euskal Herria*, iii: *El naciamiento de una nación* (Tafalla: Argitaratzea, 1995).
17. L. Mees, 'Social Solidarity and National Identity in the Basque Country: The Case of the Nationalist Trade Union ELA/STV', in Pasture and Verberckmoes (eds.), *Working-Class Internationalism and the Appeal of National Identity*.
18. M. Heiberg, *The Making of the Basque Nation* (Cambridge: Cambridge University Press, 1989).
19. P. Bew, P. Gibbon, and H. Patterson, *Northern Ireland 1921–1996: Political Forces and Social Classes* (London: Serif, 1996).
20. E. Moxon-Browne, 'National Identity in Northern Ireland', in *Social Attitudes in Northern Ireland, 1991 Edition* (Belfast: Blackstaff Press, 1991).
21. F. Moral, *Identidad regional y nacionalismo en el estado de las autonomías*, Opiniones y Actitudes, 18 (Madrid: Centro de Investigaciones Sociológicas, 1998).
22. F. J. Llera, *Los Vascos y la política* (Bilbao: Servicio Editorial, Universidad de la País Vasco, 1994).
23. A. Gurratxaga Abad, *Transformación del nacionalismo vasco: del PNV a ETA* (San Sebastian: Haranburu,1996).
24. G. Evans and M. Duffy, 'Beyond the Sectarian Divide: The Social Bases and Political Consequences of Nationalist and Unionist Party Competition in Northern Ireland', *British Journal of Political Science*, 27 (1997), 47–81.
25. Gurratxaga Abad, *Transformación del nacionalismo vasco*.

26. R. Rose, *Governing without Consensus: An Irish Perspective* (London: Faber & Faber, 1971).
27. E. Moxon-Browne, *Nation, Class and Creed in Northern Ireland* (Aldershot: Gower, 1983).
28. R. Breen, 'Who Wants a United Ireland?' Constitutional Preferences among Catholics and Protestants', in *Social Attitudes in Northern Ireland, Fifth Report* (Belfast: Appletree, 1996).
29. G. Evans and B. O'Leary, 'Frameworked Futures: Intransigence and Flexibility in the Northern Ireland Elections of May 30 1996', *Irish Political Studies* 12 (1997), 23–47.
30. Evans and Duffy, 'Beyond the Sectarian Divide'.
31. Llera, *Los Vascos y la política*.
32. Gurratxaga Abad, *Transformación del nacionalismo vasco*; Moral, *Identidad regional y nacionalismo en el Estado de las autonomías*.
33. A. Elorza, 'Introducción: Vascos guerreros', in Elorza (ed.), *La historia de ETA*.
34. J. M. Mata Lopez, *El nacionalismo vasco radical* (Bilbao: Servicio Editorial, Universidad del País Vasco, 1993).
35. P. Taylor, *Provos: The IRA and Sinn Féin* (London: Bloomsbury, 1997). This is not to say that all abuses by the security forces have been direct responses to IRA violence. Bloody Sunday in 1972 was not.
36. The irony is that, after a face-saving compromise, the government conceded the demands, thus losing the political game without gaining any practical advantage.
37. It has been said that one reason for not bombing Scotland is pressure from Scottish sympathizers, who fear opening sectarian divisions within Scotland. The IRA has certainly used Scotland as a logistical base.
38. A. Gurratxaga Abad, 'Transformación y futuro del nacionalismo vasco', in J. Beriain and R. Fernández Ubieta (eds.), *La cuestión vasca: claves de un conflicto político* (Barcelona: Proyectos, 1999).
39. Ruane and Todd, *The Dynamics of Conflict in Northern Ireland*.
40. Llera, *Los Vascos y la política*.
41. Ibid.
42. Evans and Duffy, 'Beyond the Sectarian Divide'; A. Gurratxaga Abad, *La refundación del nacionalismo vasco* (Bilbao: Servicio Editorial, Universidad del País Vasco, 1990); Gurratxaga Abad, *Transformación del nacionalismo vasco*.
43. Evans and Duffy, 'Beyond the Sectarian Divide'.
44. Llera, *Los Vascos y la política*.
45. Ruane and Todd, *The Dynamics of Conflict in Northern Ireland*.
46. Taylor, *Provos: The IRA and Sinn Féin*.
47. J. Whyte, *Interpreting Northern Ireland* (Oxford: Clarendon Press, 1990); J. McGarry and B. O'Leary, *Explaining Northern Ireland: Broken Images* (Oxford: Blackwell, 1995).

9

Making the Transition from Hegemonic Regime to Power-Sharing: Northern Ireland and Canada in Historical Perspective

S. J. R. NOEL

The idea that the conflict between Catholics and Protestants in Northern Ireland can be resolved by means of a system of power-sharing—that is, by devising new political institutions that will induce the political leaders of the two rival communities to share office in a coalition government—has continued to exert a strong hold on the imaginations of those who believe in the efficacy of constitutional engineering. Despite the failure of past power-sharing initiatives, the 1998 Good Friday Agreement once again sets out a blueprint for an elaborate constitutional edifice within which Catholic and Protestant politicians might bridge, at the elite governmental level, the deep divisions that separate their two communities.

The design is at once new and derivative. Like a piece of post-modern architecture that strives to re-create in concrete and glass a type of structure that in the original evolved as a traditional design based on the use of indigenous materials, the 1998 Constitution is inspired by an idealized model drawn from other places and times. Its intent is to re-create through international guarantees, laws, and formal institutions a system of consociational governance that is not indigenous to Northern Ireland—or Britain or Ireland—but evolved in other societies as a largely informal, pragmatic process of politically accommodating deep communal differences. Thus, the new Northern Ireland Constitution is designed to thwart majority rule and to mandate the following: executive coalition, segmental autonomy, proportionality, and minority veto.[1]

It is not my aim to discuss the specific executive and legislative arrangements that are set forth in the 1998 Agreement as these are discussed in detail elsewhere in this volume. Rather, my aim in this essay is to compare Northern Ireland and Canada with a view to determining whether

Canada's early experience of power-sharing reveals any historically identifiable determinants of success or failure that might be helpful in assessing the prospects of making a transition to power-sharing in Northern Ireland. At first glance, there would seem to be few points of comparison. Northern Ireland is a constitutional anomaly created by the partition of Ireland in 1920, a non-state, never genuinely independent or democratic, and politically the inheritor of centuries of violent Irish–English, Catholic–Protestant conflict. Canada is a long-established federation, among the world's oldest democracies, and politically the inheritor of centuries of generally successful effort to accommodate deep cleavages of ethnicity, language, religion, and region. Upon further inspection, however, there are some parallels between them that make their contrasting paths of political development all the more striking and in need of explanation.

Two Types of British Hegemony

Both Catholic–Protestant conflict in Northern Ireland and French–English conflict in Canada have their roots in wars of conquest, and in both societies historic battles have assumed mythic significance. In Northern Ireland the Battle of the Boyne in 1690, in which the Protestant forces of William of Orange defeated the Catholic forces of James II, continues to resonate in the consciousness of Ulster Protestants. Their enduring slogan ('No Surrender!') is derived from it, and their militant Orange Order faithfully commemorates its anniversary each 12 July with parades designed to intimidate Catholics by a show of Protestant power and solidarity.[2] The cultural symbolism is unmistakable: Catholics are reminded in no uncertain terms that they are not recognized either individually as equal citizens or collectively as a separate but equal community in a bicommunal or binational society.

Any reflection on ethnic relations in Canada must begin with Quebec and the famous Battle of the Plains of Abraham in 1759 in which an invading British army under General Wolfe defeated a French army under General Montcalm. But that battle has long ceased to have any symbolic meaning for English-speaking Canadians. Some may recall the first lines of *The Maple Leaf Forever* ('In days of yore, from Britain's shore | Wolfe, the dauntless hero, came'), a piece of patriotic doggerel they probably learned in school if they are over the age of 50, but they do not publicly commemorate the battle and it plays no significant part in their political identity. For

French Canadians, however, that long-ago battle on the plains above Quebec City still vividly symbolizes 'the Conquest'—the turning-point in their history from which all else followed.[3] Yet it is not without ambiguity. While the image of French Canadians as 'a conquered people' is never far beneath the surface of French–English relations, after two centuries the old symbols of defeat and conquest have been overlaid with other more positive symbols of success and power. Some of these symbols are strongly promoted by the Canadian federal government, including official bilingualism and the reflection of the 'French fact' in the country's image both at home and abroad. Other symbols are strongly promoted by the Quebec provincial government, including, paradoxically, official French *uni*lingualism within Quebec, language laws to ensure the predominance of French on commercial signs, the flying of the Quebec flag, the designation of the Quebec legislature as *l'Assemblée Nationale* and of Quebec City as *la capitale nationale*.[4] These measures reflect the national pride of the Quebec majority and their determination to ensure that Quebec retains its French character. But they are also politically charged. For many Quebec nationalists they are a reminder of their long-frustrated aspiration to secede from Canada and form an independent state. And for the English-speaking minority they are a reminder of their threatened and diminished status.

The annual St Jean-Baptiste Day parade in Montreal on 24 June is a popular celebration of Québécois nationalism. Like the Orange parades in Northern Ireland, the St Jean-Baptiste Day parade sends a message to the minority—only in Quebec it is the *English* who are a minority and for them the slogan 'le Québec aux Québécois' is a denial of their claim to cultural recognition.[5] It implies that they are not true Québécois and therefore have no claim to equal citizenship. But there any similarity with Northern Ireland ends. The St Jean-Baptiste Day parade only rarely provokes communal violence, and in recent years there have been efforts to make it more festive, more reflective of the multicultural diversity of Montreal and less exclusively French, though the English for the most part remain conspicuously aloof.

The differences between Northern Ireland and Quebec are rooted in their very different experiences of post-conquest relations with their British conquerors. British rule in Ireland has been aptly classified as a 'state-building failure' in that the British conquered Ireland militarily but failed to integrate the Gaelic Irish into the United Kingdom, as was done in the case of the Welsh and other peoples on the Celtic fringes of the British Isles.[6] The Irish were treated not as potential subjects of the English king and gradually brought under royal law and civil government, but as a wild native tribe to be subjugated by force and dispossessed of their lands by English planters. The closest parallel is with the conquest of native peoples in North and South America.

By the end of the reign of Elizabeth I, in 1603, the nature of British rule had become ingrained and resistant to fundamental change. Under Elizabeth's successor, James I, the Protestant plantation of Ulster was established by the sweeping expropriation of the lands of native Irish Catholics, thus beginning 'the fateful triangle of the modern history of Ireland, that of the English state, Irish Catholics, and Protestant settlers'.[7] The settlers were protected by military garrisons, thus creating the conditions for future cycles of armed uprisings followed by harsh measures of repression. The seventeenth century was marked by further campaigns of conquest of unrestrained brutality, most notoriously under Oliver Cromwell between 1649 and 1652, and again under William of Orange in 1690.[8] Each conquest brought new displacements of the Catholic population, until, by the end of the century, less than a fifth of Ireland's land was in Catholic hands.[9]

After 1690 the British imposed a system of draconian penal laws that stripped Irish Catholics of every remaining civil and religious right. They were excluded from all public offices and from membership in the professions; their priests were outlawed, their schools closed; even Catholic burials were legally prohibited. There were also legal restrictions placed on their ownership and transfer of property.[10] These laws, which were not finally repealed until the early nineteenth century, completed and reinforced a regime of aggressive hegemonic control of Irish Catholics by their British Protestant rulers.

The history of Quebec in the period after the British conquest is also a history of hegemonic control, but hegemonic control can take many forms, and the form imposed on Quebec was far milder than that imposed on Ireland, and hence more amenable to peaceful change. The British military regime in Quebec (1759–64) set a remarkable precedent by its respectful and sympathetic attitude towards the French population. Under Governor James Murray (a Scottish professional soldier of aristocratic background who had been one of Wolfe's brigadiers on the Plains of Abraham) French laws, customs, and institutions were left largely undisturbed; French property was protected against would-be English freebooters; and the Roman Catholic Church was scarcely more restricted in practice than under the French regime and even given financial aid to maintain its social and educational roles. Murray appointed French notables to senior administrative positions, insisted that the military pay in cash for its supplies, refused to issue warrants for forced labour, recommissioned French captains of militia, and recruited French militia volunteers on terms of service identical to those of militiamen from New York.[11]

None of these measures would have been conceivable in Ireland and, not surprisingly, they provoked astonishment and howls of protest that echoed across the Atlantic from English merchants, mainly New Englanders, who had relocated to Quebec in the expectation of easy plunder under an Irish-style regime. In Murray's opinion, the merchants were 'cruel, Ignorant, rapacious Fanatics' and 'birds of passage' who could not be trusted with political power. He was equally blunt in his affection for the French, whom he declared 'the best and bravest Race on the Globe' who would become the most loyal subjects in Britain's American empire if allowed 'a very few Privileges, which the Laws of England do not allow Catholics at home'.[12]

In unconscious parody of Ireland, it was not the French but the *English* in Quebec who complained most loudly of oppression. A royal proclamation in 1763 seemingly promised them redress, as it ordered the creation of a new civil regime in Quebec with the aim of Anglicizing the colony. But its implementation was left to Governor Murray, who undermined the intent of the proclamation by ensuring that the new system, in practice, continued to protect French interests. He refused, for example, even to summon an Assembly that would have been composed exclusively of British Protestants—in effect, of New England merchants.

Merchant complaints (backed by petitions, pleas, and even the hiring of a professional lobbyist in London) eventually led to Murray's recall, impeachment, and trial before the House of Lords on charges that included 'promoting Roman Catholicism' and issuing 'Unconstitutional, Vexious, Oppressive' ordinances—all of which were eventually dismissed by the Lords as groundless.[13]

Murray's legacy was maintained by his successors, but it also continued to be bitterly contested by the growing number of English in Quebec and their allies in the New England colonies. The Quebec Act of 1774, which codified and entrenched the recognition of French cultural and religious rights, thus putting the full force of a British statute behind the policy of conciliating the French, was the ultimate triumph of Murray's system— and the final straw for many New Englanders. It was one of the factors that precipitated the American revolution.[14]

The British regime in Quebec remained a system of hegemonic control until 1841, but one that was mitigated by legal guarantees and the practical necessity of governing with the cooperation of the Quebec elite, particularly the clergy. In effect, the British and French elites each retained what they could realistically retain: for the British, formal political control and a dominant role in business, banking, and industry; for the French, cultural and religious autonomy, political influence, a share of political patronage, access to the professions and small business, and a large measure of control over local affairs. But the cooperation of the French elite was never automatic; continual hard bargaining was necessary to secure it. Also, after the granting of representative government to Quebec in 1791, formal British political control was challenged by an elected Assembly that fell increasingly under the control of the French majority.[15] In Ireland, by contrast, British hegemony was reinforced by the abolition of the Irish Parliament (which was exclusively Protestant) under the Act of Union of 1801,[16] thereby cutting off even the possibility that Catholic representatives might one day assume a dominant place in it, as the French did in Quebec.

Various reasons may be advanced for the differences between the British regimes in Quebec and Ireland. Quebec belonged to Britain's great imperial rival, which ensured its people of a certain respect—if for no other reason than that it was entirely possible that somewhere a British colony would fall under French military rule and its colonists would wish to be treated in a similar manner. The British also quickly came to the realization that Quebec, though fairly easily conquered, would be difficult and costly to hold by military force alone if the population were provoked into a general uprising by the imposition of an Irish-style regime. Hence, to a degree unknown in Ireland, British military and civilian officials in Quebec were restrained in their use of force by both imperial policy and their need in day-to-day matters to secure at least the passive acceptance of their authority by the bulk of the French population. Above all, they needed at least some active support and participation in government by members of the French elite. Finally, the English were influenced in their attitude towards the French (and the French towards the English) by the large and threatening presence of the native Indians. Both the English and French were minorities—precarious fragments of European Christian civilization whose greatest fear was of the more numerous Indians, whom they both viewed as dangerous savages.[17] Unlike Irish Catholics, therefore, the French in Quebec were not dispossessed by the English; rather they and the English were both eager participants in the dispossession of the original inhabitants. Only after that sordid task was jointly accomplished could they safely pursue their quarrels with one another.

From Hegemony to Consociational Democracy

In any system of hegemonic rule the formative period of the regime is critical in determining its capacity for future evolution. If the early rulers are adamant in denying recognition to the subject people over whom they rule, if they treat them as aliens or enemies and refuse to accept that they have any interests in common with them, apart from the maintenance of law and order, any future transition to a consociational system is likely to be difficult and perhaps impossible.[18] If, however, the early regime extends recognition, at least to some significant degree, and bargains in good faith, at least over some matters of genuine importance, the essential prerequisites are created for a successful future transition. In the latter case, political elites acquire experience in bargaining with one another and achieve enough success to maintain the support of their respective communities. In early Canada this was the pattern that on the whole emerged—though it never ceased to be contested by influential elements within both the English and French communities.

Among the English there were many who were only nominally loyal to the British regime and who, after 1783, became increasingly enamoured of the new United States, whose aggressive tactics in dealing with troublesome minorities within its borders, and native tribes who stood in the way of its westward expansion, they particularly admired. They regarded the recognition that the British regime in Quebec extended to the French as an insult to their ethnic pride, its tolerance of the Catholic religion as a threat to their British Protestant ascendancy, and its accommodation of French interests as tantamount to treason. Among the French there were many whose national pride was expressed through resistance to the regime and all it stood for, and who condemned leaders who cooperated with it as 'vendus'—sell-outs and betrayers of their French Catholic heritage. By the 1830s the British regime in both French and English Canada was beginning to crumble under the combined force of these contradictory pressures, to which there was now added a heady mix of American ideas of popular democracy, Catholic–Protestant animosities imported directly from Ireland by a tide of immigrants, and, in the western sections, agrarian unrest. In 1837 armed rebellions broke out in both Upper Canada (Ontario) and Lower Canada (Quebec).[19] Though the rebellions were quickly put down, an alarmed British government saw them as signalling the need for sweeping constitutional change. That much they got right. Their remedy, however, was so ill conceived it could have been designed for Ireland.

The British had come to the view that the trouble with Canada was that the French had remained French and that they should, after all, be assimilated—which was no easy task, considering that they constituted a large majority in Lower Canada. The solution, which ominously echoed an earlier solution to the problem of Ireland, was an Act of Union.[20]

Under a new Constitution imposed in 1841, the two existing provinces of Upper and Lower Canada (one overwhelmingly English, the other predominantly French) were combined to form the Union of the Canadas—thus at a stroke converting the French into a permanent minority. In effect, the large and growing English population of Upper Canada was combined with the English minority of Lower Canada to produce an overall English majority. The Constitution also provided for the two sections of the Union to be equally represented in the legislature, even though Lower Canada's total population (French and English) was substantially larger than Upper Canada's. Finally, for good measure, the electoral system was rigged by gerrymandering the Montreal constituencies to ensure that in the new Parliament the French Canadians would be under-represented even in the Lower Canadian section, and the English over-represented. The intended result was to force the French at last to abandon their 'vain hopes of nationality' (in the words of Lord Durham, on whose report the policy was based)[21] and assimilate into a larger English-dominated Canada that henceforth would make no concessions whatsoever to their religion, language, or culture. In effect, the recognition of French rights was to be withdrawn and the legal and customary practices of more than eighty years were to be suddenly reversed.

The origins of modern Canada may thus be traced to a Constitution that was inherently inflammatory and so flawed in design that its likeliest outcome was civil war. Few successful democracies have ever had so unpromising a beginning. Yet a decade after its inauguration the improbable Union of the Canadas was not only still in existence but was flourishing. It had achieved a high level of democratic self-government, grown rapidly in population and wealth, and, in general, was basking in peace and prosperity. The reasons for this astonishing outcome are various and complex, but the key factor is the adoption—indeed the invention by a group of English and French Canadian politicians—of a unique system of consociational governance.

The framework of a Canadian power-sharing accord was hammered out in secret negotiations, conducted over a span of two years, between representatives of two powerful political groupings: the Upper Canadian reformers led by Robert Baldwin, and the Quebec nationalists (the 'Bleu' party) led by Louis LaFontaine.[22] Both Baldwin and LaFontaine were moderates. Baldwin was a constitutional reformer and the leading exponent of responsible parliamentary government for Canada—what in the case of Ireland would later be called 'home rule'. LaFontaine was a nationalist who advocated the pursuit of equal rights for French Canadians through constitutional means rather than through armed rebellion, a position similar to that of the Irish nationalist leader Daniel O'Connell. Both Baldwin and LaFontaine enjoyed political support in their respective communities that was widespread but uncertain, for both were vulnerable to 'outflanking' by extremists—Baldwin by agrarian radicals who favoured replacing Upper Canada's existing system of colonial government with a US-style 'Jacksonian' or 'frontier' democracy; LaFontaine by 'ultra-nationalists' who favoured the overthrow of British rule in Lower Canada and the creation of a Quebec republic. The Reform–Bleu negotiations were long, arduous, and prone to break down amid mutual suspicions and misunderstandings. Yet in the end they succeeded. That they did so owes much to the political wisdom of Baldwin and LaFontaine, but the accord was above all the achievement of Francis Hincks,[23] Baldwin's brilliant young adviser, party manager, and strategist. It was Hincks who initiated contact with LaFontaine and then persuaded Baldwin to meet with him to discuss a possible alliance. It was Hincks who possessed the imagination to visualize a future Canadian political system based on the twin principles of responsible government and power-sharing, and the political expertise to devise the compromises and trade-offs that would be necessary to make it work in practice. It was Hincks who would accept no breakdown of negotiations as final and who again and again inventively kept the process moving forward until a deal was finally reached.

Hincks's role as the creative thinker, power-broker, and *animateur* of Canadian consociationalism is little known, though it is a remarkable achievement by any standard, and perhaps all the more remarkable in view of his ethnic background—for he was by origin an Irish Protestant and had spent much of his early life in Belfast.

The effect of the Canadian consociational bargain was to stand the Constitution of 1841 squarely on its head. Baldwin and LaFontaine were soon in power as co-premiers of a Reform–Bleu government, with Hincks as 'minister of everything' ubiquitously influencing the building of the Union's new and unique political institutions. The Union had been intended to foster majority rule and exclude the French Canadians from power. Instead, it fostered a system of power-sharing in which the French Canadians were active participants and their leaders an indispensable part of every government; 'dual ministries' (French–English coalitions) soon became established as the Union's most distinctive feature, with each government headed in practice by French and English co-premiers; a rough, pragmatic proportionality became the rule in the distribution of public benefits and government patronage; English and French were both recognized as languages of parliamentary record; a large degree of segmental autonomy was observed; and in general a system of 'double majorities' or mutual veto prevailed in the legislature rather than decision-making by simple majority. Even a dispute over the location of the capital was settled in ad hoc consociational fashion when the legislators agreed to rotate it every two years between Toronto and Quebec City.

All of these practices were unprecedented in British colonial experience and so foreign to Westminster as to be incomprehensible. Within Canada consociationalism was widely accepted as necessary and widely supported, but it was not enthusiastically embraced. Though it manifestly 'delivered the goods'—that is, it produced the social peace that underpinned a burgeoning economy—it did so through decision-making processes of Byzantine complexity and compromises that disappointed many. In time its economic benefits came to be taken for granted and could even be plausibly denied by those who favoured a more decisive politics of the Westminster kind in which there would be clear winners and losers. Finally, there were powerful sectional interests that were never reconciled to power-sharing and worked ceaselessly to undermine it. The English minority in Lower Canada (Quebec) were particularly incensed, correctly believing that the Union's original purpose had been subverted, as it was they, not the French, who had been politically marginalized by it. Among the French, meanwhile, the ultra-nationalists mistrusted LaFontaine's alliance with the English and correctly regarded his and the Union's success as a greater threat to their separatist aspirations than English dominance. In Upper Canada the enemies of Baldwin and Hincks were even more numerous and extreme. Some were unreconstructed agrarian radicals who drew their inspiration from the failed rebellion of 1837, which the Baldwinites had opposed, but many more were members of a militant branch of the Orange Order who drew their inspiration directly from Ireland and who regarded the Union of the Canadas as nothing less than a French Catholic conspiracy.[24]

The Union's grand experiment with consociational democracy ultimately ended in instability and deadlock. The immediate cause was the repeated failure of the English partners in coalition ministries to maintain majority support in their section of the legislature, but there were also deeper causes. The English and French political elites had succeeded to a remarkable degree in forging bonds of trust with one another, bonds that were often cemented by long association, by the shared ups and downs of political life, and by personal friendships.[25] They had also renewed their coalition by attracting the support and advancing the ministerial careers of a group of outstanding young English and French political leaders.[26] But, ultimately, the English elite failed to maintain sufficient electoral support among the mass of the people in their section of the Union. One reason was that the new immigrants who were flooding into Upper Canada were predominantly Protestants from the British Isles, including many from Northern Ireland, and, not surprisingly, many found the Canadian system of power-sharing alien and un-British. Also, as the population of Upper Canada grew to equal, and then surpass, that of Lower Canada, the constitutionally entrenched principle of equal representation in the legislature (which the English had earlier favoured) came increasingly under attack. By 1864 the Union had reached an impasse, and in 1867 it was replaced by the larger Canadian federation.

The main consociational practices and norms that had evolved under the Union, however, were carried forward into the federation and long remained a central feature of its operation. Despite being undermined by a major constitutional change in 1982—a change ratified by every province except Quebec—and seemingly repudiated in large sections of the country in the 1990s, Canadian consociationalism continues to survive, though in a weakened condition. The current strength of separatist sentiment in Quebec may be at least partly understood as a response to the apparent embrace, by the other provinces of the federation, of the idea of majoritarian democracy—a democracy tempered by a constitutionally entrenched Charter of Rights, but with no constitutional recognition of Quebec's distinctiveness and few guarantees of consociational power-sharing.[27]

I have dwelt at length on the Union era of Canada because I believe it is essential to understand the historical roots of Canadian consociationalism in order to make any meaningful comparison with Ireland. Speaking in the House of Commons in 1837, Daniel O'Connell had expressed the view that the analogy between Canada and Ireland was close. 'In fact,' he stated, 'it was complete; and if they came to names, when they spoke of Papineau [the leader of the rebellion in Quebec] they had only to substitute another name with an 'O' at the beginning. The cases were precisely similar.'[28] They must have seemed so at the time, and not only to O'Connell. Yet a decade later they could more accurately be described as precisely the opposite.

The obvious explanation for their radically different paths of political development is that nothing remotely resembling the Union of the Canadas was allowed to develop in Ireland. To imagine such a development is to imagine a mid-nineteenth-century Ireland under home rule, peacefully governing itself through Catholic–Protestant coalitions, and perhaps even rotating its capital between Belfast and Dublin!

It must be stressed, however, that there was nothing inevitable about the development of consociationalism in Canada. Indeed, the conditions for its rise were largely absent apart from some previous experience of inter-elite bargaining,[29] and even that was supposed to be expunged by the imposition of English majority rule under the new Constitution of 1841. To withdraw legal recognition from a people after they had enjoyed it for many years is the very antithesis of consociationalism and a proven recipe for violent conflict. Had the Constitution of 1841 been implemented as intended, therefore, Canada in the 1840s could very easily have become a transatlantic equivalent of Ireland. That it instead found a way to practice power-sharing that was well suited to its particular political, social, and economic realities is a development that invites comparison with attempts to arrange a consociational solution in Northern Ireland.

The two cases, of course, are widely separated in time, and there are other factors as well that make them less than perfectly comparable. Nevertheless, there are some aspects of the process of getting a society to move from a politics of hegemonic control to a politics of power-sharing where the Canadian experience offers at least some interesting contrasts with the approach taken in Northern Ireland—and possibly some practical insights.

Conclusion

One particularly striking contrast between the Canadian and Northern Ireland cases is that they reflect two totally different outlooks regarding the role and importance of constitutions in arriving at and maintaining consociational bargains.

In the Canadian case, there was a virtual absence of concern for formal 'constitutional engineering'. The Canadian elites, French and English alike, accepted the fact that the British Parliament alone possessed the authority to enact colonial constitutions. They therefore made no attempt to negotiate a new constitution but instead concentrated on the more modest but still difficult task of negotiating a political deal—a deal to operate the new constitutional machinery that was about to be arbitrarily bestowed upon them in a way that would be to their mutual advantage. To that end, eventually, they agreed to share power by dividing ministerial offices and the spoils of patronage on a basis acceptable to both parties, to remain united in their demand for responsible government, and generally to work together in Parliament within a coalition framework. The Constitution contributed only in a negative way to this outcome: by seemingly decreeing a future of endless conflict, it ended up encouraging both sides to cooperate.

It is also noteworthy that the Canadian negotiators throughout conducted their business in secret, through private correspondence and in 'behind closed doors' meetings. They were thus able to escape the unwanted scrutiny of British officials, the press, most of their own party supporters, and the mass of the people in their respective communities. This later proved to be a weakness as it enabled extremists—Protestant sectarians in Upper Canada and French ultra-nationalists in Lower Canada—to mobilize opposition to power-sharing under the banner of popular sovereignty.[30] But at the time it contributed greatly to a successful outcome by enabling both sides to negotiate freely and make compromises.

Their meetings were informal, ad hoc affairs with no formal agenda. They took place in both Montreal and Toronto, with enough time between meetings to permit reflection and consultation. Both sides expanded the small number of participants as the discussions progressed, thus ensuring that a second tier of leaders became personally acquainted with one another, and acquired a personal stake in power-sharing, before they were called upon to become coalition partners.

In the case of Northern Ireland, the formal negotiation of a new constitution has invariably been regarded by all parties as the sine qua non of a lasting settlement and has accordingly been treated as a matter of obsessive priority. Formal constitution-making, however, is a difficult and uncertain project even under the most favourable of circumstances. The more elaborate the constitution, the more likely it is to become divorced from the concerns of the people who must live under it and the politicians who must operate it. Also, the more likely it is to generate conflict over arcane legal points and become a barrier to the rough and ready bargaining, accommodations, adjustments, and trade-offs that actual power-sharing (as opposed to theoretical or formal constitutional power-sharing) requires if it is to succeed in day-to-day reality. When negotiations are treated as a major international event, the culmination of a grandiose 'peace process' that commands the world's attention, the likelihood that the participants in such a forum will bargain freely and flexibly is extremely remote.

Given Northern Ireland's legacy of violent conflict, there can be little wonder that Catholic and Protestant political elites deeply mistrust one another. To bring them together only to negotiate a constitution—where the expectations and political stakes are dauntingly high, where media scrutiny of their every word is relentless, where any act of generosity or show of good faith across communal lines will be interpreted by 'hardliners' as a sign of weakness or betrayal—is practically to guarantee failure.

'Voluntary consociation', according to O'Leary and McGarry, 'cannot work effectively where the rival communities are fundamentally divided over their national as opposed to their linguistic or religious identities, and where they are divided over the legitimacy of the state.'[31] Such circumstances are obviously highly unfavourable to consociationalism, yet they may not be an insuperable barrier, for they were present in Canada to a large degree but were nevertheless overcome. Much of the credit for that belongs to Francis Hincks. He had started out with a vision of the economic benefits that could flow from union, and the political benefits that could flow from responsible government, but with no understanding of the depth of LaFontaine's nationalist convictions or the hatred felt by practically all French Canadians towards a state that had been designed to extinguish their national identity. Hincks learned quickly, however, and political agility was always his hallmark. Soon he was appealing to LaFontaine's nationalism, arguing that union would preserve rather than extinguish Lower Canada's French identity, if power within its government were shared, and assuring him that 'your brother reformers in Upper Canada will meet with you as Canadians, that no national animosities will be entertained, that we desire your friendship, esteem and co-operation if we can obtain them consistent with our principles'.[32] It was no small step, in the turbulent political climate of Lower Canada at the time, for LaFontaine to respond positively and with trust, but he did. Thus was set in motion the train of events that led, in September 1842, to the formation of the first Baldwin–LaFontaine administration.

Despite past failures, it is acknowledged by most serious students of Northern Ireland that some form of consociational power-sharing is essential to a peace settlement,[33] and this is also the position of both the British and Irish governments. Writing a power-sharing constitution, however, may not be the best first step. If the Canadian example offers any guidance, it is that power-sharing is only incidentally about constitutions. What it is about is developing a politics of accommodation, and that requires a willingness on the part of politicians from the different communities to meet as equals, to bargain in good faith, to think in the short term as well as the long term, and to settle for outcomes that they regard as less than ideal but that on balance are of greater benefit to the people they represent than any likely alternative. If that willingness is absent—as it has conspicuously been in Northern Ireland—it is unclear how a grand exercise in constitution-writing can bring it into existence. More modest preliminary efforts, such as building 'sites for accommodation' in local government, in non-governmental organizations, and in other arenas of limited decision-making power, where aspiring politicians might gain some practical experience of dealing with one another face-to-face, might be a more promising alternative.

Another lesson that might be learned from the Canadian experience is that the intervention of outside powers or the use of intermediaries, however well intentioned, is not necessary and might even be counter-productive.

Canadian consociationalism developed more or less in isolation. The British gave the Canadian politicians a negative incentive to negotiate, but neither the French nor the English negotiators were subject to direct pressure from an outside power, nor were their negotiations facilitated or arranged with the aid of an outside intermediary. The British government was deliberately kept in the dark, and the United States government at the time took no interest in Canadian affairs. The Canadians entered into a process of inter-elite bargaining reluctantly and with difficulty, and with many misconceptions about one another, but when they eventually did so it was on their own initiative. They therefore had no interests to consider except those of their respective communities, no third parties making threats or offering inducements, and no supposedly neutral intermediaries whom they might hope to attract to their side or whom they could blame if negotiations failed.

It is also worth noting that the Canadian elites were unencumbered by the advice of theorists, constitutional experts, or others presumed to be the repositories of greater wisdom or morality than mere politicians. Consociationalism at the time did not exist as a set of abstract propositions, nor was it a model of governance that existed somewhere else and could be held up as an exemplar. Hence the task of devising workable power-sharing arrangements was exclusively the project of a group of experienced politicians who let experience alone be their guide. In the end they accomplished a rare feat of creative political thinking, but that was not their aim, nor was it something that could reasonably have been anticipated.

By contrast, when Northern Ireland's Catholic and Protestant political elites have been brought together, it has not been on their own initiative but

rather in response to intense pressure from the British and Irish governments, and latterly from the president of the United States as well. In
1997–8 they had to be coaxed into negotiating by an American intermediary, Senator George Mitchell, and when they finally did get together they
were inundated with advice, both invited and gratuitous. The objectives set
for them were externally imposed rather than arising out of their appreciation of what might actually be possible, in view of their knowledge of local
circumstances and the pressures they were under from their followers. The
result was their seeming acquiescence in an impressive constitutional
edifice that others had constructed for them, but without the vital underpinning of a political bargain that they had worked out for themselves.

Massive, multi-government efforts to engineer a consociational settlement for Northern Ireland may therefore be misplaced. As the Canadian
experience shows, practically any constitution can be made to serve as a
vehicle for power-sharing if the leaders of the antagonistic communities are
willing and able to share power politically. Even the old Northern Ireland
Constitution (1920–72) could have been operated in a consociational fashion, if there had been any political desire to do so. Consociational systems
of government, that is to say, are quintessentially political, rather than legal
or constitutional, constructs. Hence, even the most impeccably drafted
consociational constitution will fail if it is not supported by a genuine
political bargain. The modern quest to engineer a consociational constitution for Northern Ireland cannot help but raise doubts about how well the
would-be engineers actually understand the nature of the project.

NOTES

1. These are the well-known characteristics of consociational political systems.
   See A. Lijphart, *Democracy in Plural Societies* (New Haven: Yale University
   Press, 1977); B. O'Leary, 'The Nature of the Agreement', John Whyte
   Memorial Lecture, Queen's University Belfast, 28 Nov. 1998.
2. 'Orange marches have recently been defined as an integral part of Protestant
   culture, but if this is culture it is like diplomacy, war by other means.'
   B. O'Leary and J. McGarry, *The Politics of Antagonism: Understanding
   Northern Ireland* (Atlantic Heights, NJ: Athlone Press, 1993), 140.
3. 'People are often very surprised that Quebecers say they are still affected by
   an event that took place over two hundred years ago, while other peoples
   have already overcome more recent, more devastating defeats. They forget
   the fundamental difference between defeat and conquest. A conquest is a per

manent defeat, an institutionalized defeat.' C. Dufour, *The Canadian Challenge, le defi Québécois* (Halifax: Institute for Research on Public Policy, 1990), 31.

4. Adopting the trappings and terminology of nationhood is, of course, an unsubtle way of demanding to be recognized by others as a nation. See J. Jenson, 'Naming Nations: Making Nationalist Claims in Canadian Political Discourse', *Canadian Review of Sociology and Anthropology*, 30/1 (1993), 337–57.

5. French and English claims and counter-claims to recognition are made more problematic by the fact that non-European immigration has turned Canada into an ethnically diverse country. In a notorious outburst in 1995 the then premier of Quebec, Jacques Parizeau, blamed 'money and the ethnic vote' for the narrow defeat of the 'yes' side in a Quebec referendum on sovereignty. For a perceptive analysis of multiculturalism and the politics of recognition in modern Canada, see W. Kymlicka, *Finding our Way: Re-Thinking Ethnocultural Relations in Canada* (Toronto: Oxford University Press, 1998).

6. I. Lustick, *State-Building Failure in British Ireland and French Algeria* (Berkeley: Institute of International Studies, 1985), 17–38.

7. O'Leary and McGarry, *Politics of Antagonism*, 65.

8. J. Lydon, *The Making of Ireland* (New York: Routledge, 1998), 163–217.

9. O'Leary and McGarry, *Politics of Antagonism*, 68.

10. M. Wall, 'The Age of the Penal Laws', in T. W. Moody and F. X. Martin (eds.), *The Course of Irish History* (Dublin: Mercier, 1994).

11. G. P. Browne, 'James Murray', *Dictionary of Canadian Biography*, 14 vols. (1966–98), vol. iv (Toronto: University of Toronto Press, 1979), 569–78. See also M. Wade, *The French Canadians, 1760–1967*, i (Toronto: Macmillan, 1968), 48–58.

12. *Dictionary of Canadian Biography*, iv. 575.

13. Ibid., 577.

14. Delegates to the first Continental Congress in 1774 protested against British recognition of Catholic rights in Quebec, expressing 'astonishment that a British Parliament should ever consent to establish in that country a religion that has deluged your island in blood, and dispersed impiety, bigotry, persecution, murder and rebellion through every part of the world.' *Journals of the Continental Congress*, 34 vols. (Washington: Library of Congress, 1904–37), vol. i (1904), 88.

15. Even in the first Quebec Assembly, elected in 1792, French members were in a majority, though the English retained control of the appointed Executive Council. 'Nothing can be so irksome', complained one disgruntled English assemblyman, 'as the situation of the English members—without numbers to do any good—doomed to the necessity of combatting the absurdities of the majority, without a hope of success.' Quoted in Wade, *The French Canadians*, i. 97.

16. Lydon, *The Making of Ireland*, 274–8.
17. In general, both the French and the English were bearers to the native tribes of disease, economic exploitation, fanatical variants of Christianity, and, ultimately, dispossession. The Cromwellian cry 'To Hell or Connaught!' had many parallels in North America.
18. Sir John Davies observed in 1612 that the Britain had failed to integrate Ireland because English settlers had persuaded the king 'that it was unfit to Communicate the Lawes of England unto them; that it was the best pollicie to hold them as Aliens and Enemies'. From *A Discoverie of the True Causes Why Ireland was Never Entirely Subdued*, quoted in Lustick, *State-Building Failure*, 18.
19. G. M. Craig, *Upper Canada: The Formative Years, 1784–1841* (Toronto: McClelland & Stewart, 1963), 226–51; F. Ouellet, *Lower Canada, 1791–1840: Social Change and Nationalism* (Toronto: McClelland & Stewart, 1980), 275–327.
20. For the text of the Act, see W. P. M. Kennedy (ed.), *Statutes, Treaties and Documents of the Canadian Constitution, 1713–1929* (Toronto: Oxford University Press, 1930), 433–45.
21. C. P. Lucas (ed.), *Lord Durham's Report*, 3 vols. (Oxford: Clarendon Press, 1912), 307. For the British background to the Report, see G. Martin, *The Durham Report and British Policy* (Cambridge: Cambridge University Press, 1972).
22. W. S. Cross and R. L. Fraser, 'Robert Baldwin', *Dictionary of Canadian Biography*, viii. 45–59; J. Monet, 'Louis-Hippolyte LaFontaine', *Dictionary of Canadian Biography*, ix. 440–51; J. M. S. Careless, *The Union of the Canadas: The Growth of Canadian Institutions, 1841–1857* (Toronto: McClelland & Stewart, 1967); and J. Monet, *The Last Cannon Shot: A Study of French-Canadian Nationalism, 1837–1850* (Toronto: University of Toronto Press, 1969).
23. W. G. Ormsby, 'Francis Hincks', *Dictionary of Canadian Biography*, xi. 406–16. For an account of Hincks's role in the development of Canadian consociationalism, see S. J. R. Noel, *Patrons, Clients, Brokers: Ontario Society and Politics, 1791–1896* (Toronto: University of Toronto Press, 1990), 139–75.
24. Craig, *Upper Canada*, 229–30. For the transplanting and spread of Orangeism to Canada, see H. Senior, *Orangeism: The Canadian Phase* (Toronto: McGraw-Hill Ryerson), 1972.
25. Baldwin and LaFontaine became lifelong friends. Early in their association Baldwin consulted LaFontaine on a suitable Quebec school where he might send his son. 'I must not expose him', he wrote, 'to the miserable embarrassment that I labour under myself for want of French.' Baldwin to LaFontaine, 14 August 1844, National Archives of Canada, *LaFontaine Papers*.
26. Among these were George-Étienne Cartier and John A. Macdonald, who would later become the leading architects of the Canadian federation.

27. For a lucid account of Canada's unresolved constitutional dilemma, see P. H. Russell, *Constitutional Odyssey: Can Canadians Become a Sovereign People?* (Toronto: University of Toronto Press, 1992).
28. *British Parliamentary Debates*, 6 Mar. 1837, 3rd series, V. 36, C. 1324.
29. The factors that gave rise to the sudden emergence of a well-developed system of consociational governance in the Union of the Canadas are largely a matter of conjecture. Arend Lijphart concludes that it must have been a spontaneous occurrence arising from the necessity of governing a plural society because 'not even a trace of prior consociational traditions can be detected'; A. Lijphart, *Democracy in Plural Societies*, 128–9. I have suggested that, in addition to the inter-elite bargaining that took place under the British regime in Quebec, the political and business culture of Upper Canada produced a class of talented brokers and negotiators, such as Francis Hincks, who were quick to see the advantages of power-sharing. See Noel, *Patrons, Clients, Brokers*, 171–2.
30. After the 1851 census revealed that the population of Upper Canada exceeded that of Lower Canada, 'Rep by Pop' became the cry of those whose cause was to break up the Union. See Careless, *The Union of the Canadas*, 181–2.
31. O'Leary and McGarry, *Politics of Antagonism*, 303–4.
32. Hincks to LaFontaine, 9 Sept. 1839, National Archives of Canada, *LaFontaine Papers*.
33. There is a school of thought that argues against consociationalism and in favour of 'social transformation' on the model of South Africa. See R. Taylor's contribution to this volume. For a critique of the transformationist case, see J. McGarry, 'Political Settlements in Northern Ireland and South Africa', *Political Studies*, 46/5 (1998), 853–70.

10

Northern Ireland and Island Status

ADRIAN GUELKE

When God made this country He fixed its frontiers beyond the power
of man to alter while the sea rises and falls

(Arthur Griffith in 1914)[1]

The thesis of this chapter is that the fact that Northern Ireland is the partitioned part, not just of a historical entity, but of an island, matters politically. In particular, it is argued that the norm of territorial integrity makes
the international community generally hostile to the political division of
islands. This point is illustrated by comparing Northern Ireland to other
cases in which islands have been or might be divided, or in which there is a
question mark over the island's political status. In conclusion, it is con-
tended that the acknowledgement in the Good Friday Agreement of an all-
Ireland dimension to the governance of Northern Ireland is vital to the
settlement's international legitimacy, and that this factor is likely to
influence the settlement's interpretation and development, if it survives.

The boundaries of continental states often seem arbitrary and even
artificial, as well as being most obviously man-made. By contrast, the
boundaries of islands tend to appear natural, even if the notion of natural
entities has long been discredited among political geographers.[2] Those of a
religious disposition may even see islands as God-given entities, as Griffith
did. The most obvious consequence that flows from these perceptions is
that there is a prejudice (or disposition, if a less pejorative description is
preferred) against the dividing of islands under more than one sovereignty.
That is reflected in the attitude of the international community towards
disputes involving the division of islands. As a matter of fact, too, divided
sovereignties on islands are relatively rare. Currently the only examples of
islands falling under the internationally recognized sovereignty of more
than one state are Ireland; Borneo, divided among Indonesia, Malaysia,
and Brunei; Hispaniola, divided between Haiti and the Dominican

Republic; New Guinea, divided between Indonesia and Papua New Guinea; Saint-Martin (St Maarten), divided between Guadeloupe, an overseas department of France, and Netherlands Antilles; Tierra del Fuego, divided between Argentina and Chile and Usedom (Uznam) divided between Germany and Poland. To this list one should add the cases of Cyprus and Timor and the challenge presented to the territorial integrity of Sri Lanka by that country's ethnic civil war, each of which is discussed in greater detail below.

Another consequence of the perceived wholeness of islands is to strengthen their claim to be independent entities, should a credible movement for such independent status exist.[3] To put the point another way, the pursuit of secession by an island tends to be seen in a more favourable light than that of any other part of a country. Even before the end of the cold war, when the United Nations maintained an absolute anathema against secession as in the 1970 Declaration of Principles of International Law,[4] nationalist movements seeking the independence of islands were viewed relatively tolerantly by international opinion, and in a few cases supported where a plausible case could be made that the movement in question was seeking an end to a species of colonialism. Further, as islands tend to be seen as separate entities, even islands close to large states may escape the sovereignty of the state in question. What is more, their greater legitimacy in the eyes of the international community means that they are more likely to survive absorption by even a powerful neighbour than are continental enclaves. The islands of Quemoy and Matsu very close to the coast of mainland China provide a case in point.

Defence of the territorial integrity of member states has formed an important principle of the United Nations and that has been reflected in numerous legal declarations of the General Assembly. Particularly in the years between the ending of the colonial era and the collapse of communism in eastern Europe, the effect of the principle was to freeze existing boundaries between states. There was one major exception in which the territorial status quo was not upheld in this period, and this was the emergence of Bangladesh. However, it could be rationalized as a special case for three reasons; the origins of Pakistan in partition, the large distance between the West and East wings of the country, and the fact that the people wishing to secede constituted a majority of the total population of the existing state. Further, in the circumstances of India's successful intervention and the defeat of Pakistani forces in East Pakistan, the international community's acceptance of Bangladesh amounted to little more than acquiescence in a fait accompli. Finally, it is worth stressing that though the domestic political repercussions of the emergence of Bangladesh were very considerable for the whole of the South Asian subcontinent, the change in the status of what had been the East wing of Pakistan did not entail in any other respect the redrawing of international boundaries.

By the time of the onset of the troubles, the legal position of Northern Ireland as a part of the United Kingdom was not in serious question in terms of either domestic or international law. That was one reason why the Republic of Ireland did not persist in its efforts to bring the issue before the United Nations Security Council after its initial referral of the problem to the United Nations in 1969 was shelved through the device of a motion of adjournment in the Security Council.[5] However, politically, there was widespread sympathy for the nationalist case that the root of the conflict lay in the 'illegitimate' partition of an island. The troubles themselves underscored the perception that the status quo did not enjoy widespread consent. The peculiar status of Northern Ireland as a conditional part of the United Kingdom, with its own government and different party system, suggested a colonial entity rather a subordinate element of the British political system. Such perceptions in a newly post-colonial world made unionism seem an anachronism from another age, and for its roots in the ethnic identity of Northern Protestants to be glossed over. Consequently, from the outset of the troubles nationalists found it to their advantage to promote the internationalization of the conflict. By the same token, unionists viewed external opinion with suspicion and tended to identify with others they saw as being in the same position as themselves, pariahs such as the Smith regime in Rhodesia.

After the imposition of direct rule in 1972 and the failure of the power-sharing executive in 1974, unionists became interested in another option, that of Northern Ireland's total integration into the British political system, as a way of countering nationalist demands for a settlement embracing an Irish dimension, which would, in however an attenuated form symbolize the essential unity of Ireland. However, the credibility of integration depended on the British political system's remaining highly centralized. That prospect was ended by the referendums in favour of devolution in Scotland and Wales in 1997. A further and much more effective unionist tactic in countering the nationalist insistence on the territorial integrity of the island of Ireland was to change the geographical frame of reference to that of the whole archipelago of the British Isles. This does not make partition seem more legitimate, but it places the onus for it on the secession of twenty-six counties of Ireland from the United Kingdom rather than on the exclusion of Northern Ireland from the new Irish state.

The claim that the British Isles should constitute a single political entity by reason of its map image as a 'natural' unit is at least as strong if not stronger than the geographical case for a united Ireland. However, international opinion remains firmly wedded to the united Ireland map image. The Republic of Ireland is too well-established an independent state for a perspective that casts doubt on its legitimacy to gain ground at this juncture. Further, the British Isles map image has not been very strongly articulated by any of the parties to the conflict. While use by unionists of the concept has grown, they remain divided on its exploitation, in part because of the fear that it could be used to undercut their own claim to autonomy. Lastly, it is difficult to dissociate the idea from Britain's history as a major colonial power and that is sufficient to undermine its appeal in many parts of the world.

However, nationalist opinion remains sensitive to the potential of the British Isles map image, and that is reflected in nationalist rejection of the very description 'British Isles'. Nationalists use the awkward and ambiguous description 'these islands' as an alternative. However, outside the British Isles, or these islands, if preferred, the term British Isles remains quite commonly used. An example is that when the rugby touring team consisting of the best players from England, Scotland, Wales, and Ireland (and collectively known as the Lions or the British Lions) takes part in test matches against teams from South Africa, New Zealand, or Australia, it is referred to as the team of the British Isles. Since the Lions only play outside the British Isles or these islands, the opportunity for Irish nationalists to insist that the former description should not be used has not arisen. However, a satellite television station broadcasting to Ireland was prevailed on to drop the description British Isles from its weather forecasts. Ahead of the Good Friday Agreement, the idea of a Council of the British Isles was widely canvassed, and such a council is indeed an important element in the Agreement. However, in deference to nationalist opinion it is called the British–Irish Council, while still performing the essential function of reassuring unionists that the strengthening of North–South ties in Ireland does not entail the automatic weakening of Northern Ireland's ties with other parts of the United Kingdom. The Agreement envisages that the British–Irish Council will consist of representatives of the British and Irish governments, devolved institutions in Northern Ireland, Scotland, and Wales, and others that may develop elsewhere in the United Kingdom, as well as representatives of the Isle of Man and the Channel Islands.

The fact that the archipelago of the British Isles or these islands can be so effectively counterposed to the idea of a united Ireland reflects another common aspect of island status. Some of the world's independent states are constituted from single large islands, apart from the tiny islands or islets to be found in close proximity to the coast. Iceland, Jamaica, and Madagascar are examples. However, it is also quite common for political entities to be formed from clusters of islands, in other words, from archipelagos. Japan, New Zealand, and the Philippines are obvious examples. By contrast, most continental states are constituted from a single unit of land, again exclud-ing minor features such as islets within lakes or, in the case of coastal states, small offshore islands. Contiguity tends to be the rule among continental states, especially among smaller states and land-locked states.[6] Further, this issue has a bearing on the legitimacy of political entities. One obstacle—admittedly, only one among many—to the international community's acceptance of the independent states created by South Africa under its pol-icy of apartheid was the lack of credibility as independent states of home-lands constituted from separated units of land (particularly in the case of Bophuthatswana, which was granted independence in 1977), especially as most of the several parts of the land-locked homeland were surrounded entirely by South Africa.

Because they are composed of separate units, archipelagos are more sus-ceptible to secession than are continental states. The secession at indepen-dence from France of Mayotte from the Comoros Islands, a group of four islands which had originally itself been politically attached to Madagascar, illustrates the point. Mayotte opted to stay under French rule in 1975. In 1997 two of the three remaining islands of the archipelago unilaterally declared their independence. However, their preferred option of a return to French rule is opposed by France. The Organization of African Unity has been engaged in mediation efforts among the conflicting parties. Fuller illustration of the role played by island status in the Irish question is best made through comparison of other cases of politically divided islands.

Cyprus represents in the starkest form the alternative to political accom-modation in deeply divided societies, and that is separation of the groups through partition with transfer of populations to ensure the homogeneity of the new entities. Since the completion of the process of the partitioning of the island, which took place in two phases following the invasion of Cyprus by Turkey in 1974, there has been little conflict between the Greek Cypriot and Turkish Cypriot communities. Indeed, so complete was the process of separation of the two communities through partition and the transfer of population that it left little opportunity for further intercom-munal violence to take place. Nevertheless, there remains little disposition on the part of the parties to consider the conflict resolved. Cyprus is best described today as the case of a bloodless conflict. While the outcome of partition is in line with the historical objectives of one of the communities, the Turkish Cypriot minority, in practice, the hostility of the international community and of the Greek Cypriot majority has rendered its consequences unsatisfactory even from the perspective of the minority.

At the crossroads between East and West in the ancient world, Cyprus was conquered successively by the Assyrians, the Egytians, the Persians, the Greeks, and the Romans. It was ruled from the fourth century for 800 years by Byzantium. A period of Crusader then Latin control followed before it was ceded to the Venetian Republic in 1489 and then conquered by the Ottoman Turks in 1571. The Ottomans applied the millet system to Cyprus, permitting a consolidation of the position of the previously persecuted Orthodox Church in relation to the island's ethnic Greek population. It was during this period that Turkish settlement on the island took place. In 1878 Turkey transferred administration of the island to Britain. The purpose was to provide Britain with a base to aid Turkey in the event of a Russian attack on the Ottoman empire. Ironically, this enabled Britain to annex the island in 1914 when Turkey entered the First World War on the side of Germany. Under the 1923 Treaty of Lausanne, Turkey gave up any claim to the island, and it was consequently excluded from the Treaty's provisions for a far-reaching exchange of population between Turkey and Greece.

Opposition to British rule grew after the Second World War. Early in 1950 Michael Mouskos organized a plebiscite through the Orthodox Church which produced a 96 per cent vote in favour of *enosis*, that is, union with Greece. Later that same year he was elected the head of the Orthodox Church, taking the name Archbishop Makarios III. In 1954, in reply to a debate on Cyprus, the British minister for the colonies, Henry Hopkinson, declared that there were some territories under British rule that could never expect to be fully independent. Greece sought to internationalize the issue by raising the question of the island's self-determination (in this context its right to *enosis*) in the United Nations General Assembly. The following year, 1955, a campaign of sabotage was launched by EOKA (Ethniki Organosis Kyprion Agoniston, National Organization of Freedom Fighters). This marked the start of a revolt against British rule that lasted three and a half years. Greek mobilization for *enosis* alarmed both Turkey and the Turkish minority, which constituted under 20 per cent of the island's population whereas Greeks constituted nearly 80 per cent of the population. The Turks responded to the creation of EOKA by creating the TMT (Turk Mukavenet Testikali, Turkish Defence Organization) and counterposed to the Greeks' goal of *enosis* that of *taksim*, that is, partition. Like EOKA, TMT was right-wing and anti-communist in its political ideology. One of the founders of TMT was Rauf Denktash, who was to become a figure of comparable importance among Turkish Cypriots as Makarios already was among Greek Cypriots.

A factor that exacerbated relations between the two communities was the targeting of Turkish police officers by EOKA. To EOKA, they were legitimate targets given the role they played in the execution of British security policy. But what was represented by Greeks as an attack upon colonial rule was seen very differently by the Turkish minority. In the first half of 1958 there was an escalation of intercommunal violence. It weakened the influence of institutions such as the trade unions that had succeeded in bridging the divide between the communities. The violence also prompted movement of population as people sought safety in their own communities. The effect was to increase the already high level of residential segregation. Encouragement to Turks to move north was provided by the aim of partition, since it was made clear that the Turks would claim the northern half of the island in any partition. Against the backdrop of an intensification of ethnic conflict on the island, the British government reviewed its commitment to maintaining control over the whole island. However, the British government remained opposed to *enosis*, because of the opposition of Turkey. While Turks constituted less than a fifth of the island's population, the location of Cyprus was less than fifty miles from the Turkish mainland, while 500 miles from the Greek mainland. Thus, in the power equation geography was a countervailing factor to the relative size of the two communities.

Britain's threat to partition the island persuaded Makarios to give up the aim of *enosis* and to accept independence instead. That paved the way to direct talks between Greece and Turkey over the future of the island in Zurich in February 1959, immediately followed by tripartite talks involving Britain, Greece, and Turkey in London. Out of these talks came a series of agreements that settled the island's immediate future. Under their terms Cyprus was to become an independent state on 16 August 1960. An elaborate Constitution was bequeathed to the new state to safeguard the position of the two communities. It laid down that the president of the Republic would be a Greek Cypriot with the right to choose seven of the ten ministers in the government, while the vice-president was to be a Turkish Cypriot choosing the remaining three ministers. Both were given vetoes over decisions of the Council of Ministers in respect of foreign policy, defence, and internal security. A legislature was provided for, consisting of thirty-five Greek Cypriot and fifteen Turkish Cypriot members. Any law imposing taxes or duties required the support of a majority of the representatives of each community.

The Constitution also laid down that positions in the Civil Service should be allocated to the two communities on a 70:30 ratio between the Greek Cypriot and Turkish Cypriot communities. There were similar clauses covering the composition of the security forces. The provision for a measure of over-representation for the minority was to become a cause of contention between the communities. In addition, strong protection for human rights was written into the Constitution, which ran to 199 articles. On top of all this, the Constitution was linked to three different international treaties which came into effect on the island's independence. Under the Treaty of Guarantee with Britain, Greece, and Turkey, Cyprus undertook to remain independent and to adhere to the provisions of the Constitution. Britain, Greece, and Turkey for their part guaranteed to uphold not merely Cyprus's territorial integrity but also the provisions of the Constitution. Under the Treaty of Alliance provision was made for the stationing of Greek and Turkish troops on the island for the purpose of training the Cypriot army. The Treaty of Establishment created two enclaves of British sovereign territory covering 99 square miles for use as military bases.

As Joseph points out, the settlement was 'not in accordance with UN principles of self-determination and sovereign equality of the states'.[7] Independence of the whole island had been a goal of neither of the communities, and the extent of external supervision of the Constitution was hard to reconcile with Cypriot sovereignty. The need for such extensive external supervision was itself a reflection of the reality that the settlement was in essence one that had been imposed on the local parties. Yet within two decades the territorial integrity of Cyprus was to become a cause taken up by the international community, with the consequence that all serious attempts to provide a solution to the Cyprus problem have taken as their starting-point a commitment to the nominal unity of the island. This is despite the history of the island between 1960 and 1974. The complex consociational settlement bequeathed to Cyprus quickly broke down. The conflicting aspirations of the two communities produced deadlock. As a way out of the impasse President Makarios proposed amendments to the 1960 Constitution. His proposals aroused the worst fears of the Turkish Cypriot community, and were rejected by both the Turkish Cypriot vice-president and Turkey. Tensions rose as the political crisis deepened. A minor street disturbance touched off serious intercommunal violence in the capital, Nicosia, in December 1963.

Conflict spread to the rest of the island, and in the first half of 1964 there were approximately 500 deaths as a result of political violence. Turkish Cypriot participation in the government ceased, while further impetus was given to the territorial separation of the two communities. With the threat of Turkish intervention looming in the background, the UN Security Council agreed in March 1964 to the establishment of a UN peacekeeping force, the United Nations Force in Cyprus (UNFICYP). In his appeals to the United Nations, President Makarios made great play of the defence of the territorial integrity of Cyprus against external aggression, while also insisting that the terms of the 1960 Constitution and the Treaty of Guarantee were infringements of the country's sovereignty.[8] UNFICYP did not bring about an immediate end to the violence, but it was reasonably effective in containing the conflict. Indeed, its presence on the island has been considered indispensable ever since, even after the partitioning of the island in 1974. But while international intervention helped to quell political violence, it did not restore the working of the 1960 Constitution. Mediation to get agreement between the two communities on alternative arrangements made little headway.

In April 1967 the military seized power in a *coup d'état* in Athens to forestall an expected victory by the Left in the Greek general elections. This development paradoxically appeared to improve the prospects for a political settlement in Cyprus. The hostility of the military regime in Greece to Makarios increased his determination to maintain the island's independence. However, at the same time as the prospects for negotiations taking place under the auspices of the United Nations were improving, Makarios's position was being undermined by the Greek military, which gave its support to a paramilitary organization committed to *enosis* and styling itself EOKA B. The military also used its influence in the National Guard against Makarios. At the beginning of July 1974 President Makarios demanded that the Greek junta withdraw 650 non-Cypriot officers in the National Guard. His ultimatum triggered a military *coup d'état* by the National Guard, which was supported by Greece. A notorious EOKA gunman, Nicos Sampson, was installed as president.

The prime minister of Turkey, Bulent Ecevit, sent the Greek junta an ultimatum on 18 July demanding Sampson's resignation and the withdrawal of the Greek officers from the National Guard. He received an equivocal answer from the junta, which naively believed that the United States would act to prevent a Turkish invasion, notwithstanding the extremely provocative nature of its own actions. On 20 July Turkey invaded Cyprus. The Turkish forces met fierce resistance, but succeeded in securing a wide corridor between the northern coast, where they had landed, and the capital, Nicosia. A conference of the three guarantor powers and representatives of the two Cypriot communities was held in Geneva in August. By this time the Greek military junta had collapsed, and Nicos Sampson had resigned. The negotiations reflected the shift in the balance of power between the communities as a result of the Turkish invasion. The Greek Cypriot representatives pleaded for a restoration of the 1960 Constitution, while the Turkish Cypriot representatives argued for a loose federation of two autonomous zones. In the wake of the failure of the negotiations the Turkish army took further military action, consolidating its hold on the northern part of the island. With the Turks in control of 37 per cent of the island, the process of the partitioning of the island was complete.

The very high cost of Turkey's military action in human terms, with large numbers of civilians killed and a third of the population of Cyprus turned into refugees, explains why partition accompanied by population transfer is rarely advocated as an answer to the problem of ethnic conflict. However, what has perhaps been more surprising is the attitude the international community has shown to the partitioning of Cyprus once it had become a *fait accompli*. The net result of Turkey's actions was the virtually total separation of the two communities, with Greeks constituting fewer than 1 per cent of the population in the North and Turks an even smaller proportion of the population in the South. The task of UNFICYP was greatly simplified; it had merely to police the buffer zone between the two parts of the island. However, despite the transformation of the conflict into an almost bloodless one, the international community has proved unwilling to legitimize the outcome of a permanently divided island. While the force of world opinion has not been strong enough to reverse the partitioning of Cyprus, it has proved strong enough to prevent the normalization of the situation. The result has been a continual series of negotiations to find an answer to the Cyprus problem under a variety of auspices.

In February 1975 Turkey established a Turkish Federated State in the North as a part of a putative federation. In the talks between Makarios and the Turkish Cypriot Denktash leader, Rauf in February 1977 the Greek Cypriots made an important concession to the Turkish Cypriots by agreeing to the goal of 'an independent, non-aligned, bi-communal Federal Republic'.[9] Makarios died shortly after this high-level agreement, as it was known, and the talks thereafter made little headway, as the two sides reached an impasse over issues such as freedom of movement on the island, the size of the Turkish entity, and the stationing of foreign troops on the island. In 1983 Turkey adopted a new approach to the Cyprus problem. On

15 November 1983 the area controlled by the Turks was proclaimed an independent state, the Turkish Republic of North Cyprus, with the Turkish Cypriot leader Rauf Denktash as its president. This tactic backfired. Turkey was alone in recognizing the new entity. The rest of the world continued to recognize the Greek Cypriot administration in the Southern part of the island as the legitimate government of Cyprus.

In 1988 an independent candidate with left-wing support, Georgios Vassilou, was elected president of (Greek) Cyprus, raising hopes of progress in the negotiations between representatives of the two communities. In an effort to expedite matters, the UN Secretary-General, Boutros Boutros-Ghali, summarized the possible basis for agreement between the two sides in a Set of Ideas of June 1989.[10] The essential basis of the Set of Ideas was that Cyprus would be a bizonal, bicommunal federation, and this has provided the framework for all subsequent discussion of a political settlement. However, these terms masked large differences in how these concepts were interpreted by the two sides. In 1993 Vassilou was defeated by the veteran right-wing politician Glafcos Clerides, who insisted on the unacceptability of any settlement that violated the basic right of refugees to return to the homes from which they had been driven in 1974.

A further factor that has complicated negotiations has been the hostile reaction of Turkey to a series of decisions that the European Union has made in relation to Cyprus. In 1990 the (Greek) government of Cyprus applied for membership of the European Community. In December 1997 the European Union agreed to enter into negotiations on membership with Poland, Hungary, the Czech Republic, Estonia, Slovenia, and Cyprus. At the same time the possibility of membership at a future date was held out to six other countries, Lithuania, Latvia, Slovakia, Romania, Bulgaria, and Malta. Turkey reacted with fury to this announcement. When accession talks were formally opened with Cyprus at the end of March 1998, the government of the Turkish Republic of North Cyprus threatened that the North would merge with Turkey. Substantive talks on Cyprus's accession started in November 1998, prompting further Turkish protests.[11] Concern over the unwillingness of the Turkish Cypriot authorities to participate in the talks was expressed by the governments of France, Germany, Italy, and the Netherlands, which made it clear that they considered a political settlement to be an essential precondition for Cyprus's actual membership of the European Union.

Notwithstanding such reservations, the readiness of the European Union to treat the (Greek) government of (Southern) Cyprus as the island's legitimate government is striking, as is the similar attitude of the

United Nations. This might be interpreted as demonstrating a pro-Greek bias on the part of world opinion. However, that is somewhat misleading. The international community evinced little support for the original Greek objective of *enosis*. While this may be seen as a recognition of the power realities in the eastern Mediterranean, the international community has also shown little enthusiasm for an ethnically 'fair' version of this option, double *enosis*, i.e. integration of the Southern part of the island into Greece and the Northern part into Turkey, notwithstanding interest in this option at various times among some of the parties to the conflict and among major powers such as the United States. A more accurate description of the international attitude is that it has supported the Greek Cypriot cause in so far as it became identified with the defence of the principles of the territorial integrity and sovereign equality of states. Makarios showed that he understood this well, while the Greek junta recklessly disregarded it with disastrous consequences for the Greek Cypriots in 1974.

The case of Cyprus might seem tailor-made to elicit the engagement of Irish nationalists, given what it demonstrates about the importance of the map image of an island as a single unit, but paradoxically the case has attracted more interest from unionists, notably from two senior figures in the Ulster Unionist Party, John Taylor and Ken Maginnis, who have identified themselves with the cause of the Turkish Cypriots. From a unionist perspective the durability of the Turkish Republic of North Cyprus, despite per capita incomes a quarter of those of the rest of the island, strongly demonstrates the primacy of national identity and security over other issues. The manner in which the Good Friday Agreement cuts across traditional zero-sum views of sovereignty provides a model potentially of considerable relevance to progress towards a settlement of the Cyprus problem. But there would have to be a vast improvement in relations between Greece and Turkey for that potential to become realizable.

Puerto Rico has never been partitioned and ethnicity plays little part in the island's political divisions. (Strictly speaking Puerto Rico is an archipelago because it consists of a group of islands. However, the main island is so much more important than all of the others that the point can be considered pedantic.) The obvious basis for comparison between Puerto Rico and Northern Ireland is that both are subordinate entities that form part of larger states. Further, in both Puerto Rico and Northern Ireland differences in attitudes towards the larger state provide the main basis of political divisions. Just as Northern Ireland's politics are dominated by the constitutional question, Puerto Rico's are dominated by the issue of status.

Puerto Rico was ruled by Spain from early in the sixteenth century, when the first European settlement was established on the island. It remained a Spanish colony until 1899, when it was ceded to the United States under the Treaty of Paris following the Spanish–American War. Under the Foraker Act of 1900 Puerto Rico became an 'unincorporated territory' of the United States.[12] The president of the United States appointed the island's governor, though the islanders were given the right to elect the lower chamber of the legislature, and in 1917 legislation was enacted to make Puerto Ricans American citizens. The Great Depression had a severe impact on the island's sugar-based economy, and provided the conditions for the growth of nationalism. A notable episode was the Ponce massacre, in which the police fired on a nationalist parade. Twenty people died in this incident, including two policemen. In 1938 the Partido Popular Democratico (Popular Democratic Party, PPD) was founded under the leadership of Luis Munoz Marin. In 1940 it won a narrow victory in the island's legislative elections, marking the start of Munoz Marin's domination of Puerto Rican politics, which lasted until his retirement in 1964.[13]

Following constitutional reform after the Second World War, Munoz Marin became the first elected governor of Puerto Rico in 1948, while the PPD won a landslide victory in the legislative elections. From this position of strength Munoz proposed a new constitutional dispensation for Puerto Rico. He argued that Congress would not support the total integration of Puerto Rico into the United States through statehood, and that independence would be economically disastrous. His third way was autonomy, a status encapsulated in the concept Estado Libre Asociado (literally, Free Associated State). This was translated into English as Commonwealth, masking the influence that the establishment of the Irish Free State had played in Munoz's thinking on the issue. Great care was taken in the procedure followed to put the Commonwealth into effect so that its legitimacy could not be challenged. In 1950 Congress passed Public Law 600. This allowed Puerto Rico to draw up its own Constitution in terms of Commonwealth status. Before this step took place, a referendum was held in Puerto Rico to endorse the concept of Commonwealth status. There was an overwhelming vote in favour. However, the supporters of independence boycotted the poll, and some nationalists resorted to violence in their opposition. An uprising in the interior of Puerto Rico in October 1950 resulted in twenty-seven deaths, while there was an attempt on President Truman's life by two nationalists the following month. A draft Constitution was drawn up by a Constituent Assembly elected by the islanders. It was then endorsed with some amendments by Congress and ratified in a further referendum in Puerto Rico.

Commonwealth status came into effect in July 1952 with all the outward paraphernalia of nationhood, including flag and national anthem. The United States sought international endorsement of the new dispensation at the United Nations. In a letter to the United Nations President Eisenhower pledged that if the Puerto Rican legislature adopted a resolution in favour of independence, he would recommend to Congress that its wish be granted. On this basis, the General Assembly accepted that Common-wealth status had transformed Puerto Rico into a fully self-governing territory. However, the gloss began to wear off Commonwealth status with the decolonization of the European empires. In 1960 the UN General Assembly set up the Decolonization Committee with the task of speeding the progress of dependent territories to independence. Supporters of Puerto Rican independence lobbied for the inclusion of Puerto Rico on its agenda, arguing that the need for congressional approval for any change in the island's status was a negation of the island's right to self-determination. In 1972 Puerto Rico was placed on the agenda of the Decolonization Committee and became the subject of regular resolutions calling for the ending of colonial rule on the island.

The gloss also started to come off Commonwealth status within Puerto Rico itself. There was an erosion of the island's autonomy as a result of the growth in the scope of government in Washington. However, disillusion-ment with Commonwealth status did not take the form of increased sup-port for independence. With the success of the Commonwealth's policies for economic development through tax incentives for investment by American companies, support for independence declined.[14] Instead there was increased support for the integrationist option of statehood. In a ref-erendum on the status issue in 1967, 39 per cent of voters opted for state-hood, though with 60 per cent of the vote the status quo remained the clear choice of the electorate. In November 1968 the gubernatorial election was won by Luis A. Ferre, the candidate of the pro-statehood party, the Partido Nuevo Progresista (New Progressive Party, PNP), partly as a result of a split in the PPD. He lost four years later, but in 1976 and 1980 the PNP won the governorship again. The PPD candidate won in 1984 and 1988, but that was followed by victories for the PNP candidate, Pedro Rosello, in 1992 and 1996. In a referendum on the status issue in 1993, 48.6 per cent of voters supported Commonwealth, 46.3 per cent statehood, and 4.4 per cent inde-pendence. A further non-binding referendum on the status issue with five alternatives being put before voters, including that of 'none of the above', took place on 13 December 1998. There had been considerable controversy over the definitions of the different options, with the PPD contending that they had been drawn up so as to persuade voters to opt for statehood. In particular, the PPD objected to what it saw as a colonial definition of the status of Commonwealth. In the event, statehood was defeated, with 50.2 per cent of voters opting for 'none of the above' as opposed to 46.5 per cent supporting statehood. Independence was supported by 3.5 per cent, 'free association' by 0.3 per cent, and Commonwealth by 0.1 per cent.[15] The failure yet again of the pro-statehood forces to secure a majority might suggest the need for a new approach to issues of sovereignty in Puerto Rico. However, the relative narrowness of their defeat seems to have persuaded the PNP that it should persist with the objective of statehood.

While independence has only ever enjoyed the support of a minority of Puerto Ricans, the cause has generated a measure of political violence both on the island and in the United States. In March 1954 Puerto Rican nationalists opened fire from the visitors' gallery of the United States House of Representatives, wounding five members of Congress. Puerto Rican nationalists carried out over 100 bombings in the United States in the 1970s, while a group calling itself Los Macherteros (the Machete-Wielders) was responsible for the spectacular destruction of nine planes of the National Guard in Puerto Rico in 1981. While Puerto Ricans living on the island do not have a vote in American presidential elections, they are represented in the party conventions that elect the presidential candidates of both the main parties. The attitude of American politicians towards the status issue has been equivocal. Gerald Ford was the first president to give strong support to statehood, just as he was about to leave office in January 1977. But presidential enthusiasm for statehood has not been matched in Congress, and a recurring theme on debates on the status issue in Puerto Rico is the fear that Congress might rebuff a vote in favour of statehood. At the same time, with 60 per cent of the island's population below the poverty line, Puerto Rico is massively dependent on federal aid amounting to approximately $9 billion a year, a figure almost equivalent to the total amount of American foreign aid to the rest of the world.[16]

While the aspect of partition is missing from the Puerto Rican case and there is no equivalent to Northern Ireland's sectarian divisions, there is similarity in the marginality of both entities to their respective centres. Both unionists in Northern Ireland and supporters of statehood in Puerto Rico are in the somewhat demeaning position of having to assert their national identity in the face of indifference, if not rejection, of their fellow citizens on the mainland. Constitutional and political integration to bring an end to the uncertainty over their status have been advocated in both situations as a way out of the limbo each entity occupies. However, the implementation of such a solution in Northern Ireland would require the British government to ignore the political preferences and national identity of one community in a deeply divided society, as well as much of international opinion. It is virtually inconceivable that any British government would embark on such a course of action. There are fewer barriers to the integration of Puerto Rico into the United States, even if as a small island Puerto Rico does not form part of the map image most Americans have of the United States. However, if the Good Friday Agreement is seen to be a success in redefining Northern Ireland's relationship to the United Kingdom, it is possible that American interest in alternatives to integration or Commonwealth status in its present form might grow.

The status of the island of Corsica is much clearer than that of either Puerto Rico or Northern Ireland. Corsica was annexed by France from Genoa in 1768. It was fully integrated into France in 1789. However, geographically Corsica is closer to mainland Italy than to mainland France. Further, the language of the indigenous population of the island resembles Italian, not French. In the early years of French rule there was a question mark over the island's commitment to France. It took the victory of the Bonapartists in Corsica's factional politics to lay the basis for Corsicans to become loyal subjects of France from the early nineteenth century. Corsicans took pride in their association with Napoleon Bonaparte, and their identification with France was further cemented by the employment of many Corsicans in the service of France's overseas empire and the role played by Corsicans in France's wars.

A small minority of Corsicans was attracted to nationalism at the end of the nineteenth century and again in the inter-war years.[17] In the latter period some nationalists were attracted to fascism, and put their ideological convictions into practice by collaborating with the Italians when they invaded and occupied the island in November 1942. Their actions had the effect of discrediting the espousal of any form of regionalism or nationalism for many years after the Second World War. Expressions of regionalism and nationalism only began to re-emerge during the 1960s. Factors in its re-emergence were the long-term decline in the island's population to under 250,000 as a result of its economic stagnation and resentment at the settlement of *pieds noirs* from Algeria. Hostility towards the settlers from Algeria and the workers from North Africa they employed reinforced an existing cleavage between the indigenous population and residents who had come to Corsica from mainland France and were often at the forefront of exploiting new economic opportunities on the island in the field of tourism. A group advocating independence for Corsica planted a few bombs as early as 1961. However, the violence of the 1960s was sporadic. The principal organizations committed to the use of violence to further nationalism were formed in the 1970s and for the most part separatist violence in Corsica was a phenomenon of the post-colonial era.

In 1967 the Simeoni brothers Max and Edmond founded an autonomist organization, Action Regionaliste Corse. It was banned in 1973, but reappeared as Azzione per a Rinascita Corsa (Action for a Reborn Corsica, ARC). A landmark in the development of nationalism was the seizure in 1975 of a wine depot belonging to a French Algerian, Henri Depeille, by Edmond Simeoni and fifty armed ARC militants. The aim of their action was to expose what the nationalists saw as the scandal of adulteration of wine by the settlers, whom they accused of flooding the market with cheap wine. The ARC militants held four of Depeille's Moroccan workers hostage, provoking a massive reaction from the authorities. A large contingent of police and soldiers surrounded the depot, and after the militants failed to surrender, there was a shoot-out in which two policemen were killed. Depeille's house and his wine cellar were destroyed by fire in the confrontation. Edmond Simeoni received a gaol sentence for his part in the affair. A series of explosions in 1976 marked the emergence of the Front Libération Nationale de la Corse (National Liberation Front of Corsica, FLNC) out of the merger of two existing clandestine organizations. The escalation in the level of violence led to the formation in April 1977 of another clandestine group, Front d'Action Nouvelle Contre l'Indépendance et l'Autonomie (New Action Front against Independence and Autonomy, FRANCIA). It directed its violence against the nationalists, attacking, in particular, the offices of magazines supporting the campaign for Corsican autonomy.

In response to the growth of nationalism on the island, the French authorities introduced economic reforms in 1975, but at that time made no political concessions to the nationalists. Mitterrand's election as president in 1981 resulted in much more fundamental political reform. The island was recognized as a territorial collectivity, and a directly elected Assembly was created. In the first elections to the Assembly held in August 1982, the autonomist successor to ARC, the Unione diu Populu Corsu won seven seats out of sixty-one. The majority of seats were won by candidates of parties affiliated to the national French political parties. In fresh elections to the Assembly in 1984 a party linked to the FLNC won three seats. However, in January 1983 the FLNC itself was banned. One of the principal reasons the authorities gave for taking this action was the forging of links between the FLNC and the Provisional IRA. A theme of French press comment on the violence in Corsica was the danger of the island's *irlandisation*. This was prompted as much by concern over the possibility of the conflict's internationalization as by perceived similarities between the two cases. Interest in the comparison was reinforced by the publication in 1983 of a book on the island by a Northern Ireland civil servant, Robert Ramsay. Ramsay compared the peripheral character of the two entities, while stressing the strong French commitment to Corsica both politically and economically, reflected in the proportionately much larger subsidy Corsica received from the French state. He also saw a parallel in the impact of violence in the two cases, concluding: 'Once terrorism has taken a hold in a situation in which there exists an ethnic cleavage, it is constantly reinforced by the very tensions which it creates in the community.'[18]

However, Ramsay's fears of a worsening of the situation in Corsica were not borne out. Indeed, following Mitterrand's re-election in 1988, the FLNC called a truce, which lasted a year and a half. In 1990 the FLNC split into a *canal historique* (historic wing) and a *canal habituel* (regular wing). Violence has continued sporadically. In 1997 the historic wing of the FLNC called a truce, but revoked it in January 1998. However, it denied responsibility for the most serious act of violence on the island in recent years, the murder of Claude Erignac, the prefect of Corsica, in February 1998. Responsibility for the assassination was claimed by a previously unknown separatist group, but there has also been speculation that the prefect was murdered by the Italian Mafia because of his opposition to the use of an old fortress for a casino.

Nationalists and autonomists competing under a wide variety of labels remain a significant minority of the Corsican electorate. In the elections to the Corsican Assembly in March 1998 they won in sum 17.33 per cent of the vote in the first round of voting. In the second round of voting the only remaining nationalist list, the militant Corsica Nazione, linked to the historic wing of the FLNC, won 9.85 per cent of the vote and five seats (out of fifty-one) in the regional assembly. However, in December 1988 a French court annulled the elections because of fraud and other irregularities affecting more than 1,000 ballot papers. Fresh elections were held in March 1999. In these, nationalists and regionalists did even better than they had done in 1998. Five such parties won 23.46 per cent of the vote. As in 1998, only Corsica Nazione got into the second round by winning more than 5 per cent of the vote. It won 10.41 per cent in the first round. This increased to 16.76 per cent in the second round, giving it eight seats in the Assembly and a strong bargaining position between the forces of Left and Right.[19]

At the same time the decline in the level of political violence associated with the conflict has made Corsican separatism seem less of a threat to the French state. The success of decentralization in defusing the conflict even persuaded the French government to make a highly significant symbolic concession to the islanders in 1991 by recognizing in legislation the existence of a Corsican people as a component of the French people. However, this was struck down by the Constitutional Council, which upheld the Jacobin position that acknowledged no division among the French people. Nonetheless, it is striking that even in a country as assimilationist and centralist in its traditions as France, the government should have been minded to give special recognition to the separate existence of an island minority, a step not contemplated in relation to any of France's other minorities. How successful or otherwise the Good Friday Agreement is in accommodating the different identities of people in Northern Ireland may influence French policy in Corsica, given that there already exists a strong disposition in France to compare the two cases.

The island of Timor was officially divided in a treaty between Portugal and the Netherlands in 1859 after the establishment by both countries of settlements on the islands, though it took until 1904 for the two governments to put it fully into effect. Following Japanese occupation of the island during the Second World War, the Dutch withdrew from the Western half of the island in 1949. However, the Portuguese stayed, and until 1975 the island of Timor remained divided between Indonesia and Portugal. It became clear that Portuguese colonial rule in the East of the island would be coming to an end when the army seized power in Lisbon in April 1974 in opposition to the Portuguese dictatorship's African policies. In September 1974 FRETILIN (Frente Revolucionaria do Timor Leste Independente, Revolutionary Front of Independent East Timor) was formed. It advocated complete independence for East Timor. Deriving its inspiration in part from the independence movements in other, larger Portuguese colonies, FRETILIN was left-wing in its ideological orientation. Opposing FRETILIN was a group advocating the continuation of Portuguese rule and a party that supported East Timor's integration into Indonesia.

Fighting among the factions prompted Portuguese withdrawal without the holding of planned elections. FRETILIN emerged victorious out of the ensuing conflict, and independence was declared on 28 November 1975. Indonesian forces invaded on 7 December 1975, meeting such fierce resistance that it took the Indonesian government until July 1976 to complete the process of East Timor's annexation. The annexation was a clear violation of the right of a people to self-determination within boundaries established by a colonial power. In the aftermath of the invasion the UN General Assembly passed a resolution condemning Indonesia's action by a substantial majority. However, in subsequent years the international community's opposition to the annexation waned, so that in 1982 the General Assembly passed a relatively weak resolution on the issue by a majority of only four. Cold war considerations in part account for the readiness of Western states to acquiesce in the Indonesian takeover, but the island factor was also an influence on the response of governments to what was an unambiguous violation of the prevailing interpretation of the norm of self-determination.

But despite the attitude of other governments to the annexation, Indonesia proved unable to normalize the occupation of East Timor. The major factor was continuing resistance to its rule by the people of East Timor, but non-governmental organizations in the field of human rights also played a significant role. Indeed, it was largely as a human rights issue that East Timor became and remained a focus of international concern. The scale of the killing during the Indonesian invasion of 1975 and a massacre in the capital, Dili, in November 1991 kept the issue alive, culminating in the award in 1996 of the Nobel Peace Prize to two spokespersons for the East Timorese, Bishop Bello and José Ramos-Horta. The resignation of the Indonesian dictator, President Suharto, in May 1998 created a new situation with the prospect that, in the general context of the liberalization of the Indonesian political system, the people of East Timor would be able to express their views freely for the first time on their future status. Initially, the new government of President B. J. Habibie was only ready to consider the option of the grant of a measure of autonomy to East Timor and firmly rejected calls for a referendum on the status of the territory. In November 1998 forty-four people were reported as having been killed in a military crackdown in East Timor.[20]

However, there was an abrupt change of approach by the new Indonesian government in the first months of 1999. In February 1999 President Habibie declared that Indonesia did not want to be bothered with the problem of East Timor any longer.[21] He also made it clear that he considered the only alternative to acceptance of his autonomy plan to be independence. But there were complicating factors. First, opponents of the independence organized themselves in armed militias, creating the spectre of civil war if independence was granted precipitately. Secondly, Indonesia still opposed allowing the East Timorese a straight vote for or against independence because of the demands for such referendums in other parts of the country. Eventually under an agreement with the former colonial power, Portugal, which was brokered by the United Nations, Indonesia agreed to permit the East Timorese to choose between autonomy and independence. They chose independence in the referendum of 30 August 1999. Militia violence followed, necessitating the intervention of an Australian-led peacekeeping force. The territory is being prepared for independence under the aegis of the United Nations. Indonesia comprises in total nearly 14,000 islands and islets, of which approximately 6,000 are inhabited. There is a serious challenge to Indonesian rule in Irian Jaya, the western half of the island of New Guinea, and since the fall of the Suharto dictatorship independence movements have emerged in a number of islands and groups of islands. Indonesia's readiness to give up East Timor can be seen as conceding over the issue on which Indonesia's position is weakest in the hope of saving the rest.

There are a number of resemblances among the cases of Sri Lanka, Cyprus, and Ireland. In each case the majority community in the island as a whole constitutes three-quarters to four-fifths of the island's population. The minority in each case has been concentrated in the north-east of the island. In each case it has sought to buttress its position through support outside the island from people with whom it has a cultural and national affinity. It has used the proximity of this support as a counterbalancing factor to the numerical preponderance of the majority community. There are also parallels to be drawn in the involvement of external parties in attempts to construct the framework for the resolution of conflict.[22] Conflict between the Tamils and the Sinhalese for the control of the island of Sri Lanka preceded successive periods of colonial rule, Portuguese, Dutch, and finally British. The country became independent in 1948. The Sinhalese constituted about three-quarters of the population of the island; the Tamils just under a fifth. Competition for power between Sinhala-dominated political parties led to an ethnicization of politics as the parties sought to outbid each other in asserting the interests of the Sinhalese majority, particularly in relation to language. That and anti-Tamil riots in 1956 and 1958 led to the increasing alienation of Tamils from the political system, culminating in the formation of the Tamil United Liberation Front in 1975. It quickly adopted the aim of *eelam*, or the creation of an independent state in the northern and eastern provinces of the island.

There was further serious outbursts of anti-Tamil violence in 1977, 1978, 1981, and 1983, the worst of these occurring in July 1983. In 1976 the Liberation Tigers of Tamil Eelam (LTTE) was formed. It was one of a number of paramilitary organizations to emerge as 'a militant response to state sponsored Sinhala-Buddhist chauvinism and discrimination and harassment by the Sri Lankan police and army'.[23] Indian mediation in the conflict led to the dispatch of the Indian Peace-Keeping Force (IPKF) to the island in July 1987. The political context was an accord whereby the government of Sri Lanka agreed to substantial devolution of powers to a provincial council in the north and east of the island and the LTTE agreed to a ceasefire. This initiative failed after the LTTE's defection from the agreement, resulting in its warring against the IPKF, prompting Indian withdrawal in March 1990. The current government in Sri Lanka is a left-wing coalition, the People's Alliance. It came to power in 1994 on a peace platform. However, the failure of negotiations with the LTTE to make headway has prompted the government to pursue a series of military offensives against the LTTE in an effort to force the paramilitary organization to come to terms with the government's proposals for a federal settlement.

Since 1983 over 50,000 people have died in the conflict in Sri Lanka. However, despite the scale of the conflict and its origins in violence directed against Tamils as an ethnic group, outside the important Tamil diaspora militant Tamil separatism has not won international support. While the government of Sri Lanka has been strongly criticized during the course of the conflict over gross violations of human rights by the security forces, reports of Amnesty International have been as critical of gross violations of human rights by the LTTE as they have been of the government.[24] The government has not come under pressure to give way, on the principle that the island should remain one state, though there has been widespread agreement that an important element of any settlement will be the extension of a large measure of autonomy to areas where the Tamils constitute a majority of the population. While the established unity of the island is an important difference between Sri Lanka and Ireland, there is considerable interest in Sri Lanka in the Good Friday Agreement, partly because of a recognition by the authorities that military means alone will not end the conflict.

In conflicts such as that in Sri Lanka the importance of island status tends to be implicit rather than explicit. Its unalterability makes it a factor that tends simply to be taken for granted. Its most obvious manifestation is to be found in the constant reference by those seeking to uphold the proposition that the island in question should constitute a single political unit to the principle of territorial integrity. Further, the geographical frame of reference provided by island status makes it easy to refer to the people (singular) of the island, regardless of the existence of any ethnic divisions among them. Even in the context of political settlements that explicitly recognize differences in the national identities of the inhabitants of an island, such as the Good Friday Agreement on the future of Northern

Ireland, it is striking how much importance has been attached to the settlement's endorsement by a majority of the people of the island, in this case, of Ireland. Undoubtedly, the holding of referendums simultaneously in both parts of Ireland did give added legitimacy to the Good Friday Agreement. Of course, it may be argued that amending the Constitution of the Republic of Ireland as part of the settlement made a referendum there necessary in any event, but it is worth noting that none of the parties suggested that it might be appropriate to seek the endorsement of the electorate of the whole of the United Kingdom for the innovation of a British–Irish Council under the terms of the Good Friday Agreement. Such a referendum would have smacked of treating Northern Ireland as fully integrated into the United Kingdom to nationalists, while unionists would have disliked the implication that the British electorate as a whole had a right to determine the future of Northern Ireland and thus perhaps even a right to override the unionist veto.

What remains to be seen in the case of Northern Ireland is how far island status affects the interpretation of the settlement in the long run, assuming it survives. However, on the basis of international reaction to the reaching of the Good Friday Agreement, some reasonable assumptions can be made about how island status will affect international opinion of its implementation. In particular, it is evident that the very favourable international reaction to the Agreement at the outset was critically dependent on the perceived strength of the Agreement's all-Ireland dimension. Thus, the provisions for a North–South Ministerial Council and for the setting-up of cross-border implementation bodies and the identification of other broad areas for cooperation between the two jurisdictions in Ireland under existing bodies, were crucial to undercutting any perception of the Agreement as partitionist in its implications. The corollary is that, should the North–South dimension wither because of unionist obstruction of its development or for any other reason, the international legitimacy of the settlement would be put in question. To put this another way, if the Good Friday Agreement were perceived to be incompatible with, or even perhaps simply an obstacle to, the eventual outcome of a united Ireland, international opinion would be inclined to reject it as a settlement of the conflict. That is a measure of the importance of island status.

NOTES

1. Quoted in M. Laffan, *The Partition of Ireland 1910–25* (Dundalk: Dundalgan Press, 1987), 16.
2. See the discussion on this in J. Bowman, *De Valera and the Ulster Question 1917–1973* (Oxford: Clarendon Press,1982), 11–16.
3. For a wide-ranging discussion on the impact of island status on the conduct of foreign policy, see R. T. Holt and J. E. Turner, 'Insular Polities', in James N. Rosenau (ed.), *Linkage Politics: Essays on the Convergence of National and International Systems* (New York: Free Press, 1969).
4. The full title is *Declaration of Principles of International Law concerning Friendly Relations and Co-operation among States in accordance with the Charter of the United Nations*, General Assembly Resolution 2625 (XXV), 24 Oct. 1970.
5. Boyd argues that the Irish government knew what the outcome of the referral was likely to be, but used it as a way of drawing international attention to the situation. See A. Boyd, *Fifteen Men on a Powder Keg* (London: Methuen, 1971), 328.
6. Contiguity is so much taken for granted that discussion of the issue of non-contiguity is uncommon. See R. L. Merritt, 'Noncontiguity and Political Integration', in Rosenau (ed.), *Linkage Politics*.
7. J. S. Joseph, *Cyprus: Ethnic Conflict and International Politics* (Basingstoke: Macmillan, 1997), 37.
8. Ibid., 100–2.
9. Quoted in H. S. Gobbi, *Rethinking Cyprus* (Tel Aviv: Aurora, 1993), 109.
10. The text is in Gobbi, *Rethinking Cyprus*, 93–7.
11. See e.g. 'Turkey "Bewildered" over Start of EU Talks', *Cyprus Mail*, 13 Nov. 1998.
12. See R. Carr, *Puerto Rico: A Colonial Experiment* (New York: New York University Press, 1984), 36.
13. See 'The PPD Democratic Hegemony', in A. M. Carrion (ed.), *Puerto Rico: A Political and Cultural History* (New York: Norton, 1983).
14. See R. Grosfoguel, 'The Divorce of Nationalist Discourses from the Puerto Rican People', in F. Negron-Muntaner and R. Grosfuguel (eds.), *Puerto Rican Jam: Rethinking Colonialism and Nationalism* (Minnesota: University of Minnesota Press, 1997).
15. W. Branigin, 'Puerto Rico Leader Vows to Press for Statehood', *Washington Post*, 15 Dec. 1998.
16. *New York Times*, 2 Nov. 1997.
17. J. P. Loughlin, *Regionalism and Ethnic Nationalism in France: A Case Study of Corsica* (Florence: European University Institute, 1989), 10.
18. R. Ramsay, *The Corsican Time-Bomb* (Manchester: Manchester University Press, 1983), 220–1.

19. Agence France-Presse, 'Les Nationalistes de Corsica Nazione en Position d'Arbitres', 15 Mar. 1999 (obtained through *http://www.yahoo.fr/*).
20. *Irish Times*, 23 Nov. 1998.
21. P. Shenon, 'East Timor Seems Suddenly to be on Verge of Independence', *New York Times*, 18 Feb. 1999.
22. See E. Breen, *The Three Islands: International Agreements in Northern Ireland, Cyprus and Sri Lanka*, Queen's Politics Occasional Paper, (Belfast: Department of Politics: Queen's University, Belfast, 1990).
23. P. L.de Silva, 'The Growth of Tamil Paramilitary Nationalisms: Sinhala Chauvinism and Tamil Responses', *South Asia*, special issue, 20 (1997), 110.
24. See the section on Sri Lanka in Amnesty International's annual report for 1998, obtained from Amnesty's web site at *http://www.amnesty.org*

11

Taking the Gun out of Politics: Conflict Transformation in Northern Ireland and Lebanon

KIRSTEN E. SCHULZE[*]

On 10 April 1998 Northern Ireland's political parties agreed the historic Good Friday Agreement without, as some politicians pointed out, a single bullet having been handed over by either republican or loyalist paramilitaries. The emphasis on decommissioning since the 1994 ceasefires, however, along with the widespread public belief that only physically removing weapons would end the conflict, ensured that decommissioning remained on top of the political agenda. It is thus not surprising that it became one of the focal points of the anti-Agreement campaign in the May 1998 referendum and the Assembly elections in June as well as the key obstacle to Sinn Féin taking up its seats on the new executive.

This chapter explores the parallels between the disarmament aspect of the conflict resolution processes in Lebanon and Northern Ireland. Lebanon provides an interesting and pertinent comparison because it is a recent example in which actual disarmament of paramilitary forces was relatively quickly implemented and can be considered successful in the sense that armed conflict has not re-emerged. Thus, the Lebanese example demonstrates that decommissioning is achievable and does not have to be equated with surrender. Moreover, it shows that while it is the genuine commitment to non-violence rather than the handing over of guns that signals the end to conflict, actual decommissioning, alongside civilianization and reintegration of ex-combatants, is key to establishing the necessary environment for true reconciliation. Drawing upon the Lebanese example, it will be argued here that mutual confidence-building is the crucial factor in conflict transformation and that the prolonged decommissioning debate in Northern Ireland was the result of a genuine lack of trust on the one hand and extreme politicization and the pursuit of party political strategy on the other.

The Disarmament and Dissolution of Militias in Lebanon

As a result of the breakdown of the political order in Lebanon and Northern Ireland, sub-state forces in the form of sectarian militias and paramilitary organizations were prominent in both conflicts. Their existence, their potential to undermine political negotiations, and indeed their arms needed to be addressed in the conflict resolution process. While the issues were similar in Lebanon and Northern Ireland, the respective approaches differed markedly.

The 1989 implementation of the Ta'if Accord effectively ended the violence in Lebanon. It restored a certain peace to the country by silencing the cannons and enabling civilian society to reconstitute itself.[1] The Accord explicitly included a 'declaration of the disbanding of the Lebanese and non-Lebanese militias and the transfer of weapons in their possession to the Lebanese government within six months' of the election of a president, the establishment of a national accord government, and the constitutional ratification of political reforms.[2] Underlying Ta'if was a new consensus, which had been achieved by including the leaders of the main Lebanese militias not only in the negotiations but also, by appointment, in the new government. At the heart of this new government was the notion of 'no victor, no vanquished', as well as achieving the right balance among all communities in Lebanon.

The post-Ta'if government set itself two aims with respect to militias: dissolution and disarmament and national reconciliation based on the belief that 'the cessation of internal conflict clears the way for the conversion of militiamen to civilian life'.[3] The first step in this direction was meeting with the leaders of the main militias, the Christian Lebanese Forces, Shi'a Amal, and the Druze Progressive Socialist Party (PSP).

This was followed by the Council of Ministers' announcement on 28 March 1991, dissolving the militias and reintegrating them into civilian life. The decree stated that:

- all armed organizations, Lebanese or non-Lebanese, will be considered dissolved as of 28 March 1991, and shall honour this decision immediately by taking the necessary measures within the above mentioned period (20 March–20 June 1991);
- all militias will be required to hand over their heavy and medium-sized weapons and ammunition to the Lebanese state within the specified one-month period; the Defence Ministry will form special committees to identify locations in each district where the weapons will be received; and

- some of the militia elements will be invited to join public civilian or military institutions, including the Army, the Internal Security Forces, the municipalities, the fire brigade, and others, provided they meet the conditions specified by the Ministerial committee and the qualifications for the required job. Those admitted will undergo rehabilitation and training courses.[4]

The decree further recommended legislation to penalize violations including prison sentences between five years and life for the carrying of weapons, charges of sedition and plotting against the state to be levied against armed groups who fail to deliver their arms, and prosecution of political parties which retain armed militiamen.[5] While inclusivity remained paramount—the militias had after all been brought into a national accord government—it clearly came at a price: disarmament.

Militias to be dissolved included both Lebanese and non-Lebanese organizations. On the Lebanese side the planned dissolution affected an estimated 6,000–18,000 members of the Lebanese Forces, 5,000–10,000 members of Amal, 5,000–8,500 of the PSP, and 3,000–5,000 members of Hizbollah.[6] The non-Lebanese militias were mainly the Palestine Liberation Organization (PLO) and the Iranian Pasdaran al-Islam.

The deadline for the decommissioning of medium and heavy arms was set for 30 April 1991. A ministerial committee was entrusted with the supervising of the dissolution of Lebanese and non-Lebanese militias, while a subcommittee was assigned the task of studying the possibilities of assimilating militia personnel into civilian and military institutions.[7] The committee was composed of the justice minister, the defence minister, the interior minister, and the negotiators representing the militias.[8] Together they aimed to undertake the dismantling of paramilitary structures in such a way that it would be very difficult for those organizations to return to the 'old' situation.[9]

When the deadline neared, it became clear that it would not be met as the militia leaders, the government, and the media debated this issue intensely. Some militias, such as the Lebanese Forces, argued that national reconciliation was not complete with the formation of the government as long as the boycott of the government from some sides of society (Maronite Christians) continued.[10] Others, such as Hizbollah, the PLO, and the Pasdaran asked for exemption on the grounds that they were still fighting a war of national liberation against Israel.[11]

The attitude of Lebanese society as a whole towards the dissolution of militias and their reintegration was one in which the majority favoured immediate disarmament and dissolution. Yet, many were unwilling to pay the price required for full reconciliation. The notion of rehabilitating ex-combatants and integrating militia members into government, state, and security positions was seen as unacceptable. Or, as a letter to the newspaper *As-Safir* by a concerned reader phrased it, 'I do not think you will win over many people who believe that the government of reconciliation cannot be formed without the representatives of the big militias . . . It will not be a government of reconciliation if the representatives of the big militias join it. It will be, undoubtedly, a government of national conflict.'[12]

Responding to critics of the assimilation programme, the government stated that it did not want the militias 'to feel that society had abandoned them'.[13] Lebanon's population, in the end, had no choice but to accept the government's decision despite fears that allowing the full rehabilitation of the militias would undermine Lebanon's fragile post-war political institutions. At the same time the militias had no choice but to begin voluntary decommissioning if they did not want to risk confrontation with the Lebanese and Syrian armies.[14]

In order to encourage the dissolution and disarmament process, the Council of Ministers decided upon a phased reintegration of ex-combatants on 25 May. Ten thousand members from Christian and Muslim militias were to be integrated into the army and police.[15] Candidates for such integration were to be proposed by the militias by 30 June. On 13 June 1991 Law 88 was adopted, fixing the number for the first wave to be integrated at 6,000 due to begin in September 1991. To the chagrin of the militias, their ranks were not transferred automatically. Rather, all candidates had to undergo basic training.

It was a policy described by *As-Safir* as the 'politics of [oil] refinery' that aimed at removing all complications from reaching a full settlement by 'taking in the whole and giving very little through the dropper at different phases'.[16] Such complications included some militia leaders trying to extort concessions from the state. Many of these demands were of an economic and financial nature as some of the militias had run ports and had established extensive port authority and customs structures which were now turned over to state control, depriving them of income and employment.

In May–June 1991 the Lebanese militias implemented partial voluntary disarmament. Weapons were handed over to their 'original sources' rather than as stipulated to the Lebanese government, thereby removing the association of decommissioning with surrender. This effectively meant that arms were given either to the Lebanese, Syrian, or Israeli armies. Weapons were also exported to other conflict areas such as the former Yugoslavia, Armenia, and Algeria.[17] The Lebanese Forces sent most of their medium and heavy arms to the security zone, which was under Israeli control. Others were hidden in the mountains of Kisraoun.[18] The PSP handed over some its heavy arms to the Syrian army, while burying its medium arms in the Shouf Mountains.[19] Amal agreed to deliver all heavy weapons to the Lebanese army but, in fact, moved some south for the struggle against Israel.[20] Hizbollah received its exemption and light arms were not collected at all.

Non-Lebanese militias were dissolved and disarmed according to a different agenda. While care had been taken by the Lebanese government to include Lebanese militia leaders in the decision-making in the Second Republic, to make disarmament voluntary, and to reintegrate ex-combatants so as not to signal their surrender and defeat, no such consideration was given to non-Lebanese militias. Already in April Syria and Lebanon had stated that they would approach Palestinian arms independently from Lebanese ones.[21] In effect, this meant that Palestinian guerrillas were neither bound by the same deadlines as Lebanese militias, nor were they part of any continuing discussions. Indeed, the government's move against Palestinian positions in the south and the collection of Palestinian arms with the help of Syrian troops reflected the popular consensus that the Palestinians bore much of the blame for the conflict and consequently should be 'punished'.[22] Thus the re-establishment of the rule of law was a relatively rapid affair. The speed and success, however, was principally due to the regional power context, which is essentially one in which Syria controls Lebanon, or Pax Syriana.

As the disarmament and dissolution of militias proceeded hand in hand with re-establishing the state's authority over the country, the implementation of both was phased. The first phase geographically covered Greater Beirut and Mount Lebanon, where most of the militias had their main bases. This phase aimed at assimilating 10,000 militia personnel, who after undergoing a one-year training period for professional qualifications would be able to enter civilian life. These 10,000 were to be distributed among a number of military and civilian institutions with an estimated 3,000 being integrated into the army and the security services. An estimated 4,000 would be employed in the civilian sector, half of them Muslim and the other half Christian. In an attempt at de-sectarianizing the state, those in the army would be required to serve in bases throughout all of Lebanon regardless of sectarian affiliation.[23] The largest number of new recruits was Shi'a Muslim and the smallest number was Christian because the latter tended to be less trusting of the settlement and had access to better employment opportunities.

General Nizar Abdel Kader, who was one of the key players in the integration scheme, described its aims as follows:

We thought that by recruiting them we'll enhance the army and these people weren't going to return to the militias if new troubles broke out. It would also reduce the crime level. One problem was maintaining a certain balance between factions. We did not have enough Maronite volunteers so we had to compensate with draftees, mostly females. In general, the integration went well. There were no problems in units at the academy. We did not have a single incident. There were so many Christians who'd never seen a Muslim before and were surprised. It broke down stereotypes. We transferred officers from various confessions to other areas and there were no problems—platoon leaders, captains, commanders—we rotated them all. We broke up all sectarian units.[24]

The final element in the civilianization of the militias was the August 1991 amnesty law, which gave amnesty for all crimes committed during the civil war, except murder of politicians, diplomats, and clerics. Its aim was to remove any remaining barriers for the integration of ex-combatants into society. At the same time war crimes proceedings were opened against those not exempt under the law.

The Decommissioning Debate in Northern Ireland

In Northern Ireland the issue of decommissioning paramilitary arms quickly became the focus of the peace process. It was raised by the Ulster Unionist Party (UUP) and the Democratic Unionist Party (DUP), political parties without paramilitary connections, almost immediately following the republican and loyalist ceasefires in autumn 1994, triggering a debate which not only almost brought down the negotiations before they had started, but which also complicated the implementation of the Agreement reached on 10 April 1998.

On a conceptual level attitudes in Northern Ireland resembled those in Lebanon. Parties without paramilitary wings such as the DUP believed that 'there would be no level playing field. Talks would be taking place with the IRA gun literally at the head of unionist negotiators.'[25] Or in the words of the cross-community Alliance Party:

The continued existence of illegal weapons undermines the peace process by perpetuating community fears of a return to violence, and casting doubt upon the real intentions of those who say that they have given up violence . . . The retention of illegal weapons suggests a preparedness to return to violence, and presents to those involved a temptation to fall back to violence in the event of political frustration and disappointments.[26]

These views stood in stark contrast to those held by parties with paramilitary links, which saw disarmament 'as part of the normalisation process'[27] but not as a condition for political negotiations. Moreover, the paramilitaries themselves equated demands for prior disarmament with humiliation, with surrender, with a means to differentiate the so-called constitutional parties from those with paramilitary links in order firmly to absolve the rest of society from any responsibility for the conflict, and with exclusion from politics.

Mutual distrust between loyalists and republicans as well as a more general distrust of government intentions complicated the debate further. It effectively made the loyalist decommissioning of arms dependent upon the decommissioning of republican arms, while republicans looked towards disarmament of the police and the British army. This precluded any decommissioning until after an acceptable settlement had been reached, as reflected in the IRA's position that 'there will be no hand-over of arms until a political solution has been agreed'[28] as well as in the Ulster Democratic Party (UDP) submission on 'Illegally Held Arms' in December 1995:

The arms issue is not about guns. It is about trust. Decommissioning does not eradicate the capability of violence. The decommissioning is about those who hold illegal weaponry proving their commitment to democratic methods. It is clear that while profound distrust exists it shall be unlikely that paramilitary organisations shall decide to disarm . . . Dialogue must take place to enable the necessary trust to be built which shall create the environment in which these armed groups shall feel confident to relinquish their weapons.[29]

The dynamics of the larger constitutional parties and the British and Irish governments supporting decommissioning led to the pre-negotiating agenda and the negotiations being characterized by attempts to 'impose' their will. Thus, in February 1995 decommissioning was explicitly spelled out as a precondition for negotiations in the so-called Washington Three Principles by the British government, recognizing it as the key to reassuring the unionists. These principles stated that there had to be a willingness to disarm progressively, an agreed means of doing so, and a start to demonstrate good faith and test practical arrangements.

Having achieved nothing after months of fruitless exchanges, the British and Irish governments launched a Twin Track Process on 28 November 1995, embarking upon preparatory talks in parallel with the debate on the decommissioning of arms. This was followed by the setting-up of the

International Body on Arms Decommissioning, more commonly known as the Mitchell Commission. The Commission's Report, released on 24 January 1996, reiterated the objective of the 'total and verifiable disarmament of all paramilitary organisations' and recommended that some decommissioning should take place during the process, rather than before or after.[30]

The recommendations of the Mitchell Report, however, were subsumed by the unionist call for elections to the negotiations, followed by the collapse of the IRA ceasefire with the Canary Wharf bombing on 9 February 1996 and the consequent exclusion of Sinn Féin from the negotiations. Canary Wharf confirmed unionist beliefs that decommissioning was absolutely necessary.[31] Accordingly, it became the first issue on the agenda when the multi-party negotiations began in June 1996, and remained on the agenda without solution throughout the first year of talks.

In June 1997 the parties—even without Sinn Féin—were as deadlocked as ever on the issue of disarmament, and the two governments were looking for a way out. Another independent commission was established for 'achieving further progress on decommissioning alongside progress in the three strands'.[32]

Yet when the IRA called its second ceasefire in July 1997 and Sinn Féin entered the multi-party talks the following September, progress on neither had been achieved. Ironically, sidelining the stumbling-block of decommissioning, however, had become easier with Sinn Féin's entry as it prompted the exit of the DUP and United Kingdom Unionist Party (UKUP), and, with the deadline for reaching agreement less than a year away, the negotiations refocused on less contentious issues. As a result the Good Friday Agreement was concluded in April 1998, without any decommissioning having occurred prior to or during the negotiations. The Good Friday Agreement did, however, stipulate a 'total and absolute commitment to exclusively democratic and peaceful means', that all participants should 'reaffirm their commitment to the total disarmament of all paramilitary organisations', and that all parties should 'use any influence they may have to achieve the decommissioning of all paramilitary arms within two years'.[33] Yet, while the early release of prisoners began, the Northern Ireland Assembly started to function, cross-border institutions were being devised, and a date for forming the executive was set, the handover of arms had not begun.

Politicization

One of the main problems in Northern Ireland was that decommissioning right from the beginning of the peace process became a highly politicized issue which served to prolong the debate and reinforce the impasse. For instance, some elements in unionism, foremost the DUP and UKUP, pursued decommissioning first, to claim a unionist victory over the IRA and second, to separate 'terrorists' from 'decent law-abiding citizens' with the aim of reinforcing the existing political structure focusing on the constitutional parties at the expense of the main challengers of the status quo. By adding the 'moral imperative', the demand for disarmament became the tool for attempting to exclude republican and loyalist politicians from the negotiations, for marginalizing whole segments of society, for undermining the peace process as well as political rivals, and for bringing down the Agreement. UKUP leader Robert McCartney's words several months after the signing of the Agreement leave no doubt about his broader political agenda:

The reality, as opposed to the total fiction encapsulated in the agreement, is that Sinn Féin, the PUP [Progressive Unionist Party] and the UDP are not at all the same as the other parties. These three are fronts for terrorist organisations responsible for thousands of deaths, countless hideous injuries and the mass destruction of property; organisations which to the present day are engaged in murder, shootings, brutal beatings, intimidation and criminality of every kind from drug peddling to extortion and racketeering.

. . . The Ulster Unionist leadership allowed itself to be pressured into an agreement that perpetuated the fiction of separateness of Sinn Féin and the IRA; an agreement that contained no clear and express terms that the IRA must decommission its armaments before Sinn Féin and the IRA's prisoners could benefit from the agreement's terms! By this failure they have permitted both Sinn Féin and the SDLP to use terms of the agreement to subvert the principles of democratic government itself. Decommissioning is a necessary requirement because without it real democracy is dead.[34]

McCartney raises the important issue of the incompatibility of democratic government and private armies which must ultimately be addressed through the peace process. However, his main concern clearly is not the establishment of democratic structures for Northern Ireland, but undermining the implementation of an agreement he perceives as fundamentally flawed.

A deliberate politicization of decommissioning also occurred among republicans. They, too, continued to act out the zero-sum conflict scenario of their war against the British state by demanding demilitarization. Demilitarization within the context of the decommissioning debate is equated with the disarmament of all agencies of violence and foremost the dismantling of the security apparatus of what they see as a repressive regime. British army troops should be withdrawn and the Royal Ulster Constabulary disbanded. And just as some unionists have tried to use decommissioning to vanquish the IRA and proclaim their own victory, many republicans see demilitarization as a way to de-unionize Northern Ireland and make it less British.[35]

Politicization has further taken place on a governmental level as both the British and, for a time, the Irish governments made decommissioning the touchstone for reassuring unionists throughout the peace process. In fact, British government officials repeatedly but unsuccessfully urged loyalist paramilitaries to decommission tactically during the negotiations in order to 'force' the IRA to surrender its arms.[36] The deal cut in November 1998 with the anti-Agreement Loyalist Volunteer Force (LVF) to 'make a start to decommission within a short period of its ceasefire being recognised'[37] and consequent inclusion of LVF prisoners in the Early Release Scheme is another case in point. The fact that the Ulster Volunteer Force (UVF) and Ulster Defence Association–Ulster Freedom Fighters (UDA–UFF) would not even contemplate tactical decommissioning, and that the LVF failed to honour its commitment on the date agreed but then later delivered a token amount of arms, reveals a superficial understanding of the paramilitaries by British officials. It also reveals a tendency still to see the conflict as a prolonged anti-terrorist operation against the IRA. Thus the result of politicization of the decommissioning issue at government level was an overall inflation of unionist hopes for a reduction in illegally held arms, while the paramilitaries and their political representatives were simultaneously antagonized, feeling they were being called upon to acknowledge their illegitimacy.

The key questions underlying the overall debate on disarmament after internal conflict over how far paramilitaries should be accommodated and whether full inclusion in pursuit of reconciliation underpins or undermines a political agreement are not resolved by such politicization. In fact, it could be argued that politicization is counter-productive because it distracts from other related issues such as the potential for an increase in the crime rate resulting from the retention of weapons—such as occurred in South Africa where the issue of arms was not satisfactorily resolved during the peace process—or that surplus arms could contribute to arms proliferation in other conflict areas.[38] Most importantly, however, politicization has hindered the overall process of conflict resolution by shifting the debate onto a 'moral' and 'emotional' level and retaining a zero-sum dynamic, which highlights only one of the many dilemmas of reconciling what is often an inherently 'undemocratic' conflict resolution process within a liberal-democratic context.[39]

The example of Lebanon suggests that the issue of decommissioning could have been handled differently at the outset. Indeed, Lebanon is an interesting case-study of the use and effects of politicization in the disarmament process. While the population as a whole expressed similar revulsion towards the gunmen, these sentiments did not become an issue of contention in the peace settlement. Politicization was, however, used as a means to separate the Lebanese, who collectively were cast in the role of victims from the Palestinians, who were branded as the perpetrators. Consequently, there was a comparative lack of politicization of the internal debate on the disarmament and dissolution of Lebanese militias, while at the same time there was a highly politicized discourse on the disarmament and dissolution of the Palestinian guerrilla organizations. The former served to bridge the gaps between the communities with the aim of ending the conflict and achieving national reconciliation. The latter served to marginalize the Palestinian refugee community with the long-term aim of encouraging the Palestinians to leave Lebanon.

Hillsborough, the Way Forward, and the Mitchell Review

As the implementation of the Good Friday Agreement began after April 1998 with the early release of paramilitary prisoners, the setting-up of some of the institutions such as the Assembly, and the drafting of the legislation required for others such as the North–South bodies, the debate on decommissioning shifted from attempts to link disarmament to prisoner releases to linking the handover of guns to the establishment of the executive, which was key for devolution of power from Westminster. While there was no linkage in the Agreement per se and no explicit obligation to decommission prior to the establishment of a power-sharing government, de facto linkage was soon created. The unionist position of 'no guns, no government' and Sinn Féin's position of 'no government, no guns' meant that in terms of principles democracy now clashed with inclusivity.

Three attempts were made before a mutually acceptable solution was reached. This raises two obvious questions: Why did the first two attempts—Hillsborough and the Way Forward—fail? And why did the third, the Mitchell Review, succeed?

The Hillsborough Declaration of 1 April 1999 resulted from the refusal of the Ulster Unionists in the absence of a start to decommissioning to establish the executive, which had first been scheduled for 31 October 1998 and then postponed to 10 March 1999. When both deadlines were missed in the midst of republican accusations that Ulster Unionists were 'super-imposing the demand for decommissioning as a precondition',[40] the British and Irish prime ministers decided to take matters into their own hands. They convened another round of talks set to end on the anniversary of the Good Friday Agreement. Then, drawing upon Sinn Féin leader Gerry Adams's words that he was prepared to 'reach out' and 'jump together',[41] the two governments produced a declaration based on paral-lelization. It called for nominations 'under the d'Hondt procedure of those to take up office as Ministers when powers are devolved', 'a collective act of reconciliation' which would see 'some arms put beyond use, on a voluntary basis, in a manner which will be verified by the Independent International Commission on Decommissioning', at which point 'powers will be devolved and the British/Irish Agreement will enter into force'.[42]

The Hillsborough Declaration, after some consideration, failed to get republican support. The reason given was that decommissioning had been made into a 'precondition'.[43] The real reason, however, was that Gerry Adams had indeed only managed to get 70 per cent support for the Hillsborough Declaration, and was thus unable to endorse the proposal without provoking a split.

The rejection of Hillsborough was in many ways predictable. First, despite Adams's talk of 'jumping together', fears of splits effectively meant that unionists had to jump first if the IRA was to be convinced about mak-ing any move on decommissioning. Secondly, the timing for what was essentially a compromise on republican principles was wrong as it coin-cided with the commemoration of the 1916 Easter Rising, thus making it almost the least likely date in the republican calendar on which to abandon the principle of not ever handing over guns. And thirdly, it had effectively been an 'imposed' solution rather than one negotiated between the parties who ultimately had to share power.

The next attempt to resolve the devolution–decommissioning impasse came in the form of the Way Forward proposal of 2 July 1999 and signalled a clear shift in emphasis by the two prime ministers, but not a shift in method as it was still essentially an 'imposed' solution. Having failed to convince Sinn Féin to deliver some IRA decommissioning, pressure was now put on the UUP to accept a 'fudge on arms'[44] that would allow the executive to be formed. This became evident with a draft document emerging from Downing Street on 17 May, which set the next deadline for devolution for 30 June and expected the formation of an executive on the basis of Canadian General John de Chastelain's progress report,[45] which, of course, did not equal the 'verifiable start to a process of decommissioning'[46] which the UUP wanted. The shift in emphasis was reinforced by Blair's 16 June Stranmillis speech, which stated that decommissioning was 'not a prior pre-condition of the Executive'[47] and challenged unionists to prove republicans wrong on not wanting to share power.

The Way Forward proposals tabled by the two prime ministers after this next 'absolute' deadline of 30 June had been missed saw all parties reaffirming their commitment to devolved power-sharing and decommissioning, followed by d'Hondt being triggered on 15 July, devolution being effected on 18 July, and decommissioning starting within a time specified by the International Commission on Decommissioning and to be completed by May 2000.[48] Unionist difficulties were immediately obvious. Not only were they being asked to 'jump first' into a power-sharing executive, but it was also not clear whether decommissioning would occur at all. The Report by the Independent International Commission on Decommissioning, which served as the foundation for the Way Forward, provided little conclusive evidence. Indeed, its sole basis for asserting 'that decommissioning by all paramilitary groups may now begin' was based on the fact that 'no party suggested that decommissioning ought not to happen by 22 May 2000'.[49] The Way Forward, as well as the accompanying legislation, also did not provide for an expulsion clause for Sinn Féin from the executive should decommissioning not occur, but for the automatic suspension of all institutions of the Good Friday Agreement, which Trimble saw as an 'unfair sanction' that punished the innocent along with the guilty[50] and treated democrats 'as though they were indistinguishable from terrorists'.[51] This perception of 'unfair' treatment of unionists by the British government was further compounded by the breakdown of relations between the UUP and secretary of state for Northern Ireland, Mo Mowlam. Finally, in a blunder parallel to Hillsborough, the timing of the Way Forward coincided with the height of the marching season—the Drumcree parade and the 12 July Battle of the Boyne celebrations—the time period least likely for unionist concessions. Thus it is not surprising that devolution did not occur.

Power was, however, devolved to Northern Ireland five months later, following the successful conclusion of the intense, eleven-week-long review of the peace process under the auspices of former US Senator George Mitchell. The solution agreed by Trimble and Adams in itself did not differ

significantly from what had been proposed in the Way Forward. It stipulated an inclusive executive, the decommissioning of paramilitary arms by
May 2000, and that decommissioning would be carried out in a manner
determined by the International Commission. It also resolved the sequenc-
ing stating that 'devolution should take effect, then the Executive should
meet, and then the paramilitary groups should appoint their authorised
representatives, all on the same day, in that order'.[52] Accordingly, following
the endorsement of the proposal by the Ulster Unionist Council on 27
November by a 58 per cent majority, appointments were made to the executive on 29 November,[53] and power was devolved from Westminster to
Northern Ireland on 2 December. Devolution triggered the amendment of
Articles 2 and 3 of the Irish Constitution abolishing the Republic's territorial claim, the end of the 1985 Anglo-Irish Agreement, and empowerment
of the North–South institutions and British–Irish Council. On 2 December
the IRA also appointed its interlocutor, who met with the International
Commission the following weekend for the first time to discuss the modal-
ities of decommissioning.[54] On 8 December the loyalist UFF followed suit
by appointing a five-man liaison team.[55]

Since the Mitchell Review did not change the substance or sequence
already proposed in July, the question remains what made 'government
before guns' more acceptable in November. The answer can be found in the
fact that it was the only option which could possibly achieve decommissioning and in the successful outcome of both David Trimble's and Gerry
Adams's party-political strategy of incrementally gaining sufficient support to avoid an outright split. Above all, however, the answer lies in the
changes that took place in the approach, the dynamics, and the environment.

First, the negotiations were not 'imposed' by the two prime ministers
but were directly between those who had to share power. Secondly, for the
first time there was a statement from the IRA committing itself to the
'achievement of lasting peace' and appointing an interlocutor to discuss
decommissioning,[56] in addition to Sinn Féin's statement which also for the
first time accepted that 'decommissioning is an essential part of the peace
process'.[57] The importance of these two changes for David Trimble cannot
be over-emphasized, as he himself stated that

The Way Forward was written by Tony Blair and Bertie Ahern. It was entirely what
they were saying. And when they were saying that, Pat Doherty [vice-president of
Sinn Féin] was running around saying 'this is all a cod, we're not talking about
decommissioning.' What you've got here is a statement written by Adams and
McGuinness, which is the Sinn Féin statement followed by an IRA statement. We

made it absolutely clear at the end of July that if we had an IRA statement, that that would change the atmosphere entirely. And you read the Sinn Féin and IRA statement together. We have got what amounts to a commitment to decommission from Sinn Féin. We've tied in the paramilitaries.[58]

But crucially not only had republicans said the right words to reassure their future unionist partners, but unionists too, for the first time, had publicly recognized and accepted 'that it is legitimate for nationalists to pursue their political objective of a united Ireland' and the UUP had committed itself to 'the principles of inclusivity, equality and mutual respect'.[59] This leads directly to the third change, the emerging trust, or at least the better understanding of each other's positions and difficulties, between David Trimble and Gerry Adams. Fourthly, there was a new relationship of trust between the UUP and the new secretary of state for Northern Ireland, Peter Mandelson, which dampened unionist fears of being pushed into a 'sell-out', as well as engendered confidence in the failsafe mechanism. And finally, with the backing of the Ulster Unionist Council and the post-dated resignation letters, Trimble had received sufficient support to avoid splitting the party and losing the leadership as well as providing his party with an opt-out mechanism in the form of the February review should decommissioning not occur.

Confidence-Building

In a comparison of Northern Ireland's decommissioning debate with the disarmament process in Lebanon the problems in Northern Ireland are evident immediately. The most obvious problem was the failure of mutual confidence-building. Parties with paramilitary links did not feel assured of political inclusivity, while parties without paramilitary links did not receive credible assurances that the conflict was truly over. Moreover, all parties were suspicious of the governments' intentions as well as of each other's agendas. Given this environment, the decommissioning debate could not but become highly politicized, with the effect that both sides felt that the peace process as a whole had become one-sided—in favour of the other.

Crucial for creating confidence among the paramilitaries to decommission, providing they genuinely wish to do so, is inclusivity, as the Lebanese example shows. The Ta'if Accord, which ended the Lebanese civil war in 1989, was not immediately followed by elections. Instead, the empty seats in Parliament were filled by appointment of those political representatives who had participated in the negotiations. While not being the most demo-cratic option, this ensured that all those who had committed themselves to an end to violence were included in the first post-conflict government and had a stake in maintaining peace and stability. It was exactly this inclusiv-ity in the early phase of the peace process which made decommissioning possible.

The Northern Irish negotiations, in comparison, were of equivocal inclusivity as they were contingent upon ceasefire and electoral mandate. Indeed, almost two years elapsed between the 1994 ceasefires and the beginning of the multi-party negotiations in 1996, which fostered a belief among parties with paramilitary links that the underlying agenda was to marginalize them. The missed opportunity in terms of confidence-building in the early months of the peace process ensured that paramili-taries would remain suspicious even after a political agreement had been reached.

The elections to the new Assembly only two months after the conclusion of the 1998 Good Friday Agreement further exacerbated suspicions of an exclusive agenda, particularly in loyalist paramilitary circles, as the results were in many ways predictable. Two of the smaller parties, the PUP and the UDP, which had represented Northern Ireland's largest paramilitary orga-nization the UDA–UFF at the negotiations, failed to get seats. The conse-quent disenfranchisement of a particular community, as well as the marginalization of a paramilitary actor so soon after the Agreement, led to a drop in support for the continuing political process, feelings of alien-ation, and the emergence of a source of instability as evident in the involve-ment of dissident UFF elements in violence, particularly in 1999. This also had implications for decommissioning. The UDA–UFF now had even fewer incentives to disarm, and the political marginalization of the UDP reduced the party's ability to convince the paramilitaries that decommis-sioning was in their interest. The case of the UDP further shows the difficulty some parties with paramilitary links face when operating in a democracy. Elections were accepted as necessary by all parties to the Good Friday Agreement to attain popular legitimacy. Yet, in elections there are winners and losers, making certain aspects of democratic life zero-sum.

In republican circles the Agreement did not engender confidence either, especially as republican perception was that unionists, from the conclusion of the Agreement onwards, were engaged in a process of renegotiating its terms bilaterally with the British government, as exemplified by a letter of assurance written by Prime Minister Blair in April 1998.[60] The unionist position on setting up the executive only after the decommissioning process had begun was further proof in republican eyes that unionists all along had intended to exclude Sinn Féin.

In the context of perceptions of exclusion and marginalization one particularly negative aspect was the lack of an immediate and fully fledged process of civilianization and reintegration of ex-combatants, which would have worked effectively on changing attitudes in society as a whole. Unlike the Lebanese programme for retraining and reintegration of former militia members into society, Northern Ireland moved little beyond the Early Release Scheme for paramilitary prisoners. It must, however, be pointed out that victims of paramilitary violence, too, were given little space to express their fears and pain. Consequently, true reconciliation has been elusive, and the foundations for the 'new' society envisaged by the Agreement were not adequately laid.

The fact that parties with paramilitary links perceived confidence-building to be a one-way street favouring unionists, did not, however, mean that it was. In fact, unionists perceived it to be exactly the opposite. They equated confidence-building with the appeasement of paramilitaries through the early release of prisoners, reform of the security structures, the formation of cross-border bodies, and sitting down in an Assembly with Sinn Féin and the PUP while the IRA and UVF held onto their arms. In other words, the paramilitaries were receiving concessions while violence and threat continued. Unionists saw themselves as having taken 'risks' for peace by compromising and stretching the unionist constituency in a way that other parties, most notably the Social Democratic and Labour Party, have not. Further pressure on the unionists to give in on the issue of decommissioning appeared to its supporters as the ultimate humiliation.[61]

If the early phases of the peace process were crucial for building confidence in paramilitary circles with respect to the issues of inclusivity, the period immediately following the conclusion of the Good Friday Agreement became the crucial time for building confidence within the unarmed population with respect to disarmament. In an inadvertently even-handed manner, both these crucial periods were neglected, despite the fact that the latter could have been quite simply addressed by a parallel implementation process. A start on the early release of prisoners, a start to decommissioning, a start on setting up the new political institutions, and so forth could easily have progressed alongside each other, even without formal linkage.

One of the reasons this parallelization failed to materialize was the terms of the Good Friday Agreement itself, which did not explicitly demand actual decommissioning, but only required parties to the Agreement to 'use any influence they may have to achieve the decommissioning of all paramilitary arms'. Lebanon's Ta'if Accord, in comparison, contained a declaration of the disbanding of the militias within six months of the establishment of a national accord government. This was followed by strict legislation on the disarmament and dissolution of militias and their incorporation into the state, and further legislation banning paramilitary groups and arms, arguably backed up by the threat of military force to achieve compliance. The room for a different interpretation of the letter and spirit of the Good Friday Agreement created a situation in which over a year after the Agreement more than half of all paramilitary prisoners had been released, but not one of the paramilitary organizations associated with parties supporting the Agreement had even expressed a willingness to hand over arms.

Another reason why parallelization was difficult was the inherent incentivization of violence in the process. In this respect, the process had not necessarily invited 'the elimination of armed struggle from politics, but merely displaced it to other levels, and in some ways even encouraged it'.[62] The viability of the use of force was clearly demonstrated in the 1996 breakdown of the IRA ceasefire, as well as the 1998 threat by loyalist prisoners to withdraw their support from the peace process, both of which elicited a government response of concessions to bring them back on board.[63] The selective use of violence, hinting at the possible resumption of violence, and the threat of violence were repeatedly used to manipulate the process.[64]

Unlike in Lebanon, where sanctions were included in the overall legislation on dissolution and reintegration, sanctions were rarely if ever employed against the paramilitaries by the British and Irish governments to curtail the continued violence, thus giving the unionists cause to believe that the process was just about appeasement of terrorists because there was simply no system of reward or punishment to ensure good paramilitary behaviour.[65] In this context it is not surprising that unionists suspected that parties with paramilitary links had every intention of hanging on to their private armies and that they would be 'allowed' to do so. Establishing an executive under those circumstances thus not only severely undermined democracy but also 'robbed' them of their last bargaining chip for taking the gun out of politics.

One factor that made overall confidence-building difficult was the inconsistency in the positions of the two governments, and particularly the British government. Unionist confidence was undermined as unionists saw 'prior decommissioning' turn into 'decommissioning in parallel with negotiations,' to 'decommissioning after reaching the Agreement' to 'decommissioning in parallel with setting up the new political institutions' to 'decommissioning following the establishment the Executive'. This was further exacerbated by Prime Minister Blair's letters and statements containing assurances which he could not keep as they were essentially given outside the parameters of the Good Friday Agreement. Irish Prime Minister Bertie Ahern's sudden shift from seeing Sinn Féin and the IRA as two sides of the same coin to believing they were completely separate organizations complicated the situation further.

Republican confidence was equally undermined by government inconsistency, especially Blair's assurances to the unionists, which in Gerry Adams's eyes allowed the 'UUP to open up a process of perpetual negotiation or re-negotiation'.[66] Blair's letter accompanying the 1998 Agreement stating that decommissioning would start in June, and his assertion following the 1999 Way Forward document that he could 'ensure Sinn Féin aren't in the Executive, if they are in default', are the two most obvious examples. Not surprisingly, these shifts in the governments' positions, accompanied by alternating pressure on the unionist and republican leaderships, did not result in the reconciliation of 'no guns, no government' and 'no government, no guns'.

While it may be argued that these shifts were necessary to bring and keep all parties on board until they were sufficiently 'entrapped' by the process, Blair's decision to impose an 'absolute' deadline well in advance, and outside that specified by the Agreement, in the midst of the marching season, suggests severe flaws in the Blair administration's analysis. Instead of focusing on a long-term process of mutual confidence-building aimed at unionist and republican grass roots and dissidents, it seems that Blair's policy was often no more than an exercise in brinkmanship and damage limitation, characterized by an inability to delegate, and driven by his desire to get the UK devolution project off the ground.

While the inconsistencies of the two governments undermined mutual confidence-building, the provision of detailed mechanisms of decommissioning in the proposals drafted by the Independent International Commission on Decommissioning,[67] as well as the draft decommissioning scheme for the Liaison Sub-Committee on Decommissioning,[68] even before the Good Friday Agreement had been reached, raised expectations of an imminent handover of arms. This placed emphasis on military equipment rather than the commitment to non-violence, giving the illusion that actual progress had been made, while masking the continuing lack of trust.

As the process of decommissioning was voluntary as opposed to 'coercive', the emphasis right from the beginning should have been on building up the confidence of those organizations, which would be asked to give up their arms. At the same time it should also have been made clear to the paramilitaries that decommissioning, while voluntary, was not optional, and that a commitment to non-violence included refraining from punishment beatings and shootings. This, in turn, would have served to assure the unarmed population. Indeed, the lack of clarity in the debate on decommissioning, combined with the shifts in the governments' positions, only served to exacerbate the suspicions of paramilitaries, parties, and population alike that they were all being pushed into something they had not agreed to.

Conclusion

Conflict transformation in Lebanon since 1989 and Northern Ireland since 1994 have been prolonged processes which, with regard to achieving full reconciliation, still have some way to go. The most crucial issue in both conflicts, which had been characterized by a proliferation of paramilitary organizations and the use of violence to achieve political ends, was taking the gun out of politics. In both cases, this raised the question of the compatibility of returning to democratic politics with including representatives of parties with paramilitary links in government. Yet, while the dilemma was similar in Lebanon and Northern Ireland, their respective approaches to resolve it—and consequently the lessons to be learned for conflict transformation—differed.

The Lebanese example shows that an explicit statement in the Ta'if Accord that militias had to disarm and the existence of reintegration–rehabilitation schemes for ex-combatants allowed for a speedier decommissioning process. Lebanon also demonstrates that disarmament is possible as an integral part of a mutual confidence-building process in which all aspects of the political agreement are ideally implemented parallel to each other, and that disarmament in the context of re-establishing democracy and civil society does not have to be associated with surrender.

The Northern Irish example shows the dangers of over-politicizing the issue of decommissioning in a general sense, but it also demonstrates very clearly that even in the absence of an explicit commitment to disarm in the Agreement, decommissioning is an essential part of the peace process. Northern Ireland further demonstrates that the guns and government dilemma can be managed through careful political strategy in order to overcome the lack of such an explicit commitment, but that it is an altogether much lengthier process.

And finally, both Lebanon and Northern Ireland demonstrate the importance of confidence-building as well as of some form of power-sharing for transforming paramilitary actors into constitutional political players, and that an explicit commitment to non-violence must exist as it is this commitment that determines to what extent civil society is able to re-establish itself after reaching a political agreement and to what extent a genuine peace can be achieved.

NOTES

* I would like to thank John McGarry and M. L. R. Smith for their useful comments on earlier drafts, as well as the staff research fund of the London School of Economics for enabling me to conduct research in both Northern Ireland and Lebanon.

1. J. Maila, 'The Ta'if Accord: An Evaluation', in D. Collings (ed.), *Peace for Lebanon? From War to Reconstruction* (Boulder, Colo.: Lynne Rienner, 1994), 41.
2. The Ta'if Accord, 22 Oct. 1989.
3. Maila, 'The Ta'if Accord: An Evaluation', 36.
4. Council of Ministers Decree Dissolving the Militias, *Beirut Review*, 1/2 (Fall 1991), 112–15.
5. Ibid.
6. V. Perthes, *Der Libanon nach dem Bürgerkrieg. Von Ta'if zum gesellschaftlichen Konsens?* (Baden-Baden: Nomos, 1994), 25–6; see also International Institute for Strategic Studies, *The Military Balance 1991–1992* (London: Brassey's, 1991), 111.
7. *As-Safir*, 10 Apr. 1991.
8. E. Picard, 'La Dissolution des milices dans le Liban de l'après guerre', MS, Centre for Lebanese Studies, Oxford University, 4.
9. *As-Safir*, 10 Apr. 1991.
10. *As-Safir*, 12 Jan. 1991.
11. Picard, 'La Dissolution des milices dans le Liban de l'après guerre', 3.
12. *As-Safir*, 8 Nov. 1990.
13. Ibid.
14. Interview with Nizar Abdel Kader, Beirut, 23 Mar. 1996.
15. Perthes, *Der Libanon nach dem Bürgerkrieg*, 27.
16. *As-Safir*, 11 May 1991.
17. Picard, 'La Dissolution des milices dans le Liban de l'après guerre', 15.

18. Interview with Nizar Abdel Kader, Beirut, 23 Mar. 1996.
19. Perthes, *Der Libanon nach dem Bürgerkrieg*, 26.
20. Interview with Nizar Abdel Kader, Beirut, 23 Mar. 1996.
21. *As-Safir*, 29 Apr. 1991.
22. E. Picard, *Lebanon: A Shattered Country* (New York: Holmes & Meier, 1996), 160.
23. *As-Safir*, 10 Apr. 1991.
24. Interview with Nizar Abdel Kader, Beirut, 23 Mar. 1996.
25. *Belfast Telegraph*, 24 Jan. 1996.
26. Alliance Party, *Submission to the International Body on Decommissioning* (Belfast: Alliance Party Headquarters, Dec. 1995), 3.
27. Ulster Democratic Party, *Submission on Illegally Held Arms* (Lisburn: Ulster Democratic Party Headquarters, 16 Dec. 1995), 1.
28. *An Phoblacht/Republican News*, 23 May 1996.
29. Ulster Democratic Party, *Submission on Illegally Held Arms*, 7.
30. *Report of the International Body on Arms Decommissioning* (Belfast and Dublin: International Body, 24 Jan. 1996).
31. M. L. R. Smith, 'Paradoxes of Conflict Resolution in Northern Ireland', MS, 1999.
32. *Resolving the Address to Decommissioning*, internal discussion paper (Stormont: Multi-Party Negotiations, 25 June 1997), 9.
33. Good Friday Agreement, *The Agreement: Agreement Reached in the Multi-Party Negotiations* (Belfast: Northern Ireland Office Publications, 10 Apr. 1998).
34. *Irish Times*, 17 Nov. 1998.
35. K. E. Schulze and M. L. R. Smith, 'Getting Rid of Guns', *World Today*, 54/10 (Oct. 1998), 262.
36. *Ireland on Sunday*, 15 Nov. 1998.
37. *Belfast Telegraph*, 18 Nov. 1998.
38. E. J. Laurence, *Surplus Weapons and the Micro Disarmament Process* (Bonn: Bonn International Center for Conversion, June 1995), Brief 3, p. 1.
39. Smith, 'Paradoxes of Conflict Resolution in Northern Ireland'.
40. *Irish Times*, 12 Mar. 1999.
41. *Irish Times*, 19 Mar. 1999.
42. Press release, Remarks by the Prime Minister, the Right Honourable Tony Blair MP on behalf of the UK and Irish Governments at a press conference with the Taoiseach, Bertie Ahern TD, Hillsborough Castle, Co. Down, 1 Apr. 1999.
43. *International Herald Tribune*, 14 Apr. 1999.
44. *Belfast Telegraph*, 17 May 1999.
45. *Irish Times*, 17 May 1999.
46. Ulster Unionist Party, *Latest Proposal to Resolve Decommissioning Impasse*, press release, 17 May 1999.
47. 'The Prime Minister's Speech in Full', *Irish News*, 16 June 1999.

48. *The Way Forward: A Joint Statement by the British and Irish Governments*, 2 July 1999, pub. in full in the *Belfast Telegraph*, 3 July 1999.
49. Ibid. 4.
50. 'David Trimble Exclusive', *Belfast Telegraph*, 6 July 1999.
51. D. Trimble, 'Leaping to Blair's Law Now might be a Risk too Far', *Irish Times*, 15 July 1999.
52. Statement by Senator George J. Mitchell, 18 Nov. 1999.
53. The executive: First Minister David Trimble (UUP); Deputy First Minister Seamus Mallon (SDLP); Minister of Agriculture and Rural Development Brid Rodgers (SDLP); Minister of Culture, Arts, and Leisure Michael McGimpsey (UUP); Minister of Education Martin McGuinness (Sinn Féin); Minister of Enterprise, Trade, and Investment Sir Reg Empey (UUP); Minister of the Environment Sam Foster (UUP); Minister of Finance and Personnel Mark Durkan (SDLP); Minister of Health, Social Services, and Public Safety Bairbre de Bruin (Sinn Féin); Minister of Higher and Further Education, Training, and Employment Sean Farren (SDLP); Minister for Regional Development Peter Robinson (DUP); and Minister for Social Development Nigel Dodds (DUP).
54. 'IRA Statement', *Daily Telegraph*, 5 Dec. 1999.
55. The UFF liaison team: Johnny Adair, Jackie McDonald, John White, William 'Winkie' Dodds, and John Gregg.
56. 'IRA Statement', *Irish Times*, 17 Nov. 1999.
57. 'Sinn Fein Statement', *Irish Times*, 16 Nov. 1999.
58. David Trimble, 'What we've got Amounts to a Commitment to Decommission', interview in the *Daily Telegraph*, 18 Nov. 1999.
59. 'UUP Statement', *Irish Times*, 16 Nov. 1999.
60. *Sunday Telegraph*, 12 Apr. 1998.
61. Smith, 'Paradoxes of Conflict Resolution in Northern Ireland'.
62. M. L. R. Smith, *Fighting for Ireland? The Military Strategy of the Irish Republican Movement* (London: Routledge, 1995), 227. See also K. E. Schulze and M. L. R. Smith, *Dilemmas of Decommissioning* (London: Politeia, 1999).
63. M. L. R. Smith, 'Peace in Ulster?', *Jane's Intelligence Review*, 10/7 (July 1998), 6.
64. M. von Tangen Page, 'Arms Decommissioning and the Northern Ireland Peace Agreement', *Security Dialogue*, 29/4 (1998), 412–13.
65. Smith, 'Paradoxes of Conflict Resolution'.
66. Ibid.
67. Independent International Commission on Decommissioning, *Initial Report* (Belfast and Dublin: Independent International Commission on Decommissioning, 21 Nov. 1997), and *Proposal for a Decommissioning Scheme Providing for the Destruction of Arms by those in Possession of Them* (Belfast and Dublin: Independent International Commission on Decommissioning, Dec. 1997).
68. *Draft Decommissioning Scheme for Liaison Sub-Committee on Decommissioning*, internal discussion paper (Stormont: Multi-Party Negotiations, 25 Feb. 1998).

12

Northern Ireland and South Africa: 'Hope and History at a Crossroads'

PADRAIG O'MALLEY

> Your truth that lacks the warmth of lies
> The ability to compromise.
>
> (John Hewitt)

> Whenever things threatened to fall apart during our negotiations—and they did on many occasions—we would stand back and remind ourselves that if negotiations broke down the outcome would be a blood bath of unimaginable proportions, and that after the blood bath we would have to sit down again and negotiate with each other. The thought always sobered us up, and we persisted, despite many setbacks.
>
> (President Nelson Mandela)

South African President Mandela addressed his words to the leaders of Northern Ireland's political parties, including David Trimble and Martin McGuinness, at De Hoop, a secured conference facility in Arniston, a small town in the Western Cape, on 29 May 1997. The conference was dubbed the De Hoop Indaba—*indaba* is the Zulu word for a 'meeting of the minds'. The event, which was hosted by the South African government, brought together the chief negotiators from all of Northern Ireland's political parties, both big and small, for a three-day private meeting with the people from all parties in South Africa who had negotiated the historic settlement in November 1993 that ended white minority rule, installed a non-racial transitional government, and opened the way to South Africa's first non-racial election in April 1994 and the subsequent Government of National Unity.[1]

Today President Mandela's words still resonate. Indeed, the constant refrain of the parties supporting the Good Friday Agreement in the run-up to the referendum that endorsed the Agreement was of a similar nature: If not the agreement, what is the alternative? This was a question that helped to sober up the electorate, provided them with food for thought after thirty years of conflict, and was certainly a factor in its decision to vote for the historic compromise. Eighteen months later, winding up his review of the Agreement necessitated by the impasse over the formation of a power-sharing executive that would include Sinn Féin, the political wing of the Irish Republican Army (IRA), and the decommissioning of arms by the IRA, Senator George Mitchell addressed the assembled media and warned that 'even the dogs in the street knew that without a power sharing Executive in place, there would be no decommissioning'.[2] And when the power-sharing institutions were suspended owing to the continuing impasse over decommissioning, and subsequently reconvened, politicians on both sides find they still have to address this one unchanging reality.

Northern Ireland and South Africa: Comparisons and Contrasts

Comparisons between the conflicts in South Africa and Northern Ireland should not be lightly made. However, the two share similarities that shed light on the nature of the conflict in each. Comparisons are valuable, as long as it is remembered that to compare or contrast them directly without each being put in the context of its own history would be misleading and specious. This much can be said.

The two conflicts share common structural characteristics typical of divided societies. The dominant community (Afrikaners in South Africa, Protestants in Northern Ireland) came from settler populations, and the subordinate community (blacks in South Africa, Catholics in Northern Ireland) was indigenous. In both cases, the dominant community asserted an equal claim to the land. Afrikaners trace their roots to a trading-post their forebears established on the Cape of Good Hope in 1652. Protestants trace theirs to the plantation of Ulster in 1607. In neither case is there a 'mother' country to which the designated 'settler' population can return, nor would the designated 'mother' countries regard themselves as such.

Certainly, the degree to which indigenous and settler populations live apart, the prevalence of exogamous marriage patterns, the degree to which religious or ethnic affiliations become purveyors of the perceived threats of difference rather than the perceived enrichments of diversity, and the salience of dispossession as one group's historical starting-point contribute enormously to political and socio-economic imbalances, which eventually express themselves in conflict when satisfactory forms of equilibrium among competing interests become impossible to calibrate.

Many divided society conflicts have roots in the indigenous–settler dichotomy, especially where the settlers disposed of the indigenous as the ruling elite, but this is in itself an insufficient explication of why conflict emerges in some multi-ethnic societies and not in others. There is no literature that comprehensively documents why some conflicts are more amenable to settlement—not resolution—than others. Each beats to the rhythms of its own contradictory impulses, distortions of reality, warped perceptions, and insatiable demands for revenge that are the legacy one generation bequeaths to the next. In some, the long duration of the conflicts leads to the evolution of social mechanisms to regulate and control the relationships between the parties in conflict. Unable to erase or embrace the other, they evolve relationships that prevent violence from getting out of hand.[3]

In Northern Ireland, with such social controls evolved, acceptable levels of political instability became the norm, thus reducing the pressure on the politicians to engage in the intense dialogue that is necessary to break historical logjams. In South Africa, apartheid mandated the relationships that existed between blacks and whites. When apartheid began to crumble, the absence of political and social space to create new relationships, except among certain elements of the elite, widened the divide between blacks and whites, encouraging the liberation movements to make the townships ungovernable when it became increasingly clear that the government no longer had the stomach to pay the price control of the townships required, given its own uncertainties—and divisions—with regard to the way forward. These uncertainties were reinforced by the government's reluctant conclusions in the mid-1980s that apartheid was no longer a viable proposition, nor one that could be indefinitely propped-up by made-to-order reforms.

Yet, it remained unsure what to replace apartheid with, and unwilling, or unable, to contemplate the ramifications of the inevitable—a universal franchise and a total dismantling of the apartheid apparatus; in short, the surrender of power. Nevertheless, while the social controls to regulate the conflict were deteriorating at an exponential rate, they did not collapse, and thus provided the leeway for the risks both the African National Congress (ANC) and the National Party government had to confront in their respective communities in order to convince their constituencies that neither was about to sell them out in negotiations.

A more satisfying theoretical model to explore than the indigenous-settler dichotomy is the 'narcissism of small differences', which postulates that the more objectively alike opposing groups are, the more they magnify their pseudo-differences. In South Africa marginal whites, especially Afrikaners in the lower classes who were part of the apartheid government's 'welfare state' for its own (job reservation for whites only etc.), were far more opposed to reforms that would give more opportunities to blacks than better-off whites since they would be far more likely to feel the consequences.[4] In Northern Ireland support for militant loyalism flourished in the Protestant working classes, also job beneficiaries of Protestant hegemony. They felt more threatened than their middle- and upper-class compatriots by changes that would provide more opportunities for Catholics.[5] Class differences exacerbate racial and ethnic affinities, and the consequences of radical change that would alter the balance of power among competing classes played an under-reported, often subliminal, role during negotiations in both conflicts. The elite has a highly developed propensity for protecting its own interests.[6]

As a result of the manner in which both governments tried to manage their conflicts, a number of perceptions developed that are common to both. Both governments tried to promote allegiance to the state on the basis of law rather than on the consent of the governed. Both governments pursued policies that supplemented military measures to combat political terrorism by increasing use of the judicial process, and both ended up subverting the judicial process. And because both governments went out of their way to present the problem of violence as one of law and order, of internal security or national security, Catholics and blacks alike lost faith in the police, the whole paraphernalia of the legal and judicial systems, and, therefore, in the states themselves. The perception of the Catholic community in Northern Ireland and the black community in South Africa was that the law was an instrument of the state's security and political policies rather than of justice.

Hence two antithetical perceptions of justice prevailed in each place. Northern Ireland Catholics and South African blacks regarded the administration of justice as unfair; they saw themselves as policed by the dominant Protestant and white communities respectively; in each the police was the 'enemy'. Both argued that their state's emergency powers were aimed almost exclusively against them; they saw that those who were charged with upholding the law broke it routinely and were not held accountable for their actions.

South African whites and Ulster Protestants saw the reverse: the IRA and Umkhonto we Sizwe (respectively the military wings of Sinn Féin and the ANC) were engaging in terrorist campaigns with the objective of overthrowing the state; both South African whites and Ulster Protestants feared being swamped or absorbed—whites in a South Africa ruled by an overwhelming black majority, Protestants in a united Ireland ruled by an overwhelming Catholic majority. Both regarded the security forces as too lenient with paramilitary groups; both argued that emergency laws were not sufficiently stringent and not enforced with sufficient vigour. Both saw Catholic and black unwillingness to support the police as indicative of support for the advocates of violence.

There are significant differences between the two conflicts. One involves the question of identity.

All South Africans—blacks (African, Coloured, and Indian) and whites—share a common identity: they regard themselves as South Africans. However, for whites the right to be South African was exclusive to them. Until the mid-1980s only whites were statutorily citizens; blacks were citizens of the ethnic homelands the white regime carved out for them. When that policy was revoked in 1986, it was not accompanied by the dismantling of apartheid and the all-encompassing *range of laws* that were flagrant violations of the human rights of the black community. On their side South Africa's blacks had an inclusive identity. What black liberation movements in South Africa sought was universal suffrage—one person, one vote—the recognition of their identity as South Africans, not as citizens of white-created ethnic homelands.

In Northern Ireland, which has been part of the United Kingdom since the partition of Ireland in 1921, the conflict is between two competing identities and national aspirations. Of the population of approximately 1.5 million, 40 per cent are Catholics, most of whom regard themselves as Irish and aspire to become part of the rest of Ireland, which is 95 per cent Catholic. Most Catholics in Northern Ireland have consistently made it clear that they want to pursue the aspiration to Irish unity in a peaceful manner while being able to express their Irishness and participate on the basis of equality in the government in Northern Ireland. Hence their calls for power-sharing in Northern Ireland and some institutional expression of their relationship with the rest of Ireland—the Irish dimension. The 60 per cent of the population who are Protestants regard themselves as British and want to remain part of the United Kingdom.

While these questions of identity are invariably pulled out of the hat to explain conflict in deeply divided societies and are important to take into account, at the root of conflict is fear: the fear the dominant class has of the consequences of change, whether it involves a loss of power or status, or absorption by another culture, ethos, tradition, or whatever the values and norms and particular characteristics the dominant tradition associate as being essential to its own survival.

The most profound fear of Northern Ireland's Protestants is that the two governments—the British and Irish governments—will somehow collude to deliver them into a united Ireland where they would be culturally and religiously absorbed and constitute a minority of 20 per cent. The religious component of their fears cannot be overstressed.[7]

Most white South Africans had been brain-washed into believing that the South African Communist Party (SACP) was the vanguard of Soviet expansionism into southern Africa, the crown jewel of its rapacious intentions. The threat of the 'total onslaught' from atheistic communism became ingrained in the white psyche.[8] The SACP, whites believed, was the subversive agent of the Soviets, who were using the ANC as a front to overthrow the South African government and impose a communist regime. The analogy with Protestant fears in Northern Ireland that they will somehow be coerced into a united Ireland is striking, all the more so because it, too, is irrational, the product of perceived threat rather than of actual threat. They fear being subjected to the rule of a Catholic state that takes its marching orders from Rome. A significant number of Democratic Unionist Party (DUP) supporters are members of Ian Paisley's Free Presbyterian Church or other right-wing Protestants sects. They fear negotiations, seeing them as instruments that are carefully calibrated to ensure that one day they will wake up to find themselves part and parcel of an all-Ireland state. They fear that, if such a situation were to arise, they would be absorbed into and dominated by the larger Catholic culture, and that religious and cultural absorption would inevitability lead to extinction—ethnic cleansing of a different kind.[9]

A crucial difference between the two conflicts was the measures that the dominant communities adopted to preserve their power and privilege. In South Africa the Afrikaner state implemented racial policies of apartheid and separation. These policies were implemented with methodical and brutal force, making blacks non-persons in their own country, forcing the resettlement of millions, destroying family life and undermining its social fabric, requiring them to live in under-serviced and overpopulated townships, or in white-demarcated 'Bantustans'. Blacks were totally disfranchised and denied any expression of their aspirations. Indeed, Afrikaners went one step further: They defined what black aspirations were, provided the 'homelands' in which blacks could achieve them, and forcibly moved millions into these homelands so that they might enjoy the benefits of their 'heritage'—as defined by whites.

Neither the level of subordination Catholics had to endure nor the harshness of the dominant regime ever reached the level of repression the Afrikaner regime imposed in South Africa. To say, therefore, that the situation of South African blacks and Northern Ireland Catholics was similar is to trivialize the enormous suffering South African blacks endured. Apartheid was evil, condemned by the United Nations as 'a crime against humanity'. The kinds of majority domination practised and enforced by Protestants in Northern Ireland were repulsive and wrong but hardly evil. Moreover, most of the measures of Protestant ascendancy were alleviated after the British government abolished the Ulster Parliament and introduced direct rule in 1972.

While there are common elements to the inequities both societies face as a result of the legacies of past discrimination, injustices, and being deliberately disadvantaged—either through legislative measures or wilful action on the part of the dominant group—the social and economic imbalances between Catholics and Protestants in Northern Ireland are relatively insignificant compared to the imbalances between blacks and whites in South Africa. Moreover, the emphasis put on redressing these injustices will be strikingly different. Socio-economic imbalances in Northern Ireland will be addressed in the context of similar imbalances existing in other parts of the United Kingdom. In South Africa the ANC, with its huge base of popular support, is attempting to restructure the molecular composition of society itself, to bring about a total transformation that will reach into every echelon of society. Thus, while the purpose of negotiations in both societies was to produce a settlement that would ensure that all people were treated with 'parity of esteem', the measures necessary to ensure parity will require a fundamental restructuring of South Africa on a scale that is not envisioned in the Northern Ireland settlement.

Another fundamental difference: the moral difference. The ANC represented the great majority of blacks and was engaged in a genuine war of national liberation that would give its people the voting franchise they were denied and the right to elect a government of their own choosing. It resorted to an armed struggle only as a measure of last resort when the government refused to engage in discussions.[10] It fought a just war, although the means it used to pursue a just aim were not always themselves just.[11] The IRA, on the other hand, was not fighting a war of national liberation, did not enjoy widespread support in Northern Ireland, and enjoyed next to none in the South. At best the IRA represented a minority (physical-force hardliners) of a minority (republicans) of a minority (nationalists) in

Northern Ireland, and was even more unrepresentative of the South's political proclivities.[12]

Thus while the ANC met the criteria for a just war, the IRA did not,
and the IRA used innumerable occasions to employ unjust means in the
pursuit of its unjust war. Any attempt on the part of militant republicans
to equate the actions of the IRA with the actions of Umkhonto we Sizwe
is both politically and morally indefensible. The former lacked political
legitimacy and moral standing; the latter had both. Indeed, nationalists'
demands that erupted into mass confrontations between Catholics and
Protestants in the late 1960s had been met by the British government.[13]
In this sense there never was any moral equivalence between the two
conflicts.

The Path to Negotiations

In South Africa since the mid-1980s the government had slowly come to
the conclusion that its security apparatus, despite the magnitude of the
resources at its disposal, could not defeat the liberation movement; the
ANC had slowly come to the conclusion that the armed struggle and
the internal campaign to make the country ungovernable could not defeat
the government. Their trajectories were about to intersect.[14]

In Northern Ireland the situation was more complicated. The first
traces of a peace process could only begin to emerge when Sinn Féin and
the IRA were brought to the point where they understood that: (*a*) even
though the British could not defeat the IRA, they could contain it; (*b*) the
IRA could not militarily defeat the British; (*c*) the British were not about
to withdraw from Northern Ireland; (*d*) Northern Ireland would remain
part of the United Kingdom as long as that was the wish of a majority of
the people there; (*e*) an all-Ireland state was not in the offing unless the
Catholic community could convince the Protestant community that its
future lay in it being part of some all-Ireland arrangement rather than a
peripheral part of Britain; (*f*) that might never happen and would never
happen if the IRA continued to resort to violence; (*g*) the Protestants of
Northern Ireland had the right to say no to a united Ireland; (*h*) the IRA's
targeting of members of the Royal Ulster Constabulary and the Ulster
Defence Regiment as part of the British 'killing machine' had embittered
the Protestant community to the point where reconciliation would take a
long time to achieve; and (*i*) a united Ireland was not on the cards now, in
the foreseeable future, or perhaps ever.[15] The enemy they would have to

negotiate with was not the British government but the representatives of the Protestant community in Northern Ireland—the Ulster Unionist Party (UUP), DUP, Progressive Unionist Party (PUP), and Ulster Democratic Party. If they were ever to cut a deal, these were the stakeholders they would have to cut the deal with.

For its part, the Protestant community had to rethink some of its own most sacred shibboleths: that rule by the majority in a deeply divided society was not democratic since the dominant community would always be in a position to impose its will on the minority community; that it would have to accept entrenched power-sharing between the two communities providing for parity of esteem between their respective traditions, cultures, political aspirations, and senses of national identity; that its right to say no to a united Ireland was counterbalanced by the right of Catholics to aspire to one; that special relationships existed between the two parts of Ireland that had to be accommodated in an institutional framework; and that the right of Catholics to express their Irishness had to be on an equal footing with the right of Protestants to express their Britishness.

Only when both sides had come to similar conclusions regarding the nature of the matters that had to be negotiated did a basis for negotiations exist. Both sides had legitimate rights and interests to protect; both had grievances that had to be addressed; neither owned victimhood, and neither could expect to achieve through a process of negotiations all that they had hoped for or aspired to.

Only when both could put the basis for a settlement in the perspective of what they had managed to achieve on their own behalf and what they had managed to preclude the other from achieving could there be actual, if gradual, drift towards agreement.

The Arniston Indaba

The purpose of the Arniston conference was not to proscribe, but for the South Africans to describe, share, bear witness, to their own experience that even in the most intractable of conflicts there are common denominators to the processes that must be created, the structures that must be put in place, the procedural principles that must be followed, the compromises that must be assented to, the trade-offs that must be condoned, and above all the trust that must be cultivated and blossom before negotiations can come to fruition, and a settlement, no doubt as flawed as the flawed individuals who put its fragile parts together, is agreed.

The most salient of these common denominators the South Africans identified for the Northern Irish were:

There should be transparency and openness in the negotiating process. To whatever extent possible, all stakeholders—business, unions, other institutional organs of civil society and the constituencies of the protagonists—should be made part of the process. On no account should an impression be given that deals are being made behind closed doors.

On the other hand, some deals must be done in confidence—not in secret. Confidentiality means that parties in bilateral or multilateral talks reach agreements that are not revealed at the time they are arrived at. But these agreements are ultimately part of the settlement package that is presented to the parties' constituents for their endorsement. Secret deals, on the other hand, are not put in the public domain, are only revealed in time, if at all, after a settlement is agreed but for which the public's endorsement is never sought. In the end secret deals undermine negotiated settlements, especially when each party's constituencies are fearful that their interests may be bargained away.

A secret deal on a particular issue, once it is 'sprung' on an unsuspecting public which may be accommodating itself to the new set of negotiated realities, immediately raises questions across all divides regarding what other secret deals have been cut and still remain unknown to them. There are immediate outcries of concern, whatever fears on all sides the settlement seemed to have mollified resurface, but with even greater intensity, and the whole settlement begins to unravel. In Northern Ireland British Prime Minister Tony Blair skirted with the difference between confidentiality and secrecy in the small hours of the morning of Good Friday 1998, when, in response to being informed by David Trimble and other senior members of the UUP that they could not sell the Agreement to their colleagues because of the Agreement's language on decommissioning, he reached for his pen and gave the unionists what they wanted—a reassurance that decommissioning would have to begin before the executive was formed. If the price for an agreement was a letter of reassurance on decommissioning—not made available to the other parties at this critical negotiating point—Blair was prepared to pay the price, convinced that in the end he could square the circle. In his letter of reassurance to Trimble, Blair said: 'In our view the effect of the decommissioning section of the agreement, with decommissioning schemes coming into effect in June [1998], is that the process of decommissioning should begin straight away.'[16]

That letter allowed Trimble to sell the Good Friday Agreement to a majority in his party, but did not engender unanimity of support. It ensured his leadership of the UUP, but not his command of it.

A related requirement: There must be no fudge factors. Fudge factors don't paper over differences; they dry in cement. One can tear up paper; cement you must bore through. When the cement has never hardened, it becomes impossible to bore. The language on decommissioning in the Good Friday Agreement is an indescribable mishmash of ambiguity and defensible multi-interpretations: classical avoidance that led to its own ineluctable consequences—the impasse that resulted was entirely predictable. Like most complex issues written in fudge, the fudge turned to mush. When Sinn Féin insists that the Agreement does not call for decommissioning on the part of the IRA as the price for its admission to the executive, it is perfectly correct since its frame of reference is the Agreement itself. And when the UUP insists that the Agreement calls for prior or at the very least parallel decommissioning on the part of the IRA, it, too, is perfectly correct since its frame of reference was the Agreement plus the letter of reassurance from Blair.

The South African Constitution that emerged out of the Multi-Party Negotiating Process and the deliberations of the Constituent Assembly is a model of a document whose every 'i' had been dotted and every 't' had been crossed.

Confidential talks or agreements are necessary because in a transparent environment the Heisenberg principle—the principle that the nature of an event being observed changes by virtue of the observation—becomes an integral part of the process itself. Thus, all transparent negotiations become hostage to the manner in which they are reported in the media, and thus to a propensity to negotiate sensitive issues through the media. Each party tries to put its own particular spin on matters; issues are reported in isolation from one another and without context. Agreement on a particular issue may be reported, which might make it appear that one party was making a major concession without any reciprocal concession on the part of the other. If particulars of a settlement are examined in isolation from one another, they will look very different and convey entirely different sets of implications than when they are examined as part of a package where the whole is greater than the sum of the particulars.

Progress only comes when negotiating parties learn to start trusting each other. Trust is a learned behaviour. When one party addresses another, especially in a bilateral setting, it must do so with particular sensitivity to the other party's politics and the difficulties it may be having with its own community—or even within the party's own ranks.

Parties must put themselves in the shoes of their protagonists. They must help their protagonists to bring their communities with them. In the end successful negotiations are not so much about bringing your community along with you as helping your protagonists bring their communities along with them. Respect for the others' positions is germane to the whole process. The ANC and the South African government thought they learned this at a relatively early stage in the process. They hadn't. Mistaken preconceptions on the part of both were only corrected after the protracted 'back channel' negotiations that led to a Record of Understanding. The ANC had to learn that while it was going to become the party of government, the manner in which it went about achieving this was more important than the fact that it would. The South African government had to learn the subtle fault lines between being the junior partner in a power-sharing government and the surrender of power. In Northern Ireland it took the parties that really had to learn to do so—the UUP and Sinn Féin—a lot longer to get to that point of understanding. Indeed, they both put their signatures to the Good Friday Agreement before they had done so, and it took them the better part of eighteen months to reach that pivotal fulcrum of reluctant trust that made possible the formation of the power-sharing government that the Agreement called for. But at that point reluctant trust was not sufficient, and the collapse of the arrangements agreed was for all intents and purposes a foregone inevitability.

The level of trust that develops among negotiators is a function of their ability to communicate outside the formal settings of negotiating structures at crucial points. This facilitates the alchemy of interpersonal relations, and creates empathy with the situations counterparts face—not as negotiators but as human beings with families and communities who are trying their best to grapple with problems not dissimilar from your own, and are coming up against the same kind of naysayers as you are among those on whose behalf you are negotiating. The discovery of common interests—music, books, sports, similar hobbies, children and the problems you have with them, the worries they unwittingly give you, the difficulties they have to deal with, and the fact that their futures rest in the decisions you mutually take—humanize the negotiating process and create bonds that go beyond the bonds that protracted negotiations themselves create.

If political consensus is to emerge, then mutual trust and respect, tolerance of others, and a willingness to compromise must exist at all levels. In this regard, where there is a transparent absence of trust on each side of the divide, due in part to ingrained cultural differences with regard to language and process—some of which have their origins in competing claims to legitimacy that developed over the centuries—a negotiating process that facilitates confidence-building actions is more likely to succeed than one that sets up a situation more like a poker table than a negotiating table.

Party leaders should not act as their party's chief negotiator. Their function is to appoint negotiators to act on their behalf. Negotiators are given a mandate by their parties. It is the function of negotiators to negotiate away their mandates in their quest for compromise and accommodation. It is the function of party leaders to sell their negotiators' compromises to their parties and constituents. It is also the function of a party leader to replace negotiators who fail to present the party's mandate in the most propitious light. If party leaders act as their own chief negotiators, the contradictions they force themselves to face invariably become impossible to resolve. How does one fire oneself?

At every level negotiations should involve the inherent risk of compromise; indeed, compromise is the essential ingredient of negotiations, without which there can be no negotiations. Each compromise is a building-block. As parties grow to trust each other and move from one compromise to the next, with concessions, though difficult, being made on all sides, every party becomes invested in the process, and each develops a stake in seeing the other succeed. A sum of mutual investments develops, which provides the cushion when it comes to the crunch issues.

The concept of sufficient consensus, rather than being defined in an arithmetical way, should be defined more flexibly as that level of consensus that allows the process to move on to the next stage or does not result in the process breaking down. In South Africa this meant that without the agreement of both the ANC and the South African government on a particular issue, the issue remained unresolved, irrespective of where other parties stood. While their agreement would be courted, it was no longer necessary for the process to move ahead. In Northern Ireland what began as a twosome between the UUP and the SDLP became a threesome once Sinn Féin joined the process, especially since the SDLP would not side with the UUP against Sinn Féin. This triangulation of what constituted sufficient consensus complicated the process, allowing Sinn Féin to exercise a degree of influence out of proportion to its numbers, an influence that was directly attributable to its 'influence with' the IRA, which, to complicate matters further, was not a party to the negotiations, but rather the ghost of things to come should matters come to a grinding halt. This reality made the Irish peace process less symmetrical than that in South Africa.

Timetables are important, but they should not be overriding. They concentrate minds and force participants to meet deadlines, encouraging compromise, especially when progress has been made on a number of fronts, or risk the loss of progress made up to that point. However, compromises forced on parties in order to meet arbitrarily set deadlines can create resentments that will find ways of expressing themselves that will be disruptive at some later stage. Coerced compromises are not real compromises. In the end they create the kind of backlash they were intended to avoid.

All parties must feel an equal ownership in the process. They must regard the process as their own, the result of their deliberations and agreements; governments are parties to the process, not the owners of it. Negotiations in South Africa took place in the turmoil of escalating violence. The Technical Executive Committee, a multi-party body established by the November 1993 settlement, levelled the playing-field; its inclusiveness did not obfuscate the obvious: the tacit acknowledgement on the part of all that without the ANC and the National Party government 'on side', sufficient consensus on the way forward simply didn't exist.

In Northern Ireland, violence, but especially the threat of an escalation in the scale and frequency of sectarian violence, provided the concentration of political will in London to put Northern Ireland on the political front burner rather than leave it on the back burner, where it had languished in political isolation, except for the few occasions when events, usually some particularly atrocious action by the IRA, caused it to be moved up a burner or two.

These initiatives, however, were always seriously hampered in one regard. Invariably they were government-driven. As a result the Northern Ireland parties did not fully invest in the process and were more intent on proving that they were not the ones who were to blame when things fell apart, as they always did, than on seeing themselves as the prime movers in the process and investing in it with the unqualified understanding that compromise was the indispensable ingredient of negotiation, and that without a willingness to compromise there could be no negotiations.

Negotiations break down. Indeed, breakdowns are an integral part of the process. To forestall the unforeseen consequences of such breakdowns, parties should establish back channels to each other, one or more members of their parties who iron out differences with their designated counterparts. I have already referred to the back channel established by the ANC and the South African government after the breakdown in negotiations in June 1992 (p. 285).

Technical committees are probably the most underestimated but indispensable tool of the peace process. Technical committees are made up of experts on the issues that divide parties to the conflict. They are professionals: academics, lawyers, economists, political scientists, and legal draftsmen. When a negotiating team which has responsibility for a specific issue or cluster of issues reaches broad agreement on the outlines of a compromise, it refers the matter to the technical committee that has been assembled to assist the negotiating team to find the language that will resolve their outstanding differences, close the loopholes, add caveats, insert the necessary amendments, etc.

This technical committee takes the draft agreement back to the negotiating team, who study it to determine whether it meets its specifications; if not, the team refers the matter back to the technical committee with its suggestions and reservations, and this process of going back and forth, negotiating team to technical committee and technical committee to negotiating team, continues until the negotiating team is satisfied that all its respective interests and ancillary concerns are sufficiently addressed. The technical committee searches for the precise language and measures its nuances to ensure that its principals' misgivings in the issue under discussion are met. In a sense the 'dispassionate' technical teams are the real negotiators, debating and refining the precise definitions of processes, procedures, and institutional–constitutional arrangements that will form the substance of a settlement.

Negotiators must recognize that it may not be possible to reach compromise on some positions. Thus, they agree that, when these occasions arise, they will employ agreed deadlock-breaking mechanisms to resolve the issue. This may require using parties, people, organizations, individuals, or governments who are not party to the conflict, but whose neutrality and integrity is acknowledged by all parties to the conflict.

Only win–win settlements work. If one party feels that it has been outmanoeuvred in some particular respect, or coerced into making concessions it otherwise would not have made, the resulting resentment of being perceived to be the 'loser' will find ways of expressing itself, to the detriment of the settlement.

Process is everything. Get the process right, and the substance will follow. Process takes priority over substance because without process there will be no substance. Without a context that provides the fragmentation and reintegration of the questions that form the core of the substance in a new way, the substance merely fragments.

When your party knows that an issue is 'non-negotiable' as far as the other party is concerned, never turn your knowledge of that into a demand that you know the other cannot meet. Never 'force' the other's hand. Besides the resentment it creates, the fact of one party using knowledge to which the other has made it privy in the course of confidential exchanges, for purposes that suggest a breach of confidence smacks of high-risk gamesmanship that undermines the fundamentals of the process itself.

Know thine enemy. Ironically, precisely who 'the enemy' was proved difficult for the South Africans to articulate, but more difficult still for the Northern Irish to accept—cultural and historical difference and congruencies worked at cross-purposes.

The ANC had always identified the white apartheid regime and the homeland states—the puppet black states created by the South African government as the foundation stones of grand apartheid—as the enemy that stood in the way of black liberation. One of the preconditions it had set before it would negotiate with the government was that all the homelands and the 'independent states' be dismantled and that the 'heads' of these states be given no place at the negotiating table, at least not as the representatives of legal entities. Once unbanned, the ANC abandoned this demand and began an elaborate process to 'cultivate' the very people it had condemned as 'enemies' of the people, 'collaborators' with apartheid. It identified a simple enemy—the white government that dominated every aspect of South African life. All blacks, irrespective of with whom they had made common cause prior to the ANC's unbanning, became potential allies, their 'sins' forgiven in newly formed alliances.

In Northern Ireland the enemy, especially for republicans, was the British government and its continued 'occupation' of Northern Ireland. There could only be a 'lasting' settlement when Britain recognized the 'folly' of its ways—or was brought to see this folly—and withdrew. There was a bland dismissiveness of Protestants and unionism: Protestants were simply seen as 'Brits' with a false sense of national consciousness who would roll over and passively submit to becoming part of an all-Ireland state, once British withdrawal made it inevitable.[17]

Only when a series of treaties and agreements between the British and Irish governments finally convinced the republican movement that the only obstacle to Irish unity was Protestant opposition to it, and that republicans would have to convince the Protestant community through negotiations that a united Ireland was in all their interests, were republicans finally convinced that 'the enemy' with which they would have to negotiate the future of Ireland was not the British government and its forces of 'occupation', but the Protestant community. Even at this point it is not absolutely clear that hardline republicans accept this reality[18]—which is why decommissioning will continue to be a problem.

Know thine enemy—literally. In South Africa the parties sorted this question out after an initial bout of jousting. When the posturing and put-ons were discarded, the enemy on each side knew precisely with whom it was dealing. Questions that appear to be simple turn out to be complicated. Who makes the decisions that count? Who has capacity to deliver? Who has control over the constituency it purportedly represents? There were the Inkatha Freedom Party (IFP), the Pan Africanist Congress, the Democratic Party, and infinitely many homeland and independent state parties. And then there were the National Party government and the ANC. Once the latter two stopped trying to 'woo' the IFP, real negotiations were able to start. In order to shake out the real sources of authority, you have to begin by being inclusive in every phase of the process; that having being done, you can afford the wheedling that identifies the principals to be carried along in the flood of events, not the riders of the flood.

On the Northern Ireland front such subtle distinctions were never made. Getting Sinn Féin into the process became the overriding political consideration. For obvious reasons: without Sinn Féin within the process, there would be no peace. The mistaken logic was that with Sinn Féin in the process there would be peace.

When Sinn Féin announced that it did not speak for the IRA, and could not convince it to decommission, the ingrained unionist fears began to reassert themselves. Adding to their apprehensions was the confusion of tongues over the relationship between the IRA and Sinn Féin. British Prime Minister Blair says the two are 'inextricably linked' and that Sinn Féin is the mouthpiece of the IRA. Irish Prime Minister Bertie Ahern agrees that the two are inextricably linked, but won't go so far as to say that Sinn Féin actually speaks for the IRA. Sinn Féin President Gerry Adams says a pox on both your houses, that Sinn Féin and the IRA are two separate organizations and that Sinn Féin can make no commitments on behalf of the IRA. The IRA says nothing, except for the occasional Olympian utterance—that all of this is of no concern to them[19]—which is one reason it is not a party to the Good Friday Agreement.

For example, Sinn Féin commits itself in the Good Friday Agreement to the principle of consent. Have we heard from the IRA on whether it accepts this principle? Sinn Féin accepts that all arms must be decommissioned. Have we ever heard from the IRA on this question, other than its disingenuous statements that the British government begin to disarm itself? Whose judgements do we breathlessly await? Who are they? To whom are they accountable? And, most importantly, on whose behalf do they speak? And if we do not know on whose behalf they speak, then how can we reasonably say on whose behalf they negotiate?

The process of negotiation, the South African participants told the Northern Ireland parties, is itself a captive of the random nature of events outside the control of the parties involved but which may, nevertheless, impinge on negotiations and cause parties to switch gears in order to secure their positions with their own membership. In short, the key to negotiations resulting in a settlement acceptable to all parties involved in the conflict is to create trust—far easier to objectify than to achieve, especially since the parties which must establish trust among themselves must first tear down the barriers of distrust that have separated them in the past and fuelled their conflict. Dismantling barriers of distrust creates a vacuum; how that vacuum is filled is germane to whether a propitious climate conducive to negotiations that lead to engagement can emerge. Negotiation is a necessary condition for engagement, but not a sufficient one.

Trust should not be confused with friendship or with the kinds of trust that build friendships. 'You negotiate with your enemies, not with your friends,' Mandela said at Arniston. The trust Mandela was speaking about is the product of shared understandings, belief in the integrity of the other, acknowledgement that they too are trying to the best of their abilities to come forward with ways to overcome obstacles and have an equal appreciation of the futility of a return to violence.

In South Africa the fact that this trust was established is the real miracle, especially when one considers that between 1990 and 1994—the period spanning the release of Mandela after twenty-seven years of imprisonment and the unbanning of the ANC, and the country's first non-racial, one person one vote elections—over 4,000 people became the victims of political violence resulting from the activities, often clandestine, of the state's security forces, and supporters of both the IFP and the ANC.[20]

In the end having to contemplate the alternatives to a negotiated settlement is what brought the parties in South Africa and in Northern Ireland together. In the end it is what the two conflicts had in common: situations in which neither side could prevail, in which neither side could lose. In Northern Ireland this point is understood, but not sufficiently.

At Arniston the South African participants were adamant on one thing. Even when there is an acknowledgement by all parties to a conflict that a negotiated settlement is the only alternative to continuing internecine violence which will secure 'victory' for neither side, the path to negotiations is an obstacle course that cannot be traversed in quick and easy steps. Rather it is one that throws up unexpected hurdles, one where good intentions often result in unforeseen consequences. It is a process that will stall and perhaps fail on occasion, if the role-players fail to establish the necessary trust in each other's bona fides, genuine intentions, and commitment to a negotiated settlement even in the face of misgivings and opposition among many in their own constituencies.

In South Africa the protagonists had to learn this through trial and error, and the lessons of failure were bought often at a high price. They learned that: (*a*) expressions of belligerence were often a cover for expressions of uncommitted willingness to talk about talks; (*b*) commitments to agreed settlements, no matter how well intentioned, are often mere gestures of aspirations; (*c*) aspirations cannot be transformed into realities unless the foundations are laid to build trust among former enemies; (*d*) trust is the one indispensable ingredient for successful negotiations; (*e*) building trust is a long and arduous process, the crossing of a landscape strewn with political landmines; (*f*) negotiations that lead to settlements require compromises on the part of all stakeholders, and political pain when once-cherished beliefs have to be abandoned; and (*g*) settlements should not be confused with resolution.

Resolution only emerges when settlements mature, when the accommodations that were necessary to achieve a settlement become redundant with the passage of time, with the entrenchment of trust, commitment to shared values, government that is inclusive, and processes of governance that are fully subscribed to by all former protagonists as equitable, representative, and non-discriminatory; when differences are commonplace and unencumbered by the threat of potential conflict.

Paradoxically, the outlines of settlements are usually self-apparent, although seemingly unattainable, almost always owing to the obduracy of protagonists who will not allow themselves to consider options other than outright victory. Obsession with embedded questions of identity, of righting the perceived wrongs of history, with the legacies of collective memories, and ethnicity and religion, and with issues involving the ownership of land scoured with the blood of centuries, the possession or surrender of which becomes ineluctably intertwined with questions of nationalism and sovereignty, makes the self-apparent self-emasculated.[21]

Unfortunately, in divided societies compromise and surrender are for all practical purposes one and the same thing, and the advocacy of meaningful compromise by one of the warring parties or parties supporting the same side is a political kiss of death. Thus, players in conflict situations are prisoners of the constraints forced on them by considerations of domestic politics. And, not unusually, the difficulties that pose the most serious impediments to negotiations are due more to intra-group rivalries than to inter-group differences. To be seen as the agent of 'selling out' the aspirations of one's group—ethnic, religious, linguistic, racial, or tribal—is a more damning fate than to be the instrument of a fruitless war where the only sure outcome is that nothing will be settled.

The path from the acknowledgement of the inevitability of negotiations to formal agreement on negotiation procedures, defining an agenda, implementation of complex protocols, and development of complementary institutional frameworks is invariably a long drawn-out process marked by disagreements on joint declarations on the way forward, endemic distrust papered over during negotiations, political gamesmanship, and pig-headed recalcitrance.

Trust is a learned behaviour. Learning takes time. In South Africa trust only began to develop among the main protagonists—the ANC and the National Party government—after negotiations between the two parties had broken down following the Boipatong massacre in June 1992.[22] Following the breakdown, the National Party and the ANC established a 'channel' to maintain a line of communication between the two, represented on the government side by its chief negotiator, Roelf Meyer, minister of constitutional affairs, and on the ANC side by its chief negotiator, Cyril Ramaphosa, secretary-general of the ANC. The two met on forty-eight occasions between June and September 1992, resolving outstanding issues between the parties and developing remarkable empathy for each other's party difficulties, fears, and hesitancies, and how these issues might be addressed, but more importantly developing a remarkable personal rapport. The result was the signing of a Record of Understanding between the two parties in September 1992, opening the way for the resumption of talks at the Multi-Party Negotiation Process in February 1993 and culminating in the adoption of an Interim Constitution in November 1993, and the country's first non-racial election in April 1994.

In the absence of alternatives, and with the commitment on the part of both the ANC and the National Party to a negotiated settlement, they made the tough and sometimes unpalatable compromises that resulted, in their own words, in a 'win–win' situation. Compromise, they both came to understand, was not only necessary but it was the one indispensable ingredient of a successful negotiating process; and the willingness to compromise, they also came to understand, could only reveal itself when the parties to the compromise trusted and respected each other. It is a lesson the Northern Irish understand but have yet fully to absorb.

In the end Ramaphosa and Meyer were able to imbue their parties, once the most bitter and implacable of enemies, with the trust they had carefully, if warily, nurtured. The rest, as they say, is history, but not history without pain, detours, setbacks, and rivers of blood in which the hopes and dreams of many would drown. But they pushed on because they had to; there was no going back to the 'old' ways. For both blacks and whites the waiting was over.

In the aftermath of the signing of the Record of Understanding, key members of the South African government and the ANC cemented their relationship at two *bosberaads* (meetings at undisclosed locations) in December 1992 and January 1993. For four days they lived together, ate and drank and talked together, and came to a better understanding of each other in the most casual and unceremonial of circumstances. Over the four days they stepped gingerly, and not without apprehension, across the bridges of three centuries; the informal ambience broke down formal barriers; old animosities were seen in new and less hostile lights; the rigid stereotyping that both sides had engaged in began to abate, and was slowly replaced by a new and respectful awareness of each other as individuals, which, if not fully defined or clearly understood, offered room for rapprochement if not actual friendship.

In Northern Ireland the absence of that trust is only now being addressed. Indeed, the fact that it took the provisional establishment of the power-sharing government by the Good Friday Agreement twenty months to come into being after the parties had committed themselves to the agreement can be attributed directly to the endemic distrust unionists have of Sinn Féin and the IRA.

Even when the UUP agreed to Sinn Féin taking its seats in the Assembly in September 1997, it would not talk to Sinn Féin directly. Thus there were no head-to-head bilateral talks between the two parties which held the future of Northern Ireland in their hands; they would only communicate with Sinn Féin through Senator George Mitchell. Indeed, the party leaders, Gerry Adams and David Trimble, did not shake hands until after the Good Friday Agreement had been signed. Even then, the handshake was perfunctory—more for the cameras than an expression of mutual goodwill and an intention to work together assiduously to steer the Agreement through to harmonious implementation.[23]

The failure of the two parties to resolve the impasse over decommissioning and to establish the executive forced the two parties into head-to-head discussions during Senator Mitchell's eleven-week Review of the Agreement. One benefit of the prolonged impasse over decommissioning that cannot be overestimated is that it finally compelled the UUP and Sinn Féin to face each other across a negotiating table in bilateral talks. During the long and intense review process they had to look each other in the eye. They had to talk, to develop the skeleton of relationships, to come to a better understanding of each other's predicaments, and to develop human images of the 'other'.

After Mitchell made the findings of the Review public, Sir Reg Empey, the chief unionist negotiator, told the media that unionists 'recognized the challenges and difficulties faced by the leadership of Sinn Féin/IRA'—a statement that hitherto would have been anathema, a heresy that could only be exorcised by excommunication from the party. Others were also noting the change in the relations between the two parties: indeed, in the weeks leading up to the conclusion of the Mitchell Review, the panaceas heaped on the two parties for their developing understanding of each other's problems teetered on the obsequious.[24] Mitchell himself commented on the 'reluctant camaraderie' that developed, the ineluctable result of Sinn Féin and the UUP having to work long, intensive days under sustained pressure without a break. In the statement accompanying his Review of the Agreement, Mitchell said:

Not long ago, the Ulster Unionists and Sinn Féin did not speak [to each other] directly. In the early weeks of the review, their exchanges were harsh and filled with recrimination. But gradually, as one of them put it 'trust crept in' . . . and the discussions became serious and meaningful.[25]

Later he went a step further:

The talks had been very tough until the venue moved to the US ambassador's residence in London. We sat in the ambassador's living room. We shared meals together. I insisted that there not be any discussion of issues at meals, that we just talk about other things so that they could come to view each other not as adversaries but as human beings and as people living in the same place and the same society and wanting the same thing.[26]

The *bosberaad* had come to the Court of St James. But whether it has done any good, other than to make strangers less strange to each other by fostering camaraderie that remains little more than reluctant, is problematical. But even that, in the circumstances of the fierce antagonism that exists between Sinn Féin and the unionists, was an achievement of considerable import. In the end the Mitchell Review did not produce a compromise—merely the promise of one.

With the decision by Assembly members to sanction Sinn Féin's participation in the peace process, after the IRA resumed its ceasefire in

1997, the DUP and the United Kingdom Unionist Party (UKUP) turned their backs on the process and abandoned the Assembly. Their departure, rather than bringing matters to a halt, allowed the remaining parties to get their houses in order and get down to the serious business at hand. Up to that point the party negotiators were playing at negotiations. Mitchell makes an insightful observation on the DUP–UKUP decision to quit the talks:

If their objective was, as they repeatedly insisted, to end this process, then their walk-out was a fateful error. Reaching agreement without their presence was extremely difficult; it would have been impossible with them in the room. No one can ever say for certain what might have been, but I believe that had McCartney and Paisley stayed and fought from within, there would have been no agreement. Their absence freed the UUP from daily attacks at the negotiating table and gave the party room to negotiate that it otherwise might not have had.[27]

What is perhaps most revealing about Mitchell's observation, however, is that intra-community rivalries often prove to be more troublesome to whatever parties are predisposed to negotiations than intercommunity rivalries over the division of power. Thus, moderate parties in negotiations are frequently obsessed not with positions taken by their counterparts on the other side of the divide, which they may empathize with, but with how their being seen to share similar reconciliatory positions with the 'enemy' may be used against them by parties opposing them within their own community to undermine political support among their constituents.

Hence, they find themselves having to weigh the possible impacts of proposed initiatives not because they are opposed to them but to preclude the perception of their being weak, easily manipulated, and not representing the best interests of their community. This makes the process more intricate, and makes progress slow and incremental. It underscores one of the most important principles that is the hallmark of successful negotiations: always put yourself in the shoes of your opponent, for without an understanding of the difficulties he faces in his community, you cannot help him overcome them, and hence, you cannot advance your own position.

The DUP–UKUP walkout and the consequent freeing of the UUP's hands was in a sense a replay of what had happened in South Africa.[28] The refusal of the Conservative Party to have anything to do with a negotiating process that included the ANC, and hence its decision not to participate in the Convention for a Democratic South Africa, was a catastrophic mistake on its part. More importantly, the party's refusal to participate in the April 1994 elections sounded the death-knell for the party. In the clichéd terms of the times, the train had left the station and, if you were not aboard, you were left abandoned on the platform.

The mistake worked to the advantage of the both the government and the ANC. It provided de Klerk and his negotiators with more room for manoeuvre and allowed them to use the threat of a right-wing backlash to wring concessions out of the ANC, concessions it otherwise would not have been amenable to. It spared the ANC the problems of having to put every issue to the test of 'sufficient consensus' and the guerrilla 'wordfare' the Conservative Party would have undoubtedly engaged in to make the process unworkable, the fruitless passage of time always working to its advantage.[29]

In Northern Ireland, the right-wing DUP learned assiduously from the mistakes of its South African counterparts. Although it walked out of the Assembly when Sinn Féin was admitted, it never left the process. It learned that, once a process is abandoned, the absentee party's control over its direction becomes non-existent, unless it has a paramilitary capacity to support its withdrawal (Sinn Féin always had the support of the IRA; the DUP never had the support of any Protestant paramilitary organization). Once you throw in your hand, you deal yourself out of the game, become a spectator, and watch the remaining players split the spoils.

The DUP, despite its commitment to destroy the Good Friday Agreement, never did so at the price of sacrificing the two ministerial positions its numbers entitled it to. Hence its participation in the power-sharing executive, with Sinn Féin, despite its avowals that it would never do so. It always understood the difference between 'objection' and 'absentionism'—ironically, something it took Sinn Féin over sixty years to learn.[30]

Post-Arniston

Was it a worthwhile endeavour? Did it have an impact on the negotiating process in Northern Ireland?

The following are brief quotes from the observations Northern Ireland participants and political commentators provided me with:

On the distant veld of a South Africa game park [David Trimble] began the journey in earnest from leader of one tribe to the architect of a new inclusiveness in Ulster. It was after that trip, according to one close friend 'that he knew common ground could develop between himself and [Seamus] Mallon.' (Michael Grove, *The Times*, 4 July 1998)

I [found that] I could learn to love my enemy. We had people there from the NP [National Party], the African National Congress, people from the old South African Defence Force and many of the other political parties involved in the negotiations. What I found really interesting about it was that obviously a number of years previously these people were bitter enemies, and here they were sitting together. From watching their body language it was clear that many of them actually liked each other, even loved each other. The message for me was that if they can do that, we can do that also. No party could remain unaffected by what they heard and I believe that in the weeks and months ahead we could possibly see the results of that trip. (Martin McGuinness, Sinn Féin chief negotiator, *Weekly Mail and Guardian*, 19 September 1997)

For me the real value of the trip was how the key players handled the process, how they related to each other, how they overcame difficulties in the process as they developed. (Jeffrey Donaldson MP, UUP, 7 January 1999)

Each group in South Africa, not each participant in South Africa, felt some acceptance of their identity in the final outcome. I learnt that the process was in the ownership of the participants. (Gregory Campbell, DUP, 7 January 1999)

Perhaps the most important message was to people who might be tempted to jump off [the negotiating train]. That message got through to some very important people. If you walk out of any process that's the road to ruin and marginalization. (John, Lord Alderdice, former leader of the Alliance Party, speaker of the Northern Ireland Assembly, 6 January 1999)

What we all took away were many lessons about how the South Africans had handled their process, particularly the confidence building dimension, which we hadn't fully appreciated in terms of the extent to which it could go, the significance of it, and the way in which it was subsequently built into our negotiating process. (Sean Farren, senior negotiator, SDLP, 9 January 1990

It was probably a critical turning point in our negotiations and it happened at the right time which was gratuitous inasmuch as it couldn't have been planned to have happened at the critical turning point. (Monica McWilliams, Women's Coalition, 7 January 1999)

Listening to the South African negotiators—the generals and the politicians—was vitally important to us. You had, for example, Mac Maharaj [a senior ANC operative and key negotiator]. He had the authority to re-invigorate the MK [Umkhonto we Sizwe] war. But he was redeployed to defend the peace process. That is very similar to what happened to the UVF [Ulster Volunteer Force]. The UVF had a kitchen cabinet whose job it was to escalate the war to end the war. But out of their deliberations and their analysis came an appreciation about things that were going on among Republicans and they decided it was better to have a look at these things rather than escalate the war. So there were things that had resonance. The importance of increased communication between politician and paramilitaries was something very evident when we learned how people like Matthews Phosa [another key ANC negotiator] was used to ensure that the communication levels were increased between the militarist and the politician. All had resonance for us. I think the constitutional Unionist politicians were very affected by South Africa. Trimble and Robinson were. Robinson's own admission to me on the way back in the airport at Johannesburg made it very clear that he found it a very significant journey and a very significant experience. We may not have seen that played out fully in all of his politics but the level of understanding in the period of transition was vitally important for people who knew what they would have to do but hadn't got the balls to do it. Perhaps for them to recognise that you're not alone in this world and that others have gone through it before you with more stark division and brutality and pain than we had had an impact. (David Ervine, PUP, 9 January 1999)

We came, we saw, we listened, we learned—and we applied. (Gary McMichael, UUP, 9 January 1999)

The round table seminar in South Africa, away from the media spotlight, which was attended by representatives of all the parties involved in the negotiations in Northern Ireland provided an invaluable forum for face to face discussion between parties and people who found it extremely difficult to meet on their home ground in Northern Ireland. In facilitating that process of human interaction, the South African retreat could be described as a precursor to the type of atmosphere which helped us achieve the breakthrough in the Review carried out under the chairmanship of George Mitchell. (Bertie Ahern TD, Irish prime minister, South African Institute for International Affairs, University of Witwaterstrand, 12 January 2000)

[Ahern] highlighted the round-table discussions between key Irish players, held in South Africa in 1997, as having 'heralded a breakthrough'. Ahern states that: 'It was highly complex, and South Africa went to a lot of expense to assist and show people what could be achieved, and I know that all politicians without exception who played a part in that discussion came home believing that [the Northern Ireland problem] could be cracked in some way. This was no more than two years before they made the enormous moves that they had not dared to dream about for the previous sixty to seventy years.' (Michael Morris, interview with Bertie Ahern, *Sunday Independent* (South Africa), 16 January 2000)

Some Post-Arniston Observations

Eleven problems threaten to throttle the Northern Ireland peace process with what are formidable but not insurmountable obstacles; each stands in striking contrast to the manner in which events unfolded in South Africa.

1. The absence of continuing meaningful contact between the UUP and Sinn Féin at the highest levels. Without establishing key back channels, without helping each other to bring their respective recalcitrant communities into line, the prima-facie preconditions for a durable self-sustaining accommodation will continue to be elusive. The trust that is the sine qua non for such an accommodation does not exist. Establishing it is a matter of immediate urgency.

2. The absence of contact between the IRA and any party other than Sinn Féin, making it impossible to distinguish between Sinn Féin as player and Sinn Féin as surrogate.

3. The absence of any strong belief in Northern Ireland that the suspension of the peace process will eventually result in the collapse of the process—the belief that somehow the process has become self-sustaining.

4. The absence of a belief that failure will result in some cataclysmic upheaval, that is, a bloodbath of unfathomable proportions.

5. A propensity to believe that ceasefires that have held for four years will not become casualties of prolonged stalemates; that there is no going back to 'the bad old days'.

6. The false sense of security that repeated last-minute rescue turnabouts has induced has engendered a political ennui in which people believe that the protagonists have lost the will to restart the conflict.

7. The amorphous yields of the peace dividend have dulled memories of the thirty years of violence, creating a vacuum of will.

8. An unstated but very firmly rooted belief that the process has become irreversible in the sense that the costs of going back are far greater than the imperceptible gains of going forward.

9. The millennium factor—that the last ten years of slaughter in the former Yugoslavia, for example, make the conflict in Northern Ireland look like a 'small' conflict, manageable, and therefore not a matter to become unduly concerned with, if things go slightly awry. As wars go, Northern Ireland is a third-division affair, not the stuff of the big leagues. In the 2000s it is more about nonsense than about beliefs.

10. National identities are no longer threatened or embraced in the way in which they were thirty years ago. The parades will go on and we will quarrel forever. Drumcree is war by other means.

11. Decommissioning and police reform. In South Africa the matter of decommissioning was never satisfactorily dealt with, but in a sense it didn't make any difference. In the final analysis it would have involved the ANC as liberation movement having to hand over guns to the ANC as government. In Northern Ireland the question is both quantitatively and qualita-

tively different. And it is inextricably linked with the emotion-ridden question of a police force in place that is not only acceptable, but seen to be acceptable, in every regard, to both communities.

Conclusions

There is none. The failure to resolve the matter of decommissioning resulted in the institutions of the Good Friday Agreement being suspended on 11 February 2000—in retrospect an unsurprising outcome, given the way in which the matter was handled throughout the process.[31] But it was an unfortunate one in the sense that in using legislative means to do so, the British government took ownership of the process away from the parties in Northern Ireland, thus undermining their need to understand that in the final analysis it is up to them to negotiate their differences, and that only when they acknowledge this fundamental principle, which underpins all successful peace processes, will they empower themselves to reach the necessary but unpalatable accommodations that will secure the peace.

Enforced coalitions rarely work, and never under circumstances where the partners to power-sharing have mutually opposing aspirations—antithetical to each other in the perpetuation of 'us' and 'them'. South Africa remains an experiment; Northern Ireland a laboratory test.

We can share our experiences with each other, but we cannot replicate them. Learning from others is no substitute for learning from ourselves. Voices heard are not voices listened to. In this respect the Northern Irish have a distance to travel before they can transmogrify putative trust into purposive risk-taking. The issue of decommissioning is, as Senator Mitchell insightfully pointed out, symptomatic of a larger problem: the absence of trust.

And therein lies the worm at the core. The worm, however, has many ways of wriggling.

NOTES

1. The Northern Ireland parties were the Ulster Unionist Party, the Democratic Unionist Party, the Alliance Party of Northern Ireland, the Social Democratic and Labour Party, Sinn Féin, the Women's Coalition, the Ulster Democratic Party, the Progressive Unionist Party, and the Labour Party. The major South African negotiators came from the African National Congress,

the National Party, the Pan Africanist Congress, the Freedom Front, the Inkatha Freedom Party, and the Democratic Party. For a fuller account, see P. O'Malley, *Northern Ireland and South Africa: The De Hoop Indaba* (Boston: University of Massachusetts, John W. McCormack Institute of Public Affairs, Apr. 2000).

2. The British government suspended the Good Friday Agreement's power-sharing executive and associated institutions on 11 Feb. 1999.

3. J. Darby, *Intimidation and the Control of Conflict in Northern Ireland* (Dublin: Gill & Macmillan, 1986).

4. A. Adam, F. van Syl Slabbert, and K. Moodley, *Comrades in Arms* (Cape Town: Tafelberg Press, 1997).

5. Nicholas Davies makes the claim that the Afrikaner right sold $600,000 worth of arms to the Ulster Defence Association. 'The Afrikaners', he says, 'believed they were helping their blood brothers.' See *Sunday Independent* (South Africa), 28 Nov. 1999.

6. Adam *et al.*, *Comrades in Arms*.

7. See P. O'Malley, *The Uncivil Wars: Ireland Today* (Boston: Houghton Mifflin, 1983); P. O'Malley, *Biting at the Grave: The Irish Hunger Strikes and the Politics of Despair* (Boston: Beacon Press, 1990).

8. See D. O'Meara, *Forty Lost Years* (Ohio: Ohio University Press, 1996). Also interviews with former head of the South African Defence Force, General George Meiring, and former head of the South African police General Johann van der Merwe, Pretoria, Feb. 2000.

9. The fact that the Catholic Church has relaxed its conditions regarding 'mixed' marriages—in the past the non-Catholic partner had to give an undertaking that the children of such a marriage would be raised as Catholics, which led to a steep decline in the number of Protestants in the South—has had as much impact on their thinking as the belief still prevalent among some whites in South Africa that the communist monolith is alive and well and lurking in the corridors of power, awaiting its moment to pounce upon an unsuspecting population. The reasons for Protestants being adamantly opposed to an all-Ireland state during the whole course of the conflict—opinion polls over a twenty-five-year period consistently reflect that less than 10% of Northern Ireland's Protestants would consider becoming part of an all-Ireland state under any circumstances—have never been adequately researched. Yet, this is one of the questions most germane to an understanding of the conflict.

10. Mandela himself at the Rivonia trial explained why the ANC turned to violence: 'The hard facts', he said, 'were that fifty years of non-violence had brought the African people nothing but more and more repressive legislation, and fewer and fewer rights . . . It was only when all channels of peaceful protest had been barred to us, that the decision was made to embark on violent forms of political struggle and to form *Umkhonto we Sizwe*.' (Insert 430A, folio missing) See N. Mandela, *Long Walk to Freedom* (London: Abacus, 1995), 433.

11. See *Truth and Reconciliation Commission of South Africa Report* (Cape Town: CPT Book Printers, 1998). For a critique of the Commission's Report, see A. Jeffrey, *The Truth about the Truth Commission* (Johannesburg: South African Institute of Race Relations, 1999).

12. 'The IRA gets its mandate to fight', said Gerry Adams, 'from the presence of British troops in this country [Ireland]. It doesn't seek an electoral mandate. It comes from the British claim to sovereignty over this part of Ireland [Northern Ireland].' Interview, 15 Nov. 1989. See P. O'Malley, *Questions of Nuance* (Belfast: Blackstaff Press, 1990).

 The IRA has never been convinced by the arithmetic of conventional politics. Its rationalization of its mandate for the armed struggle denies an understanding of fundamental democratic principles. Its allegiance is not to freedom but to its own conception of history. Hence the impasse on decommissioning that would bedevil the process.

 Perhaps the most eloquent statement of the IRA's position was enunciated by Thomas McDonagh at his court martial in 1916: 'We do not profess to represent the mass of the people of Ireland. We stand for the intellect and the soul of Ireland. To Ireland's soul and intellect the inert mass, drugged and degenerate by ages of servitude, must, in the distant day of resurrection, render homage and free service.'

13. See A. Pollak (ed.), *A Citizens' Inquiry: The Ophsal Report on Northern Ireland* (Dublin: Lillliput Press, 1993).

14. Interview with Neil Barnard, former head of the South African National Intelligence Service, 8 Nov. 1999. See also Mandela, *Long Walk to Freedom*.

15. As early as 1979, the British government conceded, in a report prepared by Brigadier James Glover, later general commanding officer of British forces in Northern Ireland, that 'The Provisionals' campaign of violence is likely to continue while the British remain in Northern Ireland . . . We see little prospect of political development that would seriously undermine the Provisionals' position. PIRA will probably continue to recruit the men it needs. They will be able to enhance their all-around professionalism.' See O'Malley, *The Uncivil Wars*. It took the IRA some time to catch up. See *Opsahl Report on Northern Ireland*; B. O'Brien, *The Long War: The IRA and Sinn Féin* (New York: Syracuse University Press, 1995); D. McKittrick, *The Nervous Peace* (Belfast: Blackstaff Press, 1996); K. Toolis, *Rebel Hearts* (New York: St Martin's Press, 1996); P. Taylor, *Provos: The IRA and Sinn Féin* (London: Bloomsbury, 1997); P. Bew and G. Gillespie, *Northern Ireland: A Chronology of the Troubles 1968–1999* (Dublin: Gill & Macmillan,1999); J. Holland, *Hope against History: The Ulster Conflict* (London: Hodder & Stoughton, 1999).

16. G. Mitchell, *Making Peace* (New York: Alfred A. Knopf, 1999).

17. See J. McGarry's contribution to this volume (Ch. 5) for a critique of republican thinking.

18. See the IRA's New Year message in *An Phlobacht,* 6 Jan. 2000: 'It remains our view that the ending of British government interference in Irish affairs offers the only basis for the establishment of a just and lasting peace in Ireland.'

19. One has only to review reactions to the Report of the international body chaired by Senator George Mitchell (the Mitchell Commission) to get a fix on the IRA's position. The Report, issued in Jan. 1996 made a number of suggestions ('the parties should consider . . . an approach that would represent a compromise'), not recommendations, to break the impasse on decommissioning and open the way for multi-party talks. It called on all parties to commit themselves to six principles, which included the total disarmament of all political organizations, and also suggested that decommissioning take place in tandem with talks. The IRA did not bother to respond to the Commission's compromise suggestions, leaving it to Sinn Féin to argue the issue. But Sinn Féin began to make it increasingly clear that, while it spoke to the IRA it did not speak for the IRA. See P. O'Malley, *Northern Ireland 1983—1996* (University of Massachusetts, John W. McCormack Institute of Public Affairs, Aug. 1996).

20. See A. Jeffrey, *The Natal Story: Sixteen Years of Conflict* (Johannesburg: South African Institute of Race Relations, 1995) for the most comprehensive account of the violence in KwaZulu–Natal. For a partial, but very incomplete, examination of the violence, see the Report of the Truth and Reconciliation Commission. For an examination of some of the efforts to contain the violence, see H. Ebrahim, *The Soul of a Nation* (London: Oxford University Press, 1998).

21. See L. Nieuwmeijer and R. du Toit (eds.), *Multicultural Conflict Management in Changing Societies* (Pretoria: HRSC, 1994); T. Ohlson and S. J. Stedman, *The New is not yet Born: Conflict Resolution in Southern Africa* (Washington: Brookings Institution, 1994); J. Cash, *Identity, Ideology and Conflict: The Structuration of Politics in Northern Ireland* (Cambridge: Cambridge University Press, 1996); M. W. Haughey (ed.), *New Tribalisms: The Resurgence of Race and Ethnicity* (New York: New York University Press, 1998).

22. On 17 June 1992 more than forty residents of Boipatong were massacred in a systematic attack. The ANC insisted that residents of a local hostel, controlled by the IFP, were to blame and that the police were complicit in the massacre. As a result the ANC broke off all negotiations with the government. The de Klerk government, the ANC reiterated, was ultimately responsible for the attack because of its failure to take action against those who had been involved in previous incidents of violence which the ANC had brought to its attention.

23. During July and Aug. 1999 there was a back channel of sorts between middle-level operatives in the UUP and Sinn Féin. However, the channel did not operate at the most senior level. Confidential information supplied to the author.

24. See D. de Breadun, 'Trust between SF [Sinn Féin] and the UUP Growing', *Irish Times,* 13 Nov. 1999.

25. *Irish Times*, 18 Nov. 1999.
26. *Irish Times*, 19 Nov. 1999.
27. Mitchell, *Making Peace*, 110. Robert McCartney was leader of the UKUP and the Revd Ian Paisley leader of the DUP. For Mitchell's assessment of Paisley, see Mitchell, *Making Peace*, 50–2.
28. In Mar. 1982 a rupture occurred in the National Party when a significant number of National Party MPs, under the leadership of Dr Andries Treurnicht, leader of the party in the Transvaal, abandoned the National Party, seeing the structures under consideration in the National Party for some limited form of power-sharing with Coloureds and Indians as a fundamental betrayal of the principles of Verwoerdian apartheid, and formed the Conservative Party.
29. But even though the Conservative Party was not part of the process itself, its continued barrage of criticism that the National Party was selling out the Afrikaner nation began to exact a toll on the National Party. The Conservative Party won a series of by-elections, putting it in a position to claim that the National Party no longer represented the majority of Afrikaners. De Klerk, cleverly, opted for a referendum, and put a simple question to the white electorate: 'Do you support continuation of the reform process that the state president started on 2 February and which is aimed at a new constitution through negotiations?' The wording was brilliant in its vagueness, yet so implicitly direct in the implications of a 'no' vote that it didn't give whites a choice; rather it presented them with a subliminal ultimatum: Armageddon or else. And he had the support, albeit grudgingly given, of the ANC and the media—indeed, of all institutional organs of opinion and influence. De Klerk won the referendum convincingly, and no longer had to look over his shoulder. The Conservative Party returned to the trenches and complained about the unfairness of it all. See F. W. de Klerk, *The Last Trek: A New Beginning* (London: Macmillan, 1998).
30. See P. Bew, *Irish Times*, 28 Dec. 1999. 'For some time, the DUP has been astute enough to avoid the pure logical reductionism of Mr McCartney. It has drawn the lesson from the South African experience that conservative forces cannot allow themselves to opt out of the process. Indeed, it had gone for an each-way bet: at one moment, Peter Robinson, as a responsible minister, happily drops the sour face mode to engage with Derry nationalists and republicans, on the other hand, they continue to denounce the agreement. It is a position which infuriates the Ulster Unionists. In fact, it is perfectly sustainable until the February denouement, but then whatever happens—barring a Trimble political suicide note—the DUP will have to change. Either in government or outside it—pursuing the argument on decommissioning—it will be increasingly impossible for the DUP to present Mr. Trimble as the arch-betrayer.'
31. Almost twenty months after the Good Friday Agreement was ratified, the power-sharing executive and other institutions the Agreement called for

finally came into being, but with the clear understanding on the UUP side that it would withdraw from government if the IRA had not begun to decommission its weapons by 12 Feb. 2000. To buttress his position with the Ulster Unionist Council, the governing body of the UUP, Trimble provided it with a pre-dated letter of resignation as first minister. As part of the interim arrangement the IRA agreed to appoint a representative to the International Body on Decommissioning, under the chairmanship of General John de Chastelain, in order to facilitate this process. On 5 Feb. 2000 the IRA issued a terse statement: 'We have never entered into any agreement or undertaking or understanding at any time whatsoever on any aspect of decommissioning.' Which is true—it was not a party to the Good Friday Agreement.

On 11 Feb. de Chastelain issued a second report in which he said: 'We find particularly significant and view as valuable progress the assertion made to us by the IRA representative that the IRA will consider how to put arms and explosives beyond use, in the context of the full implementation of the Good Friday Agreement, and in the context of the removal of the causes of conflict.' Which begs the obvious question: Whose causes are we talking about? On 15 Feb., in response to the suspension of the Good Friday Agreement institutions, the IRA withdrew its representative from the de Chastelain Commission. In its statement the IRA said: 'Those who have made the political process conditional on the decommissioning of silenced IRA guns are responsible for the current crisis in the peace process.'

On 20 Feb. Peter Mandelson, secretary of state for Northern Ireland, announced that the British government may release a timetable for the withdrawal of British troops from Northern Ireland. He said that the British government wanted to normalize security in the North, but added that any changes must be 'in the context of the threat [of violence] going away and politics working'. He told the *Observer* newspaper: 'The idea that the British government wants the military to hang in there and talk tough, irrespective of the political process, is nonsense. We want to normalise security. There is no pressure to keep more battalions permanently based in Northern Ireland than are strictly needed for low key patrolling purposes.' 'Withdrawal of British troops'—music to the ears of the IRA. It is what it has been after all along. See *Opsahl Report on Northern Ireland.*

13

The Tenability of Partition as a Mode of Conflict Regulation: Comparing Ireland with Palestine–Land of Israel

SAMMY SMOOHA

The British experience in Ireland is a story of failure. The British and their predecessors occupied Ireland in the twelfth century, administered it, expropriated most of its lands, Anglicized its language, partially settled it, and in the nineteenth century did their utmost to fully annex it. The Irish resisted and drove the British out of the bulk of the island by 1920. Partition turned Northern Ireland into a patrimony of the Protestant majority. The Catholic minority and the Republic of Ireland have continued to reject partition and managed to destabilize the North by the late 1960s. In 1998 a new settlement was reached that officially recognizes Ireland's involvement in the North and that promises reunification as soon as a majority in the North votes for it. The overall historical trend is disengagement and withdrawal of the British from Ireland, the weakening of partition, and the extension of Irish control over the entire island.

On the other hand, the Jewish experience in Palestine–Land of Israel is a success story.[1] The Jews settled Palestine–Land of Israel in large numbers, dispossessing and dislodging the Palestinians. When they established a state of their own on three-quarters of the territory, partition began. Since 1948 Israel has maintained a firm hold over the country, including its internal Palestinian minority. It occupied the rest of Palestine–Land of Israel in 1967, but all Jewish attempts to undo partition, namely, to settle and subdue the West Bank and Gaza Strip, have failed. The Palestinian people who rejected partition have gradually come to terms with it, and in 1993 a framework for settlement was adopted based on the legitimacy and reality of a permanent partition.

What is it that makes partition tenable in Israel–Palestine but unstable in Ireland? A comparison of Ireland and Palestine–Land of Israel will shed light on the factors explaining the differential viability of partition.

Partition as a Mode of Conflict Regulation

The boundaries of many contemporary states are largely artificial. State borders move back and forth based on shifting power balance between neighbouring states which pay little heed to ethnic demography. This is especially true for the new states of the post-Second World War period whose borders were shaped by the colonial powers. The building and break-up of multi-ethnic and multinational empires have also mixed and separated ethnic and national groups.

Because ethnically divided societies face severe problems of national integration, attempts are often made to reduce the degree of ethnic heterogeneity. Ethnic diversity may be curtailed by assimilation and population transfer, not to mention ethnic cleansing and genocide.[2] If the minorities are indigenous, they usually experience these modes of conflict regulation as involuntary and resist them actively.

Partition is another means of achieving ethnic homogeneity.[3] It can take two forms: irredenta and secession. Irredenta means the separation of a territory from one country and its attachment to a neighbouring state, whereas secession is the creation of a new independent state out of a territory torn from another country. In both forms partition derives legitimacy from the right to self-determination. It appears to be a democratic and workable solution, but it is actually troublesome. Because it usually violates the sovereignty of the state from which the territory is taken, it may be opposed vehemently. The superpowers may object lest the world state system break down in turmoil. States and international organizations may baulk at the affront to the sanctity of state boundaries. Given the extent of ethnic heterogeneity, large-scale territorial changes are often needed, not just mild border alterations. Downsizing of states may also prove economically counter-productive in times of globalization and an expanding world economic system.

The historical record is replete with both peaceful and violent partitions. To mention just a few of the successful peaceful cases, Belgium withdrew from the United Kingdom of the Netherlands in 1830–1, and the Union of Sweden and Norway was terminated in 1905. The Federation of Mali dissolved itself in 1960 into Senegal and Mali, and Singapore was separated from Malaysia in 1965. The split of Bangladesh from Pakistan in 1971 was also placid. In 1991 the Soviet Union broke up into fifteen independent states and, in a 'velvet divorce', Czechoslovakia was divided into the Czech and Slovak republics in 1993.

Other countries have been less fortunate. The division of the Indian sub-continent into India and Pakistan in 1947 brought about several wars and left Kashmir a contested territory. The de facto partition of Cyprus into Greek and Turkish parts in 1964 is still unsettling. The failed attempts of the Ibo to secede from Nigeria, the non-Muslim Southerners from Sudan, the Kurds from Iraq, and the Tamils from Sri Lanka triggered bloody civil wars. With the exception of the relatively peaceful secession of Slovenia and the former Yugoslav Republic of Macedonia, the dissolution of the Yugoslav Federation has caused considerable bloodshed and ethnic cleansing.

Drawing on these cases and theoretical considerations, it is possible to spell out several factors accounting for the use of partition as a means of conflict management and for its successful consolidation. Some of the conditions leading to partition are the following:

A conflict between two nations over the same territory. The populations to the conflict should qualify as nations claiming a right to self-determination to the same area. They are neither national minorities (a national minority is part of a nation living in the diaspora or in the homeland ruled by another nation) nor mere ethnic groups (an ethnic group is a population that shares a common descent or culture but does not claim the right of self-determination to a certain territory).

A no-win situation. The parties claiming the same territory are not able to win a decisive victory or to reduce the other side to a non-nation. As a result the conflict persists and exacts heavy price from both sides.

The international community recognizes, legitimizes, and actively supports partition. Since partition affects the world state system, the consent of the superpowers or international governing bodies is required to reach partition and to cement it.

For a partition to succeed, the following conditions should prevail:

The majorities living in any part of the partitioned territory accept or resign themselves to partition. To succeed, partition should be negotiated and agreed upon, rather than imposed unilaterally. In the post-partition states partition may fail if rejected by both or either one of the ruling majorities. Because these states continue to share regional interests, they can also agree on terms of cooperation, including a common market, a military alliance, or even a loose confederation.

The minorities living in any part of the partitioned territory are neither able nor willing to end partition. If partition is challenged by both or either one of them, it may break down. Since the minorities formed by partition pay a heavy price, they tend to fight to terminate it. Their ability to resist partition depends on many factors, among which sheer size looms largest. When minorities constitute over one-fifth of the total population, they reach a critical mass and are strongly predisposed to undo partition. Partitions that create large, unwieldy minorities are doomed to failure. Voluntary or involuntary population exchange during partition can help to reduce minorities to a manageable size.

These circumstances that favour workable partitions can be examined and elaborated in the case of the partition of Palestine–Land of Israel.

The Partition of Palestine–Land of Israel and its Lessons

In 1999 the 7.25 million Palestinians reside in three main areas: the core of 2.9 million live in the West Bank (including East Jerusalem) and Gaza Strip, 3.5 million in the Diaspora (including about 1.75 million in Jordan), and 0.85 million in Israel. About half of all Palestinians are refugees of the 1948 war and their descendants. Israel still controls most of the area that the Palestinians claim as their future state.

The history of the Jewish–Palestinian conflict is the unfolding of incompatible nationalisms claiming the same territory.[4] Zionism rose in response to rampant anti-Semitism and the Jewish predicament in Europe. It reacted to and was strongly influenced by the integral and exclusionary nationalisms of eastern Europe. It sought to form a Jewish state in Palestine–Land of Israel to which all Jews could return from the Diaspora. From the beginning the Jewish state was conceived to be fully or predominantly Jewish in population, language, institutions, and symbols. For this reason throughout one hundred years of settlement Jews have created separate localities and organizations and have shown no interest in joining forces with the indigenous population. By the end of the British mandate on 15 May 1948 Jews had managed to build a full-fledged Jewish society with little Arab involvement.[5]

Palestinian nationalism, which emerged in the 1920s as part of Arab nationalism and in reaction to Zionism, was exclusionary and rejectionist in nature.[6] It claimed exclusive rights to Palestine–Land of Israel, saw Jewish immigrants as colonial settlers, demanded a total ban on Jewish immigration and on the sale of lands to Jews, rejected the British mandate because one of its goals was to help create a Jewish homeland in Palestine, and insisted on the immediate formation of a Palestinian state in all of mandatory Palestine. The only status to be allowed to Jews in Arab Palestine was that of a traditional religious minority living under the protection and domination of the Muslim majority (Dhimmi).[7]

A 'no-win situation' has characterized relations between Jews and Palestinians throughout the twentieth century. Neither side has the power to win a decisive victory, to subdue or eliminate the other, or to control the entire area permanently. For a variety of reasons each party in the conflict always musters sufficient power to block the other. Palestine–Land of Israel was settled by the Jews at a time when it was no longer possible for Europeans to settle overseas en masse. It was controlled by imperial powers (the Ottomans and then the British) that did not permit such actions. Each side has been able to mobilize strong allies: the Palestinians continued to receive the support of the Arab world, the Muslim countries, and, after 1948, the non-aligned and communist blocs, whereas the Jews maintain the backing of the West and the Jewish Diaspora. Even when the Israelis, due to their formidable war machine, could have dealt a crushing blow to their enemy, they were precluded from doing so by international and moral restraints.

The conflict has always been internationalized. The right of both peoples to self-determination was internationally recognized. According to the 1917 Balfour Declaration, the British pledged to help the Jews build a national homeland in Palestine–Land of Israel but without prejudicing the Palestinians' rights. In 1922 the League of Nations entrusted the British with a mandate over Palestine to fulfil the same mission. The national objectives of the two peoples, to have the same territory, were evidently irreconcilable. The Palestinian and Jewish societies in Palestine–Land of Israel were separate and incompatible.

In view of the clash of rights and societies, different ideas emerged among the Jews about how to deal with the Arabs.[8] All the British and international plans for solving the problem before and after 1948, however, were various versions of partition. The idea of partition was formally introduced for the first time in 1937 by the Peel Commission. The 1947 United Nations partition resolution called for the formation of two states, one Arab (with 45 per cent of the land and 67 per cent of the population) and one Jewish (with 55 per cent and 33 per cent respectively). The Palestinians and the Arab world rejected this resolution, but the Jews accepted it in principle. In the aftermath of the Arab defeat in the 1948 war over half of the Palestinians became refugees, and the land that was earmarked for the

Arab state of Palestine was divided between Israel (ending with a total of 75 per cent of the land of mandatory Palestine), Jordan, and Egypt.[9]

The Palestinians in the West Bank and Gaza Strip during 1948–67 maintained their separate existence. This was relatively easy in the Gaza Strip because most of them were stateless refugees and encouraged by Egypt to keep their separate identity and to mobilize against Israel. On the other hand, Jordan pursued a policy of Jordanization. It annexed the West Bank, imposed Jordanian citizenship on its inhabitants, induced them to migrate to the East Bank, where development projects were launched, and discouraged them from acting against Israel. All these assimilationist efforts failed, however, because Jordan did not solve the refugee question and did not blur the basic Palestinian character of the West Bank.[10]

The Israeli occupation of the West Bank and Gaza Strip in 1967 served as the main catalyst for the resurgence of Palestinian nationalism and nation-building. The fall of pan-Arabism and the emergence of the Palestine Liberation Organization (PLO) as an internationally recognized organization provided the Palestinians with separate Palestinian national leadership, identity, and symbols. Israeli foreign rule and occupation were much clearer and more legitimate targets of resistance after 1967 than the earlier reliance on the Arab world.

During the period from 1967 to 1992 Israel's policy in the occupied territories was ambiguous, indecisive, inconsistent, and controversial. Occupation was supposed to be temporary, yet it was continuous. Military and Jordanian laws were applied to the Palestinians, while Israeli law was extended to the Jewish settlers. As investments only furthered Jewish interests, the Arab residents had no incentives to cooperate. The local economy was subordinated to the Israeli economy through regulations, dependence on Jewish employers for employment, and the prevention of economic growth. The daily military policing of the area involved frequent infractions on human rights and humiliations of the Palestinians. The widespread use of coercion, including administrative detentions, demolition of houses, and deportations, revealed the mass disaffection of the population and the inefficiency of control. The non-coercive measures of co-opting leaders and economic dependence were either not used or proved ineffective.[11]

Israel neither annexed the territories nor kept them separate. As a result they were partially incorporated into Israel. The systems of telephone, electricity, water, natural gas, oil, roads, air space, airports, and seaports were linked and subordinated to Israel. Non-private lands were allocated for establishing numerous Jewish settlements. Labour governments, which officially stood for territorial compromise, allowed the process of incorporation to occur, whereas Likud governments, which officially favoured eventual integration, launched various projects of Jewish settlement and elimination of the 1967 border.

In December 1987 the Palestinian intifada (uprising) broke out. It was a popular, semi-violent uprising against occupation and for independence. Local youths stoned and threw petrol bombs at Jewish soldiers and settlers. The Palestinian resisters sabotaged daily life by limiting shopping to several hours a day and holding frequent general strikes. They formed popular committees to run local affairs, and executed collaborators. By the end of the first two years of intifada the toll was 800 Arabs dead, 30,000 injured, and 40,000 detained. In comparison, Jewish losses were small.

As a result of the intifada, the status quo was shattered and both sides realized that they had to talk to each other to find political accommodation. The Palestinians moved away from their traditional rejectionist position and towards acceptance of partition. In late 1988 the PLO recognized Israel's right to exist, renounced terrorism, and acceded to UN Resolution 242.[12] In response the United States opened talks with PLO leaders. Jordan gave up its claims to the West Bank and endorsed the two-state solution. The Palestinian question was put on the international agenda, and Israel was pressured to start negotiations with the Palestinians. In late 1990 the Madrid Conference convened to negotiate, for the first time in the history of the conflict, a comprehensive peace settlement between Israel and the Arab parties to the conflict (Jordan, Syria, Lebanon, and the Palestinians as part of the Jordanian delegation).

The 1993 Oslo Accords were a historical breakthrough. The two peoples recognized each other's right to self-determination, accepted the government of Israel and the PLO as their legitimate representatives, and agreed to the use of peaceful negotiations as the only means to settle their differences. It was also determined that a Palestinian Authority would be established and within five years a permanent settlement would be negotiated. Although the agreement invalidated the rationale for the conflict, it left many hard issues unsettled. During the following five years a peace treaty was signed with Jordan, and hard and inconclusive negotiations were held with Syria. Several interim agreements were reached with the Palestinians that enabled Israel to withdraw from some occupied territories and to shift over 90 per cent of the Palestinians to the jurisdiction of the Palestinian Authority. This progress was made despite the right-wing opposition and its ascendance to power in 1996. The 1996–9 Likud government officially accepted the Oslo agreement but proceeded slowly and toughly with the negotiations with the Palestinians and with implementation. The return of Labour to power in mid-1999 cleared the way for the settlement of the Palestinian question.

Partition re-emerged as the best option to deal with the Palestinian predicament in the West Bank and Gaza Strip. Israel is simply unable to absorb the Palestinians who refuse to be part of Israel. At the same time Israel rejects the Palestinians as citizens lest it lose its Jewish and democratic character. Both sides have already come to terms with the forthcoming formation of a Palestinian state, and thus their political discourse has shifted towards the nature of this state. Over thirty years of Jewish settlement and integration of the occupied territories have failed to undo partition. The Jewish settlers constitute only 5 per cent of the total population (160,000 Jews versus 2.9 million Palestinians). Because most of them are concentrated in several urban clusters close to the old border, they can be annexed to Israel. A small number is dispersed in many tiny settlements that can be resettled or left where they are. The linking of the infrastructures and economies can be revamped as necessary.

Partition is also the only feasible way to handle the Israeli–Palestinian conflict because any permanent settlement must include the Palestinian Diaspora as well. Israel will not grant the Palestinian refugees a right of return to its land. Without offering hope and remedy to the Palestinian Diaspora, the solution of the Palestinian question will remain partial and fragile. The rejectionist front in the Diaspora may grow again, continue the armed struggle, and sabotage any permanent settlement. Only a Palestinian state can take responsibility for the Palestinians in the Diaspora, gradually repatriate some of the 1.7 million refugees among them, and fight the rejectionists.

The Israeli segment of the Palestinian people (16 per cent of the population) has neither opposed nor undermined partition throughout the entire period (1948–99). It lacks the capability and the will to do so. Israel declares itself to be the homeland of the Jewish people, rather than the state of and for its citizens. It is a non-liberal 'ethnic democracy', combining extension of democratic rights for all with institutionalized ethno-national dominance. It is Jewish and treats Jews preferentially in state symbols, calendar, days and sites of commemoration, national heroes, demography, language, culture, institutions, laws (regulating immigration, citizenship, and naturalization), land and settlement policy, allocation of budgets, and ties with the Diaspora. Palestinian citizens enjoy individual and collective rights, but possess a comparatively inferior status. They cannot fully identify themselves with the Jewish state, and are regarded as a security risk and discriminated against in many walks of life. These Palestinians are excluded from the national power structure (security forces, the Cabinet, the Supreme Court, high posts in the Civil Service, and top management of the economy) and are denied institutional or cultural autonomy.[13]

Israel has taken various measures to prevent Israeli Palestinians from destabilizing the state. During the initial and formative period (1948–66) they were placed under military administration, which intervened in their daily communal affairs, made them economically dependent on the Jews, co-opted their elite and leaders, and ran their institutions.[14] After the lifting of many of these restrictions by the 1970s the Arabs became organized and waged a strong struggle for peace and equality. The state responded with concessions and piecemeal change, rather than repression. To forestall the rise of a movement for autonomy or irredenta, the state has confiscated over half of the Arab lands, set up many Jewish settlements to break up Arab territorial contiguity, and invoked emergency regulations to put down seemingly subversive activities. These Arab citizens have remained weak compared with the strong state and the powerful Jewish majority. The Arab acquiescence is also a result of their sharing, though not equally, the benefits of an advanced economy, a welfare state, a viable democracy, and a modern society.

Rather than objecting to partition, Israel's Palestinian citizens firmly support it. For them, partition settles the Palestinian question and removes a critical bone of contention with the Jews. With transition to peace they will cease to be an enemy-affiliated minority and will gain the trust of the state. Their chances of facing fewer restrictions and of having better opportunities will significantly improve.

The partition of Palestine–Land of Israel has proved to be the lesser evil and the most realistic option for settling the protracted, bloody, and existential conflict between Palestinians and Jews. It withstood a vehement and long Palestinian rejection and resistance. It stood fast in the face of Israeli governments' omissions and commissions to undo or to blur it. By the late 1990s partition had been accepted by the Palestinian and Jewish mainstreams and was slowly encroaching on the broad radical periphery of both camps. Although the obstacles to reaching a final status settlement were still apparent, the historical trend was clearly towards partition.

Partition of Palestine–Land of Israel appears viable because it satisfies almost all of the above conditions leading to a workable partition. Even the crucial condition that majorities of both sides accept partition was met by the 1990s. This is why the historical trend is towards the consolidation of partition by the formation of a Palestinian state alongside Israel. Because none of these conditions obtains in Ireland, as will be shown below, it is suggested that partition there is not tenable and that the historical trend for managing the conflict is towards the weakening of partition.

The Partition of Ireland

A review of the history of Ireland will show that conditions for a stable partition were not favourable and that during the critical years from 1921 to 1972 the Protestant beneficiaries of partition in Northern Ireland failed to control the Catholic minority and to stabilize partition. The implications of the 1998 Agreement will be assessed with regard to the future of partition.

The British, the Irish, and the Partition of Ireland

The circumstances leading to the partition of Ireland after seven and a half centuries of colonial rule (1172–1921) were indeed inauspicious. Britain's consent to independence for Ireland meant British recognition of the right of the Irish to full self-determination and British renunciation of any right to Ireland. The Irish finally won the struggle against the British over the possession and control of Ireland. The Irish were accepted as a nation, and the state of Ireland was recognized as the Irish exclusive homeland. The British were a colonial power, retreating to their secure and well-established homeland on the English isle.

Rejecting the Protestants' vehement opposition to Irish independence, the British respected their desire not to be subjected to Irish Catholic rule. Yet these descendants of the seventeenth-century settlers did not see themselves, nor were they seen by the British and Irish, as a separate nation entitled to a state of its own. They were and are merely an ethnic group that did not and does not claim a right to self-determination as a nation. They feared lest an Irish state reduce them to a minority and cost them their dominant position. The movement against Irish self-determination consolidated Protestant solidarity not as a separate nationalism but, rather, as an ideology of unionism and Protestant supremacy. Because the Protestants demanded to remain part of Britain, the partition of Ireland and the conferral of autonomy on Northern Ireland were pragmatic and temporary arrangements. Moreover, because the partition of Ireland emerged as a solution for the accommodation of a minority, not for the fulfilment of the right to self-determination of a nation, it is essentially not binding and firm.

Ireland was and still is an officially irredentist state. All Irish governments since independence have demanded an end of partition. Ireland treats all the inhabitants of Northern Ireland as its full citizens with a right to Irish passports, a right to vote, and a right to stand for elections for any office in Ireland. In 1998 the state of Ireland elected a new president from the North.

From Ireland's viewpoint the granting of independence in 1921 was an incomplete act of decolonization. As a colonial power, Britain recognized the Irish's right to self-determination and granted them sovereignty. Ireland was considered an indivisible unit throughout history. The ceding of the six counties in the North was made as an expedient appeasement of the Protestants. Emerging as an artificial entity, Northern Ireland was created against the explicit will of the majority of the inhabitants of Ireland at that time. The Irish people has never approved partition in any referendum, although it ratified, in May 1998, an amendment to the Constitution which requires a majority consent in the North for unification.

From Britain's viewpoint Irish independence formally meant the secession of part of its territory and the end of a civil war in its midst.[15] A distinction in the British mind was made, however, between the British core on the English isle and the Celtic fringe on the Irish isle. The British withdrawal from Ireland did not infringe on the British nation's right to self-determination, which is fully exercised on the English isle. Had the Protestants been weaker, Britain would have withdrawn completely from Ireland. Post-war Britain lost interest in Northern Ireland, and has experienced it as a mere liability since the 'troubles' of the late 1960s. Since then the British government has declared on several occasions that Northern Ireland could freely decide to cede from Great Britain and join Ireland, thereby acknowledging the fragility of the ties between the two. Surveys in mainland Britain have repeatedly shown that the majority of the British support the idea of united Ireland, even more than the Catholics in Northern Ireland.[16]

These Irish and British viewpoints contribute considerably to Northern Ireland's lack of international legitimacy. The world community does not reject the Irish claims to sovereignty over Ulster and views Britain's hold as ambiguous, fragile, and transitory. The long and violent colonial history of Ireland and the deployment since 1969 of British troops in the North give credence to this view. One consequence of the lack of international legitimacy is the widespread belief in the final unification of Ireland among the public of both Ulster and the Republic.[17]

There is little international involvement in the affairs of the three segments of the Irish people. The core part fulfils its right to self-determination in Ireland. The lion's share, the Irish Diaspora in North America, Australia, and New Zealand, estimated at 50 million, is well settled. Only the small Irish segment in Northern Ireland is problematic. Except for the occasional opportunity to embarrass Britain, other countries have little to gain from meddling in the Northern Ireland problem.

The lack of international legitimacy and attention to Northern Ireland also implies that partition enjoys no passive or active international support. Partition is left for the direct parties (Britain, Ireland, the two communities in Northern Ireland) to decide.

On the other hand, the Irish Diaspora plays a special role against partition. It lends moral support to Ireland's claims to Ulster, contributes monies to the resistance movement, and serves as a political lobby on behalf of Ireland. Moreover, it kindles the interest of the United States in the Irish question and pushes it to take an active part in mediation and settlement.[18] Well established for generations in its newly found homelands, the Irish Diaspora's support for a united Ireland is purely sentimental and moral and detached from any stake in repatriation to the old homeland.[19]

Despite the lack of legitimacy and the involvement of the world community, Northern Ireland is internationally treated as part of Great Britain. Ireland has never tried to use force, nor even threatened to use force, to regain the North. Given its tiny army, Ireland is no match for Britain. It declares the Irish Republican Army (IRA) illegal, censures its violent actions, and tries to put it down. Although in 1969 it placed the matter of British repression of the unrest on the agenda of the United Nations Security Council and demanded that a peacekeeping force be sent to Ulster, it did not pursue the matter further when Great Britain raised objections against the external intervention in its 'domestic affairs'. As a member of the United Nations and the European Union, Ireland cannot afford to blatantly violate the sovereignty of another state.

Thus it is clear that the conditions prevalent in the partition of Palestine–Land of Israel were absent in Ireland. The Irish case is not the partition of Britain but rather the partition of Ireland with the withdrawal of the British as a colonial power. The two sides to the partition of Ireland are the Irish majority and the British minority of settlers in the North. These settlers are not a nation, with a right to self-determination, but rather a segment of the British nation, which fulfils its right to self-determination on the English isle. The partition of Ireland was a concession to accommodate the reluctant Protestant settlers of Ulster. The case of

Ireland is a 'win situation' where the Irish right to self-determination to Ireland is recognized. Partition rendered the Irish victory incomplete, however. The international community has not lent any support to the partition of Ireland, casting doubt on the legitimacy and tenability of partition.

The position of the two minorities created by the partition of Ireland remains to be examined: a Protestant minority in the South and a Catholic minority in the North. Both minorities could have played a role in the sustainability of partition. The fate of the Protestant minority in the South confirmed the need for partition. The Protestants in the Irish Republic constituted only 5 per cent of the population, enjoyed no autonomy, and lived in an inconsiderate environment. Ireland turned into a clerical Catholic state, not allowing divorce, abortions, and related freedoms. The number and influence of the Protestant minority diminished appreciably over the years, and it was too weak to challenge the Republic.[20] The fears of the Protestants in the North are reinforced by the fate of their brethren in the South.

Unlike the very small and weak minority of Protestants in the Republic, who could not and did not resist, the big and strong minority of Catholics in Ulster could and did resist.

Ethnic Democracy in Northern Ireland and its Collapse (1921–1972)[21]

From its inception Northern Ireland was established as a de facto, though not de jure, ethnic democracy. Other options were not even considered. There was nothing in the 1921 partition deal, nor in the British policy during the period from 1921 to 1972, to impose or even encourage power-sharing between Protestants and Catholics. The Protestants regarded Ulster as their patrimony, employed their numerical superiority to institute a majority dictatorship, discriminated against the Catholics, excluded them from power and privilege, and neutralized them as a menace to the regime. The Catholic minority was, however, too large and too strong to control. Consequently, ethnic democracy was crushed after fifty years of precarious partition.[22]

Although it is not clear whether Protestant nationalism or unionism is ethnically based, it is evidently exclusionary with regard to the Catholic Irish. Most Protestants see themselves as members of the British nation by descent, citizenship, and loyalty. They exclude the Catholic Irish from belonging to this nation. Protestant unionism also claims absolute and exclusive rights to Northern Ireland and negates any Irish right to the land.

Unionism separates nation from citizenship. The Catholics are seen as citizens of Britain but not members of the British nation. The government of Ulster defined its mission to preserve the distinction between nation and citizenship and avoided any attempt to incorporate the Catholics into the British nation.

From the Protestants' viewpoint Ulster belonged to the members of the British nation, not to its Protestant and Catholic citizens. Ulster was the political vehicle for the promotion of Protestant interests—keeping a Protestant majority, language, symbols, and institutions. Ulster is thus not a neutral and impartial body but rather a partisan tool in the hands of the Protestants to ensure their supremacy. Ulster was supposed to give preferential treatment to its 'owner', the Protestant majority.

Ulster mobilized the Protestants, who belong to the nation. It fostered their links to the British nation to prevent their indifference to the nation and assimilation into the Irish. It strengthened their British identity, and provided them with a favoured status to obtain their full consent, identification, support, participation, and willingness to make sacrifices for national goals. The ultimate aim was to keep Ulster Protestant and to avert a united Ireland. The Protestants were called to do their utmost to accomplish this and recieved favourable treatment in return.

This was the nationalist side of ethnic democracy in Northern Ireland, but there was also a substantial democratic dimension flowing from being a democracy. Catholics are given individual rights like all British citizens. They are also accorded the privilege of separate education that serves as a base for their separate existence. Most importantly, the Catholics are allowed to exercise their political right to conduct parliamentary and extra-parliamentary struggle. They have their own political parties and representatives in Parliament.

Minority rights were, nonetheless, quite restricted. Blatant discrimination by state institutions impaired Catholic individual rights. The Protestants scorned Catholics for being ignorant adherents of corrupting popery.[23] Catholics were also stereotyped as shiftless parasites who exploit social security benefits to raise large families. They were treated as outsiders and second-class citizens in many areas. They were deliberately excluded from policy-making positions. Discriminatory practices against them in employment, public housing, local representation, regional development, and educational funding were very much in evidence until 1968. Police mistreatment of Catholics was also widespread. Ulster did not recognize the Catholics as a national minority, and did not grant them any group rights beyond education. It neither gave them autonomy nor power-sharing. They were either excluded or limited in the Cabinet, Parliament, the courts, the security forces, and the top echelons of the civil administration. Their extra-parliamentary protest was either repressed or ignored.

The Catholic minority was perceived by the authorities as a major threat. It was defined as part of the enemy, deeply suspected of disloyalty and feared lest it undermine the territorial integrity of the country. To forestall the menace, a machinery of control was imposed on the Catholics. Their activities were a legitimate target for the security forces. Activists and leaders were closely watched and harassed. Catholic protest was monitored and checked lest it deteriorate to unrest and violence.

Control over the Catholic minority was not effective, however. From the outset Northern Ireland did not enjoy conditions conducive to effective control of minorities. Strikingly absent was a sovereign state that could manipulate its laws and agencies to control its minority effectively. Ulster lacked certain state powers and was accountable to the superior British government. Although Northern Ireland had the legal apparatus to subdue minority opposition (the Special Powers Act of 1922), its freedom to exercise authority was limited. The Stormont government always feared the reactions of the British government. For this reason it did not use its powers to intern suspects without trial during the most crucial 1968 to 1970 years.[24] The Protestant authorities lacked internal security services for effective intelligence-gathering, detection, and deterrence. The police force harassed the Catholic community instead of penetrating it. Northern Ireland also lacked a convincing ideology for legitimizing its control over the Catholic minority. Because Protestants' sectarian nationalism was equated with Protestant supremacy, it was not acceptable. Catholics' threat to security was also not credible because the Republic neither threatened to use force to undo partition nor instigated its co-ethnic members in the North to subvert the regime.

Catholics' strong institutional base, which survived partition, also defied the possibility of control. The Protestant shift from minority to majority status in Northern Ireland in 1921 did not enable the Protestant authorities to destroy the Catholics' independent bases of power, let alone to impose a military government on them. Catholics used their churches, schools, political parties, and the media as independent bases of power around which to amass public support. The IRA provided Catholics with retaliatory and disruptive powers. Protestants were unable to contain Catholic organizations. Community control gave a sense of unity to the Catholic minority, and amply rewarded the Catholic elite and leaders, preventing them from defecting from their community.

The machinery of control also lacked economic underpinnings. Ethnic stratification in Northern Ireland was not sufficiently pervasive to make Catholics economically dependent on Protestants. The increasing post-war British intervention in the Ulster economy weakened Protestant domination. Catholics also became more independent of the Protestant authorities and majority as more jobs became available to them through British investors. Growing British welfare services improved Catholic well-being, and made Stormont's regime more tractable to British pressures for reforms. The Catholic middle class has rapidly risen as a result of the expanding educational system and the mounting demand for trained and professional manpower. Instead of the traditional departure abroad, more Catholics moved to the booming urban centres. Catholic social climbers, however, soon experienced blocked mobility as the public sector remained closed to them.[25]

The unmanageable size of the Catholic minority constituted an almost insurmountable obstacle for effective control. In a formal democracy like Ulster it was difficult to neutralize, to co-opt, and to disintegrate a large minority. To accomplish such a mission, it was necessary to resort to high mobilization and tyranny of the majority, thereby exposing the injustice and illegitimacy of the regime.

These factors explain the high resistance potential of the Catholic community and the eventual collapse of control and political stability in Northern Ireland. Catholics expressed their antagonism in militant views. Most of them regarded themselves as part of the Irish nation and defined their identity as Irish, not British, and supported the idea of a united Ireland. They held annual protests against Protestant hegemony. Their backing of nationalist parties was overwhelming. A sizeable minority of Catholics was involved in resistance activities, including strikes, banned street demonstrations, secret societies, and Sinn Féin politics. The IRA enjoyed the support of as much as one-third of the Catholic population.[26]

The civil rights movement of 1968 constituted the turning-point in Catholic–Protestant relations. It started with integrationist and moderate demands, but became unruly after facing police repression and Protestant intransigence.[27] Having the strongest vested interests in the status quo, the Protestant working class spearheaded the counter-resistance. The most striking change was the deployment of British troops in Northern Ireland and the institution of direct rule from London in 1972, when it became clear that the Stormont government had lost control. This dramatic move meant the loss of ethnic democracy, which had been installed in 1921.

Consociational Democracy and the Future of Partition

The suspension of home rule in 1972 opened a new era. The British strategy has been to restore law and order, to correct the anti-Catholic biases built into the system, to replace the defunct ethnic democracy with a consociational democracy, and to soften partition by engaging Ireland in the internal affairs of the North.

Protestant supremacy received a strong blow. The British takeover undermined the Protestants' tyranny of the majority, monopoly of the state apparatus, their use of the security forces to harass the Catholics, their appropriation of a disproportional share of the societal resources (power positions, jobs, public apartments), and their attempt to legitimize hegemony by attributing disloyalty, parasitism, corrupting papal influences, and inferiority to the Catholics. As a result, the Protestants were suddenly downgraded to a status of one of two communities vying for power, rather than the group in charge.

The British met many of the Catholic demands. Almost all the civil rights inequities were rectified. Gerrymandering was terminated, allowing Catholics to take over towns where they constitute a majority. Discrimination in allocation of public housing was corrected with the formation of more accountable boards. An anti-discrimination law and an affirmative action law in employment were passed. The police forces were reorganized, a complaints commission was established, and Catholics were encouraged to join. The Catholics also greatly benefited from the expansion, with British funding, of the educational system, bringing their achievements on a par with the higher Protestant standards. The appreciable increase in the public sector and the anti-discrimination policy raised Catholic employment in the Civil Service to a proportional level. The Catholic middle class also enjoyed greater opportunities to enter technical, professional, and managerial positions.

The British took various steps towards power-sharing. Several attempts to form a coalition government during the periods 1972–4 and 1991–2 failed because of the Protestant opposition. To the Protestants' great dismay, the British also went much further in partly meeting the Catholics' nationalist demands. In 1985 the Anglo-Irish Agreement was signed, giving for the first time a consultative role to the Irish government in Northern Ireland in exchange for measures to curb terrorism from across the border.[28] Dublin was also deeply involved in the talks over power-sharing held in 1991–2.

It appears that the pressing of the nationalist claims and the official participation of Ireland in the domestic conflict contributed to greater convergence between the Irish people on both sides of the Northern divide. Irish identity and nationalism among the Catholics in the North drew them towards their brethren in the South and away from the Protestants.

By the end of 1994 a breakthrough in the stalemate and political violence in Northern Ireland took place[29] with the adoption, in February 1995, of the Joint Framework Documents by the British and Irish governments.[30] The framework introduced consociational democracy only indirectly. It conceived of Catholics and Protestants as diverse segments of a single 'people of Ireland', and called for the formation of an accountable government in Northern Ireland. The proposed package consisted of a collective executive that would include representatives of the major political parties, a legislative Assembly that would need special majorities to pass controversial legislation, and representation of the major parties in the Assembly's ten committees overseeing the governmental offices. It also provided for a bill of rights, a new police force, and novel relations, to be cemented by governing bodies, between Northern Ireland on the one hand and the Irish Republic and Great Britain on the other. The British and Irish governments agreed to amend their laws (Ireland Act of 1920 and the 1937 Irish Constitution) to ensure that unification of Ireland could come about only if a majority in Northern Ireland and a majority in the Republic accepted it. The two governments would also serve as protectors, mediators, and arbiters for the two communities of Northern Ireland.

These 1995 Joint Framework Documents endorsed a set of principles that officially terminated ethnic democracy in Northern Ireland. First, the conflict was recognized as national, and the Irish's right to self-determination (i.e. to a united Ireland) was acknowledged. Secondly, the option of a united Ireland had to be implemented through consent, not force. Thirdly, the institutions of accountable government were designed to prevent exclusion and majority monopoly. Fourthly, individual and collective rights would be protected by a constitutional charter of rights. And fifthly, the conflict was defined as 'international' and hence North–South and east–west institutions were to be constructed.

After three years of crises and setbacks the 1995 Joint Framework Documents led on 10 April 1998 to the historic breakthrough of the Good Friday Agreement, opening a new chapter in the history of Northern Ireland. During the period 1995–8 paramilitaries stopped violence, and political parties faced the Framework as a basis for negotiations over a newly restructured government. The new Agreement was negotiated by almost all the parties to the conflict and was brokered by the United States.

The 1998 Belfast Agreement is based on the same principles laid down in the 1995 Joint Framework. First is the establishment of a full-fledged consociational democracy in Northern Ireland with mandatory power-sharing in all vital areas. Power-sharing also includes the radical parliamentary representatives of both communities. The second principle is the involvement of Ireland in the internal affairs of the North through overarching bodies and mandatory consultation. The third principle is the assurance given to the Protestant majority that the status of Northern Ireland will change only through a majority approval. To make this understanding binding, Ireland agreed to amend its 1937 Constitution, and Britain agreed to repeal the Government of Ireland Act of 1920. The fourth principle is the renunciation of terrorism, the commitment to avoid violence and illegal means, and the consent to decommission arms by the paramilitaries on both sides. The Agreement was ratified by referendums in North and South, and the Irish and British Parliaments amended their laws accordingly.[31] Elections were held in 1998 for Parliament in Northern Ireland, and steps were taken for the formation of a new government and North–South and west–east intergovernmental bodies as provided by the Agreement.

Although the 1998 agreement marks a clear shift in favour of the Catholics and is obviously endorsed by them, it is necessary to account for its reluctant acceptance by the Protestants, who had successfully resisted moves towards power-sharing since 1972. John McGarry offers a convincing explanation.[32] The Protestants came to terms with the historical trend of gradually losing their majority. The Catholics have already reached 40 per cent of the population. The political Protestant majority has also been on the decline due to the defection of some Protestants to the emerging unaligned centre (the Alliance Party and the Women's Coalition). Thus majoritarian politics may no longer justify and guarantee the exclusion of Catholics, and power-sharing may be a lesser evil.[33] The flexibility shown by the nationalists also challenged and moderated the unionists. The IRA declared a ceasefire, and Sinn Féin dropped the demand for a united Ireland as a precondition for joining any agreement. But the most decisive factor in altering the Protestants' stance is their dependence on the British government. As long as they lack a real alternative of secession and see their lot and future linked to Britain, they are susceptible to British pressures. The British got their way because they designed a realistic package deal, backed by both the Conservative and Labour Parties, and endorsed by the Irish government. The package was also carefully balanced, offering Protestants non-coercive change in the North, cooperation of the Catholic minority, limited involvement of the Irish government, and protection by the British government. British resolve, concretized in the newly elected Blair government, convinced the Protestants that the new dispensation is better than the shaky status quo.

What are the options for a permanent settlement? The new Agreement can be and is interpreted in two conflicting ways. If consociational democracy functions to the satisfaction of both Catholics and Protestants, it can be consolidated and become a permanent settlement. Ireland can also feel gratified by having a say in the North and by reaching symbolic unification through the coordinating North–South bodies.

The alternative interpretation and more likely development are that consociational democracy is a transitional stage, eventually leading to a united Ireland. Following are the main factors conducive to unification:

The Catholics are likely to reach a demographic majority during the next fifteen years thanks to continued trends of high natural increase and diminishing emigration. They have already reached a majority of 52 per cent among 0–18-year-olds. When this young generation comes of age, it will probably make Catholics a majority even if their birth-rate declines to the lower Catholic rates of Ireland and the rest of Europe.[34] Their chances of becoming an electoral majority are further enhanced by the growing shift of a segment of the Protestant middle class away from unionism and towards the political and ethnically detached centre.

The 1998 Agreement will lead to greater integration between North and South. Many associations, involving Protestants from the North, already operate across the border. The new North–South Ministerial Council will create new incentives for cooperation in numerous areas, including environmental protection, agriculture, crime control, tourism, education, culture, and welfare services. Joint actions are and will be taken for pragmatic purposes on the basis of common regional interests. They will reduce Protestants' estrangement and apprehension of Ireland and improve their relations with the Catholics in the North.

Advancing European unification will gradually phase out the border and integrate the two parts of the Irish isle. The North–South economies will increasingly be integrated and tied more to the European continent, thereby becoming less dependent on Britain. The joint adoption of common European institutions, standards, and impacts will blur the differences between North and South. Furthermore, Ireland itself is changing rapidly, making Protestant objections to it less and less valid. The long-standing grounds against unification, namely, Ireland's poverty, clericalism, and unitary state structure, are receding.

Ireland is undergoing economic prosperity. Since it joined the European Union in 1973, the economy is modernizing and booming. With 62 per cent of its manpower in the services, the spread of high technologies, and the increase of investments by multinationals, Ireland has already entered the post-industrial era. In 1997 the rate of economic growth reached 6 per cent and the gross national product per capita $18,600. The standards of living and services have been on a steady rise since the early 1990s, bringing Ireland on a par with European achievements. With the advent of globalization Ireland's status and image have rightly changed from a backwater to an economic tiger. Although unemployment has remained above the 10 per cent mark, emigration slowed down appreciably, and the sparsely inhabited country has become an attractive place. The implication for Protestants is obvious: unification will not necessarily lead to a drop in their living standards and public services.

Ireland is secularizing. The 1937 Constitution institutionalized Ireland as a clerical state that bars abortion and divorce, enshrines religion, protects the family, and funds private religious schools. The church functions as the mainstay of society, a guardian of morality and collective identity, and a supplier of welfare, health, and education in addition to comprehensive religious services. Sixty years of incremental secularization opened a wide gap between reality and the constitutional vision of society.[35] Religious observance declined, the influence of the church on thinking and behaviour diminished, and the consensus on central religious values decreased to the extent that they have become the bones of contention in domestic politics. Repeated referendums on the issues of abortion and divorce demonstrate that it is only a matter of time until both become legal and common. Ireland is still much more clerical than any other member of the European Union, but it is drawing nearer every year. With Ireland's progressive secularization, Protestants will not risk religious coercion by joining it.

Because Irish society is becoming increasingly pluralistic, the unitary (nonconfederal) character of the state is diminishing. Globalization, European influences, economic growth, and secularization not only make Ireland liberal in outlooks and lifestyles, but also widen disparities between rich and poor, urban and rural, young and old, left and right, and secular and religious. Growing diversity will force people to recognize the right to be different. As a result, Ireland will follow the historical shift, prevalent in the West, from a 'republicanist Jacobean' to a multicultural democracy. A pluralistic and multiculturalist Ireland will be prepared to abandon its traditional unitary state structure and to allow Protestants and Catholics to keep their territorial autonomy, especially if successful, in the North after unification.[36] Because the Protestants will remain about one-fourth of the population of a united Ireland and a culturally distinct group, the autonomy of Ulster will be necessary and wise.

Ireland will continue to seek unification and will not rest until it accomplishes it. Unification is and will remain an integral part of the national vision, consensus, collective identity, and political culture of Ireland. It is beyond consideration of costs and benefits and is not a matter for partisan and governmental decision-making. It is even more desired than German unification because it is the last overdue step in British decolonization and in Ireland's national independence. Secularization and the decline of ethnic nationalism will not wither away the grand idea of a united Ireland. Ireland will remain irredentist in its Constitution and policies (although it is bound by its constitutional amendment to obtain a majority consent). Its irredentism is compatible with international law and world public opinion, and hence no pressure is applied to renounce it. As long as Ireland continues to pursue unification, the Catholic minority will remain republican too. Ireland and the Catholics in the North will continue to be restless until the dream of unification comes true.

Conclusion

What is in store for the partition of Palestine–Land of Israel and Ireland? It is clear, given the different historical conditions and trends, that partition will be consolidated in Palestine–Land of Israel and weakened in Ireland. The impending transformation of the Palestinian Authority into a sovereign state will resurrect the pre-1967 border and crystallize partition. The majority of Jews and Palestinians are already resigned to two independent states west of the River Jordan. The Palestinian minority within Israel also strongly favours partition. World public opinion and the superpowers fully support and endeavour to facilitate this process.

The obstacles to the consolidation of the partition of Palestine–Land of Israel are, however, still serious. The divisive issues are many, including demarcation of borders, the Arab refugees' right of return, allocation of water reservoirs, the status of Jerusalem, and security restrictions on the Palestinian state. Persistent rejectionist minorities on both sides can cause substantial trouble, including instigation of hatred and terrorism. Moreover, the peace process has thus far been proceeding without any change of the 'victim' narratives of either side, without soul-searching, without admission of guilt and wrongdoing, without mutual apology, and without feelings of compassion and reconciliation.

Partition of Palestine–Land of Israel will also raise more grave problems. How far should separation go? Should borders be widely open or strictly controlled? Should Palestinian Arabs have the right of employment in Israel? Should the infrastructures of the two countries be separated? What should be the status of the new Jewish minority in Palestine if some settlers are allowed and opt to stay in their current settlements? How will their status affect the Jewish state, the Palestinian state, and the Palestinian minority in Israel? Will the state of Palestine become irredentist, and what measures should be taken to prevent such danger? What can be done to assure the new state sufficient sovereignty not to appear as Israel's client and to be powerful and credible enough in fighting Palestinian rejectionists?[37]

On the other hand, developments in Ireland favour diminution of partition. According to a negative scenario, the new Agreement will eventually fail. The Protestants who voted against it in June 1998 will not reconcile themselves to a demoted status and will continue to resist the new regime. Even the Protestants who supported the Agreement will also be disappointed if the new coalition government is not able to keep law and order. The British will be fed up and gradually disengage, while Ireland will intervene increasingly in Northern affairs.

Another, rather positive, scenario foresees the successful implementation of the Agreement. As a result of continued consociational democracy, Ulster will lose its Protestant character and become bicultural and biconfessional. Ireland's involvement in it will broaden and deepen. North–South cooperation and the unification of Europe will remove the border barriers and further integrate the two parts of the Irish isle. It is also likely that some developments will in time make Ireland more acceptable to the Protestants. Sustained economic growth will bring Ireland on a par with Britain, blessing it with a high rate of employment, a high standard of living, and a generous welfare state. The continuing trend of secularization of the Catholic population and state will uplift Ireland to European standards of democratic liberties and freedom of religion. The growing integration of Ireland and Great Britain into the European Union will inescapably blur the border between Ulster and Ireland.

Finally, it is conceivable that the Catholics in Northern Ireland will reach a numerical and electoral majority in the foreseeable future by having greater fertility and fewer emigrants than Protestants. They will then be tempted to try to unify Ireland by democratic means. Unification will remain Ireland's national goal. It will not necessarily encounter Protestant antagonism if Ireland by then becomes a secular, well-off, and tolerant country that also grants wide autonomy to Ulster in a united Ireland.

NOTES

1. The land stretching from the River Jordan to the Mediterranean Sea is called Palestine by the Palestinians and Land of Israel (Eretz Israel) by the Jews. During the British mandate (1917–48) and at the time of its partition in 1948 the land was called and internationally known as Palestine, but the Jews continued to use the term Land of Israel and to call their community the Yishuv (Settlement). To be fair to both sides, the cumbersome term Palestine–Land of Israel is used here.

2. For a review of various modes of conflict regulation in divided societies, see S. Smooha and T. Hanf, 'The Diverse Modes of Conflict-Regulation in Deeply Divided Societies', *International Journal of Comparative Sociology*, 33 (1992), 1–2, 26–47; J. McGarry and B. O'Leary, 'Introduction: The Macro-Political Regulation of Ethnic Conflict', in J. McGarry and B. O'Leary (eds.), *The Politics of Ethnic Conflict Regulation* (New York: Routledge, 1993).

3. For detailed discussions of different forms and cases of partition, see D. Horowitz, *Ethnic Groups in Conflict* (Berkeley: University of California Press, 1985); R. R. Premdas, S. W. R. de A. Samarsinghe, and A. B. Anderson (eds.), *Secessionist Movements in Comparative Perspective* (London: Pinter, 1990); N. Chazan (ed.), *Irredentism and International Politics* (Boulder, Colo.: Lynne Rienner, 1991).

4. M. Tessler, *A History of the Israeli–Palestinian Conflict* (Bloomington: Indiana University Press, 1994).

5. D. Horowitz and M. Lissak, *Origins of the Israeli Polity: Palestine under the Mandate* (Chicago: Chicago University Press, 1978).

6. For a detailed political and social history of the Palestinians from the 1830s to the early 1990s, touching on many issues in Palestinian–Jewish relations, see B. Kimmerling and J. Migdal, *Palestinians: The Making of a People* (New York: Free Press, 1983).

7. J. Nevo, 'The Palestine Arabs' Attitude towards the Yishuv and the Zionist Movement', in S. Almog (ed.), *Zionism and the Arab Question* (Jerusalem: Zalman Shazar Center, 1983).

8. Y. Gorny, *Zionism and the Arabs, 1882–1948: A Study of Ideology* (New York: Oxford University Press, 1987).

9. A. Shlaim, *The Politics of Partition: King Abdullah, The Zionists and Palestine, 1921–1951* (Oxford: Oxford University Press, 1990); Y. Galnoor, *And the Sons Returned to their Borders* (Sde Boqer: Center for Ben-Gurion Heritage, 1994).

10. C. Bailey, *Jordan's Palestinian Challenge, 1948–1983: A Political History* (Boulder, Colo.: Westview Press, 1984).

11. S. Smooha, 'Israel's Options in Handling the Palestinians in the West Bank and Gaza Strip', in P. van den Berghe (ed.), *State Violence and Ethnicity* (Niwot: University Press of Colorado, 1990).

12. UN resolution 242 was adopted by the UN Security Council on 22 November 1967, in the aftermath of the 1967 war. It determines that 'a just and lasting peace in the Middle East' requires the 'withdrawal of Israeli armed forces from territories occupied in the recent conflict', termination of belligerence, 'acknowledgement of the sovereignty, territorial integrity and political independence of every State in the area' and the achievement of a 'just settlement of the refugees problem'. Until 1988 the PLO rejected this resolution because it falls short of calling for Israel's full retreat from all the areas seized in 1967, refers to the Palestinians as refugees, and does not recognize their national right to self-determination.

13. S. Smooha, 'Ethnic Democracy: Israel as an Archetype', *Israel Studies*, 2/2 (Fall 1997), 198–241.

14. I. Lustick, *Arabs in the Jewish State: Israel's Control of a National Minority* (Austin: University of Texas Press, 1980).

15. I. Lustick traces the process of disengagement of Britain from Ireland and compares it with the similar process that France underwent with regard to Algeria. He then draws lessons concerning the trajectory of Israel's retreat from the West Bank and Gaza Strip. See I. Lustick, *Unsettled States, Disputed Lands: Britain and Ireland, France and Algiers, Israel and the West Bank–Gaza* (Ithaca, NY: Cornell University Press, 1993). B. Neuberger compares the IRA, African National Congress, and PLO, and the nature of nationalism that they represent. See B. Neuberger, 'Nationalisms Compared: ANC, IRA and PLO', in H. Giliomee and J. Gagiano (eds.), *The Elusive Search for Peace: South Africa, Israel and Northern Ireland* (Cape Town: Oxford University Press, 1990).

16. M. Gallagher, 'How Many Nations are there in Ireland?', *Ethnic and Racial Studies*, 18/4 (Oct. 1995), 722.

17. A. Guelke, 'International Legitimacy, Self-Determination, and Northern Ireland', *Review of International Studies*, 11 (1985), 37–52.

18. A. Guelke, 'The United States, Irish Americans and the Northern Ireland Peace Process', *International Affairs*, 72/3 (July 1996), 521–36; A. J. Wilson, 'From the Beltway to Belfast: The Clinton Administration, Sinn Fein, and the Northern Ireland Conflict', *New Hibernia Review* (1997), 23–39.

19. D. H. Akenson, *The Irish Diaspora: A Primer* (Port Credit: P. D. Meany, 1993); L. J. McCaffrey, *The Irish Diaspora in America* (Bloomington: Indiana University Press, 1976).

20. J. Whyte, *Church and State in Modern Ireland, 1923–1979*, 2nd edn. (Dublin: Gill & Macmillan, 1980); K. Bowen, *Protestants in a Catholic State: Ireland's Privileged Minority* (Montreal: McGill–Queen's University Press, 1983).

21. Portions in this and next section of this chapter are adapted from S. Smooha, 'The Viability of Ethnic Democracy as a Mode of Conflict-Management: Comparing Israel and Northern Ireland', in T. M. Endelman (ed.), *Comparing Jewish Societies* (Ann Arbor: University of Michigan Press, 1997).

22. For the history of the communal conflict in Northern Ireland, see J. Darby, *Conflict in Northern Ireland: The Development of a Polarised Community* (Dublin: Gill & Macmillan, 1976); D. P. Barritt and C. F. Carter, *The Northern Ireland Problem: A Study in Group Relations*, 2nd edn. (London: Oxford University Press, 1972).

23. R. L. Harris, *Prejudice and Tolerance in Ulster* (Manchester: Manchester University Press, 1972).

24. R. Rose, *Governing without Consensus: An Irish Perspective* (Boston: Beacon Press, 1972), 432.

25. For an analysis of these liberating economic and social processes for the Catholics following the Second World War, see R. S. P. Elliot and J. Hickie, *Ulster: A Case Study in Conflict Theory* (London: Longman, 1971); R. Moore, 'Race Relations in the Six Counties: Colonialism, Industrialization and Stratification in Ireland', *Race*, 14 (1972), 21–42; P. Bew, P. Gibbon, and H. Patterson (eds.), *The State of Northern Ireland 1921–72: Political Forces and Social Classes* (New York: St Martin's Press, 1979).

26. C. C. O'Brien, *States of Ireland* (London: Hutchinson, 1972), 128–9.

27. The post-1968 period is covered by J. Whyte, *Interpreting Northern Ireland* (Oxford: Oxford University Press, 1990); T. Wilson, *Ulster: Conflict and Consent* (Oxford: Blackwell, 1989); B. O'Leary and J. McGarry, *The Politics of Antagonism: Understanding Northern Ireland* (London: Athlone Press, 1993); B. O'Leary and J. McGarry (eds.), *A State of Truce: Northern Ireland after Twenty-Five Years of War*, Ethnic and Racial Studies, special issue, 18/4 (Oct. 1995).

28. M. Connolly and J. Loughlin, 'Reflections on the Anglo-Irish Agreement', *Government and Opposition*, 21/2 (Spring 1986), 146–60.

29. P. Bew and G. Gillespie, *The Northern Ireland Peace Process: 1993–1996* (London: Serif, 1996).

30. For an analysis of the meanings and conditions leading to the Joint Framework Documents, see B. O'Leary, 'Afterword: What is Framed in the Framework Documents?', *Ethnic and Racial Studies*, 18/4 (Oct. 1995), 862–72; A. Lijphart, 'The Framework Document on Northern Ireland and the Theory of Power-Sharing', *Government and Opposition*, 31/3 (1996), 267–74.

31. With a turnout of 81% of the eligible voters in the North, 71% voted in favour: 51–3% of the Protestants and 96–7% of the Catholics. In Ireland participation was 56% and endorsement 94%.

32. J. McGarry, 'Political Settlements in Northern Ireland and South Africa', *Political Studies*, 46 (1998), 853–70.

33. J. McGarry writes: 'These demographic and electoral facts helped to undercut the traditional Unionist argument for majoritarian institutions and to make

the consociational arrangements at the heart of the Agreement palatable. They also made it increasingly rational for Unionists to seek to win Catholic support for the Union by agreeing to political concessions. And finally, the weakening unionist position made it likely that the next offer from the British and Irish governments would not be as generous as the present one'. See ibid., 866.

34. For an Irish nationalist analysis that marshals comprehensive evidence to demonstrate the 'inevitability' of the forthcoming Catholic numerical and political majority in Northern Ireland, see 'Political Demography in Northern Ireland', *http://www.geocities.com/CapitolHill/Congress.* It must be emphasized that there is nothing inevitable about (political) demography. This nationalist analysis intends to advance the goal of united Ireland by stirring a sense of hope and eventual victory among nationalists and a feeling of despair and defeatism among unionists.

35. B. Girvin, 'Church, State and the Irish Constitution: Secularization of the Irish Politics?', *Parliamentary Affairs*, 49/4 (Oct. 1996), 599–615.

36. The extended devolution of power to the Scots and Welsh in Britain, granted by the Blair government, may serve Ireland as a good example to follow.

37. In addition to the Palestinian rejectionist camp, composed of the fundamentalist Hamas and radical breakaway factions from the PLO, which opposes partition, some Israeli Arabs have been toying in the late 1990s with the idea of a binational state. Deeply disappointed with the Palestinian Authority, they fear that the new Palestinian state will be another Arab dictatorship, a corrupt regime and a sort of Bantustan. For them, consolidation of partition means despicable entrenchment of Israel as a Jewish state. They argue that partition is not a workable solution because of the de facto integration of all the area of mandatory Palestine. In the eyes of these radicals a binational state is the only pragmatic and just remedy for all the ills of partition. These anti-partition voices are isolated and devoid of any political or mass base. See e.g. N. Rouhana, 'The Test of Equal Citizenship: Israel between Jewish Ethnocracy and Bi-National Democracy', *Harvard International Review* (Spring 1998), 74–8.

INDEX